PENGUIN  CLASSIC

THE DISCOURSES

NICCOLÒ MACHIAVELLI was born in Florence in 1469 of an old citizen family. Little is known about his life until 1498, when he was appointed secretary and Second Chancellor to the Florentine Republic. During his time of office his journeys included missions to Louis XII and to the Emperor Maximilian; he was with Cesare Borgia in the Romagna; and after watching the Papal election of 1503 he accompanied Julius II on his first campaign of conquest. In 1507, as chancellor of the newly appointed *Nove di Milizia*, he organized an infantry force which fought at the capture of Pisa in 1509. Three years later it was defeated by the Holy League at Prato, the Medici returned to Florence, and Machiavelli was excluded from public life. After suffering imprisonment and torture, he retired to his farm near San Casciano, where he lived with his wife and six children and gave his time to study and writing. His works included *The Prince*; the *Discourses on the First Decade of Livy*; *The Art of War*; and the comedy, *Mandragola*, a satire on seduction. In 1520, Cardinal Giulio de' Medici secured him a commission to write a history of Florence, which he finished in 1525. After a brief return to public life, he died in 1527.

BERNARD CRICK is Emeritus Professor of Birkbeck, the University of London's college for mature part-time students. He took early retirement in 1984 to live in Edinburgh and interest himself in 'British Isles' questions. Born in 1929, he was educated at University College London, the London School of Economics and Harvard. He lived for four years in North America before teaching at the LSE and then Sheffield University. His books include *The American Science of Politics*; *In Defence of Politics*; *George Orwell: A Life*; *Political Thoughts and Polemics*; *Essays on Citizenship*, and *Crossing Borders*.

He had a long association with *The Political Quarterly* and has been a contributor to the *Observer*, the *Guardian*, the *New Statesman* and the *Independent*. He was chairman in 1998 of the government advisory committee whose report led to making Citizenship a new subject in the English national curriculum; and in 2002 he was knighted 'for services to citizenship and political studies'.

NICCOLÒ MACHIAVELLI

The Discourses

Edited with an Introduction by
BERNARD CRICK
using the translation of
LESLIE J. WALKER, S.J.
with revisions by
BRIAN RICHARDSON

PENGUIN BOOKS

In Memory of FELIX RAAB

A brilliant Australian postgraduate student who, had he not by misfortune got killed in a climbing accident, a brave but imprudent action, would surely have written a truly great and sensible, sympathetic yet critical, work on Machiavelli – as shown irrefutably in the evidence of his thesis, published posthumously as *The English Face of Machiavelli: A Changing Interpretation, 1500–1700* (London, 1964).

PENGUIN BOOKS

Published by the Penguin Group
Penguin Books Ltd, 80 Strand, London WC2R ORL, England
Penguin Putnam Inc., 375 Hudson Street, New York, New York 10014, USA
Penguin Books Australia Ltd, 250 Camberwell Road, Camberwell, Victoria 3124, Australia
Penguin Books Canada Ltd, 10 Alcorn Avenue, Toronto, Ontario, Canada M4V 3B2
Penguin Books India (P) Ltd, 11 Community Centre, Panchsheel Park, New Delhi – 110 017, India
Penguin Books (NZ) Ltd, Cnr Rosedale and Airborne Roads, Albany, Auckland, New Zealand
Penguin Books (South Africa) (Pty) Ltd, 24 Sturdee Avenue, Rosebank 2196, South Africa

Penguin Books Ltd, Registered Offices: 80 Strand, London WC2R ORL, England

www.penguin.com

Published in Pelican Books 1970
Reprinted 1974 (with corrections)
Reprinted in Penguin Classics 1983
Reprinted with new Preface and updated editorial matter 1998
Reprinted with a new Chronology and updated editorial matter 2003

054

Introduction and editorial material copyright © Bernard Crick, 1970, 2003
All rights reserved

Printed and bound in Great Britain by Clays Ltd, Elcograf S.p.A.
Set in Monotype Bembo

ISBN-13: 978-0-14-044428-5

www.greenpenguin.co.uk

MIX
Paper | Supporting responsible forestry
FSC
www.fsc.org   FSC® C018179

Penguin Books is committed to a sustainable future for our business, our readers and our planet. This book is made from Forest Stewardship Council™ certified paper.

CONTENTS

CHRONOLOGY

1469 MAY: Birth in Florence of Niccolò di Bernardo Machiavelli (M) to Bernardo and Bartolomea (née de' Nelli).

1475 Sixtus IV (della Rovere) elected Pope.

1481 With his brother Totto, M begins to attend the school of Paolo da Ronciglione.

1484 Innocent VIII (Cibo) elected Pope.

late 1480s M attends lectures by Marcello Virgilio Adriani.

1491 Savonarola as preacher begins to win influence in Florence.

1492 APRIL: Death of Lorenzo de' Medici. Piero becomes head of the family. Alexander VI (Borgia) elected Pope.

1494 NOV: Piero and the Medici are expelled from Florence. French troops enter the city.

1498 MAY: Savonarola executed for heresy.
JUNE: M is confirmed by the Great Council as second chancellor of the Republic.
JULY: M elected secretary to the Ten of War.
NOV: M is sent on his first diplomatic mission to Piombino on behalf of the Ten of War.

1499 *Discorso della guerra di Pisa* ['Report on the Pisan war']. Mission to Caterina Sforza-Riario, ruler of Imola and Forlì.

1500 JULY: Six-month mission to King Louis XII of France.

1501 M marries Marietta Corsini. (They will have six children.)

1502 Piero Soderini elected *gonfaloniere* for life.
OCT: M begins mission to the court of Cesare Borgia (Duke Valentino) at Imola.
DEC: M follows Cesare to Cesena and Senigallia.

1503 *Descrizione del modo tenuto dal Duca Valentino nell' ammazzare Vitellozzo Vitelli, Oliverotto da Fermo, il signor Pagolo e il*

Duca di Gravina Orsini ['Description of the Manner in which Duke Valentino put Vitellozzo Vitelli, Oliverotto da Fermo, Lord Pagolo and the Duke of Gravina Orsini to Death']; *Parole sopra la provvisione del danaio* ['Remarks on the raising of money']; *Del modo di trattare i sudditi della Valdichiana ribellati* ['On the method of dealing with the rebels of the Val di Chiana'].

For M's plan to assert Florentine authority over Pisa (in revolt against Florence from 1502–9), Leonardo da Vinci is consulted on a scheme to divert the river Arno around Pisa to the sea at Livorno.

APRIL: M sent on mission to Pandolfo Petrucci, ruler of Siena.

SEPT: Election of Pope Pius III (Piccolimini).

OCT: M sent on mission to Papal Court at Rome.

NOV: Election of Pope Julius II (della Rovere).

1504 *Decennale Primo* ['The First Decade'].

JAN: M's second mission to court of King Louis XII.

JULY: M's second mission to Pandolfo Petrucci.

1505 DEC: M becomes secretary to the new committee, the Nine of the Militia.

1506 *Discorso dell'ordinare lo stato di Firenze alle armi* ['Discourse on Florentine military preparation'].

JAN: M recruits for the militia in the Mugello, north of Florence.

AUG–OCT: M's second mission to the Papal Court follows Pope Julius from Viterbo to Orvieto, Perugia, Urbino, Cesena, and Imola.

1507 DEC: M sent on mission to court of the Emperor Maximilian.

1508 *Rapporto delle cose dell' Alemagna* ['Report on Germany'].

1509 *Discorso sopra le cose della Magna e sopra lo imperatore* ['Discourse on Germany and the Emperor']: *Decennale Secondo* ['The Second Decade'].

1510 JUNE–SEPT: M's third mission to the court of King Louis XII.

1511 SEPT: M's fourth mission to the court of King Louis XII.

1512 After Spanish troops invade Florentine territory – and sack Prato – Florence surrenders, Soderini is deposed and goes into exile as the Medici return to power.

[after April **1512**] *Ritratto delle cose della Magna* ['Description of German affairs'].

[after April **1512** and before August **1513**] *Ritratto delle cose di Francia* ['Description of French affairs'].

NOV: M is dismissed from the Chancery and sentenced to a year's confinement within Florentine territory.

1513 FEB: M is tried for conspiracy, tortured, and imprisoned.

MARCH–APRIL: After his release M retires to his farm at Sant' Andrea in Percussina, seven miles south of Florence.

MARCH: Election of Pope Leo X (Giovanni de' Medici).

JULY: M drafts *Il Principe* ['The Prince'].

[1514 or later] *Discorso o dialogo intorno alla nostra lingua* ['Discourse or dialogue on our language'].

1515 M joins a discussion group – interested in politics and literature – meeting at Orti Oricellari, Florence. He begins to write *Discorsi sopra la prima deca di Tito Livio* ['Discourses on the First Decade of Livy'], dedicating his commentary on the first ten books of Livy's *History of Rome* to Zanobi Buondelmonti and Cosimo Rucellai, grandson of Bernardo Rucellai who had laid out the Oricellari gardens.

[1515–20] *Belfagor* ['Belfagor'].

c. **1516** Manuscript copies of *The Prince* begin to circulate in and beyond Florence.

[1517 or 18] *L'Asino d'oro* ['The Golden Ass'].

1518 M writes his ribald play *Mandragola* ['The Mandrake Root'] and about now finishes the *Discourses*.

1520 M writes the book on military organization, *Dell' Arte della Guerra* ['The Art of War'] and *La vita di Castruccio*

Castracani da Lucca ['The Life of Castruccio Castracani of Lucca'], as well as a *Summary* of Lucca's system of government (*Sommario delle cose della città di Lucca*). He is commissioned to write the history of Florence by Cardinal Giulio de' Medici.

1519 or 1520 *Discorso delle cose fiorentine dopo la morte di Lorenzo* ['Discourse on the Florentine affairs after the death of Lorenzo'].

1521 *The Art of War* is published.

1522 *Memoriale a Raffaello Girolami* ['Advice to Raffaello Girolami'].

Cardinal Adrian Florensz is elected Pope as Adrian VI.

1523 Cardinal Giulio de' Medici is elected Pope as Clement VII.

[1524–5] *Clizia.*

1525 M visits Rome to present his finished *History of Florence* (*Istorie Fiorentine*) to Pope Clement. M's *Mandragola* is performed and acclaimed in Venice, which he later visits on a mission to settle a trade dispute for the Wool Guild of Florence.

1526 *Relazione di una visita fatta per fortificare Firenze* ['Report on the fortifications of Florence'].

M revises his play, *Mandragola.*

1527 MAY: The city of Rome is brutally sacked by the Imperialist Army of chiefly Germans and Spaniards under the Duke of Bourbon. The Medici are expelled from Florence, where the Republic adopts a new constitution.

21 JUNE: M dies and is buried in the church of Santa Croce.

1531/2 Posthumous publication of the *Discourses, The Prince* and the *History of Florence.*

(Dates in square brackets are conjectural)

PREFACE TO THE 2003 REPRINT

I MUST confess that over nearly thirty-five years my views on the nature and importance of the political have not changed, so for reasons both good and bad I have decided to let my original Introduction stand, but to shorten the original Preface and to purge and update Suggestions for Further Reading. The last thirty years have seen great advances in Machiavelli scholarship. They are most clearly encapsulated in the work of Quentin Skinner, the mentor and originating editor of the Cambridge Texts in the History of Political Thought – one of the great contemporary enterprises of historical scholarship.

Some points of my Introduction could stand revision, the references and examples could now be richer and I might claim less for Machiavelli's originality and more for his success in presenting what were becoming commonplaces of humanist thought. But while sharing many of the Cambridge school's presuppositions, I think there is something more, at least something different. There is a difference between political theory and the history of political ideas. Once a text has been placed in its context (intellectual, political and biographical) to recover the *meaning* that the concepts had to the author's contemporaries, then one can, and I believe should, move from the mode of 'history of ideas' into the mode of 'political thinking'; one should then consider the *truth* and general validity of the propositions asserted in that text. To know an author's intentions is essential, but any great thinker and writer will, in the creative activity of thinking and writing, go beyond premeditated and planned intentions and speak, in part at least, home truths to us as well as to contemporaries. Meanings change over time and are, indeed, 'essentially contestable', so to be always on guard against gross anachronism and to respect historical method; but in some texts sufficient meaning remains to justify talking of some perennial values and important theories that stand the test of time. Such a case is that very tradition of 'civic republicanism' which Professor Skinner sought to recover in Machiavelli, but is now too often and mistakenly regarded as dead. This needs reviving in an age of 'technocrats' and 'professionals' and modernizers who are so often two-faced about active citizenship.

Edinburgh,
16 December 2002   BERNARD CRICK

PREFACE

THE text used is that of Father Leslie Walker's translation from Guido Mazzoni and Mario Casella's *Tutte le opere storiche e letterarie di Niccolò Machiavelli*, published by G. Barbèra in Florence in 1929. This is used by the kind permission of Messrs Routledge & Kegan Paul.[1] Father Walker's magnificent edition is far more than a translation. His 163 pages of introduction including a large analytic table of contents, and his 390-page second volume of notes, tables and indexes, make it the most comprehensive scholarly edition in any language. The specialist and the teacher must still turn to it – as I have frequently – to pursue in depth any particular point of difficulty or delight concerning concepts quite as much as sources, borrowings or events. In comparison this is a confessedly and deliberately popular edition, but also one more concerned with the lasting stature and continued relevance of Machiavelli as a theorist of politics than with either textual scholarship or – as is the fashion of so much intellectual history at the moment – diminishing him to a precise contemporary context.

1. *The Discourses of Niccolò Machiavelli*, 2 vols. London, 1950 (still in print).

So, I have severely limited my annotations of the text to those grossest stumbling blocks of sheer meaning. Any middle path might, as Machiavelli suggests of middle paths in general, get the worst of both worlds: caviare for the general or cold mutton for the wise. What I have to say about the peculiar genius of Machiavelli, as a political theorist and as a political sociologist, neither depends on knowing who the characters in his text were nor on how accurately he uses his beloved ancient authors (nor yet on how accurate they were – there is no end to such learned pursuits). But I have retained a few of Walker's footnotes on the translation where he deals with some special difficulty about a key concept.

Machiavelli never saw an edition of either *The Prince* or *The Discourses* through the press in his lifetime, although manuscripts circulated widely. And *The Discourses on the First Ten Books of Titus Livius* (to give its full title for the first and last time) is an unfinished work. The order in which he might have placed the sections or discourses had he prepared the book for the press could be and has been questioned. But there is no certain answer. I follow Walker who in turn followed Mazzoni and Casella. And I also retain the made-up titles which Walker supplies to groups of the discourses or sections – making chapters, as it were. But beware that these are editorial intrusions – helpful over all, but sometimes a trifle leading or arbitrary when particular discourses wander through several subjects at once. So these are always printed in square brackets. The section headings are probably Machiavelli's own; and these all appear in the Table of Contents of this edition. Walker's Analytic Table of Contents is, I think, too leading. But I have followed his division of the sections into paragraphs and have thought it pedantic, for this edition, to number them; but then anyone using his indexes and this text has only to count the paragraphs to pin-point a reference.

The publishers would have commissioned a new transla-

tion, but I advised them that it would be a pedantic extravagance. However, nothing is perfect, and any good translator
can, with a fresh scholarly eye, improve on another. So I am
very grateful to Brian Richardson for checking the translation
and pointing out several score of errors and many improved
readings, all of which have been silently corrected. I think
they are all of the kind that Father Walker would have
accepted had he had the benefit of having his manuscript
closely and critically read. It has been my decision, however,
to prefer throughout to translate the key concept of *'virtù'*
either as plain 'virtue' or to leave the Italian word (for reasons
I explain on pp. 59–61).

I thank most gratefully, beside Dr Richardson, Geraint
Williams for reading the manuscript and giving me several
helpful corrections and criticisms. Sir Isaiah Berlin kindly let
me make use of his then unpublished 'The Originality of
Machiavelli', Dr Sally Jenkinson helped me prepare the manuscript and Mrs Iris Walkland was of great assistance in reading
the proofs.

As for the result? Seldom do we know, to paraphrase the
Florentine, how to be wholly good or wholly bad – which is,
to him, invariably a fatal weakness. So I beg his pardon too, for
I would try to be as Machiavellian as I can, as near to devotion
as is possible – in the circumstances – to a most worthy
humanist, a great advocate of republican government and to a
man who never preached 'the politic art' as an end in itself, but
only as the necessary means to preserve the civilized life of
cities. If this still shocks some people, or sounds very unschol-
arly to others, it is because there are so many different
Machiavellis around. It is to this question that we must turn
first.

Sheffield,
21 July 1969   BERNARD CRICK

INTRODUCTION

So Many Machiavellis

WHY should one want or feel the need to take a fresh look at Machiavelli? There's been too much brilliant originality in Machiavelli scholarship and so much downright nonsense written about him. One fears to add to it. I make no claims to originality, but only to a somewhat disingenuous common sense. I feel strongly the need to cut through many ingenious and over-elaborate discussions of the nature and alleged originality of his method, in order to show that his main substantive preoccupation, indeed his good obsession, was with the conditions for republican government. The republic to him was the best of all possible worlds and he tried to show that it had to be and could be, not merely should be, remarkably tolerant of internal conflict and dissent. Not merely does he have a coherent theory of the conditions for republican or political rule, but in some vital respects it is more fully worked out than was Aristotle's – and there is no rival in between; and, furthermore, it has a relevance to the modern world particularly because of the obvious fact, not despite it, that it can go so far without invoking industrialism.

A few years ago this might have been a reason for ignoring him or for seeing no element, even, of lasting relevance in his theories. But recently works like Wittfogel's *Oriental Despotism* (1957) and Barrington Moore's *Social Origins of Dictatorship and Democracy: Lord and Peasant in the Making of the Modern World* (1967) have at least made one suspicious, on the score of bureaucracy and of land tenure respectively, that it is possible to have exaggerated, either in a capitalist or a Marxist manner, how much industrialization has shaped the modern

consciousness. If we grow more and more sceptical of the
'convergence thesis' of industrial civilization and even come
to think in terms of 'three worlds', we cannot then use the
European industrial revolution as a sufficient explanation of
the divergence of all three patterns. Behind the 'industrial
revolution' there may be a more fundamental change in
human concepts and consciousness; perhaps the propensity to
look *forward* at all and to believe that environment can be
subject to *control* and *choice*. And among such concepts the old
tradition of an active 'citizenship', which is the central concern of Machiavelli (who was detested for being a republican
and an advocate of 'policy' quite as much as for being a pagan
or possibly an atheist), is at least as worth exploring as one of
the factors shaping the modern world as are bureaucracy, land
and the peasantry, and industrialism. Perhaps, in a word, we
should turn back to Machiavelli because 'mere political
factors' now seem a little less easy to reduce into economics or
to ignore as 'transitory phenomena'. They are likely to be with
us in any kind of society and are likely always to have more
affect than was once rashly supposed.

But if one chooses to rehabilitate Machiavelli as 'the political theorist', one must candidly admit that – and explain why
– one also can find and exaggerate, if one chooses, elements of
all kinds of things in Machiavelli. The variety of interpretations of him show that either he is supremely enigmatic ('what
is *really* in her mind?' perhaps nothing), or else someone so
important that we all have to pretend that he is unequivocably
with us or, more often, against us. The attempt to put
Machiavelli at a distance is sometimes carried to quite heroic
lengths. For to some he is the teacher of evil, 'the doctor of the
damned', as Leo Strauss and Maritain would argue – a somewhat unsubtle view of someone who so often bewails that it is
'necessary' to act in a way that is *admittedly* immoral. Others,
like Hegel and Fichte, see him as a ruthless but glorious

nationalist, while Ricci would tell sedate readers of the World's Classics that his patriotism, while intense, was democratic and humane (here would be a remarkable man indeed to anticipate nationalism by nearly three centuries). He is, in Cassirer's eyes, a cold technician, while to Croce he is an agonized humanist crucified between the conflicting intensities of his perception of the 'is' and his sense of the 'ought'. To Francis Bacon, he was the supreme realist; to Carlo Schmidt, the anticipator (since the dates don't work the other way) of Galileo's scientific method; but to Professor Butterfield he was really an *a priori* dogmatist who dressed himself up in bits of palace gossip about history and science. To some a universal genius, a fit companion among the immortals for Dante and for Leonardo; but a hostile commentator, Dr Sydney Anglo, in *Machiavelli: a Dissection* (1969), can make plain that he could have hardly hoped for a pass degree had he studied history at Swansea. To Macaulay he was an elegant, balanced and patriotic Whig; to Gramsci he was as near to a preincarnation of Lenin as any mortal man could get before the birth of Marx; and to Professors Sabine and Max Lerner, he was an American political scientist of the behavioural persuasion. Jakob Burckhardt saw him as an artist and James Burnham saw him as a managerial-bureaucrat. A funny kind of Christian, to my late friend Dante Germino – since he once preached a sermon and confessed and received absolution on his death bed, and either a pagan or an atheist to many others; a toady of princes, or a democratic satirist . . . there is no end of it, nor ever will be.[1]

1. Sir Isaiah Berlin has said that there are no fewer than twenty-five leading interpretations of *The Prince* alone – in his 'The Originality of Machiavelli', in Myron P. Gilmore (ed.), *Studies on Machiavelli*, Sansoni, Florence, 1972, which he allowed me to use in an earlier version and from which I have drawn heavily in the above paragraph. See also, on varieties of interpretation, E. W. Cochrane, 'Machiavelli: 1940–1960', *Journal of Modern History*, June 1961, pp. 113–36.

Such a fate is odd for a writer who writes well and expresses himself clearly and in propositional terms: Machiavelli is not Rousseau. He may often be wrong, but seldom deliberately obscure: Machiavelli is not Hobbes. One thing alone is clear: he raises strong emotions – mostly of doubtful relevance. It is as if everyone thinks themselves at liberty to fill in for themselves what they take to be the 'great gap' in his argument. Perhaps less liberties would have been taken with him had he, in an academic and philosophic manner – however badly – either advanced the grounds for a secular morality divorced from religion (but he did not live in the Cambridge of Leslie Stephen nor in the Bloomsbury of Leonard Woolf) or else for a complete separation of politics from all ethics (a *different question*). But he did not: he shocks or disappoints us by simply taking it for granted that there are two sets of standards. We may know what the good is, he always implies and certainly never denies; but we may not be able to act in that way: that is the whole problem. He did not go on to say that the way we have to act is good: he was not a type of romantic poet, a second-hand Nietzchean, nor yet an intellectual Fascist. Say simply, he was no philosopher; and it is as dangerous to impute a philosophy or a single method to him as it is a gratuitous and condescending insult to present him with one. He was one of those men who somehow, in a most disorderly and incoherent way, stumble upon certain truths which are important in understanding human society in its political forms. Commentators on Machiavelli should have engraved on their desks Karl Popper's dictum: 'the truth of a proposition does not depend upon its genesis'.

Some of these truths imply a way of looking at the world that we may now call 'political sociology' – an interest in the degree to which forms of regime depend upon social circumstances; and some of these truths point to the importance of, in some circumstances, conflict as a positive benefit to a society if society is seen as a whole; but this does not make him a social scientist. But it does make his conclusions of some general relevance, not because they were said by him or said in any logically consistent manner, but because they so often happen to be right or at least relevant. He is distinctively modern in a sense that predates and logically precedes both Adam Smith and Karl Marx: that man by giving thought cannot, it is true, 'add a cubit to his stature', but can, to some degree at least, effect his social environment – indeed can, within some limitations, choose to choose freely. Machiavelli loved to generalize – which to some is enough to condemn him out of hand. But there is a very high degree of consistency between his generalizations – as we will see. Thus Machiavelli was no philosopher, but he was a brilliant theorist; yet without the protection of a philosophy, his theories have been preyed upon by every kind of doctrinaire, either wishing to use his generalizations for their own purposes or finding what they seem to find in him so uncomfortable, that they dig deeper to find more than is at first apparent and to reject him utterly. Most of the 'mysteries of Machiavelli' arise in this way. ('She really is the same woman, just that you all treat her so differently.') And part of the reason why we find mysteries is because he was not a determinist: he narrows alternatives, but never removes or closes them.

The Prince *and* The Discourses

Take first the greatest and most unnecessary mystery of all: the relationship between *The Prince* and *The Discourses*. 'What do you know of Machiavelli who only *The Prince* have read?' This is one of the great stumbling blocks – a ludicrous and a silly one because *The Prince* is notorious and short, while *The Discourses* are famous but long. Biographical evidence strongly suggests that he was working on the two books at the same time.[2] And it is beyond reasonable doubt that he was not an advocate of autocracy at one period and then of republican government at another[3] (he was an advocate of either, according to the circumstances of the case). In fact, there is no essential argument in *The Prince* which is not repeated in *The Discourses*: so much for the theory that a clever and unscrupulous office seeker writes all that will please a prince, in the one, and all that will please a republic in the other (as if he wasn't going to be found out). Many things in both books would please neither; both have a definite slant, but both are incompetent if viewed as pure acts of arse-licking. There is a slant, but it is not that. Indeed, even in the first chapter of *The Prince* and the first sentence of the second chapter, the essential matter of *The Discourses* is referred to clearly:

CHAPTER I. HOW MANY KINDS OF PRINCIPALITY
THERE ARE, AND BY WHAT MEANS THEY ARE ACQUIRED

All states, all powers, that have held and hold rule over men have been and are either republics or principalities.

Principalities are either hereditary, in which the family has been long established; or they are new.

The new are either entirely new, as was Milan to Francesco

2. The first draft of *The Prince* was certainly written in 1513, and a part of *The Discourses* (to which he refers in *The Prince*) is either already written, being written or at least planned during that year. He revises *The Prince* in 1516 while still working on *The Discourses*, and in 1519 puts them aside (unfinished? certainly unrevised) for the *Art of War*, then in the following year begins the *Florentine History*. See Federico Chabod, *Machiavelli and the Renaissance* (London, 1958), pp. 31–2 fn.; Sydney Anglo's able summary of the evidence in his *Machiavelli: A Dissection* (London, 1969), chapter 3; and Roberto Ridolfi, *The Life of Niccolò Machiavelli* (London, 1963), chapter 14 and the footnotes thereto.

3. Felix Raab has shown that this radical dichotomy was a liberal, nineteenth-century gloss on Machiavelli. See his *The English Face of Machiavelli* (London, 1964), p. 255.

Sforza, or they are, as it were, members annexed to the hereditary state of the prince who has acquired them, as was the kingdom of Naples to that of the King of Spain.

Such dominions thus acquired are either accustomed to live under a prince, or to live in freedom; and are acquired either by the arms of the prince himself, or of others, either by fortune or by ability [*virtù*].

CHAPTER 2. CONCERNING HEREDITARY PRINCIPALITIES

I will leave out all discussion on republics, inasmuch as in another place I have written of them at length . . .[4]

Surely this is clear enough. He begins with a generalization, not a value judgement: that there are only two types of government. And in *The Prince*, he writes almost exclusively about the one, and in *The Discourses* predominantly about the other. But only in *The Discourse* is there any clear and explicit discussion of when it is appropriate to have personal rule and when the broader base of a republic. And only in *The Discourses* does princely power become seen not just as personal power, but as a function of all regimes – an institution. Republics need it in time of crisis, indeed 'a prince' or prince-like power is to be found in four circumstances: (i) when a man is ruthlessly determined to govern in that way and is not stopped in time; (ii) when a state is so hopelessly lacking in '*virtù*' or civic spirit that a republic would not work; (iii) when a republic is to be founded from unsuitable material; and (iv) when one is to be restored from corruption. Section 9 of Book I of *The Discourses* is headed: '*That it is necessary to be the Sole Authority if one would*

4. I use W. K. Marriott's translation of *The Prince* in the Everyman's Library edition edited by Professor H. Butterfield (1958). It is more laboured but literal than George Bull's Pelican Classics translation, but the latter is much more readable and catches the spirit of Machiavelli. I think, however, that Bull's introduction fails to see the essential unity between *The Prince* and *The Discourses*.

constitute a Republic afresh or would reform it thoroughly regardless of its Ancient Institutions.' There is no doubt where his values lie, as in the heading to the very next section: *'Those who set up a Tyranny are no less Blameworthy than are the Founders of a Republic or a Kingdom Praiseworthy.'*[5]

It all depends on circumstances. Certainly, as we will see, it is possible for a prince, one man, with *almost* super-human audacity, skill and luck to fly in the face of objective circumstances or 'necessity'. That is the point of the famous chapter in *The Prince* on Fortune – she's a fickle whore, but if she is to be mastered, it is 'necessary to beat and ill use her . . . it is seen that she allows herself to be mastered by the adventurous rather than by those who go to work more coldly . . . She is therefore', I cannot resist finishing the paragraph, 'always, woman-like, a lover of young men, because they are less cautious, more violent and with more audacity command her.' But success, will young men please note, is not guaranteed and the penalties of failure are drastic. Normally it is more prudent to see that 'our behaviour is in conformity with the times' (*Discourses* III.9).

Now the greatest feat of pure political virtuosity known to Machiavelli, and first described in *The Prince*, is to turn a flourishing republic into a principality – but the most damnable; the greatest praise is to be reserved for an almost equally difficult feat – described in *The Discourses*, the prince, hero or legislator who deliberately creates a new republic out of unlikely or ambiguous human material. But there is no doubt that Machiavelli thinks it more difficult to destroy a

5. 'Only two kinds of state', indeed; and then 'kingdoms' come up! But kings to Machiavelli are those princes who abide by the existing laws of a state: hence there is no incompatibility between having a king and being a republic, although if there never have been free institutions and the traditional laws are those of any autocracy, then the king can be the strongest and most stable kind of prince or ruler.

republic than to create one – which is why a prince may have to be so utterly ruthless. Even in *The Prince* there is this formidable testimony to republican government in chapter 5, headed '*Concerning the way to govern cities or principalities which lived under their own laws before they were annexed*':

... he who becomes master of a city accustomed to freedom and does not destroy it, may expect to be destroyed by it, for in rebellion it has always the watchword of liberty and its ancient privileges as a rallying point, which neither time nor benefits will ever cause it to forget. And whatever you may do or provide against, they never forget that name or their privileges unless they are [made] disunited or dispersed, but at every chance they rally to them, as Pisa after the hundred years she had been held in bondage by the Florentines.

But when cities or countries are accustomed to live under a prince, and his family is exterminated, they, being on the one hand accustomed to obey and on the other hand not having the old prince, cannot agree in making one from among themselves, and they do not know how to govern themselves. For this reason they are very slow to take up arms, and a prince can gain them to himself and secure them much more easily. But in republics there is more vitality, greater hatred, and more desire for vengeance, which will never permit them to allow the memory of their former liberty to rest; so that the safest way is to destroy them or to reside there.

This is the earliest statement of the great 'either/or' theme which runs through all Machiavelli's writings; but most men, he observes, choose a middle course and are undone. Nothing in *The Prince* is stronger than the advice he gives in *The Discourses* headed '*In a City or a Province which he has seized, a New Prince should make Everything New.*' (*Discourses* I.26.) New governors, new titles, 'to make the rich poor and the poor rich', to build new cities and to destroy old ones, even 'to move the inhabitants from one place to another far distant from it; in short, to leave nothing of that province intact, and nothing in it, neither rank, nor institution, nor form of government, nor wealth, except that it be held by such as recognize that it comes from you'. But *The Discourses* make clear, which *The Prince* tactfully does not, that republics are to be preferred if you can get them; and there is even an explicit argument that princes are needed to save and to create states – which calls for the sudden and ruthless concentration and use of power; but that republics normally preserve states best through long periods of time – where the problem is to spread power and to attain adaptability.

How then does one distinguish, according to Machiavelli, between the circumstances fit for republican rule and those only fit for personal rule? Or between normal times and 'states of emergency'? Enough, for the moment, to have established this as the master question – to which I will return. But this concern of Machiavelli's implies one thing: the extraordinarily high value he attaches to political stability: this is a higher value than either princely or republican rule by itself. We need not accept this as a value to see its importance as a problem and its advantage as a focus for study – it is probably the basic problem which links the practical concerns of politics with an objective scholarship. What are the main theories which seek to account for political stability and change? What were Machiavelli's theories and what is their general relevance?

Finally to ask, is it, after all, quite so abominable as it sounds to be one of those who, as a contemporary put it, 'loved their country better than the safety of their souls' (or, more soberly, to study with some special care those writers who stress survival rather than transcendence)? It depends quite as much on what one means by 'the state' as on what one believes of salvation. Again, it may be blasphemous to the Christian to treat politics as end in itself, but this should not stop us from inquiring quite what he meant by 'politics': it is unlikely that he meant quite the same thing by 'politics' as did the godly who rained abuse on the head of old *'Hatchevil* or not to be matched in evil'[6] – a far cry from that stout English Commonwealth man, James Harrington's praise of him as 'the only Politician of later Ages' and 'the sole retriever of ... *ancient Prudence.'*[7]

Republics as Mixed Government

Machiavelli is, in many respects, a very traditional writer. He cuts across the Christian tradition of natural law of St Thomas Aquinas and goes back, implicitly, to the tradition of Aristotle's *Politics* and Cicero's *Republic* and, explicitly, to the Greek historian in Rome, Polybius, and, of course, to the first ten books of Titus Livy's *History of Rome* – the nominal subject matter on which he discourses. As a theorist, he is best understood if one starts with Aristotle, but not just the Aristotle of the first four books, the apologist of the *polis* or of political rule (misleadingly seen simply as 'constitutional'), but also the Aristotle of Book V on 'Revolutions', particularly the section (which Machiavelli had obviously read) that advises a tyrant how to perpetuate his rule – if one wishes, as one should not, to govern in that way. It has often been commented that there is a Machiavellian element in old Aristotle – which is, of course, a paradoxical way of saying quite simply that there is a strong Aristotelian element in Machiavelli.

To Aristotle, the *polis*, or the best possible state, consisted in the mixture of two elements, not the philosophical or the practical dominance of a single element: aristocracy, seen in principle as the rule of the wise, constitutionally as the rule of

6. Quoted by Felix Raab, *English Face of Machiavelli, 1500–1700* (London, 1964), p. 83, from an early seventeenth-century tract.
   7. ibid., p. 187

a few and socially as the rule of the wealthy or those with property; and democracy, seen in principle as the rule of mere opinion ('the democratic belief is that because men are equal in some things, they are equal in all' – a dangerous fallacy), constitutionally as the rule of the many, and socially as the rule of the poor. Neither principle alone is likely to render either stable or just government: they need to be synthesized, and this synthesis is not a mere compromise, but the taking of the two best elements in both, wisdom and consent, and making them into a new, organic unity. So the *polis* is a state in which citizens (men fit to be citizens – a formidable reservation) 'rule and are ruled in turn'. It was from this point that Hegel took off, in his dialectic, synthesizing way, and Machiavelli more in Aristotle's. The mixture, however, in both Aristotle and Cicero is somewhat static. In Cicero it becomes almost a frozen formula of elite rule, '*Auctoritas in Senatu, Potestas in Populo*'; or the simple analysis of the basis of Roman power and expansion found on the Eagles of the legions and stamped on all military stores, 'S.P.Q.R.' – 'the Senate *and* the People of Rome'. At times a constitutional formula, but at other times simply and formidably a warning maxim addressed to the patrician political class – do not forget the dreadful power of the people if things go wrong or if agitators stir them up.

Machiavelli first introduces a dynamic element into the general theory of mixed government. He uses '*Republica*' in two senses: (i) as a general word for either of his two kinds of state whenever it is wished to stress, in the old Roman sense of *res publica*, the things that are common to a people – whether as subjects or citizens, or (put rather leadingly) the systematic relations of regime to society; and (ii) in a narrower sense, a republic specifically of the Roman kind – based upon '*uno vivere civile e politico*', a political and civic way of life, or the practice of citizenship; and he often uses '*libero*' virtually as a synonym for '*politico*'.[8] In such republics of the Roman kind, he sees three essential elements, '*qualità*' (a word with some social connotations), or '*potenza*', forces or tendencies.

These are *la potestà regia* (regal power), *la potenza degli Ottimati* (the influence of elites, plutocrats or the power hungry)[9] and *il governo popolare* ('popular government', or is it 'government of the people'? Not quite, the connotation is more like in our 'the governor' on a lorry or other engine, the

8. See instances of this in *Discourses* I.6 and I.25 and the discussion in Walker's notes, vol. I, p. 139 and vol. II, pp. 276 (on Aristotle and Machiavelli), 314 (on '*libero*') and 317 (on '*vivere*'). Walker seems to imply that the primary usage of '*libero*' is to show that a state is free from domination by other states. This is a usage, but equally often he uses it to describe the internal conditions of those states whose affairs are managed by citizens. '*Uno vivere civile*' is an independent community with its own laws, but these laws could be absolutist – unless the state is also described as '*libero*'. Indeed '*civile*' can both mean a city, any old city, and a body of citizens with legal rights which they in fact exercise. Machiavelli does, on occasion, use the bad argument (a piece of philological teleology) that the very word 'city' implies that it should be or must be a republic of citizens – just as Aristotle has a huge metaphysic to show that the *polis* exists by nature for the purpose of making people political (i.e. not servile). But both Machiavelli and Aristotle have more empirical arguments why, in the long run and other things being equal, cities are likely to survive the longest if they are governed by a civic body, and not by princes or tyrants.

9. I find Walker's translation of *Ottimati* as 'upper-class' misleading (Walker, *Discourses*, vol. II, pp. 315–16). Better is his treatment of '*Grandi*' (which Machiavelli uses almost interchangeably) as 'leading men' or 'men of standing' – despite the fact that it can in some contexts be a technical term for hereditary nobility. Machiavelli is plainly talking of the *bourgeois* or the *haut bourgeois*: the *uomini populare* or *la plebe* are a damned nuisance, though their power *has to be* taken account of, but it is the middle range of men upon whose active participation a republic depends, not the upper class alone (if one thinks in terms of a scale of three orders). If, indeed, as we will see, the upper class are '*Gentiluomini*' – landed gentry – they have to be got rid of, quick and thorough, if a republic is to flourish!

ultimate restraining force, the final limitation – but also, as we will see, the real power, both civic and military, behind republics – as distinct from principalities – if managed shrewdly by the *Ottimati* in a political manner, not by simple coercion).

What is this 'regal power' doing in a republic? Quite plainly it is not a person, but a function or institution. There has to be power like that of kings: the ability for sudden and decisive action if republics, like any other state, are to withstand emergencies. Each of these elements intermingles: those republics which have survived the longest are those which have struck upon the most appropriate combination of these three elements to different circumstances. In the Second Discourse of Book I he sets out, with some mild confusion and error, the traditional Aristotelian categories of the three good types of government and the three corrupt forms; and he comments that 'prudent legislators' have refrained from adopting any such pure form as it stood but 'chose instead one that shared in them all, since they thought that such a government would be stronger and more stable, for if in one and the same state there was principality, aristocracy and democracy, each would keep watch over the other'.

Perhaps this is slightly confusing, but the main point is clear; he uses 'aristocracy' either in an ideal sense, close to Napoleon's and Jefferson's contrast between an 'aristocracy of talent' (good) and an 'aristocracy of birth' (bad), or in the way that we would use 'elite group'. The people without leadership are helpless, and a class of leaders arises in any known society; but this is only one side of the turbulent equation: leaders need followers, or rather the state depends, at the least, on the passivity of the people, but, far better – and herein to Machiavelli the greatness of Rome – if it can mobilize the power of the people. Then, it is irresistible: far stronger and more effective than a tyranny. This I take to be a general truth of modern politics. 'The politics of the future', said Napoleon, 'will be concerned with the art of moving the masses'. And I also take it to be true that to call governments 'democratic' is always a misleading piece of propaganda – or, once-upon-a-time, abuse. It confuses doctrine with theory: we may want the democratic element in government to grow greater, but it is still only an element while it is government at all. The concept 'republican', understood in Machiavelli's sense, is much more fruitful as a basis for explanatory theory than 'democratic'.[10]

The Mixture as Adaptability

When he says of the three elements in any republic that 'each would keep watch over the other', he seems to do himself less than justice. This could sound to our ears rather Whiggish and legalistic, smacking of 'checks and balances', or at best the strange mixture of Machiavellian realism and Whiggish legalism that is found in Madison's famous *Federalist* No. 10 on the inevitability and positive utility of factions. Machiavelli is not in the least worried about restraining governments (perhaps he should be), but rather in showing that well-managed republics are actually stronger than principalities – not that strength is the only value, for it is plainly also valuable to him to involve more men rather than less in the running of a state – if circumstances allow. For political life is life at its best – here he is thoroughly Greek and Roman: private life is only possible when most men (not all) commit most of their energy (not all) to the public interest or 'civic life'.

10. See my polemics against the usefulness of the concept of 'democracy' in my *In Defence of Politics* (Pelican, 1964), pp. 56–73; 'The Elementary Types of Government', *Government and Opposition*, Winter 1968, pp. 3–20; 'Philosophy, Theory and Thought', *Political Studies*, February 1967, and *Democracy* (Oxford University Press, 2002).

Badly placed, tucked oddly away in the sections on military discipline and tactics, there are three discourses (Book III. 7, 8 and 9) which repay special study by the political and social theorist. They are concerned with the need for states to adapt themselves to circumstances. Let us only pause to say that this is part of his fundamental originality, even to raise such a question, however woolly or particular the answers. The traditional view had been that states should only adapt themselves to moral purposes, and a single true purpose at that. Here we are, for the first time, on the edge of the relativity of morals; and there is a case, gently *contra* Raymond Aron, for seeing Machiavelli rather than Montesquieu as the first master of political sociology.

Discourse III.9 is simply headed: '*That it behoves one to adapt Oneself to the Times if one wants to enjoy Continued Good Fortune*'. As he is all too prone to do, he takes the most unlikely case, that of Fabius Maximus, 'Fabius Cunctator' – the delayer, whose tactics, all authorities agreed, saved Rome from the invasion of Hannibal. But, Machiavelli points out, when Scipio wanted to take the armies to Africa, a bold attack to polish off the weary Carthaginians on their home ground, Fabius disagreed. If he had been king, says Machiavelli, he would have got his way and Rome might easily, after all that, have lost or failed to win the war 'since he was incapable of altering his methods according as circumstances changed'. But being a republic, Rome had 'diverse citizens with diverse dispositions', so they could find a man with the audacity needed to gain complete victory just as Fabius had had the admirable caution (for the time) to avoid total defeat. Now whether all this is true or not as history, let me say just once, does not matter a damn. It is a generalization, admittedly very abstract and hard to apply to individual cases (that's the practical rub), but true of human societies in general. All the lovely stuff about Fabius and Scipio could just as well be an invented example: it cannot be treated as evidence, and then rejected because of inaccuracy. In the same way, he then speculates, to give the other side of the coin, that the impetuosity, dash and audacity of Pope Julius II was all very well in the circumstances, but had he lived on and not changed his tactics in changed circumstances, then he would have been ruined. Again, this is profoundly unhistorical – how can one possibly know whether he would have adapted or not? (It is hard enough to explain what did happen, let alone to explain what did not happen.) But is it simply a truism? That if we do not adapt, we do not survive? It is not a truism while any dominant tradition of thought holds that there is a single correct solution and that it will endure if adhered to strictly and with no compromises (as true for capitalism as for Marxism). Machiavelli's argument implies that adaptability through freedom is the key to the survival of human societies, just as the anthropologist Malinowski was to argue explicitly in his great work, *Freedom and Civilization*.

So the mixture is not a static matter of checks and balances, but a dynamic blending of three elements that are needed in different proportions at different times; and a republic contains, indeed nurtures, all the three elements, whereas a principality has to suppress all but one.

... a republic has a fuller life and enjoys good fortune for a longer time than a principality, since it is better able to adapt itself to diverse circumstances owing to the diversity found among its citizens than a prince can do. For a man who is accustomed to act in one particular way, never changes, as we have said. Hence, when times change and no longer suit his ways, he is inevitably ruined. (*Discourses* III.9)

And then he gives the painful example of Piero Soderini, the Gonfalonier or chief official of the Florentine Republic, under whom Machiavelli had served. He was good-natured, shrewd, patient and humble; but when military threat demanded that he 'drop his patience and humility, he could not bring himself to do it; so that both he and his country were ruined'. He could play the Fox, but not the Lion.

In other words, it is not being 'republican' to fail to defend the republic – a point of some lasting and topical interest. A republic must contain the potentiality for *la potestà regia*, as did, of course, his beloved Rome. '*Dictatorial Authority did Good, not Harm, to the Republic of Rome: it is the Authority which Citizens arrogate to Themselves, not that granted by Free Suffrage, that is harmful to Civic Life*' (the heading of *Discourses* I.34). He interpreted the Roman dictatorship as a constitutional office: one or two men were voted absolute power by the senate solely for the duration of the emergency (if they went on beyond that they were, constitutional theory had it, *ipso facto* outlaws, marked for the knife of the patriotic assassin). Again, one could dismiss this point as realistic but obvious. 'I claim that republics which, when in imminent danger, have recourse neither to a dictatorship, nor to some form of authority analogous to it, will always be ruined when grave misfortune befalls them' (I. 34). Obvious perhaps, but seldom stated in the literature of representative government – which tends to draw all too sharp a distinction between peace and war, or between order and violence, whereas Machiavelli is concerned with all the gradations between (with what Sheldon Wolin has well called, as one of Machiavelli's major themes, 'the economy of violence').

He goes beyond, however, the simple assertion that republics must, on occasion, make use of absolute power or dictatorial authority. He believes that when they do act thus, they have actually greater power than any principality. They are both more flexible and they are able, to him the most vital point of all, to trust their own people with arms. This is an interesting thought. Think how we tended to assume in the 1920s and 1930s that 'free government' must pay a price or run a risk in terms of power and efficiency when confronted by the new dictatorships. Most writers were proudly willing to pay it, *etcetera*, but they did not doubt the claims of their enemies to be more efficient and to be able to mobilize the whole economy, not just an army. It was freedom versus efficiency! But any comparison of British and German economic planning in the Second World War must throw doubt on this common assumption.[11] (And as for the Italian mobilization of industry! It now seems only embarrassing and incredible that men like George Bernard Shaw and H. G. Wells could be taken in by Mussolini's technological claptrap.) Britain achieved a degree of mobilization of human and material resources greater than that of Germany. For here responsibility could be devolved and men would take decisions at all levels, having been used to working as a team – whereas in the new autocracy decisions had to wait, often with disastrous delay, for the *Führer* to get round to them or to be in the right mood. Failure by a subordinate leader in an autocracy is usually viewed as treachery, punishable in the harshest ways. Failure in a republic is more often punished by being given a big job in a poor colony, or by innumerable forms of being kicked upstairs, locked out but not locked up (sometimes more's the pity). And there are, after all, gradations in all these things: he had himself been put to torture when the Medici came back to power, but then they allowed him to retire to his house in the country, in modest comfort and in no fear of his life; galling for him to have no political work to do, but fortunately he solaced his boredom and tried to earn his recall by reading for and writing *The Prince* and *The Discourses*.

11. See M. M. Postan, *British War Production* (H.M.S.O., 1952); he remarks on 'the miracle of Britain's government in the war . . . a government which was largely personal and yet free from the intellectual limitation of an autocracy'. See further the discussion on p. 258 ff. of my *The Reform of Parliament*, p. 452 2nd edn (London, 1968), in relation to Professor Samuel Beer's thesis about Parliament as a device for the 'mobilization of consent'.

Adaptability as a virtue of republics included, then, dictatorship – which history was to show was indeed stronger than that of any tyranny when exercised in the name of the People; but it also included popular power or democracy. Discourses 56–8 of Book I consider the advantages of popular government. We are faced with two apparently contradictory propositions: he quotes Titus Livius to the effect that while the people as a body are courageous, yet individually they are cowardly and feeble; but the next section is roundly headed 'The masses[12] are more knowing and more constant than is a prince.' Lurid examples are quoted of the fecklessness, inconstancy, ingratitude and unpredictability of the people; but, on the other hand, the Roman populace was 'for four hundred years . . . enemies to the very name of king and lovers of glory and of the common good of their country'. The people can be inconstant and disruptive, but no more or less than princes. Both do wrong and 'to the same extent when there is nothing to prevent them doing wrong'. Here there is a hint of checks and balances, but the kind of 'wrongs' he is talking about are not civil liberties or individual rights, but mistakes which threaten the safety of the state or the city. The important thing about the mixture is not that it should restrain the other elements, but that it should push them all into the most effective and concerted direction. The masses are useless without leadership, but given leadership it is irresistible; the state that can integrate its population into public life is far stronger than those traditional autocracies who have to rely either on the passivity or the fear of the people.

And if princes are superior to populaces in drawing up laws, codes of civic life, statutes and new institutions, the populace is so superior in sustaining what has been instituted, that it indubitably adds to the glory of those who have instituted them. (*Discourses* I.58)

12. *La moltitudine* and '*plebe*' and '*populo*' get used as synonyms – they might almost, in these contexts, be simply translated as 'mob'.

'What price glory?' the Princely reader of *The Discourses* might have said. The message is plain enough: princes to create or restore states, but republics to preserve them.

So Machiavelli takes the familiar theory of mixed government, but gives it a wholly new and dynamic dimension. He justified the role of the people in terms of the superiority, harping on his oldest obsession in Florentine politics, of a citizen militia to a professional, particularly a mercenary, army. We today might want to consider the economic role of the skilled industrial worker rather than the conscript citizen-soldier: quite apart from talk of rights, all modern states depend upon him: he can be granted genuine political rights, or he can be indoctrinated and mobilized in the most elaborate and fantastic manners; but, unlike the traditional picture of the peasant, he cannot be ignored. If the object of the state is now held to be his welfare, it is equally true that the safety of the state depends upon his support – on whatever terms. That is the historical order of things, and Machiavelli sees it clearly. Government precedes consent, but those who have the active consent of the people are the most powerful.

But what actually provides the motive force of this admittedly more dynamic model of mixed government? What keeps it flexible and forces it to adapt itself? Here he provides a remarkable answer.

The Value of Conflict

Until Machiavelli every writer on politics had assumed that states cohere because of some moral unity: to Aristotle the *polis* was part of nature and existed for the purpose of unfolding the goodness potential in man; this is what Cicero means by saying that a '*consensus juris*' is a necessary condition for republican rule; and it is at the heart of the Thomist teaching on natural law. Even if Augustine can challenge Cicero and argue that this consensus is not one relating to right and justice, but solely to interest, self-love and pride – 'states cohere like bands of robbers', yet this self-interest must still be all of one piece: if the thieves fall to quarrelling among themselves, their society is lost; they must hang together or they will hang separately. Even the realism of Augustine, however, would have strained at Machiavelli's astonishing contentions that discord can actually strengthen a state and that a republic consists of at least two different '*vivere*', ways-of-life or communities, not one.

I must quote at length in case I appear to be reading too much into Machiavelli – as is so often the case, particularly on a matter, crucial to social theory, which so few historical commentators seem to notice or to think important. There is no need to go further than the heading of Book I. 4: '*That Discord between the Plebs and the Senate of Rome made this Republic both Free and Powerful.*'

He discusses the tumults that broke out in Rome between the end of the Kings and the creation of the Tribunes representative of the people – ignoring the fact, or ignorant of it, that high levels of civil disorder in the streets were typical of Roman politics at almost any period. Many have deplored such disorders, he says. And he would be, as a Florentine citizen, very much more aware than we of the presence, the pressure, the threat of the mob; of how it could sometimes break out on its own, but more often be stirred up to support one quarrelling leader against another. He had seen them support the purges of the puritanical monk, Savonarola, and then turn against him, equally savagely. But much as he disliked and feared such violence or constant threats of violence, he saw some advantages flowing from it. Our eighteenth-century ancestors in London might have shared his feelings; it is we now who are exceptionally intolerant of public disorder, both because we dislike it (which is fair enough) and because we think it a threat to the state, something that inevitably 'escalates' – which may be a quite unwarranted theory considering how ritualistic and limited most violence is, rather than explosive and comprehensive.

'Those who condemn the quarrels between the nobles and the plebs, seem to be,' he says, 'cavilling at the very things that were the primary cause of Rome's retaining her freedom.' They pay too much attention to the 'noise and the clamour' and do not see the good effects produced; 'nor do they realize that in every republic there are two different dispositions, that of the populace and that of the upper class and that all legislation favourable to liberty is brought about by the clash between them'.

Liberty itself, then, arises from conflicts, as did the popular institutions of the Roman constitution: 'Hence if tumults led to the creation of the tribunes, tumults deserve the highest praise.' But more than liberty, or as well as liberty, political power: 'every city should provide ways and means whereby the ambitions of the populace may find an outlet, especially a city which proposes to avail itself of the populace in important undertakings.' If a city wishes to use its population for war or for great public works, then it must develop strong nerves and realize that constant troubles are inherent – but that the price, compared to weakness or stagnation, may well be worth paying. He sees the connection between Roman military tactics (calling both for great discipline and great individual skill) and her qualifications for citizenship – and he was surely right. His interest in military tactics lies at the heart of his understanding of politics, so not all those long chapters are to be skipped by the modern reader. *The Art of War* repeats or assumes every essential proposition of both *The Prince* and *The Discourses* – for the art of war is an extension of the whole social condition of a society. In other words, much of what he has to say about military technology and its relationship to politics can be boldly and roughly, but helpfully, translated into modern terms of industrial technology (though even then the purely military factor is not to be forgotten). He even assumes for military factors (as Marx did for economic) that decline and eventual collapse must follow failure to expand: one can never stand still, expansion and production have mastered us.

Discourse 6 of Book I then asks the question '*Whether in Rome such a Form of Government could have been set up as would have removed the Hostility between the Populace and the Senate*'. And he answers it very precisely:

> All things considered, therefore, it was necessary for Rome's legislators to do one of two things if Rome was to remain tranquil . . .: either to emulate the Venetians and not employ its plebs in wars, or, like the Spartans, not to admit foreigners. Rome did both these things, and, by doing so, gave to its plebs alike strength, increase, and endless opportunities for commotion. On the other hand, had the government of Rome been such as to bring greater tranquillity, there would have ensued this inconvenience, that it would have been weaker, owing to its having cut off the source of supply which enabled it to acquire the greatness at which it arrived, so that, in seeking to remove the causes of tumults, Rome would have removed also the causes of expansion . . .
>
> Squabbles between the populace and the senate should, therefore, be looked upon as an inconvenience which it is necessary to put up with in order to arrive at the greatness of Rome.

Conflict can thus play a positive role in the mobilization of all the resources of a state. But how much 'squabbling' does it take to make a serious revolt or even a revolution? He gives us no criteria to judge this. He is not a modern social scientist. He is a Renaissance state-councillor in enforced retirement (and thus freed from many inhibitions) giving maxims to politicians and princes. One could reformulate the main maxim above this way, 'Don't worry in republics about inconvenience, insults or "matters of principle"; judge by the effect on liberty and on the safety and power of the state.' The maxim implies a theory, however, that republics are naturally diverse and find their strength in diversity – they can and should drive two fierce horses on a loose rein; but in a principality, *per contra*, a tight rein is called for: the smallest disorders must be struck down savagely at their first occurrence before they grow. And from this maxim, one can now attempt to formulate theories for particular eras or societies: that is now our business, and an extraordinarily difficult one. But he first pointed to the general theory: that political conflict can be functional. Far from believing that it is the business of social science to eliminate conflict, we may want, instead, to follow Machiavelli's lead and to define and study it more precisely, so many types of conflict and so many different circumstances. Plainly Machiavelli exaggerates, his instincts and situation lead him to dramatize rather than consciously to abstract and to build models of social systems and processes as do modern students of society, but he does point to a whole dimension of understanding, still not sufficiently explored, but a closed door entirely before he wrote: the civilizing of conflict, not its enervating elimination.

Factors of Social Class

The most important cause of conflict is struggle between classes. He is well aware of the importance of social composition in determining, his master question, whether a state can most easily be a republic or a principality. He considers that 'equality' is extremely important, not equality for all, remember that he was a republican and not a democrat, but the existence of a large class of equals. How large? He never tries to work this out at all precisely, but plainly a body of men too large to be managed by the informal methods of influence of a palace or a court. They may be a minority of the population, and usually will be in the pre-industrial world of republics; but they will be large enough to develop some kinds of elective institutions and a known structure of government – an electorate, an assembly and a council. Broadly speaking, he thinks that the citizen body will be the tax-paying classes (*Discourses*, I.55), who are likely to be a minority, but the largest minority. This body must guard against any of its members giving themselves the riches and airs, and finally the claims to power, of nobility; but also against any of its members, ruined by trade or ill fortune, trying to stir up the plebs to gain office for themselves (the familiar analysis of Aristotle's Book V). This is all he means by equality, equal as citizens; but with some ill-defined but definite recognition that there are extremes of real wealth and poverty, relatively conceived, which can render civic equality impossible. But, on this level of abstraction, this is all the Jacobins meant by equality. The view that anyone had the right to take part in politics, apart from any possession of property, is an extraordinarily late one – securely held no earlier than the second half of the nineteenth century, certainly neither the Americans of 1776 or the French of 1793 held it. He states:

> Let then a republic be constituted where there exists, or can be brought into being, notable equality; and a regime of the opposite type, that is a principality, where there is notable inequality. Otherwise what is done will lack proportion and will be of but short duration. (*Discourses* I.55.)

This is a very Aristotelian or a very bourgeois view of the world. But the world was and is still astonishingly like that. If this still seems too vague, some view of who he thought the citizen class were, and of how passionately he identified with them, may be inferred from his treatment of their great enemy – *gentiluomini*.

He advances the fantastic historical view that political life had continued uncorrupted in some German cities because

they did not allow any of their citizens to 'live after the fashion of gentry'; and that if any real gentry fell into their hands,
'they treat them as sources of corruption and causes of scandal,
and kill them':

... the term 'gentry' is used of those who live in idleness on the
abundant revenue derived from their estates, without having anything to do either with their cultivation or with other forms of
labour essential to life. Such men are a pest in any republic and in
any province ... (ibid.)

Notice, in passing, the moral assumption implicit in condemning people for not having to labour. Here is a bourgeois
assumption, indeed – a shift from even the Aristotelian justification of leisure, as the condition for knowledge and good citizenship, and of property as a means to that end. Machiavelli's
property, it appears, has a dynamic of its own: It is the duty of
men – just as John Locke was to argue – to use and improve
it.[13]

For such *gentiluomini*, he says, are 'particularly pernicious'
when they control castles and loyal subjects as well as the revenues from their estates. There are plenty of these men in different parts of Italy. So:

... in these provinces there has never arisen any republic or any
political life, for men born in such conditions are entirely inimical to
any form of civic government [*d'ogni civilità*]. In provinces thus
organized no attempt to set up a republic could possibly succeed. To
reconstitute them, should anyone want to do so, the only way
would be to set up a monarchy there. The reason for this is that,
where the material is so corrupt, laws do not suffice to keep it in

13. But I would not imply that Machiavelli was wholly consistent on
this point: at other times he displays the traditional scholarly or aristocratic contempt for economic activity; but always stronger against land-
lords and peasants than against city-dwellers. (But nor are any of us
consistent on this point.)

hand; it is necessary to have, besides laws, a superior force, such as appertains to a monarch, who has such absolute and overwhelming power that he can restrain excesses due to ambition and the corrupt practices of the powerful. (ibid.)

Notice, also, that he appears to shift from his basic dualistic theory of government to a tripartite one. If, the most glorious of all human actions and the most difficult, a republic is to be created from unlikely material, it calls for personal power; but the prince who takes up power in order to create a republic is then honoured with the name of monarch. But this really does call for *personal* power, whereas the third force, or the *potestà regia*, which is needed to cope with emergencies in a republic, this can be handled by a commission (rather as Hobbes hedges or admits that the terrible power of Leviathan is not necessarily that of one person), although it is ordinarily better handled by the *constitutional* office of Dictator.

So finally, his own words are better than any paraphrase:

From this discussion the following conclusion may be drawn: (i) that, where the gentry are numerous, no one who proposes to set up a republic can succeed unless he first gets rid of the lot; and (ii) that, where considerable equality prevails, no one who proposes to set up a kingdom or a principality, will ever be able to do it unless from that equality he selects many of the more ambitious and restless minds and makes of them gentry in fact and not in name, by giving them castles and possessions and making of them a privileged class with respect both to property and subjects; so that around him there will be those with whose support he may maintain himself in power, and whose ambitions, thanks to him, may be realized. As to the rest they will be compelled to bear a yoke which nothing but force will ever be able to make them endure. (ibid.)

Here is the familiar 'either/or' alternative; and then follows the most famous passage (as we will see below) about the dangers of striking any middle course; but the alternative is put, cutting in both directions, in terms of the need to change and the possibility of changing, the whole class structure of a society if one wishes (as a matter of principle presumably) to go wholly against the grain.

The Conditions for Republican Rule

The threads can now be drawn together. Machiavelli considers that republics can flourish, or that principalities can only be created with extraordinary difficulty, when six conditions exist: (i) that there is a respect for custom and tradition; (ii) that the town dominates the country; (iii) that a large middle class exists; (iv) that popular power is institutionalized; (v) that civic spirit or *virtù* has not decayed; and (vi) that there is a knowledge of these things. If these conditions prevail, he is absolutely clear that men *should* support republican government and *should not*, although it is possible, subvert it. If they do not prevail, men should not ordinarily attempt republican government – the result will be ruin for themselves and the state; but it is just possible for a really extraordinary individual to create a republic out of unlikely and rotten material, but only success can justify it: it is so difficult that Machiavelli never argues that it should be attempted, only that, if attempted and successful, it is the greatest feat in the world – the memory of those few who have done it will live for ever, they are among the Immortals. Let us say a word about each of the conditions in turn.

(i) *A respect for custom and tradition* is extremely important. However much stress Machiavelli puts on the prince or the monarch as innovator or restorer, the basic laws and customs of free government have to be there and have to be seen to be there and respected. So often does he come back to this theme of restoring ancient virtues, that one wonders if he really believed that originally all states were naturally republics, or that there have only ever been few republics, Rome above all

– remarkable and exemplary offspring of extraordinary circumstances and great men? But he has too practical and historical a mind to get involved in speculations about the origins of human society. He simply makes, on a commonsense reading, a practical and rather pessimistic point: you have to build on something. Free institutions are not a bright idea that can be dreamed up and voted in or wished on another: they must expand upon or restore some traditional institution.

This should be noted by all those who contemplate . . . setting up a new and free form; because, since novelties cause men to change their minds, you should see to it that changes retain as much as possible of what is old, and that, if changes are made in the number, the authority and the period of office of the magistrates, they should retain the traditional names.

This, as I have said, should be observed by anyone who proposes to set up a political regime, whether by way of a republic or of a monarchy. But he who proposes to set up a despotism, or what writers call a 'tyranny', must renovate everything. (*Discourses* I.25.)

(ii) *That the town must dominate the country* comes out in his contempt for both gentlemen and peasants. 'Citizen' is literally the inhabitant of a city, and inhabitants of cities should (if all these conditions prevail) have some voice in the running of their city; and only inhabitants of cities have both the will and the opportunity to do so on some regular basis. It is not true to say that Machiavelli only considered the problems of 'city states' and ignored the big kingdoms, if the contrast is then seen as between urban government and rural landowning. For he was well aware that the most powerful of the Italian city states, like his own Florence, owned large areas of the countryside and that the population of the city itself was usually a minority of the inhabitants of the state. The denunciation of the *gentiluomini* turns on this point, as does his scorn for the lack of *virtù* in the peasants. He was not limiting his sights, so much as expressing both a definite value judgement

44

and a definite theory: that civilization itself – morality, civic spirit, learning, art, science and commerce – was a product of city life; and that only in states with large and politically dominant cities have there ever been republics. (iii) *A large middle class* or a substantial equality must exist. This can be seen as equality only on a narrowly political basis (and then only for some) but also, more basically, as the absence of inequalities so great as to render men too powerful or too desperate. This has already been discussed, enough to say that the citizen class is not so large as for the state to be exclusively democratic (always republican or mixed government, never the democratic element alone), nor so small as to be able to function as an informal oligarchy.[14] He says nothing about how this 'relative equality' came to be, nor about how it can be deliberately achieved: his political theory lacks an economic basis, but it has moved forward from almost purely philosophical and moral theories.

(iv) *Popular power* must not dominate, but it must be channelled effectively, it can never be repressed if a republic is to thrive. This, as we have seen, is the heart of his theory of conflict. Each of the two classes has its peculiar characteristic and

14. I would actually prefer to beg many questions and to say 'bourgeois', for 'middle class' implies an 'upper class' whereas Machiavelli implies that his '*Grandi*' or '*Ottimati*' are better off without the *Gentiluomini*: they are only 'upper class' by contrast to the populace or lower class – a point that Walker at times confuses in his translation. But Machiavelli is not at all consistent in his vocabulary. The basic point is that he uses, as it were, a three rank scale for his general analysis of political systems – upper (as aristocratic), middle (bourgeois?) and lower, but advocates 'lopping off' the top when it comes to ensuring stability in a republic, and thereafter uses a two-rank scale. Hence he either uses '*Grandi*' (which can mean 'nobility' even) very loosely when discussing a republic, or is flattering 'the cits', or is using it to mean something like 'ruling class' irrespective of which social group is in the saddle. In fact, he seems to use it in all three ways.

function – skill and power respectively. What is to be feared is not class strife, which, if nerves are strong and the army is loyal, gives the state its vigour and dynamism, but is faction. Faction is division within classes, particularly among the *Ottimati*, and this tempts men to try to seize personal power and gives them the opportunity. Certainly, there is some idealization here – just as in Aristotle: the division of functions between the classes is too neat to be fully plausible. But if his value judgements intrude here upon his analysis, let not ours also. He is not to be rejected for being against democracy as a form of government, but respected for the clear-headed way in which he recognizes the power of the people: a republican government may have to bamboozle them, but it cannot ignore them. Republics are normally, or in the long run always, stronger than principalities because they have the people behind them. Machiavelli is well aware that power, in the (princely) sense of unchallengeability, is not the same thing as power to get things done. States that can integrate popular power in political institutions are stronger, can achieve more and are more adaptable.

(v) *Civic spirit or virtù* is the thing most difficult to create, or to destroy. The importance of individual action and the place of politics as the most important and glorious object of human activity, these themes underlie the whole set of the theoretical assumptions of *The Discourses* – so they will be discussed below. Sufficient here to say that a republic depends upon active citizens; in a principality such men either do not exist, or they have to be corrupted or destroyed.

(vi) It is not enough that these social relationships exist, *they must be known to exist*. 'Knowledge is power' is, indeed, a glove that fits. There is a rational and conscious knowledge of state-craft to be gained from history and topical examples which does help greatly (but it can never ensure) the preservation of the state, occasionally even the changing of the system of

government. In this respect he is both a Renaissance humanist and an innovator; he is not, for all his stress on tradition, a
premature conservative of the school of Burke. But, as we will
now see, the knowledge is admittedly not as precise as in the
natural sciences and is always conditional. It does not yield any
universal methodology for the study of politics, nor any single
formula for its conduct: rather, it points to relevant considerations and offers, not iron laws but probable tendencies, not
programmes for action but precepts and maxims – and always
conditional on someone wishing to take up the Greek gift of
power. For instance, it is from a knowledge of politics that
rulers of a republic, if they are wise, will make legal provision
for the institution of a Dictator in time of emergency. This is
extremely important, obviously, but it is not, as such, an
historical or sociological prerequisite for the existence of
republics, only for their preservation *if* such circumstances
arise (as they are *likely* to); nor does Machiavelli himself
generalize it, as did Bodin and Hobbes, into a theory of
'sovereignty' as a precondition for stability.

Are these criteria at all clear? How far could one use them,
then or now, to judge what form of government is possible?

Theory and Method

It may be helpful in trying to answer these questions and in
assessing what Machiavelli did and what he didn't do, to distinguish between three levels of political study. By *political
thought* I mean the ordinary opinions that people hold, their
immediate demands, assumptions and the conditioned reflec-
tions they hold about the politics of their time. In this sense,
Machiavelli's opinions are obviously interesting to the historian as a part of Italian Renaissance history, *cum grano salis* as
to how typical he was; but his two works that could be formally called political theory are no more, or no less, important

than the rest of his writings, including the many letters and diplomatic papers that survive; and these are not our particular concern.[15] By *political theory* I mean attempts to explain political attitudes and behaviour in terms of generalizations about allegedly typical relationships between concepts and circumstances. In this sense, Machiavelli is undoubtedly a political theorist: he fairly bristles with generalizations (which is what many contemporary historians have against him). Some are very conventional to the classical world if not to the middle ages of Christendom, some are new, but all have a high degree of consistency – an internal consistency at least. By *political philosophy* I mean attempts to resolve or simply to understand conflicts between political theories which might appear equally plausible as explanations of a given circumstance; and it can take two forms (not necessarily incompatible): simply an analysis of the terms and concepts used in the theories, or attempts to establish ethical criteria to judge between the desirability of different doctrines.[16] In neither of these senses can Machiavelli possibly be called a political philosopher. Better for him that he had been, even on the elementary level of clarity, more consistent in the use of key concepts like '*Fortuna*', '*Necessità*' and '*Virtù*', but he wasn't. He was simply astonishingly fertile and imaginative in the framing of hypotheses (as it is better to call generalizations which as yet lack adequate verification, or more precisely, which people still hope to disprove).

Thus it is much easier to state a reasonably clear general theory of republican and princely government from Machiavelli than it is to be clear about the logical grounds on which he reached his conclusions. In view of the many claims that

15. As they were splendidly in J. R. Hale's short and rewarding *Machiavelli and Renaissance Italy* (London, 1961).

16. I have elaborated these distinctions in my 'Philosophy, Theory and Thought', op. cit.

have been made for the originality of his method (and disputes as to what it is), as well as his own brief boasts in the Dedications to both *The Prince* and *The Discourses*, this may seem a surprising conclusion.[17] But I suspect that the constant search for THE METHOD of Machiavelli is in itself largely a misunderstanding of the nature of scientific method. A rigidity of method is attributed to him which he neither possessed nor did he pursue, and he is then criticized for not in fact proving faithful to it. And this is done both by enthusiastic social scientists, who believe in *the* scientific method, and by historians, who do not believe in that sort of thing at all, but imply that Machiavelli did, but, not unnaturally, failed in trying to apply it.[18]

17. His most extended claim for originality occurs in Chapter 15 of *The Prince*; but notice that even here the concern is basically with morality – the method is vague, unless it simply consisted in the doing without conventional morality (here I use George Bull's Pelican Classics translation): 'It now remains for us to see how a prince should govern his conduct towards his subjects or his friends. I know that this has often been written about before, and so I hope it will not be thought presumptuous for me to do so, as, especially in discussing this subject, I draw up an original set of rules. But since my intention is to say something that will prove of practical use to the inquirer, I have thought it proper to represent things as they are in real truth, rather than as they are imagined. Many have dreamed up republics and principalities which have never in truth been known to exist; the gulf between how one should live and how one does live is so wide that a man who neglects what is actually done for what should be done learns the way to self-destruction rather than self-preservation. The fact is that a man who wants to act virtuously in every way necessarily comes to grief among so many who are not virtuous. Therefore if a prince wants to maintain his rule he must learn how not to be virtuous, and to make use of this or not according to need.'

What Bull translates as 'virtuous' is '*buono*', not *virtù*, i.e. the conventional and Christian idea of goodness; and his 'according to need' tones down Machiavelli's harsh and recurrent, '*necessità*'.

18. Of which viewpoint Sir Herbert Butterfield's *The Statecraft of Machiavelli* (London, 1940) is the least extreme example.

A rigidly inductivist view is attributed to him: that theories can be derived from an unprejudiced observation of all the facts. And then, of course, it can be shown that he does not consider all the facts, gets many of them wrong, that his historical sources were unreliable and that he is also biased in favour of freedom, variety and change. Two schools of error debate with each other uselessly at this point: that his love of the ancient authors misled him into trusting their accuracy, and hence the whole thing fails; or that his 'brutal realism' should have led him, anyway, to discount history but to gather systematically aggregate data on the states of his time (and we can now do better than he in this respect, thanks to the Ford Foundation and the *American Political Science Review*).

Learning is still, in some sense, a unity – at least all of a piece. One would have thought that the inductivist fallacy could not have survived works like Sir Karl Popper's *Logic of Scientific Discovery*. What is surely important about scientific scholarship, natural or social, is the ability to frame meaningful generalizations (without which 'facts' are infinite and have no order) in such a way that they are capable of being refuted by observation and thus are, in that sense, regarded as 'verified' or as having stood the test if, after much careful observation or experiment, they have not been shown to be false. Methodologies are either a retrospective commentary upon scientific discovery or they are rules for the consolidation and extension of discoveries by deducing further hypotheses from a general theory – and testing them; they are not an *a priori* set of rules for making major discoveries and framing general theories.

Of Machiavelli's fertility as a theorist or theory-maker there can be no reasonable doubt. The manner in which he reaches these conclusions is ultimately irrelevant. It is very disputable, however (and perhaps not very important), in what sense if any he deserves to be called a political scientist or scientific historian: for despite his almost invariable habit of considering contrary instances and explaining them away, the dice are usually loaded. On the other hand, by contrast to most authors who went before, his respect for experience is great. But, as we will see in the next section, this respect is based on a very definite set of value judgements: that we should consider men as they are and government as a utilitarian, human institution; and not judge men by one set of transcendent moral standards and classify regimes by their intentions, but both by their behaviour. His is a secular and not a religious spirit, superficially at least, but this is far from saying that his works are those of Cassirer's 'cold and scientific technician'. In so far as he is a modern secularist (for he is a classical pagan as well), he holds secular values – although again, he is no philosopher, so he asserts some and assumes others, but attempts no logical justification.[19]

It is wrong, if one takes him as a whole, to put too much weight on his occasional sayings to the effect that 'human nature is everywhere the same', or that 'history repeats itself'. These remarks are almost meaningless. What does he mean by 'human nature'? This is never clear. Does he mean attitudes or behaviour? And if either, he certainly shows more evidence for variation than for fixity. Perhaps there is a 'human nature' quite apart from different and changing attitudes and behaviour? But he does not explore these deep waters of natural law or philosophical anthropology. 'History repeats itself' can simply be a warrant for drawing some lessons from past events, but if it is a rigid determinism, then his whole ethical position (as we will finally see) cuts against it.

19. 'Ah, does this make him an existentialist?' No, damn it: it just makes him this much less adequate; he just didn't get around to doing it, nor ever – probably – to understanding what needed to be done. He wasn't an anti-philosopher; he just was not a philosopher – the point that the great Leo Strauss wilfully misses in his huge and denunciatory, *Thoughts on Machiavelli* (Free Press, Glencoe, Ill., 1958).

Tendencies work in a particular direction, but it is always possible for fortune to change or for the really extraordinary leader to reshape things. 'Whosoever wishes to foretell the future must consider the past, for human events ever resemble those of preceding times.' This is common sense, if one allows 'resemble' to mean what is ordinarily meant by 'resemble'; but if one chooses to think that he meant by 'resemble' something like 'are ever determined by', then this is wrong, and it is not his view either.[20] Choices can always be made, though they may not be the right ones.

No one, however, is likely to have been so fertile as a theory-maker, so many of whose theories still appear true, without some method or typical procedure. But it was a much more informal and eclectic method than is often suggested. I cannot do better than quote Father Walker on this point:

The procedure Machiavelli himself adopts consists essentially:
(i) In looking in history for some incident likely to recur ... and in enquiring as to its consequences, *good or bad*, relative to the person

20. See, for example, *Discourses* III, 39, '*That a General ought to be acquainted with the Lie of the Land.*' He argues that hunting is a very good sport for military leaders – it gives them an exact knowledge of the particular terrain of their country and 'it also enables one who has familiarized himself with one district, to grasp with ease the details of any new region. For all countries and all their parts have about them *a certain uniformity*, so that from the knowledge of one, it is easy to pass to the knowledge of another; whereas he who has not acquired a good experience of any one, can with difficulty acquire a knowledge of another.' (my italics).
Would any one seriously argue from this passage that he believes (i) that terrain is everywhere the same, and (ii) that in the same type of terrain a hunt will always follow the same course? Specific features of the terrain and events of a hunt will not recur, but hunting is a good preparation for war just as reading history is the best preparation for politics (but equally does not provide iron laws or magic formulae, though many useful manuals can be written on both).

or persons in question and to the state; or, alternatively, in noting some consequence . . . *disastrous or beneficial*, and then enquiring into the line of conduct which brought it about.

(ii) In enquiring further whether there are any other instances of such a sequence to be found in history, of which one, at least, should have occurred in relatively modern times.

(iii) In formulating, given that such a sequence has occurred, a generalization stating that on the occurrence of the antecedent, X, the consequent, Y, always, *or often, or, in most cases*, follows; *preferably*, of course, invariably follows.

(iv) In enquiring whether there are any negative instances . . .

(v) In enquiring whether the consequence is desirable or undesirable from the standpoint of . . . specifiable inclinations and appetites; and in formulating a maxim stating . . . the line of conduct . . . to be carried out *if the consequence is desired*, or is to be avoided *if the consequence is not desired*.

(vi) The precepts of moralists . . . are to be judged by their consequences in precisely the same way as any other institution, custom or practice; and, should these consequences turn out to be politically harmful, this is to be pointed out lest, in deference to moralists, rulers should adopt a line of policy likely to end in political disaster.[21]

Such is his procedure. But it hardly tells us, still, how he seizes upon certain incidents as likely to recur. Nor does it establish any procedure for validation as elaborate as is normally implied in a scientific methodology. It looks far more rigid than it is. Essentially it is the way in which Machiavelli sets about writing, it is not the procedure by which he sets out to validate his conclusions. There is no such procedure. He read history, he took part in politics, he read every letter or report he could on the events of his times. When he went into exile, he read solidly, but read few books that he was not, in some manner, familiar with before. Many of these books he had referred to or plagiarized in his longer and more discursive

---

21. Walker, *Discourses* I, pp. 82–3, my italics.

diplomatic reports.[22] He loved and used the ancient authors then, but he no more followed them slavishly as a diplomat than he did as a scholar. He was not, in Michael Oakeshott's sense, a 'rationalist': one who might take his politics from a book – even though many people have treated him in this way.[23]

His general theory of mixed government, his subsidiary theories of the function of conflict and of types of government, these he drew from his books and his experience, both inextricably intermingled, and all seen through a pair of eyes at once remarkably cool and remarkably unconventional.[24] One more theory must be made explicit. His view of history, not as determined progression, nor as a remorseless cycle of recurring forms, but simply as constant change – to which forms of government must adjust – and uncertainty – in which any form of government must be flexible:

> Since … all human affairs are ever in a state of flux, and cannot stand still, either there will be improvement or decline, and necessity will lead you to do many things which reason does not recommend. Hence if a commonwealth be constituted with a view to its maintaining the *status quo*, but not with a view to expansion, and by necessity it be led to expand, its basic principles will be subverted and it will soon be faced with ruin. So, too, should heaven, on the other hand, be so kind to it that it has no need to go to war, it will then come about that idleness will either render it effeminate or give rise to factions; and these two things, either in conjunction or separately, will bring about its downfall. (*Discourses* I.6].

22. See Christian E. Detmold, ed., *The Historical, Political and Diplomatic Writings of Niccolò Machiavelli*, 4 vols. (Boston, 1882).

23. The criticism that he often follows Livy and Polybius so closely or plagiarizes from them, has to be balanced against the criticism that he uses his historical sources so very selectively. Both are half-truths: he took what he wanted to suit his theories and conclusions.

24. As his gay, audacious, cynical, dirty and first-class second-rate play, *The Mandragola*, well shows.

We may search for and find empirical arguments to bolster our moral objection to the view thus implied of continual military and territorial expansion, or of constant readiness for expansion. But we should also be able to find – and would we try as hard? – similar arguments today against the assumption in *both* capitalism and Marxism of constant economic expansion or bust. Most of his arguments in terms of military technology are now directly translatable in terms of economic technology. Even when we stay in the same place, we have to run pretty fast to do it. Few of us doubt that it is a 'necessary' part of the practical legitimacy of any *modern* regime that it should claim and appear effective to raise, not just maintain, the standard of living of its inhabitants or, at least, the Gross National Product. We simply assume (if, perhaps, rashly) 'political and economic development'. And we also assume (largely because Machiavelli taught us to) that forms of government are relative to circumstances.

But if no philosophy or formal methodology are to be found in Machiavelli, certain concepts recur constantly, both explicitly and implicitly binding together his theories into some sort of coherence. They are *Necessità, Fortuna* and *Virtù*.

Necessity. Many commentators reject the alleged method of Machiavelli because of his proneness to call things 'necessary'; just as many critics of Marx and Engels take their use of this term, with greater warrant, at its face value, but having, like Berlin and Popper, shown brilliantly and properly that 'necessity' can never be proved, they then neglect to ask *how true* are the actual theories, regardless of whether they are only probable rather than demonstrably 'necessary'. There is usually a good deal more rhetoric than logic about 'necessary', but this does not necessarily invalidate the conclusions, although it makes them tentative and fallible but still, perhaps, likely. In fact, Machiavelli's 'necessity' is only ever a hypothetical or consequential necessity: if you wish to achieve X, you must do Y and Z. It is 'necessary for a prince to know how to act like a beast as well as a man' – that is if he is to maintain his position. And, again from *The Prince*, chapter 18, a new prince, especially, 'is often driven (*necessitato*), in order to maintain his position, to act contrary to good faith, charity, humanity and religion: he has need of a mind ready to turn according as the winds of fortune and changes in the situation dictate'.[25] As Walker comments, 'the conflict between expediency and morality could scarce be more plainly expressed'. 'Necessity' is always political necessity in given social conditions; but this stands and falls by his moral identification with the preservation of the state as the first object of human activity: it has absolutely nothing to do with eighteenth- and nineteenth-century attempts to find objective laws of development for human society. And one *can* always avoid 'political necessity' by retirement into private life or by flight; it is simply the case that – by one scale of values – one should not. It is necessary, implies Machiavelli, for someone to get his hands dirty in running a state, or to take up the burden or the curse of political power. It depends for what sort of state. When he says in *Discourses* III.41 that when the safety and freedom of one's country are at stake, 'no attention should be paid either to justice or injustice, kindness or cruelty . . .', it is clear in the context that he means by freedom both the independence of a state and its maintenance of its own customary laws. Some might still not agree, and on one scale of values we then honour them as secular or religious saints ('Let justice be done though the heavens fall', as it improbably says above the Old Bailey Criminal Court in London); but we must then gently note that they are right outside politics. Machiavelli puts as a

25. Quoted by Walker in his admirable section on 'Necessity and Fortune' in *Discourses* I, p. 75. And see also chapter 15 of *The Prince*, quoted above p. 47.

dramatic – perhaps melodramatic – maxim what Lincoln once put as a sobering reflection: 'It has long been a grave question whether any government not too strong for the liberties of its people, can be strong enough to maintain its liberties in great emergencies.' But I suspect it was the same, essentially humanistic, dilemma of 'necessity of state' in both men.

Fortune. 'As the winds of fortune and changes in the situation dictate ...' Fortune, the woman, is ever changeable. Things rarely remain fixed for long. The politician must know this and guard against it. 'Changes in the situation' can be narrowly political, as so often in the turbulent politics of his time, but beneath this superficial level there is, as the whole stress on social classes and conflict shows, a sociological level of tendencies and shaping factors. If these tendencies are properly understood, Fortune can be guarded against and resisted. The famous passage on Fortune in *The Prince*, Chapter 25, compares Fortune to a river which, when in flood cannot be resisted and sweeps all away, but against which in fair weather men can take precautions of building embankments and dykes. These precautions may not work, but sometimes they do; and this is the path of political prudence. But if these precautions have not been taken, or prove ineffective, there is still the possibility of intense personal or princely audacity succeeding – as in the famous metaphor of Fortune the woman who must be taken by force[26] (a remote possibility,

26. See above, p. 20. Notice that the metaphors of both 'the river in flood' and '*Donna e mobile*' are marginally more voluntaristic than the traditional medieval 'wheel of fortune', which remorselessly spins the Emperor to death and the beggarman to health and long life and so on and on. However, between the *Prince* and the *Discourses* the concept varies in stress. In the *Discourses* the voluntaristic element of audacity is less (*Discourses* II.29), one man is less likely to bring about great changes, but hope lies in a more collective adaptation to Fortune (*Discourses* III.9).

but, in the circumstances, the only thing to do if an ethic of action rather than one of suffering is to be pursued). So Fortune is not necessity. It can, in theory and occasionally in practice, be resisted by men of super-abundant *virtù*. In fact, this is part of the strength of republics over principalities. If the Borgia prince, the great lion-cum-fox, is ready with his army in the hills to descend on Rome and coerce the election of the new Pope, he may be suddenly struck down by fever and reduced to a babbling impotence, recovering too late so that the whole enterprise collapses. But in a republic there would have been others to step in his place. On the other hand, it is unlikely that such an enterprise could have been launched but by one resolute man.

So Machiavelli's Fortune is not simply accident, nor is it a kind of deterministic sociology, nor yet the preordained 'Doom' of the northern myths or even the fatalism of the inactive cynic: it is the sudden, aweful and challenging piling up of social factors and contingent political events in an unexpected way. Now there is something mythological about some of the ways he uses the concept: it is part of his pagan ethic. The 'gods' or 'the heavens' send good Fortune or bad Fortune with inscrutable whimsy. It is prudent to accept Fortune as she comes; but it is heroic, and sometimes successful, to resist. Something of the god-like is attributed to the man who can rape Fortune. And this need not be mere literary imagery in Machiavelli: it is a touch of classical paganism, that men and gods are (unlike in Christianity) of one substance, so that a man who has super-abundant skill, force, manliness and all that can possibly go to make up *virtù*, becomes a demi-god.[27]

27. See, for example, *Discourses* II.2. This 'beatifying' of heroes may seem nonsense. But there is a general empirical element even here. Consider how Marxists, arguing that thought is a product of circumstances, have tried to account for the position of Marx himself – he really must have been a most extraordinary person, even though it is

Plainly there is a great unresolved muddle in Machiavelli between the concepts of Necessity and Fortune; but neither invalidate his general theories nor spoil what is, in the result, the extraordinary balance he strikes between factors of social conditioning and freedom of action.

Virtù. The last phrase of the first chapter of *The Prince* says that a prince can govern a new state, '*o per fortuna o per virtù*'. 'Either by fortune or by prowess', George Bull ingeniously renders it; W. K. Marriott's translation has it as 'ability'; Allan Gilbert's as 'strength and wisdom'; some of the older translations said simply, 'valour'; and Father Walker sometimes risks the ambiguous 'virtue' itself. The last is possibly the best solution, although in English the particular meaning of virtue implied is now somewhat archaic, but not so archaic that anyone who can read Shakespeare or the King James Bible would not be with it.[28] Better still, perhaps, to admit defeat and to regard the term, in all its rich connotations, as untranslatable.

only Stalin and Mao Tse Tung who took on many of the claims and attributes of classical demi-gods. Karl Mannheim, too, even on the purely intellectual level of his *Ideology and Utopia* and *Essays on the Sociology of Knowledge*, had to dig himself out of the pit of 'ideology' by flatteringly inventing 'free-floating intellectuals'. Hitler, wrapped up in a deterministic rhetoric, had to give himself direct insight into the intentions of Providence and the future of history. Intellectually, this shows the danger of getting into such a position to start with (and here Machiavelli's rhetoric sometimes traps him); but politically it shows clearly that Machiavelli was right to see that such a *claim* to super-human knowledge or skill can form a part of even (or especially) the most rational theories of politics.

28. See *Oxford English Dictionary*. Nothing to do with 'conformity of life and conduct with the principles of morality'; still less with 'Chastity, sexual purity'; something to do with 'An accomplishment'; but rather 'Efficacy arising from physical qualities ... (Middle English)'; and, directly on target, 'The possession or display of manly qualities; manly excellence, manliness (Middle English).'

It comes from the Roman '*vir*' (man) and '*virtus*' (what is proper to a man). But what is proper to a man? Courage, fortitude, audacity, skill and civic spirit – a whole classical and renaissance theory of man and culture underlies the word: man is himself at his best when active for the common good – and he is not properly a man otherwise: politics is not a necessary evil, it is the very life. It has little or nothing to do with the Christian concept of virtue and virtuousness – virtuosity is closer to the mark. Machiavelli, indeed, sees *virtù* and the Christian doctrines of humility as directly opposed. Usually the word is far from morally neutral. To say 'life-force', 'guts', 'will power', 'valour' or 'high spirit' helps in understanding its predominant meaning to Machiavelli, but is insufficient. Certainly there are occasions when he uses it simply to mean technique and efficiency; he is not wholly consistent. But ordinarily, as must be plain to anyone who reads *The Discourses* as well as *The Prince*, *virtù* implies a specifically civic spirit. *Virtù* is the quality of mind and action that creates, saves or maintains cities. It is not true *virtù* to destroy a city.[29] Hence it always implies a *political* morality. 'Civic spirit' is probably the best simple translation – if by 'spirit' one means spirited action,[30] like the *arete* of the early Greeks – as in Homer's

29. See Walker, *Discourses* I, pp. 99–113, particularly his discussion of the case of Agathocles (in *The Prince*, chapter 8) who, although very successful, may not be called a man of *virtù* because of his barbarous cruelty. If he had acted as he did to save a state, however, the case would be different. Compare Walker's patient elucidation of Machiavelli on this point with the carping cleverness of Sydney Anglo, *Machiavelli*, pp. 231–2.

30. I think Neal Wood goes too far (in his otherwise most useful 'Machiavelli's Concept of *Virtù* Reconsidered', *Political Studies*, June 1967, pp. 159–72) to say that *virtù* must always include actual military ability – say rather, 'militant'. A city's leaders could have *virtù* without being fit to go or ever having been to war themselves. And at least one *woman* is praised for her *virtù* – the Countess Girolamo, whose tale is told on p. 419 below.

description of Achilles as being 'a do'er of deeds and a speaker
of words'; and in Machiavelli's relishing the significance of
Achilles' tutor having been a centaur, 'half-beast and half-
man'. Lastly, while he often uses the term in a hortatory way
– people should recover their *virtù* while there is time, or
should not have let it idle away into *ozio* (indolence or corruption) – its force is as often empirical. Does a state have *virtù*
among its inhabitants or not? Are there, in a word, citizens? If
there are no or too few citizens, one is doomed to personal or
princely rule; but if many, then a republic can flourish, and
will prove – the by now familiar argument – the stronger form
of state.[31] Look around the modern world. It is a reasonably
precise criterion. To give one dangerous example. Leave aside
the rights and the wrongs of the Arab-Israeli conflict. Is it not
obvious that the weakness, for all their numbers and arms, of
the Arabs is related to the historical lack and the slow development of a class of citizens – men who combine individual
initiative with collective discipline? And that much of the
strength of Israel is related to its citizen culture as well as to
foreign subvention?

This *virtù*, if it studies necessity, can combat fortune. This is
the theory to be pursued, but there are no guaranteed methods of success or certain methods of drawing lessons from the
past: only probable ones. And these we should follow, as the
best we can do – which is a lot better than before, he modestly
implies, I, Niccolò Machiavelli, wrote my two great manuscripts.

31. Which was the essential argument which English seventeenth-
and eighteenth-century republican writers found in Machiavelli. See
Raab, *The English Face of Machiavelli*, chapters 6 and 7, and J. G. A.
Pocock's magnificent 'Machiavelli, Harrington and English Political
Ideologies in the Eighteenth Century', *William and Mary Quarterly*
(October 1965), pp. 549–83. Both are part of the history of citizenship
– which is yet to be written.

But what is it, strictly speaking, a theory of? Man? No, that is too general. I think Felix Raab is right: 'It does Machiavelli no violence to regard him as the apostle of political stability'.[32] 'Apostle'? Yes, that was his political ethic. But he is also the theorist of political stability. And we need not swallow our moral dislike of certain regimes to see that the centre of the study of politics is to understand how they are maintained, and why they change, the good, the bad and the indifferent.

But if we admitted, indeed claimed, that in this sense there is a political science, yet – for the last time – nothing Machiavelli says implies that it is certain. Yes, the criteria or conditions for republican rule which we discussed in the last section are meaningful and valid, *ceteris paribus*, or in the long run, or in normal prudence; but if Fortune can effect them, so can human will. Following the passage in *The Discourses* I.55 where he argues the necessity of getting rid of the gentry, *if* a republic is to thrive, he says:

> But since to convert a province, suited to monarchical rule, into a republic, and to convert a province, suited to a republican regime, into a kingdom, is a matter which only a man of outstanding brain-power and authority can handle, and such men are rare, there have been many who have attempted it but few who have had the ability to carry it through. For the magnitude of an undertaking of this kind is such that it breaks down at the very beginning, partly because men get terrified and partly owing to the obstacles encountered.

Politics and Morality

By now it should be clear that in no sense can Machiavelli be called a determinist. Indeed, he constantly praises free actions; only, he insists, actions takes place in some social and historical context. Necessity narrows the range of alternatives, but choices have to be made. Further, it is possible by reason

32. Raab, *The English Face of Machiavelli*, p. 249.

applied to experience to make meaningful generalizations (at some level of abstraction) about how likely certain types of action are to succeed in certain types of circumstance (but even then, there is always *Fortuna*). Those who accuse him of being a determinist have either got a crude late-Victorian view of science in their minds, and cannot distinguish between invariable relationships and statistically significant relationships (or between certainty and probability), or else they are, like so many modern historians, sceptical of all generalizations, mystic believers in something they call 'unique events'.[33]

So men, to Machiavelli, are free to choose – men with *virtù*, at least. But they must know the price of their choices. And sometimes the price of achieving one set of values is, in terms of another set of values, almost unbearable.

We have already followed his account of the ruthlessness necessary for a prince to create order in a conquered or suddenly acquired state.[34] But he adds in the same discourse (I.26):

His aim should be to emulate Philip of Macedon, the father of Alexander, who, starting as a little king, by these methods made himself prince of Greece. Of him a writer says that he moved men from province to province as shepherds move their sheep.

Such methods are exceedingly cruel, and are repugnant to any community, not only to a Christian one, but to any composed of men. It behoves, therefore, every man to shun them, and to prefer

33. If there were only unique events, such that no historical or sociological generalizations were valid at some degree of abstraction, then language itself would break down, or could never have existed.

34. This could be challenged empirically. His far more successful friend, Guicciardini, was very critical, in his 'Considerations on *The Discourses* of Machiavelli', of this (*Discourses* I.55) and all those other passages which stress the need to eliminate even potential rivals, not just known or open opponents. The ruler must also know how to be magnanimous and prudently forgiving – see Cecil Grayson, *Francesco Guicciardini: Selected Writings* (London, 1965), pp. 91–2. There is a very

to live as a private citizen than as a king with such ruination of men to his score. None the less, for the sort of man who is unwilling to take up this first course of well doing, it is expedient, should he wish to hold what he has, to enter on the path of wrong doing. Actually, most men prefer to steer a middle course which is very harmful, for they know not how to be wholly good or wholly bad.

Such actions may be, in this conditional sense, necessary or, at least, expedient, but Machiavelli will never call them good. They are neither good to Christians nor to any community of men. Better, by both moralities, to retire into private life; but do not think, in such circumstances, that such actions can be avoided by someone. Someone has to take up the dirty work.

But this, of course, is the harshest possible case. Some such ruthlessness, however, he considers is necessary also in the glorious actions, which deserve to be ever memorable, of creating or defending a republic.[35] Here we have – what? A

---

real sense in which Machiavelli's antithesis between republics and principalities, and hence the need to eliminate all possible rivals, was over-dramatized and too sharp for the politics of his time – just as no known Greek tyrant ever followed Aristotle's incredibly thorough-going advice about how tyrannies *could* be rendered permanent. Both fit far better, and astonishingly closely, the one great system of government right outside their formal classifications: modern or totalitarian autocracy. They achieved such a degree of true theoretical abstraction.

But Walker is surely right (vol. I, p. 110) to criticize the extremity and to denounce (by his standards) the morality of Machiavelli's advice, for instance, that 'the sons of Brutus', that is even those whose character might make them even potential tyrannicides, should be eliminated (*Discourses* III.3 and 4). But he forgets his own analysis of Machiavelli's 'necessity' as always conditional. *If* the regime is to be stable . . . No one has seriously attacked Aristotle for seeming to offer in his Book V equally monstrous or dangerous advice to tyrants (e.g. 'to lop off' all men of *arete*) *if* tyranny is to be perpetuated.

35. See *Discourses* 16–18, which Walker titles 'The Transition from Servitude to Freedom', particularly the passage in 18 where he bewails that too rarely is 'a good man ready to use bad methods in order to make himself prince, though with a good end in view'.

decision to take between two conflicting moralities? Or simply two conflicting moralities? I follow Sir Isaiah Berlin in thinking the latter to be true, and that this is Machiavelli's terrible originality. He never denies that what Christians call good, is in fact good: 'humility, kindness, scruples, unworldliness, faith in God, sanctity . . .'[36] But there is also the morality of the pagan world: *virtù*, citizenship, heroism, public achievement, and the preservation and the cultural enrichment of the city-state.

Father Walker does not put it quite so starkly and pithily, but essentially he agrees. For Machiavelli, he says, never 'calls right wrong or wrong right. He prefers to state boldly that if security be their aim, there are occasions on which rulers must know how to do wrong . . . He is perfectly frank, and if his very frankness makes his statements sound more shocking, it at any rate clarifies the issue. His claim is that, in the sphere of politics, a good end justifies what is morally wrong.'[37]

Actions, then, can be morally wrong by Christian standards but morally right by Pagan standards. Like both Villari, in his great biography, and Walker, the modern reader should take Machiavelli's paganism very seriously. It is in this context that his constant remarks, throughout both works, on the usefulness of religion are to be understood, and on the duty of the prince to make his people fear God. Religion helps mightily in creating civic cohesion and social discipline. But which religion?

He tells us unambiguously:

36. See Berlin's 'The Originality of Machiavelli', *op. cit.*
37. Walker, *Discourses*, pp. 118–19. Or in Machiavelli's own words: '. . . a sound maxim that, when an action is reprehensible, the result may excuse it, and, when the result is good, always excuses it.' (*Discourses* I.9.) Walker would have been wiser to say 'excuses' rather than 'justifies'.

If one asks oneself how it comes about that peoples of old were more fond of liberty than they are today, I think the answer is ... due ... to the difference between our education and that of bygone times, which is based on the difference between our religion and the religion of those days ... The old religion did not beatify men unless they were full of worldly glory: army commanders, for instance, and rulers of republics. Our religion has glorified humble and contemplative men, rather than men of action. It has assigned as man's highest good humility, abnegation and contempt for worldly things, whereas the other identified it with magnanimity, bodily strength and everything else that tends to make men very bold ... But though it looks as if the world were to become effeminate and as if heaven were powerless, this undoubtedly is due rather to the pusillanimity of those who have interpreted our religion in terms of *laissez faire* [*l'ozio*] not in terms of valour [*virtù*]. (*Discourses* II.2.)

The 'old religion' is best – for the preservation of the state and the encouragement of *virtù*. But, again, as much as Machiavelli rails against the corruption of the Papacy and the Church, he both shows respect for 'true Christians' and the ideals of the primitive church,[38] and uses Christian standards to say that many 'necessities of state' are evil actions. They are bad by one standard, but good (or pardonable if successful) by another.

There is thus something far more profound in Machiavelli than simply a distinction between what is right and what is possible, or a reminder of 'the price' we may have to pay for 'seeming good' actions. Two standards are at work simultaneously. He implicitly challenges the whole traditional view that morality must be of one piece. He is not, strictly speaking, a relativist: he only recognizes two views, but then he only really recognizes two circumstances: historically, the ancient

38. As in *Discourses* I.12: 'The first debt which we, Italians, owe to the Church and to priests ... is that we have become irreligious and perverse.'

and the modern world, and politically, the republic and the principality. He never shows the slightest wish to reinterpret morality so as to be subordinate to a theory of the state (as did Hobbes and Hegel in their different ways); and nor is he simply taking politics out of morality or putting it above morality. The sense in which, in effect, he advocates a political morality is not in terms of a divorce between ethics and politics, but in terms of the prime and heroic dignity given to politics and political action in classical pagan morality. He sees all the time two moralities side-by-side each making conflicting demands: the morality of the soul and the morality of the city.

Had he been a philosopher, he might have felt bound to try to bridge this gap – in some conventional and perhaps evasive way. But being an extremely free, original and honest mind, he did better: he noticed that in practice nearly everyone is torn in these two directions. And he saw clearly that the best kind of men of action did not simply represent the inferiority of action to morality,[39] but that they pursued different ends which called for – and certainly got – different kinds of justification. True, some men of power were so cruel and so selfish, lacking in either Roman virtues or Christian graces, that they were despicable or damned on both counts. But for most men, it was not a gap between theory and practice, but between two different theories of practice or different practices of theory. The one sought the glory, welfare and safety of the state; the other, the safety of the soul or (even in secular terms) the purity of conscience. The one sought immortality in terms of worthy public deeds that would never be forgotten by free men; the other sought immortality in terms of – to

39. That action *per se* could be superior to morality would not have entered his head. Only nineteenth-century anarchists and twentieth-century fascists (and a few intermediate forms of life today who hide behind 'the market') have ever thought that way.

men – the anonymous and unknown transactions of an individual with God.

Certainly, suspended between these two moralities, Machiavelli did achieve a radically secular viewpoint. He laid the basis for a secular study of society, and showed why in the future, more and more, the exercise of power had to be justified in secular and utilitarian terms. Politics itself emerges as a secular activity and it is, in a narrow but clear sense, *autonomous*, in that one *can* if one wishes, by the new 'politic art', and if one has both skill and will, is both a lion and a fox, change the character of human society or – and politics is the only means to this end – ensure its preservation. But *should* one wish to do so? This question is just as real to Machiavelli and the answer is quite plain: 'yes', by one set of moral standards, and 'no', by the other. Felix Raab is right to see that, for instance, 'English Machiavellianism leads to Halifax, not Locke; to a sophisticated and secular consciousness of political logic and not to a new set of normative values for society and for the state.'[40] But precisely because he did not create a new and secular moral synthesis, he left the world with what he found, recognized and dramatized – an uncomfortable and at times almost unbearable dilemma: two sets of traditional standards, often leading in completely opposite directions, but neither of them to be abandoned. There are times when it is necessary to do admittedly evil things for the preservation and the welfare of the political community – and if one is not so willing, one is simply stepping outside politics and, incidentally, abandoning it to those who have no scruples. But if one is willing, then, he seems to say, for God and man's sake, recognize that what for the moment you are doing is evil, and do not fall into calling it good. It is this radical dualism which has made him so acutely disturbing to people who insist on

40. Raab, *The English Face of Machiavelli*, p. 262.

finding a single truth, or who try to reduce all theories and doctrines to particular and contingent events – so disturbing that they plunge into so many different and fervid interpretations of Machiavelli's 'real meaning', all designed to evade this awkward duality, this ultimate incoherence, not in Machiavelli, but in our whole culture – perhaps in the nature of things. 'Machiavelli's theory was a sword which was plunged into the flank of the body politic of Western humanity, causing it to cry out and struggle with itself'.[41] The pain is still with us and if we ever cease to feel it, it will not be because the conditions that give rise to it have miraculously vanished but because our nerves have gone dead.

The Letter to Vettori

That is all I have to say by way of introduction – and perhaps too much. There are three types of introduction: (i) those which should only be read after reading a book, and are otherwise meaningless; (ii) those which are really intended to make the reading of a book unnecessary for the lazy, the hasty or the overloaded student; and (iii) those which presume to create a perspective in which it might be read – a liberty which should only be taken if the book is intrinsically difficult (which is not the case here), or full of strange and alien assumptions (of which, in this case, too much has been made), or because there are so many received opinions about it which are badly balanced, eccentric or wrong (which is very much the case here). But in attempting to create a better perspective, one is arguing against the most foolish or limited of received opinions; so one stresses those things which contradict and counter them. No introduction can or should be 'the author

41. Friedrich Meinecke, *Machiavellism: the Doctrine of Raison D'Etat and Its Place in Modern History* (London, 1957), translated by Douglas Scott.

in miniature'. So any readers naturally seeking for the second category of introduction had better be told (too late) that they have been cheated. There is no substitute for reading this book. But I have tried to correct a perspective, without, however, wanting to reduce many earlier introductions and commentaries to an unearned oblivion. But finally it is the author's own perspective that counts. So before or just after reading the text, I strongly advise reading or re-reading Machiavelli's dedicatory letter to *The Prince* and compare it to the dedication or introduction to *The Discourses* which is emphatically not to be skipped. But also read, however, this famous letter to his friend, Francesco Vettori, in which he describes his life at his small country house or farm after the Medici restoration had excluded him from public office.

I rise in the morning with the sun, and I go off to a wood of mine which I am having cut down, where I stop for two hours to see what was done the day before and to talk to the woodcutters who always have some trouble on hand either among themselves or with their neighbours ... Leaving the wood I go to a spring and thence to some bird-traps of mine. I have a book with me, Dante or Petrarch or one of the minor poets, Tibullus, Ovid or the like. I read about their amorous passions and their loves, I remember my own, and dwell enjoyably on these thoughts for a while. Then I go on to the road and into the tavern. I talk to the passers-by, I ask what news of their villages, I hear all sorts of things, and observe the various tastes and ideas of men. In the meanwhile it is time for dinner, and with my folk I eat what food this poor farm and miserable patrimony of mine provides. When I have eaten I go back to the tavern. Here I find the host and usually a butcher, a miller, and a couple of kilnmen. With them I degrade myself playing all day at *cricca* and tric-trac, and this gives rise to a thousand arguments and endless vexations with insulting words, and most times there is a fight over a penny, and we can be heard shouting from as far away as San Casciano. And so, surrounded by these lice, I blow the cobwebs out of my brain and relieve the unkïndness of my fate, content that she trample on me in this way to see if she is not ashamed to treat me thus.

When evening comes I return home and go into my study, and at the door I take off my daytime dress covered in mud and dirt, and put on royal and curial robes; and their decently attired I enter the courts of the ancients, where affectionately greeted by them, I partake of that food which is mine alone and for which I was born; where I am not ashamed to talk with them and inquire the reasons of their actions; and they out of their human kindness answer me, and for four hours at a stretch I feel no worry of any kind; I forget all my troubles, I am not afraid of poverty or of death. I give myself up entirely to them. And because Dante says that understanding does not constitute knowledge unless it is retained in the memory, I have written down what I have learned from their conversation and composed a short work *de Principatibus* . . .[42]

And his biographer, Ridolfi, adds: 'In such a mixture of happiness and unhappiness, of dream and reality, of base things and greatness, wholly resembling the man himself, *The Discourses* and *The Prince* had their origin.'

42. Quoted by Ridolfi, *Life of Niccolò Machiavelli*, translated by Cecil Grayson, pp. 151–2.

FURTHER READING

OF the making of books on Machiavelli there is no end. Achille Norsa listed over 2,100 items relating to Machiavelli in his *Il principio della forza nel pensiero di Niccolò Machiavelli* ... Milan, 1936, even before inflation set in really badly. They range from the obsessionally pedantic to the crazily polemical or cabalistic. Perhaps L. A. Burd's noble edition of *Il Principe*, Clarendon Press, Oxford, 1891, is the best representative of the former especially for those who, being able to read with equal facility Greek, Latin, French, German, Italian and Spanish of various periods, can appreciate Lord Acton's Introduction. And as representative of the latter l'abbé Aime Guillon's *Machiavel commenté par Napoleon Buonaparte*, Paris, 1816, is a forgery genially intended to blacken each name with the other.

'Machiavellianism' is traced, including many great men who covertly followed him and others, like Frederick of Prussia, who denounced him publicly as a smokescreen for their private adherence (albeit an adherence to a myth more than a man), in Friedrich Meinecke's great book, *Machiavellism: the Doctrine of Raison D'Etat and its Place in Modern History*, Routledge, London, 1957, edited by W. Stark, first published in Munich in 1924. And specifically for England, Felix Raab, *The English Face of Machiavelli: a Changing Interpretation 1500–1700*, Routledge, London, 1964. But see also the references to Machiavelli in Christopher Morris's *Political Thought in England: Tyndale to Hooker*, Oxford, 1953.

The biography is still R. Ridolfi, *The Life of Machiavelli*, Routledge, London, 1963. Scholarly and readable, well translated, this now replaces the earlier and pietistic learning of Villari (four vols. translated 1878–83). Virolo Maurizion's *Niccolo's Smile: a Biography of Machiavelli*, I. B. Tauris, London, 2001, corrects Ridolfi in some minor matters.

For his other works, all of any general interest are in Allan Gilbert, translator, *Machiavelli: the Chief Works and Others*, three vols., Duke University Press, Durham, N.C., 1965 This is extremely useful to the English reader, but the translation is an odd mixture of fustian and modern colloquial. Felix Gilbert's Introduction to Machiavelli's *History of Florence*, Harper Torchback, New York and London, 1960, is short and rewarding. Also Neal Wood's Introduction to *The Art of War*, Library of Liberal Arts, New York, 1965, is full and most interesting, but it was irresponsible not to have either redone or radically revised Farneworth's antiquated and inaccurate translation of 1762. *The Literary Works of Machiavelli*, Oxford University Press, 1961, is modestly edited and well translated by J. R. Hale, and Vicki B. Sullivan, *The Comedy and Tragedy of Machiavelli: Essays on the Literary Works*, Yale University Press, 2000, yields rich critical appreciations. Most of the main diplomatic reports and statepapers written by Machiavelli are translated in Christian E. Detmold, *The Historical, Political and Diplomatic Writings of Niccolò Machiavelli*, four vols. Boston, 1882.

Of general commentaries in English, Federico Chabod, *Machiavelli and the Renaissance*, Harper Torchbacks, London, 1965, is well balanced between 'the contemporary' and 'the universal', despite its over-great concentration on *The Prince*. J. R. Hale, *Machiavelli and Renaissance Italy*, English Universities Press, London, 1961; Garret Mattingly, *Renaissance Diplomacy*, Cape, London, 1955; and H. Butterfield, *The Statecraft of Machiavelli*, Bell, London, 1940, all argue or imply that there is nothing but context, and to Butterfield he doesn't do very well in that either. Leo Strauss's *Thoughts on Machiavelli*, The Free Press, Glencoe, Ill., 1958, hits the wrong target in the right cause – the cause is 'value-orientated' philosophy and Machiavelli is 'the teacher of evil' – as in his disciple Harvey C. Mansfield, *Machiavelli's Virtue*, University of Chicago Press, 1996 (see also his *Machiavelli's New Modes and Orders: a Study of the Discourses*, University of Chicago Press, London, 2001). Ernst Cassirer's three chapters on Machiavelli in his *The Myth of the State*, Oxford University Press, 1946, are with their stress on the cold technician, subtly wrong but challengingly thoughtful. Antonio Gramsci's posthumous *The Modern Prince* (Lawrence & Wishart) 1958, written in prison under Mussolini, argued the revolutionary implications of Machiavelli; but it is an imaginative re-enactment rather than historical restoration. A dispassionate and respectful treatment of Machiavelli, particularly on his assumptions about the ends of life and the 'manly' nature of politics, is Dr Robert Orr's 'The Time Motif in Machiavelli', *Political Studies*, June 1969. Hannah Pitkin's *Fortune is a Woman: Gender and Politics in the Thought of Machiavelli*, University of Chicago Press, London, 1999, breaks new ground contentiously.

Four from many volumes of essays are important: Myron P. Gilmore (ed.), *Studies on Machiavelli*, Sansoni, Florence, 1972 (which includes Isaiah Berlin's flamboyant tour of diverse interpretations, 'The originality of Machiavelli'); J. H. Whitfield, *Discourses on Machiavelli*, Cambridge University Press, 1969, Martin Fleischer (ed.), *Machiavelli and the Nature of Political Thought*, Atheneum, New York, 1972; and, above all, Gisela Bock, Quentin Skinner and Maurizio Viroli (eds.), *Machiavelli and Republicanism*, Cambridge University Press, 1990, especially Skinner on the '*Discorsi* and the Pre-Humanist Origins of Republican Ideas'. Of extraordinary interest and importance: J. G. A. Pocock, *The Machiavellian Moment: Florentine Political Thought and the Atlantic Republican Tradition*, Princeton University Press, 1975. A short but original introduction which sets Machiavelli clearly in precise intellectual context is Quentin Skinner, *Machiavelli*, Oxford University Press, 1981, also his still shorter *Machiavelli: a Very Short Introduction*, Oxford University Press, 2000; and his and Russell Price's edition of *The Prince*, Cambridge University Press, 1988, has invaluable editorial matter and bibliography

DISCORSI DI NICOLO MACHIAVELLI
CITTADINO, ET SEGRETARIO
FIORENTINO, SOPRA LA PRI
MA DECA DI TITO LIVIO,
A ZANOBI BVONDEL=
MONTI, ET A COSI=
MO RVCELLAI.

Con Gratie, & Priuilegi di.N.S. Clemente
VII. & altri Prencipi, che intra il termino di.X.
Anni non si stampino, ne stampati si uendino:
sotto le pene, che in essi si contengono.
M. D. XXXI.

TABLE OF CONTENTS

Book One

[THE DEVELOPMENT OF ROME'S CONSTITUTION]

[1–10 THE BEST FORM OF GOVERNMENT]

Book Two
[THE GROWTH OF ROME'S EMPIRE]

TABLE OF CONTENTS

Book Three
[THE EXAMPLE OF ROME'S GREAT MEN]

[1–5 REFORM, SECURITY, AND THE ELIMINATION OF RIVALS]

[6 ON CONSPIRACIES]

[7–9 THE NEED OF ADAPTATION TO ENVIRONMENT]

TABLE OF CONTENTS

TABLE OF CONTENTS

*Discourses on
the First Ten Books
of Titus Livy*

NICCOLÒ MACHIAVELLI TO ZANOBI BUONDELMONTI AND COSIMO RUCELLAI
GREETING

I AM sending you a present which, if it does not come up to the obligations I owe you, is at any rate the best that Niccolò Machiavelli is able to send you. For in it I have set down all that I know and have learnt from a long experience of, and from constantly reading about, political affairs. And since neither you nor anyone else can well expect more from me than this, you will not be disappointed that I am not sending you more. You may perhaps lament my lack of skill, should these my narratives be thin, and also errors of judgement, should I, in discussing things, have in many places made mistakes. If this be so, I know not which of us is less obliged to the other, I to you, for having forced me to write what I should never have written of my own accord, or you to me, if what I have written fails to satisfy you. Accept it, then, in the manner in which things are accepted amongst friends, by whom the intention of the giver is always more esteemed than the quality of the gift. And believe me when I say that I have in this just one consolation. It is that when I reflect on the many mistakes I may have made in other circumstances, I know that I have made no mistake at any rate in this, that I have chosen to dedicate these my discourses to you in preference to all others; both because, in doing so, I seem to be showing some gratitude for benefits received, and also because I seem in this to be departing from the usual practice of authors, which has always been to dedicate their works to some prince, and, blinded by ambition and avarice, to praise him for all his virtuous qualities when they ought to have blamed him for all manner of shameful deeds.

So, to avoid this mistake, I have chosen not those who are princes, but those who, on account of their innumerable good qualities, deserve to be; not those who might shower on me rank, honours, and riches, but those who, though unable, would like to do so. For, to judge aright, one should esteem men because they are generous, not because they have the power to be generous; and, in like manner, should admire those who know how to govern a kingdom, not those who, without knowing how, actually govern one. There are, indeed, writers who praise Hiero the Syracusan though but a private person, in preference to Perseus the Macedonian though he was a king, because Hiero to become a prince lacked but a principality, whereas the other had no kingly attribute save his kingdom. Entertain yourselves, then, with what you were anxious to get, whether it be good or bad; and, should you be so mistaken as to find my views acceptable, I shall not fail to follow this up with the rest of the history as I promised at the start. Farewell.

Book One

[THE DEVELOPMENT OF ROME'S CONSTITUTION]

Book One deals with 'such events due to public decrees' as the author judges to be worthy of comment, and with their consequences . . . . It treats of the constitutional development which took place in Rome from the time of the kings down to the year 387 B.C., when the conquest of Italy began, and is based on Livy, Books I to VI. The first ten chapters form an introduction.

The heading of each discourse or chapter, printed in italics, is Machiavelli's.

The division of the chapters into groups under the headings given in the Table of Contents has been introduced for the convenience of the reader.

And in like manner the titles of the three books which in the original are merely numbered.

L.J.W.

Book One

[*The Preface*]

ALTHOUGH owing to the envy inherent in man's nature it
has always been no less dangerous to discover new ways and
methods than to set off in search of new seas and unknown
lands because most men are much more ready to belittle than
to praise another's actions, none the less, impelled by the
natural desire I have always had to labour, regardless of anything, on that which I believe to be for the common benefit
of all, I have decided to enter upon a new way, as yet untrod-
den by anyone else. And, even if it entails a tiresome and
difficult task, it may yet reward me in that there are those who
will look kindly on the purpose of these my labours. And if
my poor ability, my limited experience of current affairs, my
feeble knowledge of antiquity, should render my efforts im-
perfect and of little worth, they may none the less point the
way for another of greater ability, capacity for analysis, and
judgement, who will achieve my ambition; which, if it does
not earn me praise, should not earn me reproaches.

When, therefore, I consider in what honour antiquity is
held, and how – to cite but one instance – a bit of an old statue
has fetched a high price that someone may have it by him to
give honour to his house and that it may be possible for it to
be copied by those who are keen on this art; and how the

97

latter then with great industry take pains to reproduce it in all their works; and when, on the other hand, I notice that what history has to say about the highly virtuous actions performed by ancient kingdoms and republics, by their kings, their generals, their citizens, their legislators, and by others who have gone to the trouble of serving their country, is rather admired than imitated; nay, is so shunned by everybody in each little thing they do, that of the virtue of bygone days there remains no trace, it cannot but fill me at once with astonishment and grief. The more so when I see that in the civic disputes which arise between citizens and in the diseases men get, they always have recourse to decisions laid down by the ancients and to the prescriptions they drew up. For the civil law is nothing but a collection of decisions, made by jurists of old, which the jurists of today have tabulated in orderly fashion for our instruction. Nor, again, is medicine anything but a record of experiments, performed by doctors of old, upon which the doctors of our day base their prescriptions. In spite of which in constituting republics, in maintaining states, in governing kingdoms, in forming an army or conducting a war, in dealing with subjects, in extending the empire, one finds neither prince nor republic who repairs to antiquity for examples.

This is due in my opinion not so much to the weak state to which the religion of today has brought the world, or to the evil wrought in many provinces and cities of Christendom by ambition conjoined with idleness, as to the lack of a proper appreciation of history, owing to people failing to realize the significance of what they read, and to their having no taste for the delicacies it comprises. Hence it comes about that the great bulk of those who read it take pleasure in hearing of the various incidents which are contained in it, but never think of imitating them, since they hold them to be not merely difficult but impossible of imitation, as if the heaven, the sun, the elements and man had in their motion, their order, and their potency, become different from what they used to be.

Since I want to get men out of this wrong way of thinking, I have thought fit to write a commentary on all those books of Titus Livy which have not by the malignity of time had their continuity broken.[1] It will comprise what I have arrived at by comparing ancient with modern events, and think necessary for the better understanding of them, so that those who read what I have to say may the more easily draw those practical lessons which one should seek to obtain from the study of history. Though the enterprise is difficult, yet, with the help of those who have encouraged me to undertake the task, I think I can carry it out in such a way that there shall remain to another but a short road to traverse in order to reach the place assigned.

Book One

[THE BEST FORM OF GOVERNMENT]

---

1. *Concerning the Origin of Cities in General and of Rome in Particular*

THOSE who read of the origin of the city of Rome, of its legislators and of its constitution, will not be surprised that in this city such great virtue was maintained for so many centuries, and that later on there came into being the empire into which that republic developed.

Since this first discourse will deal with its origin, I would point out that all cities are built either by natives of the place in which they are built, or by people from elsewhere. The first case comes about when inhabitants, dispersed in many small communities, find that they cannot enjoy security since no one community of itself, owing to its position and to the smallness of its numbers, is strong enough to resist the on-slaught of an invader, and, when the enemy arrives, there is no time for them to unite for their defence; or, if there be time, they have to abandon many of their strongholds, and thus at once fall as prey to their enemies. Hence, to escape these dangers, either of their own accord or at the suggestion of someone of greater authority among them, such com-munities undertake to live together in some place they have chosen in order to live more conveniently and the more easily to defend themselves.

This was the case with Athens and Venice, among many others. Athens was built under the authority of Theseus for reasons such as these by inhabitants who were dispersed; Venice by numerous peoples who had sought refuge in certain islets at the top of the Adriatic Sea that they might escape the wars which daily arose in Italy after the decline of the Roman empire owing to the arrival of a new lot of barbarians. There, without any particular person or prince to give them a constitution, they began to live as a community under laws which seemed to them appropriate for their maintenance. And this happened because of the long repose the situation afforded them in that the sea at their end had no exit and the peoples who were ravaging Italy had no ships in which to infest them. This being so, a beginning, however small, sufficed to bring them to their present greatness.

The second case occurs when a city is built by men of a foreign race. They may either be free men, or men dependent on others, as are the colonies sent out either by a republic or a prince to relieve their towns of some of the population or for the defence of newly acquired territory which they desire to hold securely and without expense. The Romans built a number of such cities, and this throughout the whole of their empire. Others have been built by a prince, not that he may dwell there, but to enhance his reputation, as the city of Alexandria was built by Alexander. And since such cities are not at the outset free, it very seldom happens that they make great progress or that of their own doing they come to be reckoned among the capitals of kingdoms.

It was thus that Florence came to be built; for – whether it was built by the soldiers of Sulla, or was built by chance by inhabitants from the hills of Fiesole who, relying on the long peace which the world enjoyed under Octavian, came to dwell in the plains above the Arno – it was built under the Roman empire, and could at the outset make no addition to its territory save such as was allowed by the courtesy of the emperor.

Free cities are those which are built by peoples who, either under a prince or of their own accord, are driven by pestilence or famine or war to abandon the land of their birth and to look for new habitations. These may be either cities they find in countries they have occupied and in which they go to dwell, as Moses did; or new cities which they build, as Aeneas did. In this case the virtue of the builder is discernible in the fortune of what was built, for the city is more or less remarkable according as he is more or less virtuous who is responsible for the start. This virtue shows itself in two ways: first in the choice of a site, and secondly in the drawing up of laws.

Since men work either of necessity or by choice, and since there is found to be greater virtue where choice has less to say to it, the question arises whether it would not be better to choose a barren place in which to build cities so that men would have to be industrious and less given to idleness, and so would be more united because, owing to the poor situation, there would be less occasion for discord; as happened in Ragusa and in many other cities built in such-like places.

Such a choice would undoubtedly be wiser and more advantageous were men content to earn their own living and not anxious to lord it over others. Since, however, security for man is impossible unless it be conjoined with power, it is necessary to avoid sterile places and for cities to be put in very fertile places where, when expansion has taken place owing to the fruitfulness of the land, it may be possible for them both to defend themselves against attack and to overcome any who stand in the way of the city's greatness. As to the idleness which such a situation may encourage, it must be provided for by laws imposing that need to work which the situation

does not impose. It is advisable here to follow the example of
those wise folk who have dwelt in most beautiful and fertile
lands, i.e. in such lands as tend to produce idleness and
ineptitude for training in virtue of any kind, and who, in
order to obviate the disasters which the idleness induced by
the amenities of the land might cause, have imposed the need
for training on those who were to become soldiers, and have
made this training such that men there have become better
soldiers than those in countries which were rough and sterile
by nature.

A case in point is the kingdom of the Egyptians which, notwithstanding the amenities of the land, imposed the need to
work so successfully by means of laws that it produced most
excellent men, whose names, if they had not been lost in
antiquity, would be even more celebrated than that of Alexander the Great, and than those of many others whose memory is still fresh. So, too, anyone who has reflected on the
kingdom of the Sultan, on the discipline of the Mamelukes,
and on that of their troops, before they were wiped out by
Selim, the Great Turk, might have noted there the many
exercises the troops underwent, and might have inferred from
this how greatly they feared the idleness to which the beneficence of the country might have led if they had not obviated
it by very strict laws.

I maintain, then, that it is more prudent to place a city in a
fertile situation, provided its fertility is kept in due bounds by
laws. When Alexander the Great was proposing to build a city
that should redound to his credit, Deinocrates, the architect,
came to him and suggested that he should build it on Mount
Athos, for, besides being a strong place, it could be so fashioned as to give the city a human form, which would be a
remarkable thing, a rare thing, and worthy of his greatness.
And on what, Alexander asked, would the inhabitants live?
Deinocrates replied that he had not thought of this. Whereupon

Alexander laughed, and, leaving the mountain alone, built Alexandria where inhabitants would be glad to live owing to the richness of the land and to the conveniences afforded by the sea and by the Nile.

For those, then, who, having examined the question how Rome came to be built, hold that Aeneas was its first founder, it will be a city built by foreigners, but for those who prefer Romulus, it will be a city built by natives of the place. But, whichever be the case, both will recognize that it began as a free city, dependent upon no one. They will also recognize, as we shall presently point out, under what strict discipline it was placed by the laws made by Romulus, Numa, and others, and that, in consequence, neither its fertile situation, the convenience afforded by the sea, its frequent victories, nor the greatness of its empire, were for many centuries able to corrupt it, but that these laws kept it so rich in virtue that there has never been any other city or any other republic so well adorned.

Wherefore since what was done by this city, as Titus Livy records it, was done sometimes in accordance with public enactments, sometimes on the initiative of private individuals, and sometimes within the city, sometimes abroad, I shall begin by discussing such of the events due to public decrees as I shall judge to be more worthy of comment, and with the events shall conjoin their consequences to which the discourses of this first book or first part will be restricted.

2. *How many Kinds of State*^a *there are and of what Kind was that of Rome*

I PROPOSE to dispense with a discussion of cities which from the outset have been subject to another power, and shall speak only of those which have from the outset been far removed from any kind of external servitude, but, instead, have from the start been governed in accordance with their wishes, whether as republics or principalities. As such cities have had diverse origins, so too they have had diverse laws and institutions. For either at the outset, or before very long, to some of them laws have been given by some one person at some one time, as laws were given to the Spartans by Lycurgus; whereas others have acquired them by chance and at different times as occasion arose. This was the case in Rome.

Happy indeed should we call that state[a] which produces a man so prudent that men can live securely under the laws which he prescribes without having to emend them. Sparta, for instance, observed its laws for more than eight hundred years without corrupting them and without any dangerous disturbance. Unhappy, on the other hand, in some degree is that city to be deemed which, not having chanced to meet with a prudent organizer, has to reorganize itself. And, of such, that is the more unhappy which is the more remote from order; and that is the more remote from order whose institutions have missed altogether the straight road which leads it to its perfect and true destiny. For it is almost impossible that states of this type should by any eventuality be set on the right road again; whereas those which, if their order is not perfect, have made a good beginning and are capable of improvement, may become perfect should something happen which provides the opportunity. It should, however, be noted that they will never introduce order without incurring danger, because few men ever welcome new laws setting up a new order in the state unless necessity makes it clear to them that there is need for such laws; and since such a necessity cannot arise

[a] *quella republica*. [Walker renders this 'Commonwealth'. Plainly in the context *republica* means any kind of state with some civic spirit or sense of *res publica* (see above, p. 24), not specifically a republican one. But 'Commonwealth' (shades of Cromwell!) sounds even more republican than 'republic'. B.R.C.]

without danger, the state may easily be ruined before the new order has been brought to completion. The republic of Florence bears this out, for owing to what happened at Arezzo in '02 it was reconstituted, and owing to what happened at Prato in '12 its constitution was destroyed.

It being now my intention to discuss what were the institutions of the city of Rome and what events conduced to its perfection, I would remark that those who have written about states[a] say that there are to be found in them one of three forms of government, called by them *Principality*, *Aristocracy* and *Democracy*,[b] and that those who set up a government in any particular state [c] must adopt one of them, as best suits their purpose.[2]

Others – and with better judgement many think – say that there are six types of government,[d] of which three are very bad, and three are good in themselves but easily become corrupt, so that they too must be classed as pernicious. Those that are good are the three above mentioned. Those that are bad are the other three, which depend on them, and each of them is so like the one associated with it that it easily passes from one form to the other. For *Principality* easily becomes *Tyranny*. From *Aristocracy* the transition to *Oligarchy*[e] is an easy one. *Democracy*[f] is without difficulty converted into *Anarchy*.[g] So that if anyone who is organizing a commonwealth sets up one of the three first forms of government, he sets up what will last but for a while, since there are no means whereby to prevent it passing into its contrary, on account of the likeness which in such a case virtue has to vice.

These variations of government among men are due to chance. For in the beginning of the world, when its inhabitants were few, they lived for a time scattered like the beasts. Then,

[a] *republiche.* [b] *uno de' tre stati, chiamati da loro Principato, Ottimati, e Popolare.* [c] *città.* [d] *sei ragioni governi.* [e] *stato di pochi.* [f] *popolare.* [g] *licenzioso.*

with the multiplication of their offspring, they drew together and, in order the better to be able to defend themselves, began to look about for a man stronger and more courageous than the rest, made him their head, and obeyed him.

It was thus that men learned how to distinguish what is honest and good from what is pernicious and wicked, for the sight of someone injuring his benefactor evoked in them hatred and sympathy and they blamed the ungrateful and respected those who showed gratitude, well aware that the same injuries might have been done to themselves. Hence to prevent evil of this kind they took to making laws and to assigning punishments to those who contravened them. The notion of justice thus came into being.

In this way it came about that, when later on they had to choose a prince, they did not have recourse to the boldest as formerly, but to one who excelled in prudence and justice.

But when at a yet later stage they began to make the prince hereditary instead of electing him, his heirs soon began to degenerate as compared with their ancestors, and, forsaking virtuous deeds, considered that princes have nought else to do but to surpass other men in extravagance, lasciviousness, and every other form of licentiousness. With the result that the prince came to be hated, and, since he was hated, came to be afraid, and from fear soon passed to offensive action, which quickly brought about a tyranny.

From which, before long, was begotten the source of their downfall; for tyranny gave rise to conspiracies and plots against princes, organized not by timid and weak men, but by men conspicuous for their liberality, magnanimity, wealth and ability, for such men could not stand the dishonourable life the prince was leading. The masses,[a] therefore, at the instigation of these powerful leaders,[b] took up arms against the prince, and, when he had been liquidated, submitted to the

[a] *la moltitudine.*   [b] *potenti.*

authority of those whom they looked upon as their liberators. Hence the latter, to whom the very term 'sole head' had become odious, formed themselves into a government. Moreover, in the beginning, mindful of what they had suffered under a tyranny, they ruled in accordance with the laws which they had made, subordinated their own convenience to the common advantage, and, both in private matters and public affairs, governed and preserved order with the utmost diligence.

But when the administration passed to their descendants who had no experience of the changeability of fortune, had not been through bad times, and instead of remaining content with the civic equality then prevailing, reverted to avarice, ambition and to seizing other men's womenfolk, they caused government by an aristocracy to become government by an oligarchy in which civic rights were entirely disregarded; so that in a short time there came to pass in their case the same thing as happened to the tyrant, for the masses, sick of their government, were ready to help anyone who had any sort of plan for attacking their rulers; and so there soon arose someone who with the aid of the masses liquidated them.

Then, since the memory of the prince and of the injuries inflicted by him was still fresh, and since, having got rid of government by the few, they had no desire to return to that of a prince, they turned to a democratic form of government, which they organized in such a way that no sort of authority was vested either in a few powerful men or in a prince.

And, since all forms of government are to some extent respected at the outset, this democratic form of government maintained itself for a while but not for long, especially when the generation that had organized it had passed away. For anarchy quickly supervened, in which no respect was shown either for the individual or for the official, and which was such that, as everyone did what he liked, all sorts of outrages were constantly committed. The outcome was inevitable. Either at the suggestion of some good man or because this anarchy had to be got rid of somehow, principality was once again restored. And from this there was, stage by stage, a return to anarchy, by way of the transitions and for the reasons assigned.

This, then, is the cycle through which all commonwealths pass, whether they govern themselves or are governed. But rarely do they return to the same form of government, for there can scarce be a state of such vitality that it can undergo often such changes and yet remain in being. What usually happens is that, while in a state of commotion in which it lacks both counsel and strength, a state becomes subject to a neighbouring and better organized state. Were it not so, a commonwealth might go on for ever passing through these governmental transitions.

I maintain then, that all the forms of government mentioned above are far from satisfactory, the three good ones because their life is so short, the three bad ones because of their inherent malignity. Hence prudent legislators, aware of their defects, refrained from adopting as such any one of these forms, and chose instead one that shared in them all, since they thought such a government would be stronger and more stable, for if in one and the same state[a] there was principality, aristocracy and democracy each would keep watch over the other.

Lycurgus is one of those who have earned no small measure of praise for constitutions of this kind. For in the laws which he gave to Sparta, he assigned to the kings, to the aristocracy, and to the populace each its own function, and thus introduced a form of government which lasted for more than eight hundred years to his very great credit and to the tranquillity of that city.

[a] *città.*

It was not so in the case of Solon, who drew up laws for Athens, for he set up merely a democratic form of government, which was so short-lived that he saw before his death the birth of a tyranny under Pisistratus; and though, forty years later, Pisistratus' heirs were expelled, and Athens returned to liberty because it again adopted a democratic form of government in accordance with Solon's laws, it did not retain its liberty for more than a hundred years. For, in spite of the fact that many constitutions were made whereby to restrain the arrogance of the upper class[a] and the licentiousness of the general public,[b] for which Solon had made no provision, none the less Athens had a very short life as compared with that of Sparta because with democracy Solon had not blended either princely power or that of the aristocracy.

But let us come to Rome. In spite of the fact that Rome had no Lycurgus to give it at the outset such a constitution as would ensure to it a long life of freedom, yet, owing to friction between the plebs and the senate, so many things happened that chance effected what had not been provided by a lawgiver. So that, if Rome did not get fortune's first gift, it got its second. For her early institutions, though defective, were not on wrong lines and so might pave the way to perfection. For Romulus and the rest of the kings made many good laws quite compatible with freedom; but, because their aim was to found a kingdom, not a republic, when the city became free, it lacked many institutions essential to the preservation of liberty, which had to be provided, since they had not been provided by the kings. So, when it came to pass that its kings lost their sovereignty, for reasons and in the manner described earlier in this discourse, those who had expelled them at once appointed two consuls to take the place of the king, so that what they expelled was the title of king, not the royal power. In the republic, then, at this stage there were the consuls and

<hr>

[a] *grandi.* [b] *universale.*

the senate, so that as yet it comprised but two of the aforesaid estates,[a] namely, Principality and Aristocracy. It remained to find a place for Democracy. This came about when the Roman nobility became so overbearing for reasons which will be given later – that the populace rose against them, and they were constrained by the fear that they might lose all, to grant the populace a share in the government; the senate and the consuls retaining, however, sufficient authority for them to be able to maintain their position in the republic.

It was in this way that tribunes of the plebs came to be appointed, and their appointment did much to stabilize the form of government in this republic, for in its government all three estates now had a share. And so favoured was it by fortune that, though the transition from Monarchy to Aristocracy and thence to Democracy, took place by the very stages and for the very reasons laid down earlier in this discourse, none the less the granting of authority to the aristocracy did not abolish altogether the royal estate, nor was the authority of the aristocracy wholly removed when the populace was granted a share in it. On the contrary, the blending of these estates made a perfect commonwealth; and since it was friction between the plebs and the senate that brought this perfection about, in the next two chapters we shall show more fully how this came to be.

3. What Kind of Events gave rise in Rome to the Creation of Tribunes of the Plebs, whereby that Republic was made more Perfect

ALL writers on politics have pointed out, and throughout history there are plenty of examples which indicate, that in constituting and legislating for a commonwealth it must

---

[a] *qualità* – here used in the sense of what is earlier called *potenza*, just as we say either 'three powers' or 'three estates'.

needs be taken for granted that all men are wicked and that they will always give vent to the malignity that is in their minds when opportunity offers.[3] That evil dispositions often do not show themselves for a time is due to a hidden cause which those fail to perceive who have had no experience of the opposite; but in time – which is said to be the father of all truth – it reveals itself.

After the expulsion of the Tarquins there appeared to be in Rome the utmost harmony between the plebs and the senate. The nobles seemed to have set aside their pride, to have become imbued with the same spirit as the populace, and to be bearable by all, even by the meanest. In this neither their deception nor the cause of it was apparent so long as the Tarquins lived; for the nobility were afraid of them and feared that, if they treated the plebs badly, it would not be friendly towards them, but would make common cause with the Tarquins, so they treated the plebs with consideration. But, no sooner were the Tarquins dead and the fears of the nobility removed, than they began to vomit forth against the plebs the poison hid in their hearts and to oppress them in every way they could.

This bears out what has been said above, namely, that men never do good unless necessity drives them to it; but when they are too free to choose and can do just as they please, confusion and disorder become everywhere rampant. Hence it is said that hunger and poverty make men industrious, and that laws make them good. There is no need of legislation so long as things work well without it, but, when such good customs break down, legislation forthwith becomes necessary. Hence when the regime of the Tarquins collapsed and the nobility were no longer kept in check by the fear of them, it became necessary to devise some new institution which should produce the same effect as the Tarquins had done in their time. Wherefore, after many disturbances, rumours, and dangers of scandal had been occasioned by the squabbles between the plebs and the nobility, for the security of the former tribunes came to be appointed, and were invested with such prerogatives and standing that henceforth they could always mediate between the plebs and the senate and curb the arrogance of the nobility.

4. *That Discord between the Plebs and the Senate of Rome made this Republic both Free and Powerful*

I MUST not fail to discuss the tumults that broke out in Rome between the death of the Tarquins and the creation of the tribunes, nor yet to mention certain facts which militate against the view of those who allege that the republic of Rome was so tumultuous and so full of confusion that, had not good fortune and military virtue counterbalanced these defects, its condition would have been worse than that of any other republic. I by no means deny that fortune and military organization had a good deal to do with Rome's empire, but it seems to me that this view fails to take account of the fact that where military organization is good there must needs be good order, and that rarely does it happen that good fortune does not also accompany it.

There are also other points to be observed in connection with this city. To me those who condemn the quarrels between the nobles and the plebs, seem to be cavilling at the very things that were the primary cause of Rome's retaining her freedom, and that they pay more attention to the noise and clamour resulting from such commotions than to what resulted from them, i.e. to the good effects which they produced. Nor do they realize that in every republic there are two different dispositions, that of the populace and that of the upper class and that all legislation favourable to liberty is brought about by the clash between them.

It is easy to see that this was the consequence in Rome; for from the days of the Tarquins to those of the Gracchi, which was more than three hundred years, tumults in Rome seldom led to banishment, and very seldom to executions. One cannot, therefore, regard such tumults as harmful, nor such a republic as divided, seeing that during so long a period it did not on account of its discords send into exile more than eight or ten citizens, put very few to death, and did not on many impose fines. Nor can a republic reasonably be stigmatized in any way as disordered in which there occur such striking examples of virtue, since good examples proceed from good education, good education from good laws, and good laws in this case from those very tumults which many so inconsiderately condemn; for anyone who studies carefully their result, will not find that they occasioned any banishment or act of violence inimical to the common good, but that they led to laws and institutions whereby the liberties of the public benefited.

But, someone may object, the means used were extraordinary and almost barbaric. Look how people used to assemble and clamour against the senate, and how the senate decried the people, how men ran helter-skelter about the streets, how the shops were closed and how the plebs *en masse* would troop out of Rome – events which terrify, to say the least, anyone who read about them. To which I answer that every city should provide ways and means whereby the ambitions of the populace may find an outlet, especially a city which proposes to avail itself of the populace in important undertakings. The city of Rome was one of those which did provide such ways and means in that, when the populace wanted a law passed, it either behaved in some such way as we have described or it refused to enlist for the wars, so that, to placate it, it had to some extent to be satisfied.

The demands of a free populace, too, are very seldom

harmful to liberty, for they are due either to the populace being oppressed or to the suspicion that it is going to be oppressed, and, should these impressions be false, a remedy is provided in the public platform on which some man of standing can get up, appeal to the crowd, and show that it is mistaken. And though, as Tully remarks, the populace may be ignorant, it is capable of grasping the truth and readily yields when a man, worthy of confidence, lays the truth before it.

Critics, therefore, should be more sparing in finding fault with the government of Rome, and should reflect that the excellent results which this republic obtained could have been brought about only by excellent causes. Hence if tumults led to the creation of the tribunes, tumults deserve the highest praise, since, besides giving the populace a share in the administration, they served as the guardian of Roman liberties, as we shall show in the next chapter.

5. Whether the Safeguarding of Liberty can be more safely entrusted to the Populace or to the Upper Class; and which has the Stronger Reason for creating Disturbances, the 'Have-nots' or the 'Haves' [a]

THOSE who have displayed prudence in constituting a republic have looked upon the safeguarding of liberty as one of the most essential things for which they had to provide, and according to the efficiency with which this has been done liberty has been enjoyed for a longer or a shorter time. And, since in every republic there is an upper and a lower class,[b] it may be asked into whose hands it is best to place the guardianship of liberty. By the Lacaedemonians, and in our day by

[a] *chi vuole acquistare o chi vuole mantenere* – those who want to acquire or those who want to keep, i.e. what we commonly call the have-nots and the haves.   [b] *uomini grandi e popolari.*

Venice, it was entrusted to the nobles, but by the Romans it was entrusted to the plebs.

It is necessary, therefore, to inquire which of these republics made the better choice. If we appeal to reason arguments may be adduced in support of either thesis; but, if we ask what the result was, the answer will favour the nobility, for the freedom of Sparta and of Venice lasted longer than did that of Rome.

Let us deal first with the appeal to reason. It may be urged in support of the Roman view that the guardianship of anything should be placed in the hands of those who are less desirous of appropriating it to their own use. And unquestionably if we ask what it is the nobility are after and what it is the common people are after, it will be seen that in the former there is a great desire to dominate and in the latter merely the desire not to be dominated. Consequently the latter will be more keen on liberty since their hope of usurping dominion over others will be less than in the case of the upper class. So that if the populace be made the guardians of liberty, it is reasonable to suppose that they will take more care of it, and that, since it is impossible for them to usurp power, they will not permit others to do so.

On the other hand, the defenders of the Spartan and Venetian systems say that to place the guardianship in the hands of the powerful has two good results. First, it satisfies their ambition more, since with this stick in their hands, they play a more important part in the republic, and so should be more contented. Secondly, it prevents the restless minds of the plebs from acquiring a sense of power, which is the cause of endless squabbles and trouble in a republic, and is enough to drive the nobility to desperate measures which in course of time have disastrous results. They cite as an instance Rome itself, where, when the plebs through their tribunes got this power into their hands, they were not content with one plebeian consul, but wanted to have both. After which they demanded the

censorship, the praetorship, and all the other great offices in
the city. Nor did this satisfy them, but, impelled by the same
mad desire, they began later on to worship any men they saw
were strong enough to get the better of the nobility. Whence
arose the power of Marius and Rome's undoing. It must be
confessed, then, if due weight be given to both sides, that it
still remains doubtful which to select as the guardians of
liberty, for it is impossible to tell which of the two dispositions
we find in men is more harmful in a republic, that which
seeks to maintain an established position or that which has
none but seeks to acquire it.

All things considered, however, and due distinctions being
made, we shall arrive in the end at this conclusion. Either you
have in mind a republic that looks to founding an empire, as
Rome did; or one that is content to maintain the *status quo*.
In the first case it is necessary to do in all things as Rome did.
In the second case it is possible to imitate Venice and Sparta,
as will be explained in the next chapter.

Turning now to the question as to which are more harmful
in a republic, the 'have-nots' who wish to have or the 'haves'
who are afraid of losing what they have, I would point out
that when Marcus Menenius was appointed dictator and
Marcus Fulvius master of horse, both of them plebeians, in
order to investigate certain conspiracies formed in Capua
against Rome, the people empowered them to inquire also
about those in Rome who, moved by ambition, had sought
to obtain the consulship and other posts in the city by other
than the accepted methods. To the nobility it looked as if the
authority thus vested in the dictator was a hit at them, so they
spread it about in Rome that it was not the nobles who had
ambitioned these positions and used out-of-the-way means to
get them, but commoners who, having neither blood nor
virtue on which to rely, sought to obtain these posts by round-
about methods, and in particular they accused the dictator of

this. So much weight was attached to this accusation that Menenius, having made a speech in which he complained about the calumnies spread by the nobles, resigned the dictatorship, and submitted his actions to the judgement of the people. He defended his own case and was acquitted.

At the trial there arose considerable discussion as to whether the 'haves' or the 'have-nots' were the more ambitious, for the appetites of both might easily become the cause of no small disturbance. Actually, however, such disturbances are more often caused by the 'haves', since the fear of losing what they have arouses in them the same inclination we find in those who want to get more, for men are inclined to think that they cannot hold securely what they possess unless they get more at others' expense. Furthermore, those who have great possessions can bring about changes with greater effect and greater speed. And yet again their corrupt and grasping deportment arouses in the minds of the 'have-nots' the desire to have, either to revenge themselves by desporting them, or that they may again share in those riches and honours in regard to which they deem themselves to have been badly used by the other party.

6. Whether in Rome such a Form of Government could have been set up as would have removed the Hostility between the Populace and the Senate

WE have just been discussing the effects produced by the controversies between the populace and the senate. Now, since these controversies went on until the time of the Gracchi[4] when they became the causes which led to the destruction of liberty, it may occur to some to ask whether Rome could have done the great things she did without the existence of such animosities. Hence it seems to me worth while to inquire whether it would have been possible to set

up in Rome a form of government which would have prevented these controversies. In order to discuss this question it
is necessary to consider those republics which have been free
from such animosities and tumults and yet have enjoyed a
long spell of liberty, to look at their governments, and to ask
whether they could have been introduced into Rome.

Among ancient states Sparta is a case in point, and among
modern states Venice, as I have already pointed out. Sparta
set up a king and a small senate to govern it. Venice did not
distinguish by different names those who took part in its
government, but all who were eligible for administrative
posts were classed under one head and called gentry.[a] This
was due to chance rather than to the prudence of its legislators; for many people having retired to those sandbanks on
which the city now stands and taken up their abode there for
the reasons already assigned, when their numbers grew to such
an extent that it became necessary for them to make laws if
they were to live together, they devised a form of government. They had frequently met together to discuss the city's
affairs, so, when it seemed to them that the population was
sufficient to form a body politic,[b] they decided that all newcomers who meant to reside there, should not take part in the
government. Then, when in course of time they found that
there were quite a number of inhabitants in the place who were
disbarred from government, with an eye to the reputation of
those who governed they called them gentlefolk and the rest
commoners.

Such a form of government could arise and be maintained
without tumult because, when it came into being, whoever
then dwelt in Venice was admitted to the government, so
that no one could complain. Nor had those who came to
dwell there later on and found the form of government firmly
established, either cause or opportunity to make a commotion.

[a] *Gentiluomini.*   [b] *vivere politico.*

They had no cause because they had been deprived of nothing. They had no opportunity because the government had the whip-hand and did not employ them in matters which would enable them to acquire authority. Besides, there were not many who came later to dwell in Venice, nor were they so numerous as to upset the balance between rulers and ruled; for the number of gentlefolk[5] was either equal to, or greater than, that of the newcomers. These, then, were the causes which enabled Venice to set up this form of government and to maintain it without disruption.

Sparta, as I have said, was governed by a king and by a small senate. It was able to maintain itself in this way for a long time, because in Sparta there were few inhabitants and access to outsiders desirous of coming to dwell there was forbidden. Moreover, it had adopted the laws of Lycurgus and shared in his repute, and, as these laws were observed, they removed all occasion for tumult, so that the Spartans were able to live united for a long time. The reason was that the laws of Lycurgus prescribed equality of property and insisted less on equality of rank. Poverty was shared by all alike, and the plebeians had less ambition, since offices in the city were open but to few citizens and from them the plebs were kept out; nor did it desire to have them since the nobles never ill-treated the plebs. This was due to the position assigned to the Spartan kings, for, since in this principality they were surrounded by nobles, the best way of maintaining their position was to protect the plebs from injustice. It thus came about that the plebs neither feared authority nor desired to have it, and, since they neither feared it nor desired it, there was no chance of rivalry between them and the nobility, nor any ground for disturbances, and they could live united for a long time. It was, however, mainly two things which brought this union about: (i) the smallness of Sparta's population, which made it possible for a few to rule, and (ii) the exclusion of foreigners from the state, which gave it no chance either to become corrupt or to become so unwieldy that it could no longer be managed by the few who governed it.

All things considered, therefore, it is clear that it was necessary for Rome's legislators to do one of two things if Rome was to remain tranquil like the aforesaid states: either to emulate the Venetians and not employ its plebs in wars, or, like the Spartans, not to admit foreigners. Rome did both these things, and, by doing so, gave to its plebs alike strength, increase and endless opportunities for commotion. On the other hand, had the government of Rome been such as to bring greater tranquillity, there would have ensued this inconvenience, that it would have been weaker, owing to its having cut off the source of supply which enabled it to acquire the greatness at which it arrived, so that, in seeking to remove the causes of tumults, Rome would have removed also the causes of expansion.

So in all human affairs one notices, if one examines them closely, that it is impossible to remove one inconvenience without another emerging. If, then, you want to have a large population and to provide it with arms so as to establish a great empire, you will have made your population such that you cannot now handle it as you please. While, if you keep it either small or unarmed so as to be able to manage it, and then acquire dominions, either you will lose your hold on it or it will become so debased that you will be at the mercy of anyone who attacks you. Hence in all discussions one should consider which alternative involves fewer inconveniences and should adopt this as the better course; for one never finds any issue that is clear cut and not open to question. Rome might indeed have emulated Sparta, have appointed a prince for life, and have made its senate small; but it would not in that case have been able to avoid increasing its population with a view to establishing a great empire; nor would the appointment of a king for life and of a small number of senators have been of much help in the matter of unity.

Should, then, anyone be about to set up a republic, he should first inquire whether it is to expand, as Rome did, both in dominion and in power, or is to be confined to narrow limits. In the first case it is essential to constitute it as Rome was constituted and to expect commotions and disputes of all kinds which must be dealt with as best they can, because without a large population, and this well armed, such a republic will never be able to grow, or to hold its own should it grow. In the second case it might be constituted as Sparta and Venice were, but, since expansion is poison to republics of this type, it should use every endeavour to prevent it from expanding, for expansion, when based on a weak republic, simply means ruin. This happened both in Sparta's case and in that of Venice. For of these republics the first, after having subjugated almost the whole of Greece, revealed, on an occasion of slight importance in itself, how weak its foundation was, since, when Thebes revolted at the instigation of Pelopidas and other cities followed suit, this republic entirely collapsed. In like manner Venice, having occupied a large part of Italy, most of it not by dint of arms, but of money and astute diplomacy, when its strength was put to the test, lost everything in a single battle.

I am firmly convinced, therefore, that to set up a republic which is to last a long time, the way to set about it is to constitute it as Sparta and Venice were constituted; to place it in a strong position, and so to fortify it that no one will dream of taking it by a sudden assault; and, on the other hand, not to make it so large as to appear formidable to its neighbours. It should in this way be able to enjoy its form of government for a long time. For war is made on a commonwealth for two reasons: (i) to subjugate it, and (ii) for fear of being subjugated by it. Both these reasons are almost entirely re-

moved by the aforesaid precautions; for, if it be difficult to
take by assault owing to its being well organized for defence,
as I am presupposing, rarely or never will it occur to anyone
to seize it. And, if it be content with its own territory, and it
becomes clear by experience that it has no ambitions, it will
never occur that someone may make war through fear for
himself, especially if by its constitution or by its laws expansion is prohibited. Nor have I the least doubt that, if this
balance could be maintained, there would be genuine political
life and real tranquillity in such a city.

Since, however, all human affairs are ever in a state of flux
and cannot stand still, either there will be improvement or
decline, and necessity will lead you to do many things which
reason does not recommend. Hence if a commonwealth be
constituted with a view to its maintaining the *status quo*, but
not with a view to expansion, and by necessity it be led to
expand, its basic principles will be subverted and it will soon
be faced with ruin. So, too, should heaven, on the other hand,
be so kind to it that it has no need to go to war, it will then
come about that idleness will either render it effeminate or
give rise to factions; and these two things, either in conjunction or separately, will bring about its downfall.

Wherefore, since it is impossible, so I hold, to adjust the
balance so nicely as to keep things exactly to this middle
course, one ought, in constituting a republic, to consider the
possibility of its playing a more honourable role, and so to
constitute it that, should necessity actually force it to expand,
it may be able to retain possession of what it has acquired.
Coming back, then, to the first point we raised, I am convinced that the Roman type of constitution should be adopted,
not that of any other republic, for to find a middle way
between the two extremes I do not think possible. Squabbles
between the populace and the senate should, therefore, be
looked upon as an inconvenience which it is necessary to put

up with in order to arrive at the greatness of Rome. For, besides the reasons already adduced to show that the authority of the tribunes was essential to the preservation of liberty, it is easy to see what benefit a republic derives when there is an authority that can bring charges in court, which was among the powers vested in the tribunes, as will be shown in the following chapter.

7. How necessary Public Indictments are for the Maintenance of Liberty in a Republic

No authority more useful and necessary can be granted to those appointed to look after the liberties of a state[a] than that of being able to indict before the people or some magistrate or court such citizens as have committed any offence prejudicial to the freedom of the state.[b] Such an institution has two consequences most useful in a republic. First, for fear of being prosecuted, its citizens attempt nothing prejudicial to the state, and, if they do attempt anything, are suppressed forthwith without respect to persons. Secondly, an outlet is provided for that all feeling which is apt to grow up in cities against some particular citizen, however it comes about; and, when for such ill feeling there is no normal outlet, recourse is had to abnormal methods likely to bring disaster on the republic as a whole. Hence nothing does so much to stabilize and strengthen a republic as some institution whereby the changeful humours which agitate it are afforded a proper outlet by way of the laws.

This can be shown by numerous examples, and especially by one that Titus Livy adduces, namely, that of Coriolanus. Livy tells us that, when the nobility were annoyed with the plebs because it seemed to them that the plebs had too much authority owing to the appointment of tribunes to protect them, and when, besides this, there was a great scarcity of provisions in Rome and the senate had to send to Sicily for corn, Coriolanus, who was hostile to the popular faction, suggested that the time had come to punish the plebs and to deprive them of the authority they had assumed to the prejudice of the nobility. Hence he advised that they should be kept hungry and that the corn should not be distributed among them. When this came to the ears of the populace, indignation against Coriolanus grew so intense that, as he was leaving the senate, he would have been killed in the tumult if the tribunes had not cited him to appear in his own defence. One notes in this incident what has been said above, namely, how useful and necessary it is for republics to provide a legal outlet for the anger which the general public has conceived against a particular citizen, because when no such normal means are available, recourse is had to abnormal means, which unquestionably have a worse effect than does the normal method.

The reason is that, though wrong may be done when a citizen is punished in the normal way, scarce any disorder, or none at all, is brought about in the republic; for in carrying out the sentence no appeal is made either to private or to foreign forces, and it is these that entail the downfall of civic liberties. On the contrary, such force as is employed, is employed by public authority which functions within specified limits, and does not, overstepping them, go on to do things which ruin the republic.

There is no need to corroborate this view by citing further examples from olden times in addition to that of Coriolanus. In his regard, however, all should reflect on the evils that might have ensued in the Roman republic had he been tumultuously put to death, for this would have given rise to private feuding, which would have aroused fear; and fear would have led to defensive action; this to the procuring of partisans; partisans would have meant the formation of factions[a] in the city; and factions would have brought about its downfall. As, however, the matter was settled by persons vested with the requisite authority, no opening was provided for the evils that might have resulted had the matter been settled by private authority.

In our own times we have seen disturbances introduced into the republic of Florence owing to the inability of the masses to find a normal outlet for the animus aroused by one of its citizens – as for instance happened at the time when Francesco Valori's standing in the city was akin to that of a prince.[6] He was regarded by many as an ambitious man, likely, owing to his audacity and animosity, to resort to unconstitutional methods. As there was no way of resisting him save by forming a rival party, it came about that he began to collect supporters to defend himself since he had nothing to be afraid of unless extraordinary steps were taken. On the other hand, since to his opponents no ordinary means of suppressing him were available, they made up their minds to use other means, and eventually took up arms. Had it in this case been possible to oppose Valori by constitutional methods, an end would have been put to his authority without harm to anybody but himself; but since it had to be done by unconstitutional methods, harm resulted not only to him, but to many other noble citizens.

One might also cite in support of the conclusion just reached an incident that also happened in Florence. It concerns Piero Soderini, and was entirely due to the absence in this republic of any means whereby legal action might be taken against the ambition displayed by powerful citizens. For to indict a powerful citizen before eight judges is inadequate. There should have been plenty of judges, for the few always act as the few are wont to act. Had this been the case, the citizens would either have indicted him, if his conduct had been bad,

[a] parti.

PUBLIC INDICTMENTS   I.7

and in this way would have found an outlet for the animosity
without getting a Spanish army to intervene; or, if his conduct
had not been bad, would not have dared to take action against
him for fear that they themselves should be indicted. Thus in
either case the appetite which occasioned the trouble would
have ceased to operate.

We thus reach the conclusion that, whenever one finds outside forces called in by a party of men residing in a city, it
may be taken for granted that this is due to a defect in its
constitution in that it comprises no institution which provides
an outlet for the malignant humours to which men are prone,
without their taking unconstitutional action. Adequate provision for this is made when there are many judges before
whom indictments may be made, and when judgeship is
looked on as an honourable post.

Such matters were so well provided for in Rome that in the
great disputes which arose between the senate and the plebs,
never did either the senate, the plebs, or any private citizen,
contemplate the calling in of outside forces, because, there
being a remedy at home, there was no need to seek one
abroad. And, though the examples already cited should suffice
to prove my case, I am going to give you yet another, taken
from Titus Livy's history. In it he relates how in Clusium – in
those days the most noble city in Tuscany – a sister of Aruns
had been violated by Lucumon, and how Aruns, unable to
obtain justice owing to the power of her ravisher, went to the
Gauls who then controlled the province we now call Lombardy, and besought them to bring armed forces to Clusium,
pointing out that it would be to their own advantage to
avenge the injustice done to him; and how if Aruns had seen
how to obtain justice by appeal to the city's laws he would
not have invoked barbarian forces. But if such indictments are
of advantage to a republic, calumny is not only useless, but
harmful, as we shall show in the next chapter.

8. *Calumnies are as Injurious to Republics as Public Indictments are Useful*

ALTHOUGH the virtue of Furius Camillus, who had freed Rome from the yoke of the Gauls, had caused all the citizens of Rome to give him precedence without its appearing to them that, by so doing, they were diminishing their own repute or rank, none the less Manlius Capitolinus could not bear that so much honour and glory should be ascribed to Camillus, since it seemed to him that his own merits were as great as those of Camillus, since it was he who had saved the Capitol, nor was he inferior to Camillus in other praiseworthy military exploits. Consequently, so fraught was he with envy, that he could not remain tranquil while Camillus had such glory, but, realizing that he could not sow discord among the patricians, he turned to the plebs and disseminated among them diverse sinister rumours. Among other things, he said that the treasure which had been collected to give to the Gauls, had not been given to them, but had been appropriated by private citizens, and that, if it could be recovered, it might be used to the advantage of the public either in lessening the taxation of the plebs or in the discharge of certain private debts. This speech had a considerable effect on the plebs, who began to hold meetings and to raise numerous tumults in the city as it pleased them. This displeased the senate, to whom it appeared to be a serious matter and dangerous, so they appointed a dictator who should take cognizance of the situation and restrain the impetuosity of Manlius. The dictator accordingly cited Manlius to appear in public, where they confronted one another, the dictator surrounded by the nobles and Manlius surrounded by plebeians. Manlius was asked to state in whose hands the treasure was of which he had spoken, for the senate was as desirous to be informed of this as was the plebs. In his reply Manlius gave no details, but evaded the issue, saying that it was unnecessary to tell them what they already knew. So the dictator sent him to prison.

It is clear from this incident in what detestation calumnies should be held in free cities and in all other forms of society, and how with a view to checking them no institution which serves this end should be neglected. Nor for their prevention can there be anything better than an institution which provides adequate facilities for charges to be brought, because indictments are as helpful to republics as calumnies are harmful. The difference between them is this. There is no need of witnesses or of any other corroboration of the facts to set calumnies going, so that anybody can be calumniated by anybody else. But one cannot in this way be indicted, for indictments must be corroborated and circumstances be adduced to prove the truth of the indictment. Indictments are made before magistrates, before the people, and before courts. Calumnies are circulated in the squares and the arcades. Calumnies are more prevalent in cities in which less use is made of public accusations, and in which less provision has been made for receiving them. He, therefore, who constitutes a republic should do it in such a way that charges may be brought against any citizen without fear of any kind and without respect to persons. Where provision for this has been made, and due recourse is had to it, calumniators should be severely punished. Nor can they complain of such punishment, since they had an opportunity to make charges openly against those whom they calumniated in private. But where adequate provision for this has not been made, there invariably ensue considerable disorders. For calumnies do not castigate citizens, they do but exasperate them; and, since hate is more quickly aroused than is fear, they think, when exasperated, how to get their own back for what has been said against them.

This eventuality, as has been said, was adequately provided for in Rome, but was ever badly provided for in our city of

Florence. And, as in Rome such provision did much good. the lack of it in Florence did much harm. Anyone who reads the history of that city will notice how at all times calumnies have been spread against such of its citizens as were employed in important public affairs. Of one they said that he had embezzled the public funds; of another that he had failed in some undertaking because he had been bribed; of yet another that through ambition he had caused such and such an inconvenience. It thus came about that hatred arose on all sides; whence came divisions; from divisions factions, and from factions ruin. Whereas, if in Florence provision had been made for the accusing of citizens and for the punishment of calumniators, there would not have ensued the innumerable scandals that did ensue. For citizens, whether condemned or acquitted, would not have been able to harm the city, and there would have been fewer people indicted than there were calumniated, since, as I have said, it is not possible to bring an indictment against anyone as it is to calumniate anyone.

Calumnies, too, are among the various things of which citizens have availed themselves in order to acquire greatness, and are very effective when employed against powerful citizens who stand in the way of one's plans, because by playing up to the populace and confirming the poor view it takes of such men, one can make it one's friend. Of this it would be possible to adduce numerous examples, but I propose to confine myself to just one. The Florentine army was encamped about Lucca, under the command of Messer Giovanni Guicciardini, its commissary. Owing either to mismanagement or to misfortune, the taking of that city did not come about. Anyhow, whichever was the case, Messer Giovanni took the blame for it, since it was said that he had been suborned by the Lucchese. This calumny, fostered by his enemies, almost drove Messer Giovanni to utter despair. For, although, to justify himself, he offered to place himself in the hands of the 'Captain',[7] he none the less was unable ever to justify himself, since in that republic there were no means of doing so. This gave rise to considerable indignation alike among Messer Giovanni's friends, who comprised most people of standing, and among those who desired to introduce innovations in Florence. The affair, for this reason and others like it, grew to such dimensions that it led to the downfall of that republic.

Manlius Capitolinus, then, was a calumniator, not an accuser; and the Romans have shown us in his case precisely how calumniators should be punished. They should be made to bring a formal charge, and, when the charge is borne out by the facts, should be rewarded or at any rate not punished; but, when it is not borne out by the facts, they should be punished, as Manlius was.

9. That it is necessary to be the Sole Authority if one would constitute a Republic afresh or would reform it thoroughly regardless of its Ancient Institutions

To some it will appear strange that I have got so far in my discussion of Roman history without having made any mention of the founders of that republic or of either its religious or its military institutions. Hence, that I may not keep the minds of those who are anxious to hear about such things any longer in suspense, let me say that many perchance will think it a bad precedent that the founder of a civic state, such as Romulus, should first have killed his brother, and then have acquiesced in the death of Titus Tatius, the Sabine, whom he had chosen as his colleague in the kingdom. They will urge that, if such actions be justifiable, ambitious citizens who are eager to govern, will follow the example of their prince and use violence against those who are opposed to *their* authority. A view that will hold good provided we leave out of consideration the end which Romulus had in committing these murders.

One should take it as a general rule that rarely, if ever, does it happen that a state, whether it be a republic or a kingdom, is either well-ordered at the outset or radically transformed *vis-à-vis* its old institutions unless this be done by one person. It is likewise essential that there should be but one person upon whose mind and method depends any similar process of organization. Wherefore the prudent organizer of a state whose intention it is to govern not in his own interests but for the common good, and not in the interest of his successors but for the sake of that fatherland which is common to all, should contrive to be alone in his authority. Nor will any reasonable man blame him for taking any action, however extraordinary, which may be of service in the organizing of a kingdom or the constituting of a republic. It is a sound maxim that reprehensible actions may be justified by their effects, and that when the effect is good, as it was in the case of Romulus, it always justifies the action. For it is the man who uses violence to spoil things, not the man who uses it to mend them, that is blameworthy.

The organizer of a state ought further to have sufficient prudence and virtue not to bequeath the authority he has assumed to any other person, for, seeing that men are more prone to evil than to good, his successor might well make ambitious use of that which he had used virtuously. Furthermore, though but one person suffices for the purpose of organization, what he has organized will not last long if it continues to rest on the shoulders of one man, but may well last if many remain in charge and many look to its maintenance. Because, though the many are incompetent to draw up a constitution since diversity of opinion will prevent them from discovering how best to do it, yet when they realize it has been done, they will not agree to abandon it.

That Romulus was a man of this character, that for the death of his brother and of his colleague he deserves to be excused, and that what he did was done for the common good and not to satisfy his personal ambition, is shown by his having at once instituted a senate with which he consulted and with whose views his decisions were in accord. Also, a careful consideration of the authority which Romulus reserved to himself will show that all he reserved to himself was the command of the army in time of war and the convoking of the senate. It is clear, too, that when the Tarquins were expelled and Rome became free, none of its ancient institutions were changed, save that in lieu of a permanent king there were appointed each year two consuls. This shows that the original institutions of this city as a whole were more in conformity with a political and self-governing state than with absolutism or tyranny.

I might adduce in support of what I have just said numberless examples, for example Moses, Lycurgus, Solon and other founders of kingdoms and republics who assumed authority that they might formulate laws to the common good; but this I propose to omit since it is well known. I shall adduce but one further example, not so celebrated but worth considering by those who are contemplating the drawing up of good laws. It is this. Agis, King of Sparta, was considering how to confine the activities of the Spartans to the limits originally set for them by the laws of Lycurgus, because it seemed to him that it was owing to their having deviated from them in part that this city had lost a good deal of its ancient virtue, and, in consequence, a good deal of its power and of its empire. He was, however, while his project was still in the initial stage, killed by the Spartan ephors, who took him to be a man who was out to set up a tyranny. But Cleomenes, his successor in that kingdom, having learned from some records and writings of Agis which he had discovered, what was the latter's true mind

and intention, determined to pursue the same plan. He realized, however, that he could not do this for the good of his
country unless he became the sole authority there, and, since
it seemed to him impossible owing to man's ambition to help
the many against the will of the few, he took a suitable
opportunity and had all the ephors killed and anybody else
who might obstruct him. He then renewed in their entirety
the laws of Lycurgus. By so doing he gave fresh life to
Sparta, and his reputation might thereby have become as
great as that of Lycurgus if it had not been for the power of
the Macedonians and the weakness of other Greek republics.
For, after Sparta had thus been reorganized, it was attacked
by the Macedonians, and, since its forces proved to be inferior
and it could get no outside help, it was defeated, with the
result that Cleomenes' plans, however just and praiseworthy,
were never brought to completion.

All things considered, therefore, I conclude that it is
necessary to be the sole authority if one is to organize a state,
and that Romulus' action in regard to the death of Remus and
Titus Tatius is excusable, not blameworthy.

10. *Those who set up a Tyranny are no less Blameworthy than are the Founders of a Republic or a Kingdom Praiseworthy*[8]

OF all men that are praised, those are praised most who have
played the chief part in founding a religion. Next come those
who have founded either republics or kingdoms. After them
in the order of celebratees are ranked army commanders who
have added to the extent of their own dominions or to that
of their country's. With whom may be conjoined men of
letters of many different kinds who are each celebrated
according to their status. Some modicum of praise is also
ascribed to any man who excels in some art and in the

practice of it, and of these the number is legion. On the other hand, those are held to be infamous and detestable who extirpate religion, subvert kingdoms and republics, make war on virtue, on letters, and on any art that brings advantage and honour to the human race, i.e. the profane, the violent, the ignorant, the worthless, the idle, the coward. Nor will there ever be anyone, be he foolish or wise, wicked or good, who, if called upon to choose between these two classes of men, will not praise the one that calls for praise and blame the one that calls for blame.

And yet, notwithstanding this, almost all men, deceived by the false semblance of good and the false semblance of renown, allow themselves either wilfully or ignorantly to slip into the ranks of those who deserve blame rather than praise; and, when they might have founded a republic or a kingdom to their immortal honour, turn their thoughts to tyranny, and fail to see what fame, what glory, security, tranquillity, conjoined with peace of mind, they are missing by adopting this course, and what infamy, scorn, abhorrence, danger and disquiet they are incurring.

Nor is it possible for anybody, whether he be but a private citizen living in some republic, or has been fortunate enough or virtuous enough to have become a prince, to read history and to make use of the records of ancient deeds, without preferring, if he be a private citizen, to conduct himself in his fatherland rather as Scipio did than as Caesar did, or, if he be a prince, as did Agesilaus, Timoleon and Dion, rather than as did Nabis, Phalaris and Dionysius, for he could not but see how strongly the latter are dismissed with scorn, and how highly the former are praised. He would also notice that Timoleon and the like had no less authority in their respective countries than had Dionysius or Phalaris in theirs, and would observe that they enjoyed far greater security.

Nor should anyone be deceived by Caesar's renown when

he finds writers extolling him before others, for those who praise him have either been corrupted by his fortune or over-awed by the long continuance of the empire which, since it was ruled under that name, did not permit writers to speak freely of him. If, however, anyone desires to know what writers would have said, had they been free, he has but to look at what they say of Catiline.[9] For Caesar is the more blame-worthy of the two, in that he who has done wrong is more blameworthy than he who has but desired to do wrong. Or, again, let him look at the praise bestowed on Brutus: Caesar they could not find fault with on account of his power, so they cry up his enemy.

Let he who has become a prince in a republic consider, after Rome became an Empire, how much more praise is due to those emperors who acted, like good princes, in accordance with the laws, than to those who acted otherwise. It will be found that Titus, Nerva, Trajan, Hadrian, Antoninus and Marcus, had no need of soldiers to form a praetorian guard, nor of a multitude of legions to protect them, for their defence lay in their habits, the goodwill of the people, and the affection of the senate. It will be seen, too, in the case of Caligula, Nero, Vitellius and other bad emperors, how it availed them little to have armies from the East and from the West to save them from the enemies they had made by their bad habits and their evil life.

If the history of these emperors be pondered well, it should serve as a striking lesson to any prince, and should teach him to distinguish between the ways of renown and of infamy, the ways of security and of fear. For of the twenty-six emperors from Caesar to Maximinus, sixteen were assassinated and only ten died a natural death. And, if some of those who were killed were good men, as Galba and Pertinax were, their death was due to the corruption which their predecessors had introduced among the troops. While, if among those who died ordinary deaths, there was a wicked man, like Severus, it must be put down to his great good luck and to his 'virtue', two things of which few men enjoy both. It will be seen, too, from a perusal of their history on what principle a good kingdom should rest; for all the emperors who acquired imperial power by inheritance were bad men, with the exception of Titus; those who acquired it through adoption, were all good, like the five counting from Nerva to Marcus; and when it fell to their heirs a period of decadence again ensued.

Let a prince put before himself the period from Nerva to Marcus, and let him compare it with the preceding period and with that which came after, and then let him decide in which he would rather have been born, and during which he would have chosen to be emperor. What he will find when good princes were ruling, is a prince securely reigning among subjects no less secure, a world replete with peace and justice. He will see the senate's authority respected, the magistrates honoured, rich citizens enjoying their wealth, nobility and virtue held in the highest esteem, and everything working smoothly and going well. He will notice, on the other hand, the absence of any rancour, any licentiousness, corruption or ambition, and that in this golden age everyone is free to hold and to defend his own opinion. He will behold, in short, the world triumphant, its prince glorious and respected by all, the people fond of him and secure under his rule.

If he then looks attentively at the times of the other emperors, he will find them distraught with wars, torn by seditions, brutal alike in peace and in war, princes frequently killed by assassins, civil wars and foreign wars constantly occurring, Italy in travail and ever a prey to fresh misfortunes, its cities demolished and pillaged. He will see Rome burnt, its Capitol demolished by its own citizens, ancient temples lying desolate, religious rites grown corrupt, adultery rampant throughout the city. He will find the sea covered with exiles and the rocks stained with blood. In Rome he will see countless atrocities perpetrated; rank, riches, the honours men have won, and, above all, virtue, looked upon as a capital crime. He will find calumniators rewarded, servants suborned to turn against their masters, freed men to turn against their patrons, and those who lack enemies attacked by their friends. He will thus happily learn how much Rome, Italy, and the world owed to Caesar.

There can be no question but that every human being will be afraid to imitate the bad times, and will be imbued with an ardent desire to emulate the good. And, should a good prince seek worldly renown, he should most certainly covet possession of a city that has become corrupt, not, with Caesar, to complete its spoliation, but, with Romulus, to reform it. Nor in very truth can the heavens afford men a better opportunity of acquiring renown; nor can men desire anything better than this. And if in order to reform a city one were obliged to give up the principate, someone who did not reform it in order not to fall from that rank would have some excuse. There is, however, no excuse if one can both keep the principate and reform the city.

In conclusion, then, let those to whom the heavens grant such opportunities reflect that two courses are open to them: either so to behave that in life they rest secure and in death become renowned, or so to behave that in life they are in continual straits, and in death leave behind an imperishable record of their infamy.

Book One

---

11. *Concerning the Religion of the Romans*

THOUGH the first person to give Rome a constitution was Romulus, to whom, as a daughter, it owed its birth and its education, yet, since heaven did not deem the institutions of Romulus adequate for so great an empire, it inspired the Roman senate to choose Numa Pompilius as Romulus's successor, so that the things which he had left undone, might be instituted by Numa. Numa, finding the people ferocious and desiring to reduce them to civic obedience by means of the arts of peace, turned to religion as the instrument necessary above all others for the maintenance of a civilized state, and so constituted it that there was never for so many centuries so great a fear of God as there was in this republic.

It was religion that facilitated whatever enterprise the senate and the great men of Rome designed to undertake. Whoever runs through the vast number of exploits performed by the people of Rome as a whole, or by many of the Romans individually, will see that its citizens were more afraid of breaking an oath than of breaking the law, since they held in higher esteem the power of God than the power of man. This is clearly seen in the case of Scipio and of Manlius Torquatus. For, after the defeat which Hannibal had inflicted on the

Romans at Cannae, many of the citizens got together and, despairing of their fatherland, decided to abandon Italy and to transfer themselves to Sicily. When Scipio heard of this, he sought them out, and, sword in hand, forced them to swear that they would not abandon their country. Again, Lucius Manlius, the father of Titus Manlius, afterwards called Torquatus, had been indicted by Marcus Pomponius, the plebeian tribune. Before the case came up for trial, Titus went to Marcus, threatened to kill him if he did not swear to withdraw the charge against his father, and forced him to take an oath to this effect. Having taken the oath out of fear, Marcus withdrew the charge. Thus were those citizens whom neither love for their country nor the laws of their country sufficed to keep in Italy, kept there by an oath which they had been forced to take; and thus did a tribune set aside the hatred which he had for the father, and the injustice which the son had done him, together with his honour, for the sake of the oath he had taken. All of which was due to nothing else but the religion which Numa had introduced into that city.

It will also be seen by those who pay attention to Roman history, how much religion helped in the control of armies, in encouraging the plebs, in producing good men, and in shaming the bad. So that if it were a question of the ruler to whom Rome was more indebted, Romulus or Numa, Numa, I think, should easily obtain the first place. For, where there is religion, it is easy to teach men to use arms, but where there are arms, but no religion, it is with difficulty that it can be introduced. Thus, one sees that in establishing the senate and introducing other civic and military institutions, Romulus did not find it necessary to appeal to divine authority; but to Numa it was so necessary that he pretended to have private conferences with a nymph who advised him about the advice he should give to the people. This was because he wanted to introduce new institutions to which the city was unaccustomed, and doubted whether his own authority would suffice.

Nor in fact was there ever a legislator who, in introducing extraordinary laws to a people, did not have recourse to God, for otherwise they would not have been accepted, since many benefits of which a prudent man is aware, are not so evident to reason that he can convince others of them. Hence wise men, in order to escape this difficulty, have recourse to God. So Lycurgus did; so did Solon, and so have many others done who have had the same end in view. Marvelling, therefore, at Numa's goodness and prudence, the Roman people accepted all his decisions. True, the times were so impregnated with a religious spirit and the men with whom he had to deal so stupid that they contributed very much to facilitate his designs and made it easy for him to impress on them any new form. Doubtless, too, anyone seeking to establish a republic at the present time would find it easier to do so among un-cultured men of the mountains than among dwellers in cities where civilization is corrupt; just as a sculptor will more easily carve a beautiful statue from rough marble than from marble already spoiled by a bungling workman.

All things considered, therefore, I conclude that the religion introduced by Numa was among the primary causes of Rome's success, for this entailed good institutions; good institutions led to good fortune; and from good fortune arose the happy results of undertakings. And, as the observance of divine worship is the cause of greatness in republics, so the neglect of it is the cause of their ruin. Because, where the fear of God is wanting, it comes about either that a kingdom is ruined, or that it is kept going by the fear of a prince, which makes up for the lack of religion. And because princes are short-lived, it may well happen that when a kingdom loses its prince, it loses also the virtue of its prince. Hence kingdoms which depend on the virtue of one man do not last long, because they lose their virtue when his life is spent, and it seldom happens that it is revived by his successor; for, as Dante has wisely remarked:

Rarely to the branches
Does human worth ascend; for 'tis the will
Of its donor that men may recognize it as his gift.[10]

The security of a republic or of a kingdom, therefore, does not depend upon its ruler governing it prudently during his lifetime, but upon his so ordering it that, after his death, it may maintain itself in being. And, though it is easier to persuade rude men[a] to adopt a new institution or a new standpoint, it does not follow that it is impossible to persuade civilized men to do so, i.e. those who do not look on themselves as rude men. It did not seem to the people of Florence that they were either ignorant or rude, yet they were persuaded by Friar Girolamo Savonarola that he had converse with God. I do not propose to decide whether it was so or not, because of so great a man one ought to speak with reverence; but I do say that vast numbers believed it was so, without having seen him do anything out of the common whereby to make them believe; for his life, his teaching and the topic on which he preached, were sufficient to make them trust him. Let no one despair, then, of being able to effect that which has been effected by others; for, as we have said in our preface, men are born and live and die in an order which remains ever the same.

12. How Important it is to take Account of Religion, and how Italy has been ruined for lack of it, thanks to the Roman Church

THOSE princes and those republics which desire to remain free from corruption, should above all else maintain incorrupt the ceremonies of their religion and should hold them always in veneration; for there can be no surer indication of the decline of a country than to see divine worship neglected.

a uomini rozzi.

THE IMPORTANCE OF RELIGION

This is easy to understand provided one knows on what basis the religion of a man's homeland is founded, for every religion has the basis of its life rooted in some one of its main institutions. Thus religious life among the gentiles was based on the responses given by oracles and upon a body of sooth-sayers and diviners. All the rest of its ceremonies, sacrifices and rites depended on these, for it was easy to believe that the god who can predict your future, be it good or evil, could also bring it about. Hence there came to be temples in which the gods were venerated by sacrifices, supplications and ceremonies of all kinds; and also the oracle of Delos, the temple of Jupiter Ammon, and other well-known oracles, which filled the world with wonder and devotion. But when the oracles began to say what was pleasing to the powerful, and this deception was discovered by the people, they became incredulous and inclined to subvert any good institution.

The rulers of a republic or of a kingdom, therefore, should uphold the basic principles of the religion which they practise in, and, if this be done, it will be easy for them to keep their commonwealth religious, and, in consequence, good and united. They should also foster and encourage everything likely to be of help to this end, even though they be convinced that it is quite fallacious. And the more should they do this the greater their prudence and the more they know of natural laws. It was owing to wise men having taken due note of this that belief in miracles arose and that miracles are held in high esteem even by religions that are false; for to whatever they owed their origin, sensible men made much of them, and their authority caused everybody to believe in them.

There were plenty of such miracles in Rome, among them one that happened when Roman soldiers were sacking the city of Veii. Some of them went into the temple of Juno and, addressing her image, said: '*Do you want to come to Rome?*' To some it seemed that she nodded. To others that she answered, Yes. The reason was that the men were so deeply imbued with religion; for, as Livy points out, on entering the temple, they did not create a disturbance but behaved devoutly and displayed the greatest reverence. Hence it seemed to them that they heard the answer they wanted the goddess to give and had taken for granted when they approached her. Such beliefs and such credulity was studiously fostered and encouraged by Camillus and by the rest of the city's rulers.

If such a religious spirit had been kept up by the rulers of the Christian commonwealth as was ordained for us by its founder, Christian states and republics would have been much more united and much more happy than they are. Nor if one would form a conjecture as to the causes of its decline can one do better than look at those peoples who live in the immediate neighbourhood of the Church of Rome, which is the head of our religion, and see how there is less religion among them than elsewhere. Indeed, should anyone reflect on our religion as it was when founded, and then see how different the present usage is, he would undoubtedly come to the conclusion that it is approaching either ruin or a scourge.

Many are of opinion that the prosperity of Italian cities is due to the Church of Rome. I disagree, and against this view shall adduce such reasons as are necessary, two of them so potent that, in my opinion, it is impossible to gainsay them. The first is that owing to the bad example set by the Court of Rome, Italy has lost all devotion and all religion. Attendant upon this are innumerable inconveniences and innumerable disorders; for as, where there is religion, it may be taken for granted that all is going well, so, where religion is wanting, one may take for granted the opposite. The first debt which we, Italians, owe to the Church and to priests, therefore, is that we have become irreligious and perverse.

But we owe them a yet greater debt, which is the second

cause of our ruin. It is the Church that has kept, and keeps, Italy divided. Now of a truth no country has ever been united and happy unless the whole of it has been under the jurisdiction of one republic or one prince, as has happened to France and Spain. And the reason why Italy is not in the same position, i.e. why there is not one republic or one prince ruling there, is due entirely to the Church. For, though the Church has its headquarters in Italy and has temporal power, neither its power nor its virtue has been sufficiently great for it to be able to usurp power in Italy and become its leader; nor yet, on the other hand, has it been so weak that it could not, when afraid of losing its dominion over things temporal, call upon one of the powers to defend it against an Italian state that had become too powerful. There is abundant evidence of this in times gone by. For instance, with the help of Charles the Great, it drove out the Lombards who had established a sort of kingship over the whole of Italy. So, too, in our own day, it stripped Venice of its power with the help of France, and, later on, drove out the French with the help of the Swiss.[11]

The Church, then, has neither been able to occupy the whole of Italy, nor has it allowed anyone else to occupy it. Consequently, it has been the cause why Italy has never come under one head, but has been under many princes and *signori*, by whom such disunion and such weakness has been brought about, that it has now become the prey, not only of barbarian potentates, but of anyone who attacks it. For which our Italians have to thank the Church, and nobody else. Should anyone want to prove the truth of this by actual experience, he would need to have such power that he could send the Roman Court, together with the authority it has in Italy, to dwell in the territories of the Swiss, who are the only people who today, with respect both to religion and to military institutions, live as the ancients did. He would then find that

the evil ways of this court would cause before long more
disorders in that country than any that any other event at any
time whatsoever has been able to bring about.

13. What Use the Romans made of Religion in reorganizing the City, in prosecuting their Enterprises, and in composing Tumults

IT does not seem to me foreign to my purpose to adduce some
examples of how the Romans used religion in reforming their
city, and in prosecuting their wars. In Titus Livy there are
many examples of this, but I shall be content with the following. The Roman people, having created tribunes with consular
power, all of whom, save one, were plebeians, there occurred
in that year pestilences and famine, and certain prodigies took
place. Availing themselves of this opportunity in the next
appointment of tribunes, the nobles said that the gods were
angry with Rome for having abused the majesty of her
authority, and that the only way to placate them was to
restore the election of tribunes to its proper position. The
result was that the plebs, terrified by this appeal to religion,
appointed only nobles as tribunes.

One notes also in the siege of the city of Veii how the army
leaders used religion in order to keep the troops keyed up for
attack. During the year, the Alban lake had risen in an extraordinary way, and the Roman soldiers, tired of the long siege,
were desirous of returning to Rome when it was discovered
that Apollo and certain other oracles had said that the city of
Veii would be taken in the year in which Lake Alba over-
flowed. This report made the soldiers endure the fatigues of
the siege, since they now felt sure that they would capture the
town. Contentedly, therefore, they went on with the attack
until Camillus was made dictator and took the city after it
had been besieged for ten years. Thus religion, when properly

used, helped both towards the taking of a city and towards the restoring of the tribunate to the nobility; which it would in both cases have been difficult to carry out save by these means.

I must not omit to add yet another relevant example. There had arisen in Rome a number of tumults occasioned by Terentillus, a tribune, who wanted to propose a certain law, for reasons which will be given later in their proper place. One of the first remedies the nobility used was religion, of which they availed themselves in two ways. First they got someone to look up the Sibylline books, which told them, so they said, that, owing to sedition, the city would be in danger of losing its liberties that very year. Though the tribunes exposed the fraud, it none the less put such fear into the breasts of the plebs that they refrained from following their lead.

Another way in which they used religion was when one Appius Herdonius, with a crowd of exiles and slaves, numbering four thousand men, seized the Capitol by night; which made people afraid lest the Aequi and the Volsci, Rome's perpetual enemies, should come and capture Rome. In spite of this, the tribunes obstinately persisted in pushing forward the Terentillian law, alleging that the aforesaid attack was a fabrication, and that it was not true. Then from the senate came one Publius Ruberius, a grave man and a citizen of considerable authority, who, in a speech that was half friendly, half threatening, pointed out the dangers to the city and the inopportuneness of their demand to such effect that he got the plebs to swear to abide by the decision of the consul; with the result that the now obedient plebs recovered the Capitol by force. However, in the course of the attack, Publius Valerius, the consul, was killed, and forthwith Titus Quintius was reappointed in his stead, so the latter, giving the plebs no time for rest or to think of the Terentillian law, bade them go forth against the Volsci, alleging that by the oath they had made not to abandon the consul, they were obliged to follow him. The tribunes objected to this on the ground that the oath had been given to the dead consul and not to him. None the less, Titus Livy shows how the plebs, out of reverence for religion, preferred rather to obey the consul than to believe the tribunes; and on behalf of the ancient religion uses these words: 'Not as yet was there that negligence of the gods which now pre- vails in the world, nor did the individual put upon oaths and laws his own interpretation.' This made the tribunes afraid lest they should now lose the whole of their standing, so they agreed to remain obedient to the consul, and not to raise the question of the Terentillian law for a year, and the consuls agreed not to take the plebs off to the war for a year. Religion thus enabled the senate to overcome these difficulties, which, otherwise, they would never have succeeded in doing.

14. *The Romans interpreted their Auspices in accordance with their Needs, were wise enough ostensibly to observe Religion when forced to ignore it, and punished those who were so rash as to disparage it*

AUGURIES were not only in large part the basis of the ancient religion of the gentiles, as we have remarked in a previous discourse, but they also contributed to the well-being of the Roman republic. Hence the Romans took more care in regard to them than in regard to any other institution in that repub- lic. They made use of them in the election of consuls, in entering upon military enterprises, in leading forth their armies, on engaging in battles, and in all their important enterprises, whether civic or military. Never would they set forth on an expedition until they had convinced the troops that the gods had promised them victory.

Among other exponents of augury they had in their armies certain officials concerned with the taking of auspices,

who were called poultrymen; and whenever they had to fix
the day for an engagement with the enemy, they requested
the poultrymen to take the auspices. If the poultry pecked, the
augury was good and they fought; if they didn't peck, they
abstained from battle. Nevertheless, when reason told them
that a thing had to be done, they did it anyhow, even should
the auspices be adverse. But, so adroit were they in words and
actions at giving things a twist that they did not appear to
have done anything disparaging to religion.

Adroitness of this kind was used by Papirius, the consul, in
an important battle which he fought with the Samnites, after
which the latter were left extremely weak and dispirited. For,
when Papirius was encamped opposite to the Samnites, and it
seemed to him that in battle he would certainly win, in order
that he might choose the day for this he told the poultrymen
to take the auspices. But the poultry did not peck. Observing,
however, the army's great eagerness to fight and that alike
the commander and all the troops thought they would win,
the head-poultryman in order not to deprive the army of so
good an opportunity for the work in hand, sent word to the
consul that the result of the auspices had been favourable. So
Papirius ordered the troops to fall in. But meanwhile some of
the poultrymen let it out to some soldiers that the poultry had
not pecked; and they told Spurius Papirius, the consul's
nephew, who passed it on to the consul. Whereupon the
consul told him to mind his own business and to mind it well,
and that, as for himself and the army, the auspices had been
good, and that, if the poultryman had told a lie, that was his
look-out. That the result should agree with the prognostica-
tion, he then told the legates to put the poultrymen in the
forefront of the battle. Whence it came about that, when they
attacked the enemy, the head-poultryman was accidentally
killed by a javelin thrown by a Roman soldier. When the
consul heard of this, he said that all was going well, thanks be

to the gods; for by the death of this liar the army had been
purged of any blame and any wrath which it had incurred in
the sight of the gods. Thus, through knowing how to accommodate nicely his plans to the auspices, he engaged the enemy
and beat them without the army's suspecting that he had in
any way neglected what was prescribed by their religion.

In Sicily during the first Punic war Appius Pulcher acted
very differently. When about to engage with the Carthaginian army, he had the auspices taken by the poultrymen, and,
when they reported that the poultry would not peck, he
exclaimed 'Let's see if they won't drink!', and had them
thrown into the sea. He then made the attack and lost the
day. For which he was condemned at Rome and Papirius
honoured; not so much because the one had been victorious
and the other had lost, as because the one, in contravening the
auspices, had been prudent and the other rash. Nor did this
custom of consulting the auspices tend to produce any result
save to cause troops to go confidently into battle, the which
confidence almost always leads to victory. Nor yet was it
only the Romans who used it, but also foreigners, of which I
think I will give an example in the following chapter.

15. The Samnites had recourse to Religion as a last Resort when their Affairs were going badly

AFTER the Samnites had been defeated several times by the
Romans and had been finally destroyed in Tuscany, their
army and its officers killed, their allies such as the Tuscans,
Gauls and Umbrians conquered, 'they could rely now neither
on their strength nor on that of others, yet they did not withdraw from the war, so far were they from becoming weary
of defending liberty even without success, and so much did
they prefer to be beaten rather than not try to win'. They
determined, therefore, to make a final effort; and, since they

knew it was necessary to instil into the minds of the soldiers
an obstinate will to conquer, and that, to instil it, there were
no better means than religion, they decided on the advice of
Ovius Paccius, their priest, to revive one of their ancient
sacrifices. The ritual they observed was as follows. Having
offered a solemn sacrifice, and made all the officers of the
army stand between the dead victims and the flame-lit altars
and swear that they would never abandon the fight, they
called up the soldiers one by one, made them stand between
the altars in the midst of a number of centurions with drawn
swords in their hands, and first of all swear that they would
not reveal anything which they saw or observed. They then
made them promise the gods with curses and the most
terrible incantations that they would be ready to go wherever
the generals ordered, that they would never flee from the
battle, and that they would kill anyone whom they saw
running away, and, if they did not do this, they prayed that
the curse might fall on the heads of their family and on their
children. Some of them, terrified, were reluctant to take the
oath, and were at once killed by the centurions. All those who
came after them, frightened by the ferocity of the spectacle,
then took the oath. To make this, their assemblage of forty
thousand men, yet more magnificent, they clad half of them
in white, with crests and plumes on their helmets; and, thus
arrayed, the army took up its position near Aquilonia.

Papirius went to meet them, and, to encourage his troops,
told them that 'crests do not cause wounds, and the Roman
javelin goes through painted and gilded shields'. Then, in
order to dispel any false impression his own troops might have
formed of the enemy owing to the oath they had taken, he
said that its effect would be to make them afraid, not to
strengthen them, since at one and the same time they were
afraid of their fellow citizens, of the gods, and of the enemy.

When the engagement took place, the Samnites were overcome, because the virtue of the Romans and the fear caused by past defeats more than counterbalanced any obstinacy they might have derived from the virtue of religion and from the oath they had taken. Nevertheless, it is clear that to them there did not appear to be anything else to which they could have recourse or any other remedy they could try in the hope of recovering the virtue they had lost. This bears striking witness to the magnitude of that confidence which religion gives when properly used.

And, though, perhaps, it might have been better to discuss the question under the head of foreign affairs, yet it is concerned with one of the most important institutions of the Roman Republic, and so seems to me to belong here, since otherwise I should have to deal with this topic in parts and to return to it several times.

Book One

[THE TRANSITION FROM SERVITUDE TO FREEDOM

---

16. *A People accustomed to live under a Prince, should they by some Eventuality become free, will with Difficulty maintain their Freedom*

How difficult it is for a people accustomed to live under a prince to preserve their liberty, should they by some accident acquire it as Rome did after the expulsion of the Tarquins, is shown by numerous examples which may be studied in the historical records of ancient times. That there should be such a difficulty is reasonable; for such a people differs in no wise from a wild animal which, though by nature fierce and accustomed to the woods, has been brought up in captivity and servitude and is then loosed to rove the countryside at will, where, being unaccustomed to seeking its own food and discovering no place in which it can find refuge, it becomes the prey of the first comer who seeks to chain it up again.

The same thing happens to a people which has been accustomed to live under foreign rulers and so has taken no thought for either public defence or offence and is acquainted with no princes nor yet are any acquainted with it; it forthwith returns to the yoke, and ofttimes to a heavier one than that which, a

153

while back, it threw off its neck. This difficulty may occur, no matter how free the material be from corruption. But, since a people which has become wholly corrupt, cannot even for a brief space, no, not even for a moment, enjoy its freedom, as we shall show later, we shall confine ourselves in the present discourse to peoples in whom corruption has not advanced too far, and in whom there is still more goodness than rottenness.[12]

In addition to the difficulty already mentioned there is yet another. It is that the government of a state which has become free evokes factions which are hostile, not factions which are friendly. To such hostile factions will belong all those who held preferment under the tyrannical government and grew fat on the riches of its prince, since, now that they are deprived of these emoluments, they cannot live contented, but are compelled, each of them, to try to restore the tyranny in order to regain their authority. Nor, as I have said, will such a government acquire supporters who are friendly, because a self-governing state[a] assigns honours and rewards only for honest and determinate reasons, and, apart from this, rewards and honours no one; and when one acquires honours or advantages which appear to have been deserved, one does not acknowledge any obligation towards those responsible for the remuneration. Furthermore, that common advantage which results from a self-governing state is not recognized by anybody so long as it is possessed – the possibility of enjoying what one has, freely and without incurring suspicion for instance, the assurance that one's wife and children will be respected, the absence of fear for oneself – for no one admits that he incurs an obligation to another merely because that other has done him no wrong.

It is, then, as I have said. The government of a state which is free and has been newly formed, will evoke hostile factions but not friendly factions. If then one desires to remedy these

[a] *il vivere libero.*

154

difficulties and to cure the disorders which the aforesaid difficulties bring about, there is no way more efficient, more sure, more safe or more necessary, than to kill the sons of Brutus, who, as history shows[13] would not together with other Roman youths have been induced to conspire against their country if it had not been that, under consuls, they could not attain to an outstanding position, as they could under the kings; so that the freedom of the people was, from their point of view, but servitude.

He then who sets out to govern the masses, whether in a free state or in a principality, and does not secure himself against those who are hostile to the new order, is setting up a form of government which will be but short-lived. True, I look upon those rulers as unhappy who, to make their government secure, have to adopt abnormal methods because they find the masses hostile; for he who has but the few as his enemies, can easily and without much scandal make himself secure, but he who has the public as a whole for his enemy can never make himself secure; and the greater his cruelty, the weaker does his regime become. In such a case the best remedy he can adopt is to make the populace his friend.

Though to speak now of a prince, now of a republic is to distort the plan of this discourse, I propose, none the less, to talk of princes that I may not have to return to this topic. If, then, a prince wants to make sure of a populace that might be hostile to him – I speak of such princes as have become tyrants in their own country – what I say is that he ought first to ask what it is that the people desire, and that he will always find that they desire two things: (i) to avenge themselves against the persons who have been the cause of their servitude, and (ii) to regain their freedom. The first of these demands the prince can satisfy entirely, the second in part.

Of the first demand there is an example much to the point. When Clearchus, tyrant of Heraclea, was in exile, it happened that in Heraclea a controversy arose between its populace and the upper class who were in the weaker position, and so decided to support Clearchus and, despite the popular feeling, swore to bring him back and to deprive the populace of its freedom. It thus came about that Clearchus found himself between an arrogant upper class which he could in no way either satisfy or correct, and a raving populace who could not stand having lost its freedom. He decided therefore at one stroke to free himself from the vexations caused by the leading men and to win over the populace. So, choosing a suitable opportunity, he cut to pieces all the nobles to the immense satisfaction of the popular party, and in this way satisfied one of the demands of the populace, namely, the demand for vengeance.

As to the second popular demand – the restoration of freedom, since this the prince is unable to satisfy, he should inquire as to the grounds on which the demand for freedom is based. He will find that a small section of the populace desire to be free in order to obtain authority over others, but that the vast bulk of those who demand freedom, desire but to live in security. For in all states whatever be their form of government, the real rulers do not amount to more than forty or fifty citizens and, since this is a small number, it is an easy thing to make yourself secure in their regard either by doing away with them or by granting them such a share of honours, according to their standing, as will for the most part satisfy them. As for the rest, who demand but to live in security, they can easily be satisfied by introducing such institutions and laws as shall, in conjunction with the power of the prince, make for the security of the public as a whole. When a prince does this, and the people see that on no occasion does he break such laws, in a short time they will begin to live in security and contentment.

This is exemplified by the kingdom of France, in which

people live in security simply because its kings are pledged to observe numerous laws on which the security of all their people depends. It was the intention of the founder of this state that its kings should do as they thought fit in regard to the use of arms and to finance, but that in other respects they should act as the laws required.[14] That prince, therefore, or that republic which has not made its government secure at the outset, must take the first opportunity of doing so, as the Romans did. He who fails to do this will repent too late of having omitted to do what he ought to have done.

Thus, since the Roman people were not as yet corrupt when they regained their freedom, they were able to maintain it when the sons of Brutus were dead and there was an end of the Tarquins, by means of those methods of government and those institutions which are discussed elsewhere. On the other hand, had this people already become corrupt, neither in Rome nor anywhere else would remedies adequate for its maintenance have been found, as will be shown in the next chapter.

17. *A Corrupted People, having acquired Liberty, can maintain it only with the Greatest Difficulty*

IN Rome it was inevitable, in my opinion, that either the kings should be removed or that in a very short time the state would have become weak and of no account; because, if one considers how corrupt the kings had become, it is clear that in the course of two or three generations the corruption inherent in the kingship would have begun to spread to the members, and, when the members had become corrupt, it would no longer have been possible to reform them. But, since the head was lost while the trunk remained whole it was easily possible to recover a free and ordered mode of life. It should be assumed, then, as a basic and established principle that to a state[a] which has been under a prince and has become corrupt, freedom cannot be restored even if the prince and the whole of his stock be wiped out. On the contrary, what will happen is that one prince will wipe out another, and without the creation of a new lord it will never settle down unless indeed the goodness of some one man, conjoined with virtue, should keep it free. Such freedom, however, will last only so long as he lives. This happened to Syracuse in the case of Dion and of Timoleon, whose virtue was such that on both occasions the city remained free so long as they lived, but when they were dead returned to its ancient tyranny.

Nor can any better example of this be found than in Rome, which, when the Tarquins were expelled, was able forthwith both to acquire and to maintain its liberty; yet, when Caesar was killed, and Gaius Caligula and Nero were killed, and the whole of Caesar's stock was exterminated, was not only unable ever to maintain liberty, but could not even make a start. Results so diverse in one and the same city are caused by nought else but that in the time of the Tarquins the Roman populace was not yet corrupt, but in the later period was extremely corrupt. For in the former case, in order to stiffen the people up and to keep them averse to a king, it sufficed to make them swear never to consent to any king ruling in Rome. But in the other period the authority and severity of Brutus, backed by all the legions of the East, did not suffice to keep them disposed to desire that liberty to be maintained which he, after the manner of the first Brutus, had introduced. This was due to the corruption with which the Marian faction had impregnated the populace. For, when Caesar became the head of this faction, he so successfully blinded the masses that they were unaware of the yoke which they themselves had placed on their necks.

Though the example of Rome is preferable to any other,

[a] *città* – 'state', and so throughout.

yet I propose to add to it further examples with which those who live at the present time will be familiar. I assert, then, that nothing that befell Milan or Naples, however grave and however violent in character, could ever bring them freedom, since their members were wholly corrupt. This is apparent after the death of Filippo Visconti, for, though it was proposed to introduce freedom in Milan, it could not be done, nor could any means of maintaining it be devised. Rome, then, was extremely lucky in that its kings quickly became corrupt, with the result that they were expelled before their corruption had penetrated to the bowels of that city. This absence of corruption was, in fact, the reason why the numerous tumults which took place in Rome, instigated by men of good intentions, did no harm, but, on the contrary, were an advantage to that republic.

It is possible, then, to arrive at this conclusion: when the material is not corrupt, tumults and other troubles do no harm, but, when it is corrupt, good legislation is of no avail unless it be initiated by someone in so extremely strong a position that he can enforce obedience until such time as the material has become good. Whether this has ever happened or whether it is possible for it to happen I do not know. For, as I have just said, it is clear that, if in a state which is on the decline owing to the corruption of its material a renaissance is ever to be brought about, it will be by the virtue of some one person who is then living, not by the virtue of the public as a whole, that good institutions are kept up, and, as soon as such a person is dead, they will relapse into their former habits.[15]

This happened at Thebes, which, thanks to the virtue of Epaminondas, successfully maintained a republican form of government as long as he lived, but, on his death, forthwith returned to its former disorderly state. The reason is that no individual can possibly live long enough for a state which has long had bad customs to acquire good ones. Unless a man living for a very long time or one virtuous man succeeded by another, organize it on their passing away, as we have said, there would be a collapse, unless the renaissance is brought about at considerable risk and with no small blood-shedding. For corruption of this kind and ineptitude for a free mode of life is due to the inequality one finds in a city, and, to restore equality it is necessary to take steps which are by no means normal; and this few people either know how to do or are ready to do, a point that will be dealt with in detail in another place.[16]

18. *How in Corrupt Cities a Free Government can be maintained where it exists, or be established where it does not exist*

IT will not, I think, be foreign to my purpose nor contrary to the plan of my previous discourse to consider whether in a corrupt city it is possible to maintain a free government[a] where it exists, and whether, when there has been none, it can be set up. In regard to this question I maintain that in either case it will be a very difficult thing to do. It is, moreover, almost impossible to lay down rules, for the method to be adopted will of necessity depend upon the degree of corruption. None the less, since it is well to take account of all cases, I do not propose to shelve the question. I suppose then an exceedingly corrupt state, whereby the difficulty will clearly be intensified, since in it there will be found neither laws nor institutions which will suffice to check widespread corruption. Because, just as for the maintenance of good customs laws are required, so if laws are to be observed, there is need of good customs. Furthermore, institutions and laws made in the early days of a republic when men were good, no longer serve

[a] *uno stato libero* – free in the sense that citizens are free to choose their own government.

their purpose when men have become bad. And, if by any chance the laws of the state are changed, there will never, or but rarely, be a change in its institutions. The result is that new laws are ineffectual, because the institutions, which remain constant, corrupt them.

In order to make this point more clear I would point out that in Rome there was a constitution regulating its government, or rather its form of government, and then laws enabling the magistrates to keep the citizens in order. To the constitution determining its form of government pertained the authority vested in the people, the senate, the tribunes, and in the consuls, the method of applying for and of appointing to magisterial posts, and its legislative procedure. These institutions underwent little or no change in the course of events, whereas there were changes in the laws which kept the citizens in order. There was, for instance, the law concerning adultery, the sumptuary law, a law concerning ambition, and many others. These laws were introduced step by step as the citizens became corrupt. But since the institutions determining its form of government remained unchanged and, when corruption had set in, were no longer good, these modifications of the laws did not suffice to keep men good, though they might have helped had the introduction of new laws been accompanied by a modification of the institutions.

That it is true to say that such institutions would not be good in a corrupted state is clearly seen in two important cases, in the appointing of magistrates and in the making of laws. The Roman people had never given the consulate or any other important office in the city except to such as had applied for the post. This institution was at the outset good, because only such citizens applied for posts as judged themselves worthy to fill them, and to be rejected was looked upon as ignominious; so that everybody behaved well in order to be judged worthy. This procedure, when the city became corrupt, was extremely harmful; because not those who had more virtue, but those who had more power, applied for magistracies, and the powerless, though virtuous, refrained from applying through fear. This inconvenience did not come about all at once, but by stages, as is the case with all inconveniences. For when the Romans had conquered Africa and Asia, and had reduced the greater part of Greece to subjection, they had become secure as to their liberty nor had they any more enemies whom there was ground to fear. This sense of security and this weakness on the part of their enemies caused the Roman people in appointing to the consulate to consider not a man's virtue, but his popularity. This drew to that office men who knew better how to get round men, not those who knew better how to conquer enemies. They then turned from those who had more popularity and gave it to those who had more power. Thus owing to the defectiveness of this institution it came about that good men were wholly excluded from consular rank.

Again, a tribune or any other citizen could propose to the people a law, in regard to which every citizen was entitled to speak either in favour of it or against, prior to a decision being reached. This institution was good so long as the citizens were good, because it is always a good thing that anyone anxious to serve the public should be able to propose his plan. It is also a good thing that everyone should be at liberty to express his opinion on it, so that when the people have heard what each has to say they may choose the best plan. But when the citizens had become perverse, this institution became a nuisance; because only the powerful proposed laws, and this for the sake, not of their common liberties, but to augment their own power. And against such projects no one durst speak for fear of such folk; with the result that the people were induced, either by deceit or by force, to adopt measures which spelt their own ruin.

In order to maintain Rome's liberty, therefore, when corruption had set in, it was necessary in the course of its development to introduce new institutions just as there had been made
new laws; for different institutions and a different procedure
should be prescribed for the governed according as they are
good or bad, since similar forms cannot subsist in matter which
is disposed in a contrary manner. Now defective institutions
must either be renovated all at once as soon as the decline from
goodness is noticed, or little by little before they become
known to everybody. Neither of which courses is possible, I
maintain. For if the renovation is to take place little by little,
there is need of someone who shall see the inconvenience
coming while yet it is far off and in its infancy. But it may
quite easily happen in a state that no such person will ever
arise, or, should he arise in point of fact, that he will never be
able to persuade others to see things as he does himself; for men
accustomed to a certain mode of life are reluctant to change it,
especially when they have not themselves noticed the evil in
question, but have had their attention called to it by conjectures. While with regard to modifying institutions all at
once when everybody realizes that they are no good, I would
point out that, though it is easy to recognize their futility, it is
not easy to correct it; for, to do this, normal methods will not
suffice now that normal methods are bad. Hence it is necessary
to resort to extraordinary methods, such as the use of force and
an appeal to arms, and, before doing anything, to become a
prince in the state, so that one can dispose it as one thinks fit.

But, to reconstitute political life in a state presupposes a
good man, whereas to have recourse to violence in order to
make oneself prince in a republic supposes a bad man. Hence
very rarely will there be found a good man ready to use bad
methods in order to make himself prince, though with a good
end in view, nor yet a bad man who, having become a prince,
is ready to do the right thing and to whose mind it will occur

to use well that authority which he has acquired by bad means.

It is on account of all this that it is difficult, or rather impossible, either to maintain a republican form of government in states which have become corrupt or to create such a form afresh. Should a republic simply have to be created or to be maintained, it would be necessary to introduce into it a form of government akin rather to a monarchy than to a democracy, so that those men whose arrogance is such that they cannot be corrected by legal processes, may yet be restrained to some extent by a quasi-regal power.[17] To try to make them become good in any other way would be either a most brutal or an impossible undertaking – the kind of thing that Cleomenes did, as I said above; for that he might rule alone, he killed the ephors, and for the same reasons Romulus killed his brother and Titus Tatius killed the Sabine, and afterwards both of them made good use of their authority. It should, however, be noted that neither the one nor the other had subjects steeped in corruption, which in this chapter we have taken as the basis of our argument; so that both were able to resolve on such steps, and, having done so, to camouflage their plan.

Book One

---

19. A Weak Prince who succeeds an Outstanding Prince can hold his own, but a Weak Prince who succeeds another Weak Prince cannot hold any Kingdom

THE virtue and the methods of Romulus, Numa and Tullus, the first three kings of Rome, show how extremely fortunate Rome was to have had first a fierce and warlike king, then a peaceful and religious one, and thirdly a king with the military ardour of Romulus and a lover of war rather than peace. For it was essential to Rome in its early days that there should arise a legislator to give it a civic constitution, and it was also necessary that there should be others who would again display the virtue of Romulus, since, otherwise, the city would have become effeminate and have fallen a prey to its neighbours. In which connection it may be noted that a prince who is less virtuous than his predecessor can hold a state thanks to the virtue of its previous ruler and can enjoy the fruits of his labours; but, should he happen to live a long time or should there not arise another who again displays the virtue of the first, the kingdom must needs be ruined. And, conversely, if of two princes who come one after the other both are conspicuous for virtue, it is frequently found that they perform magnificent exploits and that their fame reaches to the uppermost limits of the heavens.

David no doubt was a very fine man, alike as soldier, teacher and judge; and his virtue was such that, having beaten and conquered all his neighbours, he left to his young son, Solomon, a peaceful kingdom, which he could maintain by peaceful instead of warlike methods, and there enjoy happily the fruits of his father's virtue. He could not, however, leave it just so to Rehoboam, his young son, who, since he lacked his grandfather's virtue and also his father's good fortune, with difficulty remained heir to a sixth part of the kingdom.[18]

Bajazet, Sultan of the Turks, a man who loved peace more than war, was able to enjoy the fruits of his father, Mahomet's, labours; for the latter, like David, had defeated his neighbours, and left to him a strong kingdom which he could easily maintain by peaceful methods. Had, however, his son, Selim, the present ruler, been like his father, not like his grandfather, this kingdom would have been ruined. Actually, however, he seems to be out to excel the glory of his grandfather.

I claim, then, in view of these examples, that a weak prince who succeeds an able prince can hold his own; but that if a weak prince succeeds another weak prince, he cannot keep any kingdom going, unless, as in France, there are ancient institutions which keep things going. By 'weak' princes I mean those who are not prepared for war.

I conclude with these remarks. The virtue of Romulus was so great that he made it possible for Numa Pompilius to rule for many years by peaceful methods. He was then succeeded by Tullus whose repute for ferocity rivalled that of Romulus. Then came Ancus whose natural talents were such that he could avail himself of peace and also carry on war. At first he was inclined to keep to the ways of peace; but when one fine day he discovered that his neighbours thought him effeminate and held him in little esteem, he at once decided that, if he wanted to keep Rome, he must resort to war and emulate Romulus rather than Numa.

From these examples let all princes who have dominions learn that, if they emulate Numa, they will hold them or fail to hold them according to the times or the fortune that befalls them. Whereas if they emulate Romulus and, like him, rely both on prudence and on arms, they will hold them in any case, unless some obstinate and overwhelming force takes them away. It is highly probable that if it had not been Rome's lot to have in her third king a man who knew how to use armed forces to maintain her reputation, she would never, or would with the utmost difficulty, have established her position, nor would she have succeeded in effecting what she did effect. Thus, while Rome was subject to kings, she was exposed to dangers that might have ruined her had she been under a weak or malevolent king.

20. Two Virtuous Princes, of whom one immediately succeeds the other, do Great Things: and, as in Well-ordered Republics there is of necessity such a Virtuous Succession, their Acquisitions and their Increase also is great

WHEN Rome got rid of her kings, with them vanished the dangers entailed by the accession of a weak or a bad king. For the sovereign power was now vested in consuls, who acquired it not by heredity or by trickery or by violence inspired by ambition, but came into this power by the free votes of the people, and withal were very able men. Under their virtuous rule Rome thrived and fortune favoured her time and again, so that she attained to her highest pitch of greatness in as many years again as she had been subject to kings.

How this came about is clear. For, if the immediate succession of one virtuous prince by another suffices for the conquest of the world, as it did in the case of Philip of Macedon and Alexander the Great, a republic should be all the more successful, since, thanks to its practice of electing its rulers, it has not merely a succession of two highly virtuous rulers, but an infinite number each succeeding the other; and this virtuous succession may always be kept up in a well-ordered republic.

21. *Princes and Republics which have not their own Armed Forces are highly reprehensible*

PRESENT-DAY princes and modern republics which have not their own troops for offence and defence ought to be ashamed of themselves. They should consider the example set by Tullus, and should ascribe this defect not to lack of men fit to become soldiers, but to their own fault in that they have neglected to train men to be soldiers. Rome had been at peace for forty years when Tullus succeeded to that kingdom and he found there no man who had ever been to the wars. None the less, when he was making plans for war, he did not consider making use of the Samnites or of the Tuscans or of others who were accustomed to the use of arms, but decided, like a prudent man, to avail himself of his own people. And so great was his virtue that in a brief space under his rule he was able to make excellent soldiers. It is indeed the truest of truths that if, where there are men, there are not soldiers, it is their ruler's fault, not the fault of the situation or of nature.

Of this there is quite a recent instance. For everyone knows how a short time ago the king of England attacked the kingdom of France, and took with him none but his own people as troops. It being more than thirty years since this kingdom had been engaged in war, there were neither soldiers nor officers who had ever seen military service. Yet with such troops the king did not hesitate to attack a kingdom in which there were plenty of officers and of good troops who had been con-

tinuously under arms in the wars in Italy. All this was due to
the king's being a prudent man and to his kingdom being in
good order, for in times of peace it had not dropped the
institutions associated with war.[19]

When the Thebans, Pelopidas and Epaminondas, had
liberated Thebes and delivered it from servitude under the
Spartan empire, they found themselves in a city accustomed
to servitude and amidst an effeminate populace. Yet, such
was their virtue that they did not hesitate to put the populace
under arms nor with such troops to scour the countryside in
search of the Spartan army, which they defeated. With
reference to this a writer says that these two showed in a
short time that it was not only in Lacaedemonia that warriors
are born, but wherever men are born, provided there be
those who know how to give the military training, as we have
seen that Tullus did in the case of the Romans. This view
could not be expressed better than it is by Virgil, nor does any
remark put it so neatly as he does when he says of Tullus:

> And his slothful men
> Will Tullus rouse to arms.

22. What is worthy of Note in the Case of the Three Roman Horatii and of the Three Alban Curiatii

TULLUS, king of Rome, and Mettius, king of Alba, made a
pact to the effect that whichever of these two sets of three men
should win, their people would become lords over the other
people. All the Alban Curiatii were killed, and of the Roman
Horatii only one survived. Consequently Mettius, the Alban
king, together with his people, became subject to the Romans.
When the victorious Horatius returned to Rome he met one
of his sisters who was married to one of the three Curiatii

who had been slain. She was bewailing her husband's death, so he killed her. For this delinquency Horatius was brought to trial, and after much disputing was set free, not so much on account of his merits as on account of his father's intercession.

There are three things to be noted here:

(i) that never should one risk the whole of one's fortune on the success of but a part of one's forces;

(ii) that in assigning rewards and punishments in a well-ordered city never should blameworthy actions be counterbalanced by deserts;

(iii) that it is never wise to adopt a course if there is reason to doubt, or if there be doubt, whether the other party will observe his engagements. For that one city should become subject to another is a matter of such consequence that it was incredible that any king or any people should have rested content if the issue depend on three of their citizens being vanquished. This is illustrated by the conduct of Mettius, who, when the Romans won, at once admitted his own defeat and promised obedience to Tullus, yet in the first expedition which the Romans undertook against the Veientes, is found contriving how to let them down, like a man who comes to see too late how rash is the course he had adopted.

In regard to this third point enough has been said, so in the next two chapters I shall speak only of the other two points.

23. That One should not stake the Whole of One's Fortune except on the Whole of One's Forces; and that, consequently, it is frequently Harmful to defend Passes

IT has never been thought a wise course to risk the whole of your fortune without employing all your forces. This may be done in several ways. One way is to act as Tullus and Mettius did when they entrusted the whole of their country's fortune and the virtue of all the troops each of them had in his army to the virtue and fortune of three of their citizens, who came to but a tiny fraction of the forces each had at his disposal. Nor did they realize that in adopting such a course they were treating as of no account all the pains to which their ancestors had put themselves in order so to organize the commonwealth that it might enjoy a long life of freedom and that the citizens of each might be themselves the defenders of their freedom, for it lay within the power of so few to lose it. Than this these kings could hardly have done anything more stupid.

Those also almost always incur an inconvenience of this kind who, when the enemy is at hand, decide to hold difficult positions and to defend passes; for such a decision is almost always harmful unless the difficult position is such that you can conveniently hold it with all your forces. In that case this course should be adopted. But if the place is so awkward that it will not hold all your forces, such a course is dangerous. What leads me to think so is that those who have been attacked by a powerful foe in a land surrounded by mountains and in an Alpine terrain, have never attempted to engage the enemy in their passes and their mountains but have gone forth from them to meet him beyond them; or, when reluctant to do this, have awaited him behind their mountains, but in open country, not in country of the Alpine type. The reasons for this are, as has been said, that it is not easy to bring many men to the defence of an Alpine terrain, both because there is not enough for them to live on for very long, and because, the place being confined and capable of holding but a few, it is not possible to withstand an enemy who comes with a large force to attack it; and for the enemy to come with a large force is easy since his purpose is to get through, not to make it a stronghold. Nor is it possible for the defender to await in force, since he does not know when the enemy intends to pass that way, and so must find accommodation for a lengthy period in places which I am supposing to be both confined and sterile. When, therefore, the pass which you proposed to hold and on which your people and your army were relying, has been lost, your people and what remains of your forces will more often than not be so filled with terror that they will give up without awaiting a further chance of putting their valour to the test. You will thus have lost your whole fortune though you have employed but a part of your forces.

Everybody knows how difficult Hannibal found it to cross the Alps which separate Lombardy from Gaul and again how difficult he found it to cross those which separate Lombardy from Tuscany. Yet the Romans, in spite of this, awaited him first on the Ticinus and afterwards in the plain of Arezzo, for they preferred their army to be wiped out by the enemy in a place where it had a chance of winning rather than to lead it up the Alps to be destroyed by the malignant situation.

He who reads with appreciation history as a whole will find that very few generals of any virtuosity have attempted to hold such passes, both for the aforesaid reasons and because it is impossible to close them all, for in mountains, as in open country, there are not only the commonly frequented routes, but many others which, if not known to foreigners, are known to peasants, whose help you can always enlist in any place to the discomfiture of your opponent.

Of this quite a recent example may be cited. In 1515 when Francis, king of France, was intending to cross into Italy in order to regain control of Lombardy, the chief objection raised by those who were averse to the undertaking was that the Swiss would be a menace to the passes over their mountains. But experience showed that the objection was without foundation for, avoiding the two or three places which the Swiss were guarding, the king came by another route of which they were unaware, and was in Italy and down on them before they knew of it. Whereupon the Swiss in their alarm retreated on Milan, and the whole population of Lombardy came out to welcome the French forces when they found they were mistaken in thinking that the French would be held up in their mountains.

24. Well-ordered Republics, in assigning Rewards and Punishments, never balance one against the Other

VERY great were the merits of Horatius by whose virtue the Curiatii had been overcome; yet so abominable was his crime of killing his sister and so distressed were the Romans by this murder, that they tried him for his life, despite his deserts which were both great and recent. Superficially this would seem to be an instance of the ingratitude of the populace. But if one examines the case more carefully, bearing in mind the kind of institutions that a republic should have, it will be seen that the populace was more to blame for letting him off than for wanting to condemn him. The reason is that no well-ordered republic allows the demerits of its citizens to be cancelled out by their merits; but, having prescribed rewards for a good deed and punishments for a bad one, and having rewarded someone for doing well, if that same person afterwards does wrong, it punishes him, regardless of any of the good deeds he has done. And, when such ordinances are duly observed, the city long enjoys freedom, but otherwise will always be ruined. Because if a citizen who has rendered some signal service to the state, acquire thereby not merely the repute which the affair has brought him, but is emboldened to expect that he can do wrong with impunity, he will soon become so insolent that civic life in such a state will disappear.

It is highly necessary, therefore, that if punishment is to be assigned for evil deeds, rewards should be made for good ones, as actually was the case in Rome. Even though a republic be poor and able to give but little, it should not withhold that little, because every little gift awarded to someone in recognition of services however great, will always be highly esteemed and treasured by the recipient.

The story of Horatius Cocles and that of Mucius Scaevola is well known. The first held the enemy in check on a bridge until at length it was cut down. The other burnt the hand that had erred when he was going to assassinate Porsenna, king of the Tuscans. For these two deeds of outstanding merit, they each received a public grant of two half-acres of land.

The story of Manlius Capitolinus is also noteworthy. For having saved the Capitol from the Gauls who were encamped before it, his fellow-citizens who were being besieged together with him, gave him a small measure of corn. This reward was considerable in view of fortunes then current in Rome. It was also such that, when Manlius, out of envy or because his nature was bad, started a sedition in Rome and tried to win over the populace, not the least attention was paid to his merits, but he was thrown headlong from the Capitol which he had once saved with such renown.

Book One

---

25. He who proposes to change an Old-established Form of Government in a Free City should retain at least the Shadow of its Ancient Customs

HE who desires or proposes to change the form of government in a state and wishes it to be acceptable and to be able to maintain it to everyone's satisfaction, must needs retain at least the shadow of its ancient customs, so that institutions may not appear to its people to have been changed, though in point of fact the new institutions may be radically different from the old ones. This he must do because men in general are as much affected by what a thing appears to be as by what it is, indeed they are frequently influenced more by appearances than by the reality.

For this reason the Romans, on acquiring freedom, recognized the need of this from the start; and when in place of a king they appointed two consuls, they decided that the latter should not have more than twelve lictors, so as not to exceed the number which had ministered to the kings.

Furthermore, since when a commemorative sacrifice was offered it could only be offered by the king in person, and they did not wish the absence of the kings to arouse in the people a desire for anything pertaining to the past, they appointed a 'master of ceremonies' whom they called the 'sacrificial king' and put him under the high priest. It thus came about that the populace were content with this sacrifice, and had no occasion, for lack of a king, to desire that he should return.

This should be noted by all who contemplate abolishing an ancient form of constitution in a city and setting up a new and free form; because, since novelties cause men to change their minds, you should see to it that changes retain as much as possible of what is old, and that, if changes are made in the number, the authority and the period of office of the magistrates, they should retain the traditional names.

This, as I have said, should be observed by one who proposes to set up a political regime,[a] whether by way of a republic or by way of a monarchy. But he who proposes to set up a despotism,[b] or what writers call a 'tyranny',[20] must renovate everything, as will be said in the next chapter.

26. In a City or Province which he has seized, a New Prince should make Everything New

SHOULD anyone become the ruler either of a city or of a state, especially if he has no sure footing in it and it is suited neither for the civic life characteristic of a monarchy nor yet that of a republic, the best thing he can do in order to retain such a principality, given that he be a new prince, is to organize everything in that state afresh; e.g. in its cities to appoint new governors, with new titles and a new authority, the governors themselves being new men; to make the rich poor and the poor rich; as did David when he became king, 'who filled the hungry with good things and the rich sent empty away'[21]; as well as to build new cities, to destroy those already

_____
[a] uno vivere politico.   [b] una potestà assoluta.

built, and to move the inhabitants from one place to another far distant from it; in short, to leave nothing of that province intact, and nothing in it, neither rank, nor institution, nor form of government, nor wealth, except it be held by such as recognize that it comes from you.

His aim should be to emulate Philip of Macedon, the father of Alexander, who, starting as a little king, by these methods made himself prince of Greece. Of him a writer says that he moved men from province to province as shepherds move their sheep.

Such methods are exceedingly cruel, and are repugnant to any community, not only to a Christian one, but to any composed of men. It behoves, therefore, every man to shun them, and to prefer rather to live as a private citizen than as a king with such ruination of men to his score. None the less, for the sort of man who is unwilling to take up this first course of well doing, it is expedient, should he wish to hold what he has, to enter on the path of wrong doing. Actually, however, most men prefer to steer a middle course, which is very harmful; for they know not how to be wholly good nor yet wholly bad, as in the next chapter will be shown by means of an example.

27. *Very rarely do Men know how to be either Wholly Good or Wholly Bad*

POPE JULIUS II, on going to Bologna in 1505 to expel from that state the house of Bentivogli, who had held that city as a principality for a hundred years, resolved also to remove Giovampagolo Baglioni from Perugia, where he was ruling as a tyrant, for the Pope had sworn to be rid of all tyrants who had seized the estates of the Church. Being thus minded and for this purpose, as everyone knew, he hurried to Perugia and did not wait for the army which was to protect him before entering the city, but entered it unarmed, in spite of the fact that Giovampagolo was there in person with a strong body of troops which he had collected for his defence. Carried away by that impetuosity which characterized all his actions, he thus placed himself and the simple guard he had with him in the hands of his enemy; yet took his enemy away with him, and left in the city a governor who should be responsible to the Church.

Prudent men who were with the Pope were astonished at the pope's rashness and at the cowardice displayed by Giovampagolo; nor could they understand how it came about that the latter did not acquire perpetual fame by getting rid of his enemy at a single stroke and enriching himself with the booty; for with the Pope were all the cardinals in all their splendour. They could not believe that it was any good motive, or his conscience, that held him back, for the heart of a criminal who had committed incest with his own sister and to gain the throne had put to death his cousins and his nephews, could scarce be influenced by any pious consideration. So they concluded it must be due to men not knowing how to be either magnificently bad or perfectly good; and that, since evil deeds have a certain grandeur and are open-handed in their way, Giovampagolo was incapable of performing them.

Thus Giovampagolo, who thought nothing of incest or of publicly murdering his relatives, knew not how, or better, did not dare, to avail himself of an excellent opportunity to do what would have caused everyone to admire his courage and would have gained for him immortal fame, since he would have been the first to show prelates how little men are respected who live and rule as they do, and would have done a thing the greatness of which would have obliterated any infamy and any danger that might arise from it.

Book One

---

28. What made the Romans less ungrateful to their Citizens than were the Athenians?

WHOEVER reads of the doings of republics will find in all of them some sort of ingratitude in the way in which they deal with their citizens, but in Rome will find less than in Athens, and perhaps than in any other republic. If one inquires how this comes about in the case of Rome and Athens, I believe that it was due to Rome's having less ground for mistrusting her citizens than had Athens. For in Rome one sees that from the expulsion of the kings to the time of Sulla and Marius, she was never deprived of liberty by any of her citizens so that in her case there was no great reason to be suspicious of them, and, in consequence, rashly to give them offence.

The contrary was noticeably the case in Athens, for it was deprived of liberty by Pisistratus during its most flourishing period owing to its mistaken notion of what was good for it. Thus, when it again became free, mindful of the injuries done to it and of its past servitude, it very quickly became vengeful, not only when its citizens made mistakes, but even the semblance of mistakes. Hence the banishment and execution of so many of its best citizens. Hence the institution of ostracism and other forms of violence used at various times in that city against its upper class. Quite rightly do writers on civic government say that peoples bite more savagely when they have just recovered their liberty than when they have had it for some time.

In view, therefore, of what has been said, one can neither blame Athens nor praise Rome for what happened, but should ascribe it simply to necessity, a necessity that was brought about in these cities by events which differed in kind. For if one looks into things closely, one will see that, if Rome had been deprived of her liberty as Athens was, she would not have shown more respect for her citizens than did Athens. This becomes highly probable if we bear in mind what occurred, after the expulsion of the kings, in the case of Colla- tinus and Publius Valerius; of whom the first, although he was one of those who had helped to liberate Rome, was banished simply because he bore the name of Tarquin, while the second narrowly escaped being made an exile merely because he became suspect on account of a house he had built on the Caelian hill. The mistrust and the severity which Rome displayed against these two men leads one to think that Rome would have shown the same ingratitude as Athens, had she, like Athens, in her early days and before she grew, been injured by her own citizens. That there may be no need to return to this question of ingratitude, I shall make such further remarks as are necessary in the next chapter.

29. Which is the more ungrateful, a People or a Prince?

WITH respect to the topic under discussion it seems to me relevant to inquire whether ingratitude is better exemplified by a people or by a prince. The better to discuss this I premise that the vice of ingratitude arises either from avarice or from suspicion. For when a people or a prince has entrusted the command of an important enterprise to one of their generals and he is victorious and so acquires much glory, that prince or that people is under an obligation to reward him for this. Hence if, instead of rewarding him, they are discourteous to him or give him offence, and it be avarice that moves them to it in that it is greed that restrains them from giving effect to their desire to satisfy him, in acting thus they commit an error for which there is no excuse, and which is attended with lasting infamy. Yet there are found many princes who offend in this way. Cornelius Tacitus tells us the cause of this when he says 'One is more inclined to repay injuries than benefits; for it is burdensome to grant favours, but revenge is profitable.'

But when their motive for not rewarding him, or rather for giving him offence, is not avarice, but suspicion, there is in that case some excuse both for a people and a prince. Of ingratitude arising from this cause numerous examples are to be found in history, for the general who by his valour[a] has extended his lord's dominions, vanquished his enemies, won glory for himself and riches for his troops, must needs acquire such a reputation alike with his troops, with the enemy, and with that prince's own subjects, that the victory may not look so good to the lord under whose orders he acted. And because men are by nature both ambitious and suspicious, and know not how to use moderation where their fortunes are concerned, it is impossible that the suspicion aroused in a prince after the victory of one of his generals should not be increased by any arrogance in manner or speech displayed by the man himself. This being so, the prince cannot but look to his own security, and to this end consider putting him to death or depriving him of the standing he has thus obtained with his army and with his people by industriously pointing out that the victory was not gained by the general's valour, but by luck, or by the

[a] *virtù* – valour, and so throughout the chapter, though competence, and this in the service of one's country, is also connoted.

cowardice of the enemy or by the prudence of other officers associated with him in the action.

When Vespasian, then in Judea, was proclaimed emperor by his army, Antonius Primus, who found himself with another army in Illyria, took Vespasian's part and came to Italy to attack Vitellius, who was ruling in Rome. With the utmost virtuosity he broke two of Vitellius's armies and occupied Rome. Hence Mucianus, Vespasian's deputy, found that through Antonius's valour everything had been acquired and all difficulties overcome. The reward which Antonius got was at once to be deprived of his command of the army by Mucianus, and step by step to be reduced to a position of no authority in Rome. When he went to see Vespasian, who was still in Asia, his reception was such that before long he became just a nobody and died in despair.

History is full of such cases. Everybody at present alive knows how in our time Gonsalvo Ferrante, when fighting against the French in the kingdom of Naples on behalf of Ferdinand, king of Aragon, by his industry and valour conquered and overcame that kingdom; and how the reward he got for his victory was that, when Ferdinand left Aragon and came to Naples, he relieved him of his command of the army in the field, then took from him the fortresses and brought him with him to Spain, where shortly afterwards he died in ignominy. This natural suspicion is, therefore, in princes so intense that there is no defence against it, and it is impossible for princes to show gratitude to those who by victory have made great conquests under the flag of their prince.

Since a prince cannot help himself in this matter it is not to be marvelled at, nor is it a matter more worthy of remark, if a people cannot help itself. Because a city in which freedom prevails has two ends in view. One is to enlarge its dominions; the other is to keep itself free. In both it can err by excess. The errors made in expanding will be discussed in their proper place.[22] The errors made in the cause of liberty are, among others, these: giving offence to citizens who should be rewarded, and the suspecting of citizens in whom confidence should be placed. Both lines of conduct in a republic which is already corrupt may occasion great evils and the coming of tyranny is thereby often accelerated, as happened in Rome when Caesar took by force what ingratitude had denied to him. Nevertheless in a republic which is not corrupt they are highly beneficial and promote the cause of freedom, for owing to the fear of punishment men stay better and less ambitious for a longer time.

Of all peoples who have ever had an empire, Rome was the least ungrateful for the reasons given above, of its ingratitude but one instance can be cited, that of Scipio. For Coriolanus and Camillus were banished on account of the injuries which in each case they had done to the plebs. Moreover, though one of them was not pardoned owing to his having always maintained a hostile attitude towards the populace, the other was not only recalled, but during the rest of his life was treated like a prince. The ingratitude with which Scipio was treated, on the other hand, arose from the suspicion which the citizens began to have of him, but which they had not felt towards others. This was due to the greatness of the enemy which Scipio had defeated, to the reputation which he had acquired by his victory after so long and so dangerous a war, to the speed with which he had gained it, and to the favours which his youth, his prudence, and his other remarkable virtues were winning for him. All this was so striking that to say the least the magistrates grew afraid of his authority. This displeased the wiseheads since it was a thing to which Rome was unused. So extraordinary, indeed, did his career seem to be that Cato the Elder, reputably a holy man, was the first to criticize him on the ground that a city could not be called free in which there was a citizen of whom the magistrates were afraid.

Hence, if the people of Rome took in this matter the same view as Cato, there is some excuse for them, as I have said above of those peoples and those princes whose ingratitude is due to suspicion.

In bringing this discourse to a close, then, I say that since this vice of ingratitude is occasioned either by avarice or by suspicion, it will be found that peoples never display it owing to avarice, and that, owing to suspicion, they display it much more rarely than do princes, because peoples have less ground for suspicion, as will be explained later.[23]

30. *What Steps should be taken by a Prince or by a Republic to avoid this Vice of Ingratitude, and what should be done by a General or by a Citizen who does not want to suffer from it*

To avoid the necessity of having to spend his life suspecting people and displaying ingratitude, a prince should go in person on any expedition, as in the beginning the Roman emperors did, as in our day the Turk does, and as courageous princes both have done and still do. Because, if they win, both the glory and the territory gained is wholly theirs; but, if they are not there, the glory is another's, and they feel the glory of that other, they cannot make use of the acquisition until they obliterate a glory which they did not know how to acquire. So they become ungrateful and unjust, and thus unquestionably lose more than they gain. But when they stay idly at home owing to negligence or lack of prudence, and send a general in their stead, I have no maxim to give them other than that which they can find out for themselves. .

But to the general I would point out that, since he cannot in my opinion escape the jaws of ingratitude, he should do one of two things. Either he should, immediately after the victory, quit the army and place himself in the hands of his prince, abstaining from any act savouring of arrogance or ambition, so that his prince may have no ground for suspicion and in consequence will either reward him or at least refrain from harming him. Or, if this does not appear to him to be the thing to do, let him strenuously do just the opposite, i.e. use every means he thinks appropriate to make the acquisition his own and not his prince's: ingratiate himself with soldiers and with subjects, enter into friendly relations with neighbouring powers, put his own men in possession of fortresses, corrupt the leading officers of his army, and make sure of those whom he cannot corrupt; and in such-like ways seek to punish his master for the ingratitude he might perhaps display towards him. There are no other alternatives. But, as has already been remarked, men know not how to be either wholly bad or wholly good. Hence it always happens that after a victory generals are loath at once to give up their command and find it impossible to behave modestly, yet hesitate to resort to violent measures which may win him honour so that owing to the ambiguity of their position while they hesitate and doubt, they are overcome.

For a republic which desires to avoid the vice of ingratitude, it is not possible to prescribe the same remedies as for a prince, i.e. that they should accompany, not send out, expeditions, for they are obliged to put one of their citizens in command. The remedy I should prescribe in their case, therefore, is that they should keep to the methods used by the republic of Rome, methods which caused it to display less ingratitude than any other. This was the result of the way in which it was governed, for in time of war it availed itself of everybody in the city, whether they were nobles or not nobles, and in consequence there was always to be found in Rome at any given epoch so many virtuous men[a] with various victories to

[a] *uomini virtuosi*, where the context shows that their 'virtue' was no mere valour nor yet mere competence.

their name that the people had no cause to be dubious in regard to any of them, since there were so many that one looked after the other. In fact, so carefully did they maintain their integrity and so studious were they to avoid the least semblance of ambition lest it should cause the populace to attack them as ambitious persons, that, when there came to be a dictator, he acquired the more fame the sooner he resigned. Wherefore, since behaviour of this kind could not render men suspect, they did not evoke ingratitude. A republic, then, which does not want to have ground for ingratitude, should be governed as Rome was governed; and a citizen who wishes to escape the jaws of ingratitude should keep within the bounds to which Roman citizens kept.

31. *Roman Generals were never punished with Extreme Severity for their Mistakes; nor yet were they ever punished for Ignorance or Bad Judgement even though it caused Harm to the Republic*

THE Romans, as we have said in an earlier discourse, were not only less ungrateful than other republics; they were also more considerate and more careful in punishing the commanders of armies than was any other republic. For even if they had made a mistake with evil intent, their punishment was still humane; while, if it was due to ignorance, the Romans did not punish, but rewarded and honoured the person concerned. This mode of procedure met with their approval because they held it to be of supreme importance to those who commanded their armies, that in mind they should be free and unembarrassed, and should not have to concern themselves with irrelevant matters in arriving at their decisions, for they did not wish to add fresh difficulties and dangers to what was already a difficult and dangerous task, since, were they thus encumbered, there would be none who would ever act virtuously. Take, for instance, the army they sent against Philip of Macedon in Greece,[24] or against Hannibal in Italy, or against the peoples whom first they conquered. The commander who was put in charge of such an expedition had enough to do with the cares attendant upon such a grave and highly important undertaking. Now, if to such cares had been added the recollection of cases in which the Romans had crucified or otherwise put to death those who had lost the day, it would have been impossible for a general, with such a prospect in mind, to give his whole attention to the matter in hand. It was held, therefore, that to such men the ignominy of having lost would be a sufficient punishment, so they preferred not to alarm them by imposing other and greater punishments.

Here is an example of an error which was not committed through ignorance. Sergius and Virginius were encamped before Veii, each in charge of a section of the army. Sergius was on a route along which the Tuscans might come to attack him. Virginius was on the other side of the city. What happened was that, when Sergius was attacked by the Falisci and other tribes, he let himself be put to rout rather than ask Virginius for help; and, on his part, Virginius, anticipating Sergius' humiliation, preferred to witness his country's dishonour and the destruction of Sergius' army rather than come to his assistance. It was a case of obvious misconduct of which notice must be taken, and one that would give a bad impression of the Roman republic if neither of the two commanders had been punished. Actually, whereas any other republic would have inflicted capital punishment, Rome imposed on them a fine. This was not because their offences did not merit a greater punishment, but because the Romans preferred in this case, for the aforesaid reasons, to abide by their ancient customs.

Of errors due to ignorance there is no finer example than that of Varro, owing to whose rashness the Romans were routed by Hannibal at Cannae, whereby the freedom of that republic was endangered. None the less, because he was guilty of ignorance, not malice, not only did they not punish him, but they honoured him, and everyone of senatorial rank went to meet him on his return to Rome. Since on the battle they could scarce congratulate him, they congratulated him on his return and on his refusal to regard Rome's situation as desperate. When Papirius Cursor wanted to put Fabius to death for having engaged the Samnites contrary to his orders, among other arguments used by Fabius' father to combat the dictator's obstinacy, he urged that when defeats had been incurred by their commanders, the Roman people had never done what Papirius wanted to do on the occasion of a victory.

32. Neither a Republic nor a Prince should put off conferring Benefits on People until danger is at hand

ADMITTEDLY the Romans were fortunate in that they managed to be generous to the populace when danger arose. Thus, when Porsenna came to attack Rome to restore the Tarquins and the senate doubted whether the plebs would not prefer to welcome back the kings rather than go to war, for security's sake it remitted the duty on salt and other burdens, alleging that the poor did enough to help the public cause by bringing up their children; and admittedly by conferring this benefit it induced them to stand siege, hunger and war. Let no one, however, relying on this case, put off making sure of the populace until the time of danger arrives, because he may not, as the Romans did, succeed in this. For the people as a whole will not consider that they owe this benefit to you, but rather to your enemies, and, since they cannot but fear that, when the need has passed, you may deprive them of what you have been compelled to give, will in no way feel obliged to you.

The reason why the Romans turned this question to good account, was because the government was new and not yet stabilized. The populace had seen how laws had already been made to their advantage, for instance the right of appealing to the plebs, so that it was possible to persuade it that this benefit had been conferred not so much because the enemy were at their gates as because the senate was inclined to confer benefits on it. Besides this, it still retained a vivid recollection of the kings by whom it had been downtrodden and maltreated. But, since such causes are rarely operative, it will rarely happen that such remedies are of avail.

Hence every government, whether it be republican or of the princely type, should consider beforehand what adverse times may befall him and on what people it may have to rely in time of adversity, and should in its dealings with them act in that way in which it judges that it will be compelled to act should misfortune befall. A government which acts otherwise – whether it be a prince or a republic, but especially if it be a prince, – i.e. a government which thinks that it is only when danger has arisen that it should win men over by the conferring of benefits, is mistaken; for not only will it fail to win them over, but it will hasten its own ruin.

Book One

[THE USE AND ABUSE OF DICTATORSHIP]

---

33. *When either within a State or against a State an Inconvenience has made Headway, the Safer Course is to temporize, not to suppress it*

WHEN the Roman republic grew in reputation, power and dominion, its neighbours, who had not at first thought this new republic would do them much harm, began too late to realize their mistake, and, with a view to remedying what they had not remedied at the outset, they formed a league of full forty peoples against Rome. Whereupon from among the remedies which they were accustomed to use when danger was imminent, the Romans chose to appoint a dictator, i.e. to give power to some one man to make decisions without consulting others and to carry them out without anyone having the right to appeal. This remedy not only proved useful at the time, and enabled them to overcome the dangers still threatening, but was always of the greatest help in all those eventualities which from time to time betokened ill to the republic as its empire grew.

In regard to such events the first thing to notice is that, when an inconvenience which has arisen within a republic, or is affecting it adversely owing either to internal or external causes, has become so great that everybody begins to get alarmed, by far the safer course is to temporize in its regard, and not try to eradicate it straightway. For, as usual, those who try to suppress it, cause it to grow stronger and speed up the evils which they anticipate and dread.

Events of this kind are more often due in a republic to an internal cause than to an external, for in it very often either a citizen is allowed to acquire more power than is reasonable, or corruption is introduced in the administration of some law on which the nerve and life-blood of freedom depends; and this blunder is allowed to go on till it reaches such a pass that to attempt to remedy it is more harmful than to let it take its course. To discern such inconveniences in their initial stage is the more difficult the more men are by nature inclined to look with favour on new enterprises; a favour which is likely to be bestowed, above all else, on enterprises which seem to have in them a certain virility^a and which are taken up by young men. For, if in a republic there appears some youth of noble birth and outstanding virtue, the eyes of every citizen at once turn towards him, and without further consideration they agree to show him honour; so that, if in him there is a spark of ambition, the favours bestowed on him by nature conjoin with these events to place him in such a position that, when the citizens come to see their mistake, there is but small chance of their putting it right; and any attempt to apply such remedies as they have, does but tend to establish more quickly his power.

Of this it would be possible to adduce plenty of instances, but I propose to give only one from in our city. Cosimo de' Medici, with whom the greatness of the house of Medici in this our city began, acquired great repute thanks to favours gained by his own prudence and through the ignorance of the

^a *virtù.*

citizens. He thus began to arouse alarm for the security of its government; with the result that his fellow-citizens thought it dangerous to touch him, and still more dangerous to let him alone. But there lived in those days one, Niccolò da Uzzano, who was looked on as an expert in politics. He had made the first of the above mistakes in that he had not recognized the dangers to which Cosimo's reputation might lead, but while he lived he never allowed the second one to be made; that is, that anyone should attempt to get rid of him; since he was convinced that such an attempt would mean the utter ruin of their government, as in fact it was seen to do after his death. For the citizens who survived him failed to follow his advice, grew bold in their opposition to Cosimo, and drove him out of Florence. It thus came about that his faction, resenting this injustice, recalled him shortly afterwards, and made him the 'prince' of that republic, a rank to which he would never have been able to rise except for this open opposition.

The same thing happened at Rome in the case of Caesar, whose virtue won for him such favour with Pompey and others that before long this favour gave place to fear; to which Cicero bears witness when he says that Pompey had too late begun to fear Caesar. This fear caused people to look for remedies, but the remedies they applied did but accelerate the ruin of their republic.

I claim, therefore, that since it is difficult to recognize such evils in the initial stage owing to the false impression new enterprizes make on you at the outset, when they are recognized the wiser course is to temporize rather than to oppose them by force. Because, if one temporizes, either the trouble disappears of its own accord, or at least disaster is postponed for a considerable time. In all such matters rulers who plan to remedy the evils or to attack them direct by means of force, should keep their eyes open lest, instead of causing them to decrease, they cause them to increase, and in the belief that they are

repelling them make them grow, – as if one could suffocate a
plant by sprinkling it with water. Rather should the strength
of the disease be considered well, and, if you see that you can
cure it, you should set about it without further ado. But otherwise should let it be, and in no wise interfere, lest that happen
which, as we have said above, happened to Rome's neighbours, for whom it would have been safer when Rome's
power had grown so strong, to have sought by peaceful
methods to placate it and hold it back, rather than by preparing
for war to make Rome think out new institutions and new
plans for her defence. For by this league of theirs all they did
was to make the Romans more united, more on their guard,
and more keen on finding new devices whereby the more
quickly to increase their power. Among which was the
appointment of a dictator, whereby the Romans were enabled
not only to overcome their present dangers, but to obviate a
multitude of evils which would have befallen that republic
had not this remedy been available.

34. *Dictatorial Authority did Good, not Harm, to the
Republic of Rome: it is the Authority which
Citizens arrogate to Themselves, not that
granted by Free Suffrage, that is harmful
to Civic Life*

THOSE Romans who were responsible for the institution of a
dictatorship in Rome are condemned by some Roman
writers who find in the dictatorship the cause which eventually
led to tyranny in Rome. They point out that the person who
became its first tyrant, had authority there in virtue of his title
as dictator, and assert that, if it had not been for this, Caesar
would not have succeeded under any other public title in
making his tyranny look honest and above board.

The case, however, was not well examined by the person who held this view, and the view has been accepted without good ground. For it was neither the name nor the rank of the dictator that made Rome servile, but the loss of authority of which the citizens were deprived by the length of his rule. If in Rome there had been no such rank, the dictator would have found some other; for it is easy for force to acquire a title, but not for a title to acquire force.

It is clear that the dictatorship, so long as it was bestowed in accordance with public institutions, and not assumed by the dictator on his own authority, was always of benefit to the state. For it is magistrates that are made and authority that is given in irregular ways that is prejudicial to a republic, not that which is given in the ordinary way, as is clear from the fact that during a very long period in Rome's history, no dictator ever did anything but good to that republic.[25]

The reasons for this are obvious. First, if a citizen is to do harm and is to obtain extraordinary authority, he must have many attributes which in a republic that is not corrupt it will be impossible for him to acquire; for he will need to be very rich and to have numerous adherents and partisans, which he cannot have so long as the laws are observed; and, even if he had them, men of this kind are so dreaded that people would not freely vote for him.

Furthermore, a dictator was appointed for a limited time, and for the purpose of dealing solely with such matters as had led to the appointment. He had authority to make what decisions he thought fit in order to meet a definite and urgent danger, and to do this without consultation; and anyone he punished had no right of appeal. But he could do nothing to diminish the constitutional position of the government, as would have been the case if he could have taken away the authority vested in the senate or in the people, or have abolished the ancient institutions of the city and made new ones. Wherefore, in view of the short duration of the dictatorship, of the limited authority which the dictator possessed, and of the fact that the Roman people were not corrupt, it was impossible for the dictator to overstep his terms of reference and to do the state harm. On the contrary, experience has shown that the dictatorship was always useful.

Actually, then, of Rome's various institutions this is one that deserves to be considered and ranked among those to which the greatness of Rome's vast empire was due. For without such an institution cities will with difficulty find a way out of abnormal situations. For the institutions normally used by republics are slow in functioning. No assembly nor magistrate can do everything alone. In many cases they have to consult one another, and to reconcile their diverse views takes time. Where there is question of remedying a situation which will not brook delay, such a procedure is most dangerous.

Republics, therefore, ought to have among their institutions some device akin to this. The republic of Venice, which ranks high among modern republics, has reserved to a few of its citizens authority to deal with urgent questions with regard to which, if they all agree, they can make decisions without reference to any other body. Whereas in a republic in which no such provision is made, it is necessary either to stand by the constitution and be ruined, or to violate it and not be ruined. But that events should happen in a republic which have to be dealt with by extraordinary measures, is not desirable; for though the extraordinary measures may do good at the time, the precedent thus established is bad, since it sanctions the usage of dispensing with constitutional methods for a good purpose, and thereby makes it possible, on some plausible pretext, to dispense with them for a bad purpose. No republic is ever perfect unless by its laws it has provided for all contingencies, and for every eventuality has provided a remedy and determined the method of applying it.

In conclusion, then, I claim that republics which, when in imminent danger, have recourse neither to a dictatorship, nor to some form of authority analogous to it, will always be ruined when grave misfortune befalls them.

In the matter of this new institution, the great wisdom which the Romans displayed in the method of electing to it, is to be noted. For, since the appointment of a dictator was in a way a reflection on the consuls, who, though at the head of the state, had to obey like everyone else, and since it was assumed that this might arouse resentment among the citizens, the Romans decided that the power to appoint a dictator should lie with the consuls; for they thought that, when circumstances became such that Rome had need of this royal prerogative, they would have to make the appointment of their own accord, and, since they themselves had made the appointment, it would pain them less. Because wounds and other ills which are inflicted of one's own accord and choice, grieve you much less than those that are inflicted on you by others. Besides, during the last period, instead of appointing a dictator, the Romans used to invest the consul with dictatorial authority, with the words: 'Let the consul see to it that the republic takes no harm.'

I close with a remark relevant to the matter we are discussing. It was Rome's neighbours who in their desire to crush her, caused her to set up institutions which not only enabled her to defend herself but also to attack them with greater force, counsel and authority.

35. How it came about that the Appointment of the Decemviri in Rome was harmful to that Republic in spite of their having been appointed by Free and Public Suffrage

To what was said in the preceding discourse as to the authority which is seized with violence, not that which is obtained by suffrage, being harmful to republics, the election of the ten citizens which the Roman people instituted that they might draw up laws for Rome, appears to be incompatible; for in course of time they became tyrants, and, regardless of everybody and everything, deprived Rome of her liberty. The way in which the authority was conferred and the period for which it was granted must here be taken into account. When unrestricted authority is given for a long time, where by a long time I mean a year or more, it may always be dangerous, and will produce good or bad effects according as those to whom it is given are evil or good. Now, if we look at the authority which the Ten had and at that which the dictators had, it will be seen that the authority of the Ten was incomparably greater. For, when a dictator was appointed, the tribunes, the consuls, the senate, with their respective powers, remained; nor could the dictator take them away. He had, indeed, the power to deprive any one person of the consulate or of his senatorial rank, but he could not annul a decree of the senate, nor could he make new laws. The result was that, as the authority of the senate, the consuls and the tribunes still stood, they came to be, as it were, his guardians, to see that he kept to the straight path. Quite the contrary happened when the Ten were appointed; for the appointment of consuls and tribunes was suspended, and the Ten were given power to make laws and in general to act as if they were the Roman people. So that, finding themselves on their own, without consuls, without tribunes, and without there being any appeal to the people, and that, in consequence, there was no one to look after them, they were able in their second year, urged on by the ambition of Appius, to become arrogant.

It should be noted, then, that in saying that authority, granted by free suffrage, never harms any republic, it is presumed that a people is never persuaded to give it except under certain conditions and for a specified time. But when, whether by mistake or owing to some other contributory cause, a republic is persuaded to give it imprudently, in the way in which the Roman people gave it to the Ten, the same thing will happen as happened in their case. This is easily proved if we consider what causes kept dictators good and what made the Ten bad; and if we consider further how those states which are looked upon as well-ordered, acted when they gave a long-termed authority, as the Spartans did to their kings and as the Venetians do to their doges. For it would appear that in both these cases supervisors were appointed to see to it that they should not be able to abuse their authority. Nor to the autocrat is it of any consequence whether the material be corrupt, for absolute power will very soon corrupt it by making friends and partisans. Nor yet does it hurt him to be poor or without lineage, for riches and every other advantage will at once accrue to him, as will be shown when we come to discuss in detail the aforesaid Decemviri.

36. *Citizens who have held Higher Posts should not disdain to accept Lower*

IN the consulship of Marcus Fabius and G. Manlius the Romans gained a most glorious victory over the Veientes and the Etruscans, in which Quintus Fabius, the consul's brother, was killed. Quintus had been consul in the previous year.

It may be seen from this how well the institutions of this city were adapted to make it great, and how mistaken are other republics which dispense with this procedure. For, though the Romans had a great esteem for glory, yet they did not deem it an unworthy thing to obey one who had previously been under their command, nor to serve in an army of which they had formerly been commanders in chief.

In the views, institutions, and practice of citizens in our day, this custom is reversed. Venice even makes the mistake of thinking that a citizen who has held high office, should be ashamed to accept a lower; and the state is content that he should decline to accept it. This course, though it may be honourable from the standpoint of a private citizen, is of no use whatsoever from the public standpoint. For a republic rightly places more hope and confidence in a citizen who from a high command descends to a lower, than in one who from a lower command rises to a higher; since on the latter they cannot reasonably rely unless in his entourage they see men so respected and of such virtue that by their advice and authority his inexperience[a] may be corrected.

Had there been in Rome the custom which obtains in Venice and in other modern republics and kingdoms, that a person who had once been consul would never want to serve in the army except as consul, numberless events might have happened which would have endangered its freedom, both through the mistakes which the new men would have made, and through the ambition to which they could have the better given rein had they not had around them men in whose presence they were afraid to do wrong. For in that case they would have been more free, and might have used their power to the detriment of the public.

[a] *novità.*

Book One

---

37. On the Troubles to which the Agrarian Laws gave rise in Rome; and how great is the Trouble given in a Republic by passing a Law that is too Retrospective and Contravenes an Ancient Custom of the City

ANCIENT writers were of opinion that men are wont to get annoyed with adversity and fed up with prosperity, both of which passions give rise to the same effects. For, whenever there is no need for men to fight, they fight for ambition's sake; and so powerful is the sway that ambition exercises over the human heart that it never relinquishes them, no matter how high they have risen. The reason is that nature has so constituted men that, though all things are objects of desire, not all things are attainable; so that desire always exceeds the power of attainment, with the result that men are ill content with what they possess and their present state brings them little satisfaction. Hence arise the vicissitudes of their fortune. For, since some desire to have more and others are afraid to lose what they have already acquired, enmities and wars are begotten, and this brings about the ruin of one province and the exaltation of its rival.

I have made these preliminary remarks because the Roman plebs were not content with having made their position secure in regard to the nobles by the creation of tribunes, which necessity constrained them to demand; but, having acquired them, at once began to quarrel with the nobles out of ambition, and to demand also a share in the distribution of honours and of property[a] than which man esteems nothing more highly. This grew into a disease, which led to the dispute about the Agrarian Law and in the end caused the destruction of the republic.

Now, in as much as well-ordered republics have to keep the public rich but their citizens poor,[26] it looks as if in the city of Rome this law was defective, either because it had not been so made at the outset as to prevent the need of going back on it, or because the making of it had been so long deferred that to deal now with an old difficulty gave trouble, or because, though well drawn up at the outset, in practice it had become corrupted. Anyhow, it came about that, whenever this law was mentioned in Rome, everything was turned topsy-turvy in that city.

The provisions made by this law fell under two heads. It provided first that no citizen should be allowed to possess above so many acres of land; and, secondly, that all the lands that were taken from an enemy should be divided among the Roman people. This gave offence to the nobility in two ways; for those who possessed more land than the law allowed – and they were the greater part of the nobility – were to be deprived of the overplus; and the sharing of enemy goods among the plebs put a stop to their chance of enriching themselves. Wherefore, since these provisions gave offence to powerful men, and it seemed to them that, in opposing the law, they were acting in the public interest, whenever the question cropped up the whole city was turned topsy-turvy,

[a] *la sustanze.*

as has been said. Patiently and industriously the nobles sought to put the matter off, either by setting out with an army for foreign parts, or by setting up another tribune against the tribune who proposed the law, or sometimes by a partial concession, or again by sending a colony out to the place where the land was to be distributed. This happened, for instance, in regard to the lands round about Antium, which had given rise to a controversy about the law; for a colony, drawn from Rome, was sent there, to which the lands in that neighbourhood were assigned. In regard to this Titus Livy makes a remark worth mentioning. He says that in Rome it was difficult to get men to put their names down to go with the colony, and observes that the plebs were much more keen on voicing in Rome their desire for things than they were in taking possession of them at Antium.

Dissatisfaction with this law for a time went on causing trouble in Rome, until the Romans began to lead their armies to the more remote parts of Italy, and beyond it, when for some time it seems to have ceased. This was because the lands which the enemies of Rome possessed, being far away from where any of its plebs lived and in places where it was not easy to cultivate them, the plebs came to be less keen on having them; and again because the Romans were less severe in punishing their enemies by such deprivations, and because, when they did despoil a place of the lands in its neighbourhood, they were distributed among colonists. This being so, the Agrarian law lay dormant until the time of the Gracchi, and, when they raised it again, it spelt the complete destruction of Rome's liberty. For by that time the power of its adversaries was twice as great, and, as a result, the mutual hatred existent between the plebs and the senate was so intense that it led to armed conflict and bloodshed, in which neither moderation nor respect for civic customs was shown. So that, the public magistrates being unable to find a remedy and none of the

RETROSPECTIVE LEGISLATION   I.37

factions having any longer any confidence in them, recourse
was had to private remedies, and each party began to look
out for some chief to head and defend it.

In this scandal and disorder the plebs took the first step by
staking its reputation on Marius, to such effect that it made
him four times consul. His consulship was in fact continuous,
except for short intervals, and this enabled him on his own
authority to appoint himself consul on three other occasions.
As the nobility had no other remedy whereby to counteract
this pest, they took to backing Sulla, and, when he was made
the head of their party, civil war broke out, and in it, after
much bloodshed and many changes of fortune, the nobility
got the upper hand.

These animosities were revived in the time of Caesar and
Pompey. For, when Caesar became the head of the Marian
party and Pompey the head of Sulla's, they came to blows,
and Caesar got the best of it, and so became Rome's first
tyrant. After which that city never again recovered its
liberties.

Such, then, was the beginning, and such the end of the
Agrarian law. Elsewhere we have shown that it was enmity
between the senate and populace of Rome that kept Rome free,
because it was owing to this that laws were made in favour of
liberty. And, though with this conclusion the result of the
Agrarian Law may seem to be incompatible, I must confess
that I am not on this account inclined to change my opinion,
for, so great is the ambition of the great that unless in a city
they are kept down by various ways and means, that city will
soon be brought to ruin. Hence, if it was fully three hundred
years before the Agrarian Law led to the servitude of Rome, it
would, perchance, have led to servitude much sooner, had not
the plebs by means of this law and by other demands prompted
by their appetites, always kept the ambition of the nobles in
check.

It is also clear from this that men set much greater store on property than on honours. For the Roman nobility always gave way to the plebs in the matter of honours without causing serious troubles; but, when it came to property, so great was the obstinacy with which they defended it, that in order to satisfy their appetites the plebs had recourse to those irregular means which have been mentioned above. To this disorderly conduct they were moved by the Gracchi, whose intention is more praiseworthy than was their prudence. For to seek to remove a disorder which has grown inveterate in a commonwealth by making a law that is too retrospective is not a wise course to adopt, and, as has been explained at length above, serves but to accelerate the evil to which the disorder is urging you on; whereas, by temporizing, either the evil will be postponed, or by this means it will in course of time spend itself before it reaches a head.

38. Weak Republics suffer from Irresolution and cannot reach Decisions; and, when they do arrive at one, it is due rather to Necessity than to Choice

WHEN there was a very great pestilence in Rome and for this reason it seemed to the Volsci and the Aequi that the time had come for them to be able to overcome Rome, these two peoples got together a very big army, attacked the Latins and the Hernici, and laid waste their territory, so that they were forced to turn to Rome and to beg the Romans to defend them. The Romans, burdened by the epidemic, replied that the Latins and the Hernici had better look to their own defence, using their own forces, since they were unable to defend them. This shows the generosity and the prudence of the Roman senate; and how, whatever happened, it always wanted to take the lead in the decisions which those dependent on it had to make and how it was never ashamed to adopt a course which was contrary to its usual procedure and to other decisions it had made, when necessity required it.

I say this because on other occasions the same senate had forbidden these peoples to arm in their own defence, so that by a senate less prudent than was this, it would have been regarded as a loss of dignity to allow them thus to defend themselves. The Roman senate, however, always faced facts as they should be faced, and always took the lesser evil to be the better alternative. For bad as it felt it to be not to be able to defend its own subjects, and bad as it felt it to be that subjects should have recourse to arms without them, none the less for the reasons given and many others that are obvious, recognizing that with the enemy at their doors they must needs fly to arms in any case, it did the honourable thing, preferring that what they had to do should be done with Rome's permission, so that having disobeyed because needs must, they should not get into the habit of disobeying by choice.

But though it would seem that this alternative ought to be adopted by any republic, the fact remains that weak and ill-advised republics neither know how to adopt it nor how to derive honour from such occasions of necessity. Duke Valentine had taken Faenza and made Bologna submit to his terms. Then, since he wanted to return to Rome *via* Tuscany, he sent one of his men to Florence to ask leave for himself and his army to pass through. A consultation was held in Florence as to what should be done in the matter, and no one advised that leave should be granted. Now, this was not in accord with Roman procedure; for the Duke had armed forces of very great strength, whereas the Florentines were so badly armed that they could not prevent his passage. Hence it would have accorded far better with their honour to have seemed to allow his passage of their own accord, rather than be forced to it; for, whereas it brought on them nothing but shame, there would have been less of it had they managed things differently.

But the worst thing about weak republics is that they are irresolute, so that all the choices they make, they are forced to make: and, if they should happen to do the right thing, it is force, not their own good sense, that makes them do it. I will give two examples which occurred in our day to the government of our city.[a]

In 1500 King Louis XII of France, having retaken Milan, was ready to restore Pisa for the fifty thousand ducats which had been promised to him by the Florentines on its recovery. So he sent his armies to Pisa under the command of Monsieur de Beaumont, who, though a Frenchman, was none the less a man in whom the Florentines had considerable trust. The army and its commander took up a position between Cascina and Pisa, that they might proceed to attack its walls. While waiting a day or so to prepare for the attack, Pisan envoys came to Beaumont and offered to surrender the city to the French troops on these terms: he was to promise, on the king's word, not to hand the city over to the Florentines for four months. This offer was turned down altogether by the Florentines, so that the net result was a journey to lay siege to Pisa and their departure in shame. The only reason for declining this offer was that the Florentines did not trust the king's word. Their policy had been so weak that they had been forced to put themselves in the king's hands, yet they did not trust him. Nor did they see that it was better for the king to be in Pisa and to hand that city over, or, by failing to do so, to disclose his intentions, than for him to promise it them when he hadn't yet got it, and for them to be forced to pay for the promises. Hence they would have done much better to have agreed to Beaumont's taking it under whatever conditions.

[a] *nello stato della nostra città.*

A similar incident occurred afterwards in 1502, when Arezzo was in revolt, and the Kings of France sent Monsieur Imbault with a French army to the help of the Florentines. Having reached the neighbourhood of Arezzo, he began before long to discuss terms with the people of Arezzo, who were ready to surrender the town under certain conditions, just as the Pisans had been. In Florence the offer was turned down. When Monsieur Imbault saw this, it seemed to him that the Florentines had not shown much sense, so he began to discuss terms on his own account, without informing the commissioners. In this he was so successful that a treaty was made to his liking, under which he entered Arezzo with his army, and gave the Florentines to understand that they were mad and had no understanding of the ways of the world. If they wanted Arezzo, they should apply to the king, who was in a better position to give it them now that his army was in the city, than when it was outside. In Florence there was no end to the cutting remarks and vituperation showered on Imbault; nor did it stop until at length they realized that, if Beaumont had been like Imbault, they might have had Pisa as well as Arezzo.

In regard, then, to the question under discussion, irresolute republics never choose the right alternative unless they are driven to it, for their weakness does not allow them to arrive at a decision where there is any doubt; and, unless this doubt is removed by some compelling act of violence, they remain ever in suspense.

39. *To Different Peoples the same sort of Thing is often found to happen*

IF the present be compared with the remote past, it is easily seen that in all cities and in all peoples there are the same desires and the same passions as there always were. So that, if one examines with diligence the past, it is easy to foresee the future of any commonwealth, and to apply those remedies which were used of old; or, if one does not find that remedies were used, to devise new ones owing to the similarity between events. But, since such studies are neglected and what is read is not understood, or, if it be understood, is not applied in practice by those who rule, the consequence is that similar troubles occur at all times.

Since the city of Florence after '94 lost part of its dominions, e.g. Pisa and other towns, it had to make war on those who had occupied them. And, because those who had occupied them were powerful, the result of the war was considerable expense and no fruit; from the expense there resulted heavy taxation; and from the heavy taxation endless complaints by the populace. Since this war was administered by a magistracy consisting of ten citizens, called 'the Ten of War', the public in general began to be disgusted with it in that it was responsible both for the war and for the expense. They were convinced that, if this magistracy was abolished, there would be an end to the war; so, when the time came to re-elect it, instead of making new appointments they let it lapse, and entrusted their affairs to the Signoria. This decision was so disastrous that not only did it fail to stop the war, as the public in general had expected, but it removed the very men who had been administering it wisely, and led to such confusion that, in addition to Pisa, Arezzo was lost, and many other places. Consequently the people repented their mistake, and since the cause of the trouble was the malady, not the doctor, they reappointed the magistracy of the Ten.

The same passion was aroused in Rome by the title of consul. For, when the people saw one war following on another, and that they never got any rest, they ought to have ascribed it to the ambition of neighbours who were seeking to crush them, whereas they thought it was due to the ambition of nobles who, unable to chastise the plebs within the state where they were protected by the power of the tribunes, were anxious for them to be led forth under consuls that they might oppress them where there was no one to help. For this reason they thought it necessary either to abolish the consuls, or so to regulate their power that they should have no authority over the populace either abroad or at home. The first to propose such a law was Terentillus, a tribune. He proposed that five men should be appointed to investigate the consular power and to set limits to it. This incensed the nobles not a little, for it looked to them as if the majesty of government would vanish altogether, and that to the nobility there would no longer remain any status in the republic. The obstinacy of the tribunes was none the less such that the title of consul was abolished, and, after certain other ordinances had been made, they were at length content to appoint tribunes with consular power instead of consuls, so that what they had really hated was the title rather than the authority of the consuls. This custom was observed for a long time, but at length, realizing their mistake, they again appointed consuls, just as the Florentines returned to the 'Ten'.

Book One

[SUNDRY REFLECTIONS BASED ON THE DECEMVIRATE]

---

40. *The Appointment of the Decemvirate in Rome and what is Noteworthy about it; in which will be considered, among other Things, how such an Incident may lead either to a Republic's Salvation or to its Subjection*

SINCE I am proposing to discuss in detail the events which led to the appointment of the Decemvirate in Rome, it will not be amiss, I think, first to state all that followed on such an appointment, and then to discuss such points as are noteworthy in the behaviour of those concerned; and there are many worthy of a careful consideration alike by those whose aim is to maintain the freedom of a republic and by those who plan to bring it into subjection. For such a discussion will bring to light many mistakes made by the senate and people which were prejudicial to liberty, and many mistakes made by Appius, the head of the Decemvirate, which were prejudicial to the tyranny which he was proposing to set up in Rome.

After many disputes and much conflict between the senate and the populace in Rome in regard to the drawing up of new laws whereby the freedom of that state might be the better stabilized, it was agreed to send Spurius Postumius with two other citizens to Athens for copies of the laws which Solon had given to that city, so that upon them they might base the Roman laws. After their return from this journey, the next step was to appoint men for the purpose of examining and codifying these laws. Ten citizens were appointed for a year; among them Appius Claudius, a sagacious man, but restless. That they might draw up these laws without reference to anyone else all other magistrates in Rome were suspended, in particular the tribunes and the consuls. The right of appeal to the people was also suspended, with the result that his magistracy came to all intents and purposes to be a prince-dom in Rome. Whereupon, so favoured was Appius by the plebs that the whole authority of his colleagues came to be vested in him; for so popular had he made himself by the attitude he adopted that it looked as if in some extraordinary way he had suddenly acquired a new nature and a new charac-ter, for up to this moment he had been a cruel persecutor of the plebs.

The Ten governed at first with due decorum, and had no more than twelve lictors who marched in front of the Decemvir who was acting as president. And, although they had absolute authority, when they had to punish a citizen for homicide they cited him to appear before the people, and left it to them to pronounce judgement. Their laws they wrote on ten tables, and, before they were confirmed, they set them before the public so that everyone might read and discuss them to see if there were any defects, with a view to their being amended before the laws were ratified.

Apropos of this Appius caused a rumour to spread through Rome to the effect that, if to these ten tables two more were added, it would make the codex complete. This suggestion provided the populace with an opportunity to re-appoint the Ten for another year; to which they readily agreed, because consuls would not in that case be re-appointed, and because they thought they could get along without tribunes now that they themselves were judging causes, as has been said above. When, then, the decision had been taken to re-appoint the Ten, all the nobility were keen on getting these honours, with Appius among the foremost, and such was the good-will he displayed towards the plebs during his election-campaign that his colleagues began to grow suspicious of him. 'They thought that in view of his great arrogance this hail-fellow-well-met attitude could scarce be genuine.' Hesitating to oppose him openly, they decided to do it by artifice so, though he was junior to all in point of time, they authorized him to propose the future Ten to the people, thinking that, like others, he would observe the conventions and not propose himself, since in Rome this was not done and was looked on as not quite the thing. 'Appius, however, seized what was meant to be an obstacle as an opportunity', and put his own name at the head of the list, to the astonish-ment and consternation of all the nobility; and after it placed nine other names suited to his purpose.

This fresh appointment, made for another year, began to show the people and the nobility the error of their ways. For at once 'Appius dropped the disguise he had been wearing', and began to display his innate arrogance. Nor was it long before his colleagues took up the same line. To overawe the people and the senate they appointed a hundred and twenty lictors instead of the usual twelve.

Fear at this juncture was shared by all alike. Then the Ten began to play up to the senate and to ill-treat the plebs; and, should anyone who had been ill-treated by the one appeal to the other, he was treated worse on appeal than in the first instance. So that the plebs, realizing their mistake, began in their sore affliction to look to the nobles in the hope 'of regaining a breath of liberty from the source from which they had so dreaded servitude that they had brought the state to this pass'. But to the nobility their affliction was a pleasing sight, for it was likely 'that, disgusted with the present situation, they would want the consuls back'.

When the second year came to an end, the two tables of laws were ready but had not been published. This provided the Ten with an excuse for continuing their magistracy, and they began to act with violence in order to maintain their status. They made youthful nobles their satellites, and bestowed on them the goods of those they had condemned. 'With which gifts the youth were corrupted, and preferred licence for themselves to liberty for all.'

It happened at this juncture that the Sabines and the Volsci started to make war on the Romans, and the fear which resulted was such that the Ten began to realize the weakness of their status; for without the senate they could not make preparations for war, and, if they summoned the senate, it looked as if they would lose their position. Actually necessity drove them to adopt this latter course. When the senators had assembled many of them spoke against the arrogance of the Ten, particularly Valerius and Horatius; and there would have been an end altogether to their authority if the senate out of envy for the plebs had not wanted to show its power, for they thought that, if the Ten resigned the magistracy of its own accord, they might be able to prevent the reappointment of tribunes of the plebs. They decided, therefore, on war. Two armies set out, led in part by members of the Ten. Appius remained behind to govern the city. It thus came about that he fell in love with Virginia, whom he was intending to seize by force, but her father, Virginius, killed her in order to save her from this. Disturbances followed alike in Rome and in the armies; which joined with what was left of the Roman plebs, and retired to Mons Sacer, where they remained until the Ten gave up their magistracy and tribunes and consuls were appointed and Rome recovered the form of her ancient liberty.

In the incidents here related it should, therefore, be noticed first of all that the inconvenience involved in the establishment of this tyranny was due to the same causes as are most tyrannies that are set up in cities, namely to the excessive demand of the people for freedom and to the excessive demand to dominate on the part of the nobles. For, when they fail to agree in making a law conducive to liberty, and, instead, one or other of the parties uses its weight to support a particular person, tyranny at once arises. The populace and the nobility in Rome agreed to appoint the Ten, and to invest them with such great authority, owing to the desire which each party had, one to get rid of consular rank and the other to get rid of the tribunate. When they had been appointed and it seemed to the plebs that Appius had become a demagogue and was out to down the nobility, the populace turned to him and gave him its support. But when a people is induced to make the mistake of holding someone in high esteem because he is down on those whom they hold in detestation, and *that* someone has his wits about him, it will always happen that a tyranny will arise in that city. For he will wait until, with the support of the populace, he has got rid of the nobility, and will not begin to oppress the people until he has got rid of it, by which time the populace will have come to realize that it is a slave and will have no way of escape.

This method has always been adopted by those who have established tyrannies in republics; and, if Appius had kept to it, his tyranny would have had a longer lease of life and would not have collapsed so soon. But he did just the opposite, and could not have behaved more unwisely. For in order to maintain his tyranny he made enemies of those who had given it to him and were able to maintain him in it, and enemies of those who had not been ready to give it to him and who would not have been able to maintain him in it. In this way he lost those who had been his friends, and tried to make friends with those who could not be his friends. For though nobles desire to tyrannize, that part of the nobility which finds itself left out in a tyrannical regime, is always the tyrant's enemy. Nor can he win them all over, for so great is the ambition and the avarice with which they are imbued, that no tyrant can have enough riches and enough honours to satisfy all. Hence Appius in deserting the populace and courting the nobles made a very obvious mistake, alike for the reasons given above and because an attempt to hold anything by sheer force postulates that he who uses force be more powerful than those upon whom force is used.

It follows that those who have the public as a whole for their friends and the great ones for their enemies are the more secure, in that their violence is backed by a greater force than it is in the case of those who have the populace for an enemy and the nobility for a friend.[27] For, if the people be friendly, internal forces suffice for their preservation, as they sufficed in the case of Nabis, tyrant of Sparta, when the whole of Greece and the Roman people attacked him; for Nabis, having made sure of the few nobles, and having the people as his friend, with their help defended himself, which he would not have been able to do had they been enemies. But in the alternative case in which one has but few friends at home, internal forces do not suffice, and one has to seek outside help. This has to be of three kinds: first, foreign satellites to protect your person; secondly, the arming of the countryside to do what should be done by the plebs; and, thirdly, a defensive alliance with powerful neighbours. He who adopts these precautions and does it well, even if his people are hostile, should in some fashion be able to look after himself. But Appius could not manage to make sure of the countryside, for the countryside was the same thing as Rome; and he didn't know what to do, so that he was done for from the very start.

The senate and the people also made a very great mistake in appointing the Decemviri, for, in spite of what has been said earlier in the discourse which dealt with dictators, to the effect that self-appointed magistrates, not those appointed by the people, are prejudicial to liberty, the people should, none the less, in appointing magistrates, create them so that they hesitate to turn to evil ways. And, whereas they should have appointed guardians to see that they behaved properly, the Romans took the guardians away, for they made the Decemvirate the sole magistracy in Rome, and annulled all others, owing, as we have said above, to the excessive desire of the senate to get rid of tribunes and of the plebs to get rid of consuls, a desire so strong that it blinded them, and caused them to cooperate in the disorderly procedure. For men, as king Ferdinand used to say, resemble certain little birds of prey in whom so strong is the desire to catch the prey which nature incites them to pursue, that they do not notice another and a greater bird of prey which hovers over them ready to pounce and kill. This discourse should make plain, as I promised at the start, the mistake the Roman people made in their endeavour to save their freedom, and the mistakes that Appius made in his endeavour to set up a tyranny.

41. A Sudden Transition from Humility to Pride or from Kindness to Cruelty without Appropriate Steps in between is both Imprudent and Futile

AMONG other stupid things which Appius did in order to maintain his tyranny, his too sudden change from one character to another is of no small moment. He did well in being so astute as to deceive the plebs by pretending that he was a man of the people. He also effectively employed the means he used to get the Decemviri re-elected. He did well, too, in being so bold as again to stand for office, contrary to the expectation of the nobility. He did well again to appoint colleagues that suited his purpose.

But, though in this he did well, he did not do at all well, as I have pointed out above, in suddenly changing his character from that of a friend of the plebs to that of an open enemy, from being humane to being arrogant, from being easy going to being difficult; and in doing this so quickly that no one had any excuse for failing to recognize the crookedness of his mind. For he who has at one time seemed to be good, and proposes for his own purposes to become bad, should make the change by appropriate stages, so adapting his conduct to circumstances that, before the change in character has robbed you of your old supporters, it may have brought you so many new ones that your power will not be lessened. Otherwise you will find yourself at large without friends, and so will be undone.

42. *How easily Men may be Corrupted*

IT should be noted, too, in the affair of the Decemviri how easily men are corrupted and in nature become transformed, however good they may be and however well taught. Consider, for instance, how the young men whom Appius chose as a bodyguard, soon became the friends of tyranny for the sake of the small advantages which accrued; and how Quintus Fabius, one of the second Ten, though an excellent fellow, was after a while blinded by a little ambition and, under the evil influence of Appius, changed his good habits for bad and became like him.

Due consideration of this will cause all legislators, whether in a republic or a kingdom, to be all the more ready to restrain human appetites and to deprive them of all hope of doing wrong with impunity.

43. *Those who fight for Glory's Sake make Good and Faithful Soldiers*

ANOTHER point to be considered in connection with the above discourse is what a difference there is between a contented army which fights for the glory of the thing and one that is ill disposed and fights to help on someone's ambition. For, whereas the Roman armies were accustomed to being victorious under the consuls, under the Decemviri they always lost.

This shows, among other things, the reason why mercenary troops are useless, for they have no cause to stand firm when attacked, apart from the small pay which you give them. And this reason is not and cannot be sufficient to make them loyal, or to make them so much your friends that they should want to die for you. For in armies in which there is no affection for him for whom they are fighting such as would make them his partisans, it will be impossible for them ever to have virtue enough to withstand even a moderately valorous foe. Since neither the requisite love nor the requisite enthusiasm can be aroused except in your own subjects, it is necessary if one desires to retain a form of state, i.e. desires to uphold either a republic or a kingdom, to arm oneself with one's own subjects, as it is manifest that all have done who by means of armies have reaped great profit.

Under the Ten the Roman armies had the same valour as before, but, because they had not the same disposition towards their rulers, they did not produce the same effect as usual. Whereas as soon as the administration of the Ten was abolished and they began to fight as free men, they recovered the same old spirit, and, in consequence, their attacks produced the same happy results as they had always done.

44. A Crowd[a] is useless without a Head;
nor should it first use Threats and then appeal for the
Requisite Authority

THE plebs of Rome, owing to what had happened to Virginia, withdrew under arms to Mons Sacer.[28] The senate sent messengers to inquire by what authority they had deserted their officers and retired to the Mountains; and so great was the respect which the plebs had for the authority of the senate that, since they had none of their leaders with them, no one ventured to reply. Not, says Titus Livy, that they lacked material for a reply, but that they lacked the men to make it. This shows at once how useless a crowd is without a head.

Virginius recognized this confusion and by his instructions twenty military tribunes were elected that the plebs might have leaders who could discuss matters with the senate and come to some agreement. When they asked that Valerius and Horatius should be sent to them that they might explain what they wanted, they declined to go until the Ten had been deprived of their magistracy. When they arrived at the Mountain where the plebs were assembled, they were told that what the plebs wanted was the appointment of plebeian tribunes, the right of appeal from any magistrate to the people, and the handing over to them of all the Ten, whom they proposed to burn alive.

Valerius and Horatius approved their first demands, but deprecated the last as barbarous, remarking: 'you condemn cruelty, yet lapse into cruelty'. They recommended them to drop the question of the Ten, and to look instead to the reestablishment of their own authority and power, for afterwards they would not lack the means of obtaining satisfaction.

This teaches us plainly how stupid and foolish it is, when

---

[a] una moltitudine.

asking for something, to announce 'I propose to do such and such a wrong thing with it.' For one should not declare one's intentions, but should seek to get what one desires anyhow. There is, for instance, no need in asking someone for a weapon to say 'I propose to kill you with it', since you can satisfy your appetite once you have the weapon in your hands.

45. It is a Bad Precedent to break a New Law, especially if the Legislator himself does it; and daily to inflict Fresh Injuries on a City is most Harmful to him that governs it

WHEN agreement had been reached and Rome had returned to its ancient form of government Virginius cited Appius to appear before the people to defend his case. He appeared in the company of many nobles. Virginius ordered him to be put in prison. Appius began to protest loudly, and appealed to the people. Virginius said that he was not worthy to have the right of appeal since he had abolished it, or to have as his defenders a people whom he had ill treated. Appius replied that the people ought not to violate the right of appeal which they had been so keen on instituting. He was none the less imprisoned, and killed himself before the trial came on. Appius by his wicked life no doubt merited the severest punishment. But it scarce accorded with civic custom to violate the law, especially a law that had just been made. For I do not think a worse example can be set in a republic than to make a law and not to observe it; and when it is not observed by the man who made it so much the worse.

After '94 the government of Florence was reconstituted with the aid of Friar Girolamo Savonarola, whose writings attest the learning, prudence, and virtue of his mind. For the security of the citizens he had made, among other constitutions, a law which allowed an appeal to the people from a judgement which, in cases of treason, the Eight and the Signoria had passed. He had advocated this law for some time, and with the greatest difficulty got it accepted. Shortly after it had been sanctioned, it happened that five citizens were condemned to death by the Signoria for treason. When they wished to appeal they were not allowed to do so, and the law was not observed. This did more to lessen the reputation of the Friar than anything else that befell him. For, if the right to appeal was worth having, he ought to have seen that it was observed. If it was not worth having, he should not have forced it through. The event attracted more notice in that this Friar in not one of the many sermons which he preached after the law had been broken, ever condemned the breach or offered any excuse. For, since it suited his purpose, to condemn it he was unwilling, and to excuse it he was unable. Since this made it plain to all that at heart he was ambitious and a party-man, it ruined his reputation and brought on him much reproach.

It does considerable harm to a state to arouse every day fresh discontent in the minds of your citizens by inflicting fresh injuries on this or that person, as happened in Rome after the fall of the Decemviri. For all ten of them, and other citizens besides, were at various times accused and condemned, so that the whole nobility was in a state of extreme terror, since they thought there would be no end to such condemnations until the whole of the nobility was destroyed. This would have caused great inconveniences in the city if Marcus Duilius, a tribune, had not made provision against it by issuing an edict which made it unlawful for anyone to cite or accuse any Roman citizen for the space of a year; whereby the whole nobility was reassured.

This shows how harmful it is to a republic or to a prince to keep the minds of their subjects in suspense and fear by continually inflicting punishment and giving offence. Than this there is unquestionably no practice more pernicious. For when men begin to suspect that evil may befall them, they take any means to protect themselves and grow more bold and less restrained in attempting a revolution. It is necessary, therefore, either never to injure anyone, or to inflict the injuries at one go, and then to reassure men and give them ground to expect peace and security.

Book One

---

46. Men pass from one Ambition to Another, and, having first striven against Ill-treatment, inflict it next upon Others

WHEN the Roman people recovered its liberty and returned to its pristine state which was now the greater in that many new laws had been made whereby its power was strengthened, it looked as if Rome for the time being would be tranquil. Experience, however, showed that this was not to be, for daily fresh tumults and fresh discords arose. How this came about Titus Livy has cleverly explained. Hence it seems to me relevant to cite here his remarks on this point. He says that either the populace or the nobility always became arrogant when the other party was humbled; that when the plebs was quiet and kept its place, the young nobles began to treat it badly, and that the tribunes could do little to mend matters because violence was being used also against them. On the other hand, though to the rest of the nobility it seemed that their young men were going too far, it was none the less to their liking that, if excesses had to be committed, their own men should commit them rather than the plebs. Thus the desire for liberty caused each party to oppress the other in so

223

far as it got the upper hand. And the sequence in which these events occur is such that men seek first to be free from apprehension, then make others apprehensive, and that the injuries of which they had ridded themselves, they proceeded to inflict on others. It was as if it were necessary either to treat others ill or to be ill-treated.

In this we see one of the ways in which republics come to be dissolved; and how men pass from one ambition to another; and how true is the saying which Sallust puts into the mouth of Caesar 'that all bad examples arise from good beginnings'. The first thing which these citizens who live ambitiously in a republic seek, is, as I have said, not to be ill-treated, neither by private persons nor yet by the magistrates. To obtain this security they form friendships by ways seemingly honest, such as giving pecuniary assistance or protection against the powerful. And, since this appears to be a virtuous act, everyone is easily deceived and so does nothing about it, with the result that such men, persevering and meeting no obstacle, acquire a position of which private citizens are afraid and which the magistrates respect. When they have risen thus far and no obstacle has yet been placed in the way of their greatness, they arrive ultimately at a position which it is very dangerous to . assail for the reasons I have already given, namely, the danger of removing an inconvenience from a state in which it has already grown to considerable dimensions. So that in the end it comes to this: either you must look for a way of removing the person concerned with imminent danger of ruin, or you must let him go on, with the prospect of manifest servitude unless death or some accident sets you free. For when a man has reached the stage at which both the citizens and the magistrates are afraid of offending him and his friends, it is not very difficult after that for them to do just what they please and to give offence in their own turn.

A republic, therefore, ought to have some institution whereby to prevent its citizens from doing wrong under pretence of doing right, and to see that their popularity is helpful, and not harmful to liberty – a point which we shall discuss further in its proper place.[29]

47. *Though Men make Mistakes about Things in General, they do not make Mistakes about Particulars*

THE Roman people, as I have already said, came to look on the consular office as a nuisance, and wished this office to be thrown open to plebeians, or, alternatively, that the authority of the consuls should be reduced. To prevent the authority of the consuls from being sullied by the adoption of either of these alternatives, the nobility suggested a middle course, and agreed to the appointment of four tribunes with consular power who might be either plebeians or nobles. With this the plebs was content, since it was tantamount to abolishing the consulate, and in the highest office of the state they had a share. An event now took place which is noteworthy. When it came to electing these tribunes, though they might have elected plebeians in all cases, all those the Roman people elected were nobles. On this Titus Livy remarks that 'the result of these elections shows that the attitude adopted in the struggle for liberty and honour was different from that adopted when the struggle was over and gave place to unbiased judgement'.

If one asks how this could have come about, I believe it came about because men make quite a number of mistakes about things in general, but not so many about particulars. In general the Roman plebs thought that they deserved the consulate because they were the more numerous party in the city, because it was they who had been exposed to greater danger in the wars, because it was they who by brawn and muscle had kept Rome free and made it powerful. And since, as I have said, this desire appeared to them reasonable, they were determined to acquire this authority by some means or other. But when it came to deciding which particular members of their party to elect, they recognized their weakness and judged that no one of them was worthy of that of which all of them, taken together, had seemed to be worthy; so that being ashamed of their own people, they had recourse to those who were worthy of the office. It is no wonder Titus Livy is astonished at this decision, and remarks: 'Where today will you find in anyone that modesty, fairness and highmindedness which the whole people then displayed?'

In confirmation of this may be adduced another notable instance which occurred in Capua after Hannibal had routed the Romans at Cannae. By this disaster the whole of Italy was stirred, and Capua was again on the brink of tumult owing to the hatred which existed between the populace and the senate. Pacuvius Calavius, who at the time was the city's chief magistrate and realized the danger the city was in, considered how best he could use his position in order to reconcile the plebs with the nobility. This was the plan he adopted. He summoned the senate, told them of the hatred which the populace had for them, and that this meant they were in danger of being killed and of the city's being handed over to Hannibal, so sorry was the plight the Romans were in. He then added that, if they would leave it to him to deal with the matter, he would do it in such a way that they should again be reunited, but he proposed to lock them up in the palace, and, in order to save them, to appeal to the power which the populace would thus have of chastizing them. The senators yielded to his advice. So when he had locked the senate up in the palace he called a meeting of the populace, and told them that the time had come when they could humble the pride of the nobility and obtain vengeance for the injuries done them, since the whole senate was locked up in his custody. He was sure, however, that they would not want their city to remain without a government, so that, if they proposed to kill the old senators, it would be necessary to appoint new ones. With this end in view he had put the names of all the senators in a bag, from which he would proceed to draw them in their presence. He would then put to death those whose names had been drawn, one after the other, as soon as they had found for each a successor. He then began by drawing out one name. On hearing the man's name an uproar was raised, and they called him a proud and cruel and arrogant fellow. Pacuvius then called on them to appoint someone in his stead; whereupon the shouting subsided altogether, and after a pause one of the plebs was nominated. At his name some began to hiss, some to laugh, some to abuse him in one way, some in another. And so it went on, time upon time, till all who had been nominated had been judged to be unworthy of senatorial rank. Pacuvius then took occasion to remark: since you think this city cannot get on without a senate, but are not agreed as to who should replace the old senators, I think the best thing is for you to become reconciled; for the fear which has been hanging over the senators will have so humiliated them that you will find in them now that considerateness for which you have been looking elsewhere. To this they agreed, and unity in this institution was thus brought about, so that the mistake they had been making was discovered as soon as they were forced to get down to particulars. Other mistakes that are made by the populace in judging of things and of the properties of things in general also vanish when they come to study them in detail.

After 1494 when those who had been princes in Florence were expelled from that city, and there was no proper government, but rather a state in which anarchy and ambition were commingled and public business was going from bad to worse, many belonging to the popular party, seeing the city going to ruin and discerning no other cause for it, laid the blame on those powerful citizens who had fomented the disturbances that they might be able to set up the kind of state they wanted and take away liberty. They advocated these views in the colonnades and squares, spoke ill of many citizens, and threatened that if ever they got into the Signoria they would show them their mistake and would chastise them.

It has often happened that a man of this sort has risen to the highest office, and, when he has got there, has looked at things more closely and so has come to recognize the source of the disorders, the dangers which they entail, and the difficulty of putting matters right. Realizing that it is circumstances,[a] not men, that have brought the disorders about, he has then quickly changed both his mind and his line of conduct; for acquaintance with things in detail has removed the wrong impression that had been taken for granted when only general considerations were taken into account. Consequently those who have heard such a one speak when he was a private person, and, later on, have noticed how silent he remained when he held high office, have ascribed this not to his better acquaintance with affairs, but to his having been suborned and corrupted by the great. It is the sort of thing that happens to many and on many occasions. Hence the proverb which says: 'He is of a different opinion in the market place from what he is in the palace.'

In view of all that has been said in this discourse, it should be clear, then, that it is possible to make the populace open its eyes as soon as a way can be found of making it see that it is a mistake to generalize, and that it ought to get down to particulars, as Pacuvius made it do in Capua, and the senate in Rome. We may infer, I think, too, that a wise man will not ignore public opinion in regard to particular matters, such as the distribution of offices and preferments; for here the populace, when left to itself, does not make mistakes, or, if some-

[a] *i tempi.*

times it does, its mistakes are rare in comparison with those that would occur if the few had to make such a distribution. Nor will it be superfluous, I think, for me to point out in the next chapter the means taken by the senate to delude the populace when it was making its appointments.

48. *To prevent an Official Appointment being given to a Base and Wicked Fellow, either an Exceedingly Base and Wicked Man should be put forward as a Candidate or an Exceedingly Noble and Good Man*

WHEN the senate half expected that plebeians would be made tribunes with consular power, it adopted one of these two expedients. Either it put forward as candidates the most reputable men in Rome, or on the other hand, it took suitable means to suborn some rascally and insignificant plebeians and to cause them to mingle with plebeians of higher standing who in the ordinary course would stand as candidates, so that they should stand as candidates together. This second expedient made the plebs ashamed to give a man the office, while the first made them ashamed not to give it.

This all bears out the proposition laid down in the preceding discourse that, if the populace makes mistakes about generalities, it does not make mistakes about particulars.

49. If those City-States which from the Outset have been Free, as Rome was, find it difficult to formulate Laws whereby to maintain Liberty, those which have just been servile are faced with a Quasi-impossibility

How difficult it is in constituting a republic to foresee all the laws required for the maintenance of liberty, is clearly shown in the development of the Roman republic; in which, notwithstanding that many laws were laid down first by Romulus, then by Numa, Tullus Hostilius, and Servius, and finally by the ten citizens appointed for this purpose, in the managing of this city new needs continually cropped up and it was necessary to introduce new institutions. An instance of this occurred when they instituted censors. This was one of those provisions which helped to keep Rome free at a time when it was actually enjoying freedom. For in that the censors became the arbiters of Roman customs, they constituted a very powerful instrument which the Romans used in order to postpone the advent of corruption.[30] At the outset, however, they made a serious mistake in the creating of this magistracy in that the censors were appointed for five years. But, before very long, this was corrected by the prudence of the dictator, Mamercus, who by a new law reduced the term of their office to eighteen months. This the censors, who were on the watch, took so ill that they deprived Mamercus of his senatorial rank, an action of which both the plebs and the patricians strongly disapproved. That history does not tell us whether Mamercus was able to do anything to defend himself, is due either to an omission on the part of historians, or to Rome's institutions being in this respect defective; for it is not well that the procedure of a republic should be such that a citizen can be impugned without redress for promulgating a law in conformity with civic life and liberty.

But to return to the question at issue in this discourse. I say that in the creation of this new magistracy the point to notice is that, if in a state which had been free from the outset and had directed its own affairs, as Rome did, there was great difficulty in devising good laws whereby to maintain liberty, it is no wonder that a city which at the outset was in servitude to another, should find it not merely difficult, but impossible, ever to draw up a constitution that will enable it to enjoy tranquillity in the conduct of its affairs.

This is illustrated by what happened to the city of Florence, which, owing to its having been at the outset under the dominion of the Roman empire, and to its having always lived under foreign rule, remained for a time abject and without thought for its own condition. Later, however, when it got time to breathe, it began to make its own institutions; but found it impossible to make good ones for they were mixed up with the old ones, which were bad. It carried on thus for two hundred years, of which there are reliable records, without ever getting a form of government such as would entitle it rightly to be called a republic. The difficulty which it experienced, all states experience which have had a like beginning. And although time and again, ample authority was given by free and public suffrage to a few of its citizens to reform it, they never used it to draw up a constitution to the common advantage, but always in the interests of their own party; with the result that not order, but greater disorder, was brought about in that city.

Take, for instance, one particular point. I maintain that one of the things that has to be taken into account by one who is drawing up a constitution for a republic, is the question into the hands of what men should authority to inflict punishment on its citizens be placed. Rome's institution here was a good one, for an appeal to the people was ordinarily allowed, and if an important case arose in which to defer action, pending an appeal, was dangerous, they had recourse to a dictator who dealt with it straightway; but to this remedy they never had recourse unless driven to it by necessity. Whereas Florence, and other cities which came into being in the same way, being servile, vested this authority in a foreigner, who fulfilled this function as his prince should direct. When, later on, they obtained their freedom, they continued to give this authority to a foreigner whom they called the 'Captain'; which was a most pernicious practice, seeing how easily such an official could be corrupted by powerful citizens. But later still, owing to a change in the form of government a change took place in this institution and they appointed eight citizens to fulfil the function of the captain. This institution was bad and became worse, for reasons which have been given elsewhere, namely, that the few were always the servants of the few, and these the more powerful men.

Against this abuse the city of Venice has safeguarded itself by having ten citizens who are empowered to punish any citizen without appeal; and, lest the ten should not suffice for the punishing of the powerful, though they have authority to do this, they have set up the tribunal of Forty and, yet further, have decided that the Court of Rogation, which is the Greater Council, shall have power to punish them; so that there is no shortage of judges there to keep the powerful in check, given that there be no shortage of accusers.

Seeing, then, that in Rome, which had its own constitution drawn up by so many wise men, there were ever arising fresh causes which forced it to introduce new institutions in support of the liberties it enjoyed, it is no wonder that in other cities which were more lacking in order at the start, there should arise such difficulties that they can never be reconstituted aright.

Book One

[THE MANAGEMENT OF THE POPULACE]

---

50. *No One Department[a] and no One Official[b] in a State[c] should be able to hold up proceedings*

WHEN Titus Quintius Cincinnatus and Gaius Julius Mento were consuls in Rome, they fell out, and thus stopped all proceedings in that republic. When the senate, seeing this, advised the appointment of a dictator to do what the quarrel between the consuls prevented them from doing, the consuls, though they disagreed in everything else were in agreement about just one thing – not wanting to appoint a dictator. So the senate, having no other remedy, had recourse to the tribunes for help, who, with the authority of the senate behind them, forced the consuls to submit.

Here should be noted first the utility of the tribunate, for it was useful not only in bridling the ambition of the powerful which militated against the plebs, but also in bridling the ambition which they displayed one against the other. Secondly, it is to be noted that in a state there should never be an institution which allows the few to decide on any matter which in the ordinary course of things is essential to the maintenance

---

[a] consiglio.   *[b] magistrato.*   *[c] città.*

of the commonwealth. For instance, if you empower a council to distribute preferments and emoluments, or a magistracy to administer some department, it is expedient either to make it necessary for them to take action or to arrange for someone else to have the power and duty of acting, should they be unwilling to act. Otherwise the institution will be defective and dangerous, as it would have been in Rome if it had not been possible to overcome the obstinacy of the consuls by the authority of the tribunes.

In the republic of Venice the Great Council distributes preferments and emoluments, and at times it has happened that at their general meeting, owing either to annoyance or to a misapprehension, they failed to appoint successors to some of the city magistrates and to those who administered their dominions elsewhere. This caused much disorder because all at once subject territories and the city itself lacked legally constituted judges. Nor was there any redress so long as this council at its general meeting remained dissatisfied and failed to realize its mistake. This inconvenience would have reduced that city to sore straits, if some prudent citizens had not met the case by passing on a suitable occasion a law prohibiting all magistrates from vacating any office to which they had been, or should be, appointed within and without the city, till they had been relieved and their successors appointed. This council was thus deprived of the privilege of being able to hold up public business to the danger of the republic.

51. *A Republic or a Prince should ostensibly do out of Generosity what Necessity constrains them to do*

PRUDENT men always and in all their actions make a favour of doing things even though they would of necessity be constrained to do them anyhow. The Roman Senate made good use of prudence deciding to use public money to pay

men on military service. It had been the custom for soldiers to
pay their own expenses, but the senate saw that in such case
they could not make war for long, and, in consequence,
would neither be able to lay siege to towns, nor to lead their
armies far afield. Since, therefore, they thought it necessary
to be able to do both these things, they decided that the
troops should be paid a stipend; but did it in such a way that
they made a favour of doing what necessity had constrained
them to do.

So acceptable was this gift to the plebs that Rome went mad
with delight; for it seemed to them that they had received a
great benefaction which they had never expected, and which
they would never have asked for themselves. And, though
the tribunes tried hard to remove this impression, pointing out
that it would increase the burden on the plebs instead of light-
ening it since it would be necessary to levy taxes to be able to
defray the cost; none the less they were quite unable to
prevent the plebs welcoming the change. It was made the
more welcome, too, by the way in which the taxes were
distributed; for those imposed on the nobility were heavier
and greater, and they had to be paid first.

52. *The Safer and Less Scandalous Way to repress the*
Arrogance of One who has risen to Power in a
Republic is to forestall him in the Methods he
uses to come by this Power

WE have seen in the last chapter what credit the nobility
acquired with the plebs by their seeming bounty of granting
the soldiers pay, and by the way in which taxes were levied.
Had the nobility kept up this practice, they would have
prevented any tumult in the city, would have deprived the
tribunes of the credit they had with the plebs, and so would
have deprived them of their authority. For certainly in a

republic, and especially in a corrupt republic, there cannot be a better, less scandalous, or easier way of thwarting the ambition of any citizen than by forestalling him in the routes he traverses to get to the goal he proposes to reach.

If this method had been adopted by the enemies of Cosimo de' Medici it would have been much better than driving him out of the city. For had his competitors among the citizens adopted his style and played up to the populace they would have taken out of his hands the weapons which availed him most, and there would have been no tumults and no violence. Piero Soderini had acquired great repute in the city of Florence simply by using this method, i.e. playing up to the public, who thus came to look upon him as a man who was devoted to the liberty of the city. It would certainly have been much easier, much more honest, less dangerous and less harmful to the republic, had those citizens who were envious of his greatness, forestalled the methods by which he made himself great, instead of opposing him in such a way that they ruined themselves, and, in doing so, brought ruin also on everybody else in the republic. For, if they had taken from his hands the weapons he used to make strong his position – which they could easily have done – they would have been able to oppose him on all councils and in all public debates without incurring suspicion and without regard for anybody. And, should anyone answer that, if the citizens who hated Piero made the mistake of not forestalling the methods whereby he had acquired repute with the people, Piero himself had made the same mistake in that he had not forestalled the methods used by his adversaries in order to frighten him, there was in Piero's case an excuse. For it would have been difficult to do; and such methods were in his eyes dishonest because the methods they used in attacking him consisted in playing up to the Medici, with whose help they got the better of him and in the end ruined him. Piero, therefore, could not in decency play such a part, which would have meant destroying not only his good name, but the liberty of which he had been appointed the guardian. Nor could he have supported the Medici in secret and for the time being, since this would have been most dangerous in his case; for, should he have been discovered to be the friend of the Medici, he would at once have become suspect and odious to the populace; and this would have made it yet easier for his enemies to attack him than it had been before.

Men ought, therefore, in choosing between alternatives, to consider the snags and the dangers involved, and not to adopt that which may entail more danger than advantage, even though they have the backing of an assembly in what they have decided upon. Because, if they do otherwise, it may well happen in their case as it did in that of Tullius [Cicero], who, in attempting to remove those who favoured Mark Antony, did but increase their numbers. For Mark Antony had been declared by the senate to be an enemy of the state, and had collected together a large army consisting for the most part of soldiers who had espoused Caesar's cause. In order to deprive him of these soldiers, Tullius advised the senate to give preferment to Octavian, and to send him with the consuls, Hirtius and Pansa, against Mark Antony; alleging that, as soon as the soldiers who were following Mark Antony heard the name of Octavian, who was Caesar's nephew and had adopted the name of Caesar, they would leave the former and join him; which would leave Mark Antony devoid of supporters, so that it would be easy to overcome him. The result was just the opposite; for Mark Antony won over Octavian, who left Tullius and the senate in the lurch, and joined him. This affair led to the utter destruction of the aristocratic[a] party.

This might easily have been foreseen. The senate ought not

[a] *della parte degli Ottimati* – 'Optimates' being the technical term then in use for the wealthier and more aristocratic party.

to have given credence to Tullius's arguments, but should have borne ever in mind that name which had so gloriously wiped out its enemies and acquired the princedom of Rome. Nor should they have expected to be able to do anything consistent with the name of liberty with the help of his relatives and his supporters.

53. *The Populace, misled by the False Appearance of Advantage, often seeks its own Ruin, and is easily moved by Splendid Hopes and Rash Promises*

WHEN the city of Veii had been taken it occurred to the Roman populace that it would be of advantage to the city of Rome if half its inhabitants went to live in Veii; for it was argued that, since Veii was situated in a rich neighbourhood, was full of buildings and near to Rome, one half of Rome's citizens might prosper there, and yet not be so near to Rome as to interfere with its civic proceedings. The project seemed to the senate and to wiser folk in Rome to be so futile and so likely to do harm that they openly declared that it would be better to suffer death than to agree to such a plan. The result was that, when the matter came up for discussion, the plebs became so incensed against the senate that there would have been an armed conflict and bloodshed, had not the senate been shielded by some citizens of mature age and high repute, and had not the plebs been deterred by the respect it had for them from proceeding further with its impertinence.

Two things here are noteworthy. First of all, the populace, misled by the false appearance of good, often seeks its own ruin, and, unless it be brought to realize what is bad and what is good for it by someone in whom it has confidence, brings on republics endless dangers and disasters. Again, when by ill chance the populace has no confidence in anyone at all, as sometimes happens owing to its having been deceived in the past either by events or by men, it spells ruin, and necessarily so. Apropos of which Dante said in the discourse he made *On Monarchy* that the populace often used to cry Long live its death! and Death to its life!

From this unreadiness to trust anybody it sometimes happens that a republic fails to reach the right decision, as has been said above of the Venetians, who, when attacked by numerous enemies, could not decide whether or not to save the situation by restoring what they had taken from others – for it was this that had led to the war and caused princes to form the League against them – until ruin came upon them.

Turning now to the question of what it is easy and what difficult to persuade a people, this distinction may be made. Either that of which you have to persuade it looks at first sight like a sure thing, or it looks like a lost cause, or, again, it may seem to it a bold thing or a cowardly thing to do. When proposals which have been laid before the populace look like sure things, even though concealed within them disaster lies hid, or when it looks like a bold thing, even though concealed within it lies the republic's ruin, it will always be easy to persuade the masses to adopt such a proposal. And, in like manner, it will always be difficult to persuade them to adopt a course which seems to them cowardly or hopeless, even though safety and security lie hid beneath it.

What I have said is borne out by numerous instances, Roman and non-Roman, modern and ancient. For instance, it was in this way that a poor view came to be taken in Rome of Fabius Maximus, who failed to persuade the Roman people that the republic would do well to go slowly with the war against Hannibal and to act on the defensive instead of attacking him; for that people thought such a course cowardly and saw no advantage in it, nor had Fabius reasons enough to make them see his point. So blind indeed are peoples in matters concerning their own safety that, although the Roman people had made the mistake of authorizing Fabius's master of horse to attack, contrary to Fabius's wish, and although by the action, thus authorized, the Roman army would have been routed had not Fabius had the prudence to come to the rescue, yet so little did they profit by this experience that they afterwards made Varro consul, not on the score of merit, but because he had gone about everywhere proclaiming in the squares and public places that he would break Hannibal if they would but give him the command. The result was the battle and rout at Cannae, which almost ruined Rome.

Let me give yet another instance of such conduct in Rome. Hannibal had been in Italy for eight or ten years and had slaughtered Romans right and left throughout the whole of this province, when Marcus Centenius Penula, a low born fellow – though he had held some rank in the forces – came to the senate and offered, if they would authorize him to form an army of volunteers drawn from any place he pleased in Italy, to present them in a very short time with Hannibal either dead or alive. To the senate this rascal's request seemed foolhardy; yet, in view of the fact that, if they refused it and the populace got to know of their decision, there would be disturbances and the odium would fall on those of senatorial rank, they granted it, preferring to expose to danger all who should follow him, rather than to arouse fresh resentment in the populace, for they knew how eagerly such a course would be welcomed and how difficult it would be to dissuade them. So the rascal went with a disorderly and undisciplined mob to look for Hannibal, and was defeated and killed, together with all his followers, at the first encounter.

In Greece, in the city of Athens, Nicias, a man both of weight and wisdom, could never persuade the people of that city of the folly of invading Sicily, with the result that against the advice of those who knew better, they took a decision which led to the total ruin of Athens.

When Scipio became consul and was keen on getting the province of Africa, promising that Carthage should be completely destroyed, and the senate would not agree to this because Fabius Maximus was against it, he threatened to appeal to the people, for he knew full well how pleasing such projects are to the populace.

One might cite relevant instances from our own city. For example, when Messer Ercole Bentivoglio, commander of the Florentine forces, together with Antonio Giacomini, after they had defeated Bartolommeo d'Alviano at San Vincenti, went to besiege Pisa, this attack was decided upon by the populace in view of Messer Ercole's bold promises though many wise citizens were against it. Nor was there any way out since the project had been put forward by the general will, based as it was on the assurances given by the commander of the army.

I claim, then, that there is no easier way of bringing disaster on a republic in which the populace has authority, than to engage it in undertakings which appear bold, for, if the populace is of any account, it is bound to be taken up; nor will those who are of a different opinion be able to do anything to stop it. But if this brings ruin to a city it brings ruin still more frequently to the particular citizens put in charge of such an enterprise. For the populace having taken victory for granted, when defeat comes, do not blame it on fortune or on the helplessness of the person in command, but on his malevolence or his ignorance. Hence usually he gets either killed or imprisoned or exiled, as happened to numberless Carthaginian generals and to many Athenians. Nor does it help such a one to have won victories in the past, for the present disaster cancels them all out. This was what happened to our friend, Antonio Giacomini. For, when he failed to take Pisa, as the populace expected and as he had promised to do, he fell into such disgrace with the populace that, notwithstanding his countless services in the past, he owed his life rather to the compassion of those in power than to any cause which weighed in his favour with the populace.

54. How Great an Influence a Grave Man may have in restraining an Excited Crowd

THE second thing to be noted in regard to the incident related in the last chapter is that nothing is more suitable to restrain an excited crowd than respect for some man of gravity and standing who in person confronts them. Hence not without reason does Virgil say:

> If then some grave and pious man appear
> They hush their noise and lend a listening ear.

This being so, a person who has command of an army or who finds himself in a city where a tumult has arisen should present himself before those involved with as much grace and dignity as he can muster, wearing the insignia of whatever rank he holds in order to impress them.

A few years ago Florence was divided into two factions, the Frateschi and the Arrabbiati, as they were called. When they came to blows the Frateschi were overpowered, among whom was Pagolantonio Soderini, a citizen of considerable repute in those days. During the disturbance the populace, having armed itself, went to his house to pillage it. In the house they found by chance Messer Francesco, his brother, then bishop of Volterra, and now a cardinal. On hearing the noise and seeing the crowd, he at once donned his most magnificent robes, put his episcopal rochet over them, confronted the armed crowd, and by his presence and his words held them up. This event was talked of and applauded for several days throughout the whole of the city. I conclude, therefore, that there is no surer or more necessary means of restraining an excited crowd than the presence of a man, worthy of its respect, who appears before it in person.

If then we turn to the aforesaid incident, one notices how obstinately the Roman plebs had taken up the suggestion that they should go to Veii because they thought it advantageous and did not perceive the harm which it involved; and how, when disturbances arose, trouble would have ensued if the senate had not, by means of grave and highly respected men, restrained their madness.

55. That it is very easy to manage Things in a State in which the Masses are not Corrupt; and that, where Equality exists, it is impossible to set up a Principality, and, where it does not exist, impossible to set up a Republic

THOUGH what is to be feared and what is to be hoped for in states[a] that are corrupt has been sufficiently discussed elsewhere,[31] it does not seem to me irrelevant to consider here a decision made by the senate in regard to the vow which Camillus had made to give a tenth part of the booty taken from the Veientes to Apollo. This booty had come into the hands of the Roman plebs; and, since there was no other way of obtaining an account of it, the senate made an edict requiring everyone to bring to the public treasury a tenth part of what he had seized. This decision was not carried into effect since the senate later adopted other ways and means of rendering to Apollo the satisfaction which was due from the plebs. It is apparent, none the less, from this decision what trust the senate had in the goodness of the plebs in that it felt sure that no one would fail to bring forth immediately all that the edict prescribed. It shows, too, that the plebs had no thought of

[a] *cittadi*, as in the title of the chapter.

acting fraudulently in regard to the edict by handing over less than was due. What they did, instead, was to get rid of the edict by showing plainly how indignant they were with it.

This example, and many others which have already been cited, show how great was the goodness and the respect for religion which then prevailed among the Roman people, and how much could be expected of them. For where such goodness prevails one cannot but anticipate good conduct. It cannot, on the other hand, be expected in these days in territories which are obviously corrupt, as is Italy above all other lands. France and Spain, too, share in this corruption; and if in these countries disorders are apparently not so great as those that occur daily in Italy, this is not so much due to the goodness of the people there – for in goodness they are notice-ably lacking – as to their having a king who keeps them united, not merely by his personal virtues, but by constitutional methods, which in those kingdoms as yet are not corrupt.

In the province of Germany it is quite clear that goodness and respect for religion are still to be found in its peoples, with the result that many republics there enjoy freedom and observe their laws in such a way that neither outsiders nor their own inhabitants dare to usurp power there.[32]

And that it is true of these republics that in them there still prevails a good deal of the goodness of ancient times, I propose to make clear by giving an example similar to that related above of the Roman senate and people. When these republics have need to spend any sum of money on the public account, it is customary for their magistrates or councils, in whom is vested authority to deal with such matters, to impose on all the inhabitants of a town a tax of one or two per cent of the value of each one's property. The decision having been made, each person presents himself to the tax-collectors in accordance with the constitutional practice of the town. He then takes an oath to pay the appropriate sum, and throws into

a chest provided for the purpose the amount which he con-
scientiously thinks that he ought to pay; but of this payment
there is no witness save the man who pays. This is an indication of how much goodness and how much respect for
religion there still is in such men; for presumably each pays
the correct sum, since, if he did not do so, the tax would not
bring in the amount estimated on the basis of previous col-
lections made in the customary way, and failure to realize it
would reveal any fraud, and in that case some other method of
collecting the tax would have been adopted.

This goodness is the more to be admired in these days in that
it is so rare. Indeed, it seems to survive only in this province.
This is due to two things. In the first place the towns have but
little intercourse with their neighbours, who seldom go to
visit them, or are visited by them, since they are content with
the goods, live on the food, and are clothed with the wool
which their own land provides. The occasion for intercourse,
and with it the initial step on the road to corruption, is thus
removed, since they have no chance of taking up the customs
either of the French, the Spaniards or the Italians, nations
which, taken together, are the source of world-wide corruption.

The second reason is that those states where political life
survives uncorrupted, do not permit any of their citizens to
live after the fashion of the gentry.[a] On the contrary, they
maintain there perfect equality, and to lords and gentry
residing in that province are extremely hostile; so that, should
any perchance fall into their hands, they treat them as sources
of corruption and causes of trouble, and kill them.[33]

To make it clear what is meant by the term 'gentry', I would
point out that the term 'gentry' is used of those who live in
idleness on the abundant revenue derived from their estates,
without having anything to do either with their cultivation or

[a] *a uso di gentiluomo.*

with other forms of labour essential to life. Such men are a pest
in any republic and in any province; but still more pernicious
are those who, in addition to the aforesaid revenues, have
castles under their command and subjects who are under their
obedience. Of these two types of men there are plenty in the
kingdom of Naples, the Papal States, the Romagna and
Lombardy. It is owing to this that in these provinces there has
never arisen any republic or any political life, for men born
in such conditions are entirely inimical to any form of civic
government. In provinces thus organized no attempt to set up
a republic could possibly succeed. To reconstitute them,
should anyone want to do so, the only way would be to set
up a monarchy there. The reason for this is that, where the
material is so corrupt, laws do not suffice to keep it in hand;
it is necessary to have, besides laws, a superior force, such as
appertains to a monarch, who has such absolute and overwhelming power that he can restrain excesses due to ambition
and the corrupt practices of the powerful.

This argument is borne out by the case of Tuscany, in whose
territory, small as it is, one finds that there have long been
three republics, Florence, Siena and Lucca; and that the other
cities of this province, though in a way servile, yet are of such
a mind and have such a constitution that either they maintain
their freedom, or would like to do so. All of which is due to
there being in Tuscany no baronial castles, and either none or
very few gentry, and to the presence there of so great an
equality that a wise man, familiar with ancient forms of civic
government, should easily be able to introduce there a civic
constitution.[a] But, so great has been Tuscany's misfortune that
up to the present she has come across nobody with the
requisite ability and knowledge.

From this discussion the following conclusion may be

[a] *uno vivere civile*. [i.e. if 'constitution', then in a very broad sense,
better to say 'way of life'. B.R.C.]

drawn: (i) that, where the gentry are numerous, no one who proposes to set up a republic can succeed unless he first gets rid of the lot; and (ii) that, where considerable equality prevails, no one who proposes to set up a kingdom or principality, will ever be able to do it unless from that equality he selects many of the more ambitious and restless minds and makes of them gentry in fact and not in name, by giving them castles and possessions and making of them a privileged class with respect both to property and subjects; so that around him will be those with whose support he may maintain himself in power, and whose ambitions, thanks to him, may be realized. As to the rest they will be compelled to bear a yoke which nothing but force will ever be able to make them endure. Between force and those to whom force is applied a balance will thus be set up, and the standing of every man, each in his own order, will be consolidated. But, since to convert a province, suited to monarchical rule, into a republic, and to convert a province, suited to a republican regime, into a kingdom, is a matter which only a man of outstanding brain-power and authority can handle, and such men are rare, there have been many who have attempted it but few who have had the ability to carry it through. For the magnitude of an undertaking of this kind is such that it breaks down at the very beginning, partly because men get terrified and partly because it hampers them.

With my thesis that where there are gentry it is impossible to set up a republic, the experience of the Venetian republic may, perhaps, appear to be incompatible, for in that republic no man may hold any office unless he be a 'gentleman'. To which the answer is that this case in no way conflicts with my thesis, since 'gentlemen' in this republic are so in name rather than in point of fact; for they do not derive any considerable income from estates: their great wealth is based on merchandise and movable goods. Moreover, none of them have castles, nor have they any jurisdiction over men. The name 'gentle-man' in their case is but a title, indicative of their standing. It is not based on any of the grounds which lead other cities to call people 'gentlemen'. Just as in other republics different classes go by different names, so in Venice the population is divided into 'gentlemen' and 'commoners'; and it has decided that of these the former alone shall hold, or be eligible for, office, from which the latter are wholly excluded. Why this does not cause disorder in that town has already been explained.

Let, then, a republic be constituted where there exists, or can be brought into being, notable equality; and a regime of the opposite type, i.e. a principality, where there is notable inequality. Otherwise what is done will lack proportion and will be of but short duration.[34]

Book One

---

56. *Before Great Misfortunes befall a City or a Province they are preceded by Portents or foretold by Men*

HOW it comes about I know not, but it is clear both from ancient and modern cases that no serious misfortune ever befalls a city or a province that has not been predicted either by divination or revelation or by prodigies or by other heavenly signs. There is no need to go far afield to prove this. Everybody knows how, before king Charles VIII of France came to Italy, his coming was frequently foretold by Friar Girolamo Savonarola, and how, in addition to this, it was said that armed hosts had been heard and seen in the sky above Arezzo fighting one with the other. Everybody knows, too, how before the death of Lorenzo de' Medici the elder, the upper part of the cathedral was struck by a thunderbolt which did much damage to that edifice. Everybody knows also how a short time before Piero Soderini, who had been made gonfalonier for life by the people of Florence, was banished and stripped of his rank, the palace was in like manner struck by lightning.

Plenty of further examples might be cited, but I pass them over lest I should bore you. I shall mention only what Titus

Livy has to say about what happened before the Gauls came to Rome; namely, that a plebeian called Marcus Caedicius reported to the senate that, as he was going along the *Via Nova*, he heard in the middle of the night a voice, louder than a man's voice, bidding him to go and inform the magistrates that the Gauls were coming to Rome.

The cause of such events should be discussed and explained, I think, by some one versed in things natural and supernatural, and this we are not. It may be, of course, as some philosophers would have it, that the atmosphere is full of spirits, endowed by nature with the virtue to foresee the future, who out of sympathy for men give them warning by means of such signs so that they may look to their defence. Anyhow, whatever be the explanation, there is evidence showing that such things happen, and that, after them, in all provinces there supervene extraordinary and novel events.

57. *The Plebs United is Strong, but in Itself it is Weak*

IN consequence of the ruin wrought in their country by the incursions of the Gauls there were many Romans who went to live in Veii, despite the decree and the orders of the senate. To remedy this disorder the senate by public edicts required everyone within a specified time and under specified penalties to return to Rome and to reside there. Those against whom these edicts were proclaimed, at first made fun of them, but, when it came to the point, all of them obeyed. Whereupon Titus Livy makes this remark: 'As a crowd they were a fierce lot, but, as individuals each was so afraid that he obeyed.'

It would, indeed, scarce be possible to describe better the natural behaviour of a crowd in such circumstances than it is described in this passage. For, in criticizing the decisions of their ruler the masses are often bold; but when they see before their eyes the penalty attached, each mistrusts the other, and they hasten to obey. This shows beyond a doubt that scant

attention should be paid to what the people says about their
own good or evil dispositions, provided your regime be such
that you can hold it if it be well disposed, and, if ill disposed,
can see to it that it does you no harm. By 'ill disposed' I mean
here a disposition that arises from some cause other than that of
having lost its freedom, or having lost a prince who was
beloved and is still alive; because ill dispositions which arise
from such causes are more formidable than anything else
whatsoever, and to hold them in check great precautions are
required; whereas its other ill dispositions are easy to handle
when there are no leaders to whom the populace can appeal.
Because, though in one sense there is nothing more formidable than the masses[a] disorganized and without a head, in
another sense there is nothing more weak. For it should be
easy to restore order, even though they have arms in their
hands, provided you have some stronghold in which to seek
refuge from their first onslaught, since, when their ardour
cools off a little, and each sees the other turning back to go
home, they begin to lose confidence and to look to their own
safety either by taking flight or by coming to terms.

If, then, an excited crowd wants to avoid these dangers, it
should at once make one of its members a leader so that he
may correct this defect, keep the populace united, and look to
its defence; as did the Roman plebs, when, after the death of
Virginia they quitted Rome and for safety's sake appointed
twenty of their members as tribunes. If this be not done, what
Titus Livy says in the passage quoted above, always comes
about, i.e., when together all are strong, but when each begins to
consider the danger he is in, they become cowardly and weak.

[a] *una moltitudine.* The terms '*plebe*', '*popolo*', '*una moltitudine*' and '*la
moltitudine*' are used here as more or less synonymous. One might almost
translate 'the mob'. [Walker had translated 'a crowd', which is too
neutral, although 'mob' is too pejorative. I prefer 'masses' (as he
himself renders *moltitudine* in the next section); some shades of meaning
are important: Machiavelli is really saying that 'the masses can never
become a people while they act like a mob'. B.R.C.]

58. *The Masses*[a] *are more Knowing and more Constant than is a Prince*

NOTHING is more futile and more inconstant than are the masses. So says our author, Titus Livy, and so say all other historians. For in the records of the actions men have performed one often finds the masses condemning someone to death, and then lamenting him and ardently wishing he were alive. The Roman people did this in Manlius Capitolinus's case: first they condemned him to death, then urgently wished him back. Of this our author says that 'soon after he had ceased to be a danger, the desire for him took hold of the people'. And again, when describing the events which happened in Syracuse after the death of Hieronymus, the nephew of Hiero, he says: 'It is of the nature of the masses either servilely to obey or arrogantly to domineer.'

I know not whether the view I am about to adopt will prove so hard to uphold and so full of difficulties that I shall have either shamefully to abandon it or laboriously to maintain it; for I propose to defend a position which all writers attack, as I have said. But, however that may be, I think, and always shall think there can be no harm in defending an opinion by arguments so long as one has no intention of appealing either to authority or force.

I claim, then, that for the failing for which writers blame the masses, any body of men one cares to select may be blamed, and especially princes; for anyone who does not regulate his conduct by laws will make the same mistakes as the masses are guilty of. This is easily seen, for there are and have been any number of princes, but of good and wise ones there have been but few. I am speaking of princes who have succeeded in breaking the bonds which might have held them

[a] *la moltitudine.*

in check; among which I do not include those kings who were born in Egypt when that most ancient of ancient realms was governed in accordance with the law, nor those born in Sparta, nor those born in France in our own times, for the kingdom of France is better regulated by laws than is any other of which at present we have knowledge. Kings who are born under such conditions are not to be classed among those whose nature we have to consider in each individual case to see whether it resembles that of the masses; for, should there be masses regulated by laws in the same way as they are, there will be found in them the same goodness as we find in kings, and it will be seen that they neither 'arrogantly dominate nor servilely obey'. Such was the Roman populace which, so long as the republic remained uncorrupt, was never servilely obsequious, nor yet did it ever dominate with arrogance: on the contrary, it had its own institutions and magistrates and honourably kept its own place. But when it was necessary to take action against some powerful person, it did so, as is seen in the case of Manlius, of the Ten, and in the case of others who sought to oppress it. Also, when it had to obey dictators or consuls in the public interest, it did so. Nor is it any wonder that the Roman populace wanted Manlius Capitolinus back when he was dead, for what they wanted was his virtues, which had been such that his memory evoked everyone's sympathy, and would have had power to produce the same effect in a prince, for all writers are of opinion that virtue is praised and admired even in one's enemies. Again, had Manlius, in response to this desire, been raised from the dead, the Roman populace would have passed on him the same sentence as it did, have had him arrested and, shortly after, have condemned him to death: though, for that matter, one also finds that reputedly wise princes have put people to death and then wished them alive again; Alexander, for instance, in the case of Cleitus and other of his friends, and

Herod in the case of Mariamne. But the truth is that what our historian says of the nature of the masses is not said of the masses when disciplined by laws, as were the Romans, but of undisciplined masses, like those of Syracuse, which made the same kind of mistakes as do men when infuriated and undisciplined, just as did Alexander the Great and Herod in the cases cited.[35]

The nature of the masses, then, is no more reprehensible than is the nature of princes, for all do wrong and to the same extent when there is nothing to prevent them doing wrong. Of this there are plenty of examples besides those given, both among the Roman emperors and among other tyrants and princes; and in them we find a degree of inconstancy and changeability in behaviour such as is never found in the masses.

I arrive, then, at a conclusion contrary to the common opinion which asserts that populaces, when in power, are variable, fickle and ungrateful; and affirm that in them these faults are in no wise different from those to be found in certain princes. Were the accusation made against both the masses and princes, it would be true; but, if princes be excepted, it is false. For when the populace is in power and is well-ordered, it will be stable, prudent and grateful, in much the same way, or in a better way, than is a prince, however wise he be thought. And, on the other hand, a prince who contemns the laws, will be more ungrateful, fickle and imprudent than is the populace. Nor is inconstancy of behaviour due to a difference in nature, for they are pretty much the same, or, if one be better than the other, it is the populace: it is due to the greater or less respect which they have for the laws under which both alike are living.

If we consider the Roman populace it will be found that for four hundred years they were enemies to the very name of king and lovers of glory and of the common good of their country. Of both characteristics the Roman populace affords

RELIABILITY OF PRINCES AND PEOPLES   I.58

numerous and striking examples. And, should anyone bring
up against me the ingratitude the populace displayed towards
Scipio, my answer is that I have already discussed this question
at length and have there shown the ingratitude of the populace
to be less than that of princes. While in the matter of prudence
and stability I claim that the populace is more prudent, more
stable, and of sounder judgement than the prince. Not without
good reason is the voice of the populace likened to that of
God; for public opinion is remarkably accurate in its prognos-
tications, so much so that it seems as if the populace by some
hidden power discerned the evil and the good that was to
befall it. With regard to its judgement, when two speakers of
equal skill are heard advocating different alternatives, very
rarely does one find the populace failing to adopt the better
view or incapable of appreciating the truth of what it hears.
While, if in bold actions and such as appear advantageous it
errs, as I have said above, so does a prince often err where
his passions are involved, and these are much stronger than
those of the populace.

It is found, too, that in the election of magistrates the
populace makes a far better choice than does the prince; nor
can the populace ever be persuaded that it is good to appoint
to such an office a man of infamous life or corrupt habits,
whereas a prince may easily and in a vast variety of ways be
persuaded to do this. Again, one finds that when the populace
begins to have a horror of something it remains of the same
mind for many centuries; a thing that is never observed in the
case of a prince. For both these characteristics I shall content
myself with the evidence afforded by the Roman populace,
which in the course of so many hundreds of years and so
many elections of consuls and tribunes did not make four
elections of which it had to repent. So much, too, as I have said,
was the title of king hated that no service rendered by one of
its citizens who ambitioned it, could render him immune

from the penalties prescribed. Besides this, one finds that cities in which the populace is the prince, in a very short time extend vastly their dominions much more than do those which have always been under a prince; as Rome did after the expulsion of the kings, and Athens after it was free of Pisistratus.

This can only be due to one thing: government by the populace is better than government by princes. Nor do I care whether to this opinion of mine all that our historian has said in the aforesaid passage or what others have said, be objected; because if account be taken of all the disorders due to populaces and of all those due to princes, and of all the glories won by populaces and all those won by princes, it will be found that alike in goodness and in glory the populace is far superior. And if princes are superior to populaces in drawing up laws, codes of civic life, statutes and new institutions, the populace is so superior in sustaining what has been instituted, that it indubitably adds to the glory of those who have instituted them.

In short, to bring this topic to a conclusion, I say that, just as princely forms of government have endured for a very long time, so, too, have republican forms of government; and that in both cases it has been essential for them to be regulated by laws. For a prince who does what he likes is a lunatic, and a populace which does what it likes is unwise. If, therefore, it be a question of a prince subservient to the laws and of a populace chained up by laws, more virtue will be found in the populace than in the prince; and if it be a question of either of them loosed from control by the law, there will be found fewer errors in the populace than in the prince, and these of less moment and much easier to put right. For a licentious and turbulent populace, when a good man can obtain a hearing, can easily be brought to behave itself; but there is no one to talk to a bad prince, nor is there any remedy except the sword. From which an inference may be drawn in regard

to the importance of their respective maladies; for, if to cure
the malady of the populace a word suffices and the sword is
needed to cure that of a prince, no one will fail to see that
the greater the cure, the greater the fault.

When the populace has thrown off all restraint, it is not the
mad things it does that are terrifying, nor is it of present evils
that one is afraid, but of what may come of them, for amidst
such confusion there may come to be a tyrant. In the case of
bad princes it is just the opposite: it is present evils that are
terrifying, but for the future there is hope, since men are
convinced that the evil ways of a bad prince may make for
freedom in the end. Thus one sees the difference between the
two cases amounts to the same thing as the difference between
what is and what must come to be. The brutalities of the masses
are directed against those whom they suspect of conspiring
against the common good; the brutalities of a prince against
those whom he suspects of conspiring against his own good.[36]
The reason why people are prejudiced against the populace is
because of the populace anyone may speak ill without fear and
openly, even when the populace is ruling. But of princes people
speak with the utmost trepidation and the utmost reserve.

Nor does it seem to me foreign to my purpose, since I find
the topic attractive, to discuss in the next chapter on which
more reliance can be placed, on confederations made by a
republic or on confederations formed by a prince.

59. What Confederations or Leagues can be trusted most; those made with a Republic or those made with a Prince

SINCE it happens every day that a prince forms a league or
an alliance with another prince, or a republic with some other
republic; and in like manner confederations and agreements
are made between a republic and a prince: I should, I think,

inquire which contracts are the more stable and on which ought more store to be set, on those made by a republic or on those made by a prince. All things considered, I believe that in many cases they are alike, but that in some there is a difference. Furthermore, I believe that forced agreements will be kept neither by a prince nor by a republic. I believe that when they come to be afraid for the safety of their estate, both the one and the other, rather than lose it, will break their agreement with you, and treat you with ingratitude.

Demetrius, who was called the conqueror of cities, had conferred endless benefits on the Athenians. But, when, later, he was beaten by his enemies and sought refuge in Athens, a friendly city which was under an obligation to him, it refused to admit him, a thing that caused him more pain than did the loss of his people and the loss of his army.

After Pompey was beaten by Caesar in Thessaly, he sought refuge with Ptolemy in Egypt, whom, earlier on, he had reinstated in his kingdom; and was killed by him. These events were clearly due to the same causes; yet more consideration and less injustice was displayed by the republic than by the prince.

It will be found, then, that where there is fear there is in fact the same attitude towards contracts. And, should one find either a prince or a republic facing ruin in order to keep a contract, this, too, may be due to like causes. It may well happen, for instance, in the case of a prince that he is the ally of some powerful prince who has no opportunity of defending him at the time, but by whom he may hope to be restored to his principality in due course; or, again, having acted as one of his partisans, he may think it impossible to find one of the prince's enemies with whom he can make an agreement or come to terms.

This was the lot of all those princes of the kingdom of Naples who espoused the cause of the French. It was also, in the case of republics, the lot of Saguntum in Spain which saw itself ruined because it had espoused the cause of Rome; and of Florence owing to her having in 1512 remained loyal to the cause of the French.

If all things be taken into account, however, I am of opinion that in cases in which there is imminent danger, republics will be found to be more reliable than princes. For though republics may have the same intention and the same desire as a prince, they are slower to act and take more time than a prince in arriving at a decision. Consequently they take more time over the breaking of a treaty than does a prince. Confederations are dissolved for the sake of some advantage, and in this republics abide by their agreements far better than do princes. Instances might be cited of treaties broken by princes for a very small advantage, and of treaties which have not been broken by a republic for a very great advantage.

This happened in regard to a proposal which Themistocles laid before the Athenians, to whom he announced in a speech that he had a piece of advice to give them which would be of great advantage to their country, but that he dare not mention it in public, for, if he did, it might spoil their chance of acting on it. Hence the Athenians deputed Aristides to hear what he had to say, and to decide what to do about it according to what he thought of the proposal. Themistocles then pointed out that the warships of all Greece, with respect to which they had treaty obligations, lay in a place where they could easily get hold of and destroy them, which would make the Athenians masters of that country. When Aristides reported to the people that Themistocles' plan was highly advantageous, but extremely dishonest, the people on this account would have nothing at all to do with it.

Philip of Macedon would not have acted thus.[37] Nor would other princes who in their enterprises and conquests have gained more by breaking their word than by any other device.

I say nothing of pacts which are allowed to lapse through non-observance, since this is the ordinary thing. I am speaking of those which are broken for some reason outside the ordinary; and with respect to these am of opinion, in view of what I have said above, that the populace is guilty of fewer faults than is the prince, and that, in consequence, it is more to be trusted than is a prince.

60. *That the Consulate and all Other Offices in Rome were conferred without Respect to Age*

IT is attested by historical records that after the consulate had been thrown open to the plebs the Roman republic granted it to its citizens without respect either to age or to birth. In Rome indeed no attention had ever been paid to age: what it had always looked for was virtue, whether in the young or in the old. Valerius Corvinus, who was made consul in his twenty-third year, bears witness to this, for he said in a speech to his troops, that the consulate was 'the reward of virtue, not of birth'.

Whether this practice is to be commended or not is open to no small question. It was necessity that constrained the Romans to disregard birth; and the necessity Rome experienced should be operative in every state that would meet with the same success that Rome had, as has been remarked on other occasions. For one cannot put men to inconvenience without rewarding them, nor can they be deprived of the hope of obtaining the reward without danger. It soon became expedient, therefore, to give the plebs cause to hope for the consulate, a hope which it entertained for a while without having the consulate. This then failed to suffice, and it became expedient to give it effect. Should a state not avail itself of its plebs in any glorious undertaking, it can treat it as it likes, – a point we have made elsewhere. But if it wants to do what Rome did, it must make no such distinction.

This being granted, nothing can be adduced in favour of a distinction in regard to age. On the contrary, it is necessary to disregard it; for in appointing a young man to a post which demands the prudence of an older man, it will be found that, should the masses have to elect, they will give the post to one who has performed some noteworthy actions. And when a young man is of such virtue that some noteworthy deed of his has become a matter of public knowledge, it would be most harmful if the state could not then avail itself of him, but should have to wait till he had grown old and had lost that vigour of mind and that expeditiousness of which his country at the time could have made good use. Thus Rome made use of Valerius Corvinus, of Scipio, of Pompey and of many others who won triumphs as very young men.

Book Two

Book Two is concerned with 'the means Rome took to increase its Empire'. It is based on the account Livy gives of
the wars in which Rome was engaged.

As in Book One the Discourses have been grouped under
headings which are not to be found in the text.

L.J.W.

Book Two

[THE GROWTH
OF ROME'S EMPIRE]

[*The Preface*]

MEN always, but not always with good reason, praise bygone days and criticize the present, and so partial are they to the past that they not only admire past ages the knowledge of which has come down to them in written records, but also, when they grow old, what they remember having seen in their youth. And, when this view is wrong, as it usually is, there are, I am convinced, various causes to which the mistake may be due.

The first of them is, I think, this. The whole truth about olden times is not grasped, since what redounds to their discredit is often passed over in silence, whereas what is likely to make them appear glorious is pompously recounted in all its details. For so obsequious are most writers to the fortune of conquerors that, in order to make their victories seem glorious, they not only exaggerate their own valorous deeds, but also magnify the exploits of the enemy, so that anyone born afterwards either in the conquering or in the conquered province may find cause to marvel at such men and such times, and is bound, in short, to admire them and to feel affection for them.

Another reason is that, since it is either through fear or through envy that men come to hate things, in the case of the past the two most powerful incentives for hating it are lacking, since the past cannot hurt you nor give you cause for envy. Whereas it is otherwise with events in which you play a part and which you see with your own eyes, for of these you have an intimate knowledge, are in touch with every detail, and in them find, mingled with the good, also much which displeases you; so that you cannot help thinking them far inferior to the remote past, even though in fact the present may be much more deserving of praise and renown. I am not here referring to what pertains to the arts, for in themselves they have so much lustre that time can scarce take away or add much to the glory which they themselves deserve. I am speaking of things appertaining to human life and human customs, the evidence for whose merit is not so clear to one's eyes.

My answer is, then, that it is true there exists this habit of praising the past and criticizing the present, and not always true that to do so is a mistake, for it must be admitted that sometimes such a judgement is valid because, since human affairs are ever in a state of flux, they move either upwards or downwards. Thus one sees a city or a province that has been endowed with a sound political constitution by some eminent man, thanks to its founder's virtue for a time go on steadily improving. Anyone born in such a state at such a time, is wrong if he gives more praise to the past than to the present, and his mistake will be due to the causes we have mentioned above. But those who are born in this city or province later on, when there has come a time in which it is on the decline and is deteriorating, will not then be in error.

When I reflect that it is in this way that events pursue their course it seems to me that the world has always been in the same condition, and that in it there has been just as much good as there is evil, but that this evil and this good has varied from province to province. This may be seen from the knowledge we have of ancient kingdoms, in which the balance of good and evil changed from one to the other owing to changes in their customs, whereas the world as a whole remained the same. The only difference was that the world's virtue first found a home in Assyria, then flourished in Media and later in Persia, and at length arrived in Italy and Rome. And, if since the Roman empire there has been no other which has lasted, and in which the world's virtue has been centred, one none the less finds it distributed among many nations where men lead virtuous lives. There was, for instance, the kingdom of the Franks; the kingdom of the Turks, [i.e.] that of the Sultan; and today all the peoples of Germany. Earlier still there were the Saracens, who performed such great exploits and occupied so much of the world, since they broke up the Roman empire in the East. Hence, after ruin had overtaken the Romans, there continued to exist in all these provinces and in all these separate units, and still exists in some of them, that virtue which is desired and quite rightly praised. If, then, anyone born there praises the past over and above the present, he may well be mistaken; but anyone born in Italy who has not become at heart an ultramontane, or anyone born in Greece who has not become at heart a Turk, has good reason to criticize his own times and to praise others, since in the latter there are plenty of things to evoke his admiration, whereas in the former he comes across nothing but extreme misery, infamy and contempt, for there is no observance either of religion or of the laws, or of military traditions, but all is besmirched with filth of every kind. And so much the more are these vices detestable when they are more prevalent among those who sit on the judgement seat, prescribe rules for others, and expect from them adoration.

But to return to our main point, I maintain that if man's judgement is biased when he tries to decide which is the better, the present age, or some past age of which he cannot have so perfect a knowledge as he has of his own times precisely because it is long since past, this ought not to bias the judgement of old men when they compare the days of their youth with those of their old age, for of both they have had the same knowledge and experience. Nor would it in point of fact, if during the various phases of their lives men judged always in the same way and had the same appetites. But, as men's appetites change, even though their circumstances remain the same, it is impossible that things should look the same to them seeing that they have other appetites, other interests, other standpoints, from what they had in their youth. For, since, when men grow old, they lack energy but increase in judgement and prudence, it is inevitable that what in their youth appeared to be tolerable and good, in their old age should become intolerable and bad; so that, instead of blaming the times, they should lay the blame on their own judgement.

Furthermore, human appetites are insatiable, for by nature we are so constituted that there is nothing we cannot long for, but by fortune we are such that of these things we can attain but few. The result is that the human mind is perpetually discontented, and of its possessions is apt to grow weary. This makes it find fault with the present, praise the past, and long for the future; though for its doing so no rational cause can be assigned. Hence I am not sure but that I deserve to be reckoned among those who thus deceive themselves if in these my discourses I have praised too much the days of the ancient Romans and have found fault with our own. Indeed, if the virtue which then prevailed and the vices which are prevalent today were not as clear as the sun, I should be more reserved in my statements lest I should fall into the very fault for which I am blaming others. But as the facts are there for any one to see, I shall make so bold as to declare plainly what I think of those days and of our own, so that the minds of young men who read what I have written may turn from the one and prepare to imitate the other whenever fortune provides them with occasion for so doing. For it is the duty of a good man to point out to others what is well done, even though the malignity of the times or of fortune has not permitted you to do it for yourself, to the end that, of the many who have the capacity, some one, more beloved of heaven, may be able to do it.

Having, therefore, in the discourses of the last book spoken of the decisions the Romans came to in regard to the internal affairs of the city, in this we shall speak of the measures the Roman people took to increase their empire.

Book Two

[METHODS OF EXPANSION]

---

1. Whether Virtue or Fortune was the Principal Cause of the Empire which Rome acquired

MANY are of opinion, and among them Plutarch, a writer of great weight, that the Roman people was indebted for the empire it acquired rather to fortune than to virtue. Among other reasons he adduces he says that the Roman people by their own confession admit this since they ascribed all their victories to fortune, and erected more temples to Fortune than to any other god. It would seem that with this view Livy also agrees, for rarely does he put into the mouth of any Roman a speech in which he tells of virtue without conjoining fortune with it.

With this view I cannot by any means agree, nor do I think it can be upheld. For if there is nowhere to be found a republic so successful as was Rome, this is because there is nowhere to be found a republic so constituted as to be able to make the conquests Rome made. For it was the virtue of her armies that caused Rome to acquire an empire, and it was her constitutional procedure and the peculiar customs which she owed to her first legislator that enabled her to maintain what she had acquired, as will be explained at length in many of the discourses which follow.

The aforesaid writers claim that Rome's never having been engaged in two very big wars at one and the same time was due to the fortune, not to the virtue, of the Roman people; for there was no war with the Latins until Rome had so thoroughly beaten the Samnites that she had to go to war in their defence. Nor did the Romans fight the Tuscans until the Latins had been subjugated and the Samnites were almost entirely exhausted by frequent defeats; yet had two of these powers, while yet intact and vigorous, united together, it is easy to conjecture, nor can one doubt, that it would have meant ruin for the Roman republic. Anyhow, however it came about, it is a fact that the Romans never had two very big wars going on at the same time; on the contrary, one finds that either when one began the other faded out, or that when one faded out the other began. This can easily be seen from the order in which their wars took place. For, setting aside those waged before Rome was taken by the Gauls, we see that, while they were fighting with the Aequi and the Volsci, no other people attacked them so long as the Aequi and Volsci were strong. It was only after they were beaten that the war with the Samnites arose; and although before this war was over the Latin peoples rebelled against the Romans, yet, when this rebellion occurred, the Samnites were already in alliance with Rome and with their armies helped the Romans to subjugate Latin insolence. When they had been subjugated, the war with Samnium flared up again. And when the forces of the Samnites were beaten owing to the many routes inflicted on them, war with the Tuscans broke out; and, when this was settled, the Samnites started a fresh one, owing to the arrival of Pyrrhus in Italy. On Pyrrhus being repulsed and sent back to Greece, they started on their first war with the Carthaginians; and, scarce was this war over, when all the Gauls, both from this and from the other side of the Alps, conspired against the Romans, with the result that they were defeated with immense slaughter between Popolonia and Pisa, where the tower of St Vincent now stands. When this war ended, they had no war of any importance for the space of twenty years, for they fought with no one except the Ligurians and what remained of the Gauls in Lombardy. Matters stood thus until the second Punic war, which led to Italy's being occupied for sixteen years. When this came to an end amid great glory, the Macedonian war broke out, and, when this was over, there came the war with Antiochus and with Asia. After which victories there remained in the whole world neither princes nor republics which, either alone or all together, could successfully oppose the forces of Rome.

If, before the final victory, we consider well the order in which these wars took place and the Roman method of procedure, it will be seen that in them, mingled with fortune, was virtue and prudence of a very high order. Hence, if one looks for the cause of this fortune, it should be easy to find. For it is quite certain that, when a prince and a people has acquired such repute that each of the neighbouring princes and peoples is afraid to attack it and fears it, no one will ever assault it unless driven thereunto by necessity; so that it will be open, so to speak, to that power to choose the neighbour on which it seems best to make war, and industriously to foster tranquillity among the rest. In this, owing in part to the respect they have for its power, and in part to their being deceived by the means it takes to lull them to sleep, they readily acquiesce. For other powers, which are farther away and have no intercourse with it, look on the affair as remote from their interests and as no concern of theirs; and in this error they remain until the conflagration is at their doors. Nor, when it arrives, have they any means of stopping it except by their own forces, which will then be inadequate, since the state in question has now become very powerful.

I do not propose to deal with the Samnites, who stood by, watching the Roman people overcome the Volsci and the Aequi; and lest I should be too prolix, only the Carthaginians, who were already a great power and in great esteem when the Romans were fighting the Samnites and the Tuscans, for they held the whole of Africa, held Sardinia and Sicily, and had dominion over part of Spain. This their power, conjoined with the fact that they were remote from the confines of the Roman people, accounts for their never having thought of attacking the Romans, or of helping the Samnites and Tuscans. On the contrary, they acted as men do when things seem to be moving rapidly in another's favour, namely, came to terms with her, and sought her friendship. Nor was the mistake thus made at the outset realized until the Romans had conquered all the peoples that lay between them and the Carthaginians and they began to contend with each other for the dominion of Sicily and Spain. The same thing happened to the Gauls, to Philip, king of Macedon, and to Antiochus as happened to the Carthaginians. Whilst Rome was engaged with some other state, each of them thought the other state would beat Rome, and that they had time enough to protect themselves against her either by peaceful or by warlike methods. I am of opinion, therefore, that the fortune which Rome had in these matters, all rulers would have who should emulate Roman methods and should be imbued with the same virtue.

I should point out in this connection how the Romans behaved on entering foreign provinces, had I not spoken of it at length in my treatise on principalities,[38] for I have there discussed the question fully. Here I shall make but this remark in passing. The Romans always took care to have in new provinces some friend to act as a ladder up which to climb or a door by which to enter, or as a means whereby to hold it. Thus we see that with the help of the Capuans they got into Samnium, of the Camertini into Tuscany, of the Mamertini into Sicily, of the Saguntines into Spain, of Masinissa into Africa, of the Aetolians into Greece, of Eumenes and other princes into Asia, of the Massilians and the Aedui into Gaul. Hence they never lacked supporters of this kind to facilitate their enterprise alike in acquiring the province and in holding it. Peoples who observe such customs will be found to have less need of fortune than those who do not observe them well.

That everyone may the better know how much more virtue helped the Romans to acquire their empire than did fortune, we shall in the next chapter discuss the character of the peoples with whom they had to fight, and show how obstinate they were in defending their liberty.

2. Concerning the Kind of People the Romans had to fight, and how obstinately they defended their Freedom

NOTHING made it harder for the Romans to conquer the peoples of the central and outlying parts of Italy than the love which in those times many peoples had for liberty. So obstinately did they defend it that only by outstanding virtue could they ever have been subjugated. For numerous instances show to what dangers they exposed themselves in order to maintain or to recover it, and what vendettas they kept up against those who had taken it away. The study of history reveals, too, the harm that servitude has done to peoples and to cities. There is, indeed, in our own times only one country which can be said to have in it free cities, whereas in ancient times quite a number of genuinely free peoples were to be found in all countries. One sees how in the times of which we are speaking at present the peoples of Italy from the Apennines which now divide Tuscany from Lombardy, right down to its toe, were all of them free. The Tuscans, the Romans, the Samnites were, for instance, and so were many other peoples who dwelt in other parts of Italy. One never hears of there being any kings, apart from those who reigned in Rome, and Porsenna, the king of Tuscany, whose stock became extinct, though history does not tell us how. It is quite clear, however, that at the time when the Romans laid siege to Veii, Tuscany was free. Moreover, it enjoyed its freedom so much, and so hated the title of prince, that, when the people of Veii appointed a king in that city for the purpose of defence, and asked the Tuscans to help them against the Romans, the Tuscans after many consultations had been held, decided not to give help to the people of Veii so long as they lived under a king, since they held that they could not well defend a country whose people had already placed themselves in subjection to someone else.

It is easy to see how this affection of peoples for self-government[a] comes about, for experience shows that cities have never increased either in dominion or wealth, unless they have been independent. It is truly remarkable to observe the greatness which Athens attained in the space of a hundred years after it had been liberated from the tyranny of Pisistratus. But most marvellous of all is it to observe the greatness which Rome attained after freeing itself from its kings. The reason is easy to understand; for it is not the well-being of individuals that makes cities great, but the well-being of the community; and it is beyond question that it is only in republics that the common good is looked to properly in that all that promotes it is carried out; and, however much this or that private person may be the loser on this account, there are so many who benefit thereby that the common good can be realized in spite of those few who suffer in consequence.

The opposite happens where there is a prince; for what he does in his own interests usually harms the city, and what is done in the interests of the city harms him. Consequently, as

[a] *del vivere libero.*

soon as tyranny replaces self-government ^a the least of the evils which this tyranny brings about are that it ceases to make progress and to grow in power and wealth: more often than not, nay always, what happens is that it declines. And should fate decree the rise of an efficient^b tyrant, so energetic and so proficient in warfare^c that he enlarges his dominions, no advantage will accrue to the commonwealth, but only to himself, for he cannot bestow honours on the valiant and good citizens over whom he tyrannizes, since he does not want to have any cause to suspect them. Nor yet can he allow the cities he acquires to make their submission to, or to become the tributaries of, the city of which he is the tyrant, for to make it powerful is not to his interest. It is to his interest to keep the state divided so that each town and each district may recognize only him as its ruler. In this way he alone profits by his acquisitions, not his country. Should anyone desire to confirm this view by a host of further arguments, let him read Xenophon's treatise *On Tyrannicide*.[39]

It is no wonder, then, that peoples of old detested tyrants and gave them no peace, or that they were so fond of liberty and held the word itself in such esteem, as happened when Hieronymus, the grandson of Hiero, the Syracusan, was killed in Syracuse, and the news of his death came to his army which was then not very far from Syracuse. At first there was a tumult, and men took up arms against those who had killed him, but when they perceived that in Syracuse the cry was for liberty, they were so delighted to hear the word, that all became quiet, and, setting aside their anger against the tyrannicides, they began to consider how self-government could be organized in that city.

Nor is it surprising that peoples are so extraordinarily revengeful towards those who have destroyed their liberty. Of this there are numerous examples, but I propose to give

^a *uno vivere libero.* ^b *virtuoso.* ^c *per virtù d'arme.*

but one, which happened in Corcyra, a city of Greece, during the Peloponnesian war. Greece was then divided into two parties, of which one supported the Athenians, the other the Spartans. The result was that in many cities internal dissensions arose, some advocating an alliance with Sparta, others an alliance with Athens. This happened in Corcyra, where the nobles got the upper hand, and deprived the populace of its liberty. But with the help of the Athenians the populace regained their strength, laid hands on all the nobles, and shut them up in one prison which held them all. Then they took them, eight or ten at a time, on the plea of banishing them to various parts, and then to set an example put them to death with much cruelty. When those who were left heard of this, they considered whether there was any possible way in which they could escape this ignominious death. So, having armed themselves with anything at hand, they defended the entrance to the prison, and fought with those who tried to get in. The result was that, when rumours of this reached the populace, they came in a crowd, removed the upper storey and roof from the building, and smothered the inmates beneath the ruins. Many well-known instances of a like horrible nature happened later in this country. We thus see how true it is that a liberty which you have actually had taken away is avenged with much greater ferocity than is a liberty which someone has only tried to take away.

If one asks oneself how it comes about that peoples of old were more fond of liberty than they are today, I think the answer is that it is due to the same cause that makes men today less bold than they used to be; and this is due, I think, to the difference between our education and that of bygone times, which is based on the difference between our religion and the religion of those days. For our religion, having taught us the truth and the true way of life, leads us to ascribe less esteem to worldly honour. Hence the gentiles, who held it in high

esteem and looked upon it as their highest good,[a] displayed
in their actions more ferocity than we do. This is evidenced
by many of their institutions. To begin with, compare the
magnificence of their sacrifices with the humility that
characterizes ours. The ceremonial in ours is delicate rather
than imposing, and there is no display of ferocity or courage.
Their ceremonies lacked neither pomp nor magnificence, but,
conjoined with this, were sacrificial acts in which there was
much shedding of blood and much ferocity; and in them
great numbers of animals were killed. Such spectacles,
because terrible, caused men to become like them. Besides,
the old religion did not beatify men unless they were replete
with worldly glory: army commanders, for instance, and
rulers[b] of republics. Our religion has glorified humble and
contemplative men, rather than men of action. It has assigned
as man's highest good humility, abnegation, and contempt
for mundane things,[c] whereas the other identified it with
magnanimity, bodily strength, and everything else that
conduces to make men very bold. And, if our religion
demands that in you there be strength, what it asks for is
strength to suffer rather than strength to do bold things.[40]

This pattern of life, therefore, appears to have made the
world weak, and to have handed it over as a prey to the
wicked, who run it successfully and securely since they are
well aware that the generality of men, with paradise for their
goal, consider how best to bear, rather than how best to
avenge, their injuries. But, though it looks as if the world
were become effeminate and as if heaven were powerless,
this undoubtedly is due rather to the pusillanimity of those
who have interpreted our religion in terms of *laissez faire*,[d]
not in terms of *virtù*. For, had they borne in mind that
religion permits us to exalt and defend the fatherland, they

[a] *il sommo bene* – the 'summum bonum', a technical scholastic term.
[b] *principi.*   [c] *cose umane.*   [d] *l'ozio.*

would have seen that it also wishes us to love and honour it, and to train ourselves to be such that we may defend it.

This kind of education, then, and these grave misinterpretations account for the fact that we see in the world fewer republics than there used to be of old, and that, consequently, in peoples we do not find the same love of liberty as there then was. Yet I can well believe that it was rather the Roman empire, which, with its armed forces and its grandiose ideas, wiped out all republics and all their civic institutions, that was the cause of this. And though, later on, Rome's empire disintegrated, its cities have never been able to pull themselves together nor to set up again a constitutional regime,[a] save in one or two parts of that empire.

Anyhow, however this may be, the Romans encountered in all parts of the world, however small, a combination of well-armed republics, extremely obstinate in the defence of their liberty; which shows that, if the virtue of the Roman people had not been of a rare and very high order, they would never have been able to overcome them. Of instances which bear this out, I shall cite but one case, that of the Samnites. It is a remarkable thing, as Livy admits, that they should have been so powerful and their arms so strong that they were able to withstand the Romans right up to the time of Papirius Cursor, the consul, son of the first Papirius; i.e. to withstand them for the space of forty-six years in spite of many disastrous defeats, the destruction of towns and the slaughter of the inhabitants of their country, a slaughter so great that this country, in which there were formerly seen so many cities and so many inhabitants, was now almost deserted, whereas at one time, it was so well ordered and so strong that it would have been insuperable if it had not been confronted with a virtue such as Rome's.

[a] *riordinare alla vita civile.* [Again, this is 'constitution' as a way of life, not simply as legal powers. B.R.C.]

It is easy, moreover, to see whence arose that order and how this disorder came about. For it is all due to the independence which then was and to the servitude which now is. Because, as has been said before, all towns and all countries that are in all respects free, profit by this enormously. For, wherever increasing populations are found, it is due to the freedom with which marriage is contracted and to its being more desired by men. And this comes about where every man is ready to have children, since he believes that he can rear them and feels sure that his patrimony will not be taken away, and since he knows that not only will they be born free, instead of into slavery, but that, if they have virtue, they will have a chance of becoming rulers. One observes, too, how riches multiply and abound there, alike those that come from agriculture and those that are produced by the trades. For everybody is eager to acquire such things and to obtain property, provided he be convinced that he will enjoy it when it has been acquired. It thus comes about that, in competition one with the other, men look both to their own advantage and to that of the public; so that in both respects wonderful progress is made. The contrary of this happens in countries which live in servitude; and the harder the servitude the more does the well-being to which they are accustomed, dwindle.

Of all forms of servitude, too, that is the hardest which subjects you to a republic. First because it is more lasting, and there is no hope of escape; secondly because the aim of a republic is to deprive all other corporations of their vitality and to weaken them, to the end that its own body corporate may increase. A prince who makes you his subject, does not do this unless he be a barbarian who devastates the country and destroys all that man has done for civilization, as oriental princes do. On the contrary, if his institutions be humane and he behave constitutionally, he will more often than not be equally fond of all the cities that are subject to him, and will leave them in possession of all their trades and all their ancient institutions. So that, if they are unable to increase, as free cities do, they will not be ruined like those that are enslaved. I refer here to the servitude that befalls cities which are subject to a foreigner, for of those that are subject to one of their own citizens I have already spoken.

He who reflects, therefore, on all that has been said, will not wonder at the power the Samnites had when free, or at the weakness that befell them later, when they became a subject state. This Titus Livy attests in several places, particularly in his account of the war with Hannibal, where he shows how the Samnites, when they had been maltreated by a legion which lay at Nola, sent messengers to Hannibal to ask him to come to their aid. In their address they told him that for a hundred years they had been fighting the Romans with their own troops and their own officers, and that often they had held up two consular armies and two consuls, but that now they had come to such a pass that they could scarce hold their own against the small Roman legion that was at Nola.

3. Rome became a Great City by ruining the Cities round about her, and by granting Foreigners Easy Access to her Honours

'Rome meanwhile grows on the ruins of Alba.' Those who plan to convert a city into a great empire should use every available device to fill it with inhabitants; for unless a city has a large male population it cannot do much. There are two ways of acquiring a large population, by friendliness and by force. It is done by friendliness when the road is kept open and safe for foreigners who propose to come and dwell there so that everybody is glad to do so. It is done by force, when neighbouring cities are destroyed and their inhabitants are sent to dwell in your city. This custom was so studiously observed in Rome that, in the time of its sixth king, there dwelt in Rome eighty thousand men bearing arms. For in this the Romans sought to do as a good farmer does, who, that a plant may grow big and produce and mature its fruit, cuts off the first branches that are put forth so that its roots may gather virtue and in due course may produce greener and more fruitful branches.

That this method of providing for expansion and a future empire was both necessary and good is shown by the example of Sparta and Athens, two republics which were very well armed and governed by the best laws, yet never attained the greatness of the Roman empire, though Rome appears to have been more tumultuous and not so well governed as they were. For this no reason can be assigned other than that already adduced. For Rome, by pursuing these two ways of enlarging the composition of her city, was able to put under arms two hundred and eighty thousand men, whereas Sparta and Athens could never muster twenty thousand each. This was not due to Rome's being in a more advantageous position than was theirs, but simply to the difference in their modes of procedure. For Lycurgus, the founder of the Spartan republic, thought nothing more likely to frustrate his laws than the admixture of new inhabitants, and so did everything he could to prevent foreigners having any intercourse with the citizens. Not only was intermarriage forbidden, but also the admittance to civic rights and other forms of intercommunication which bring men together. In addition to which he instituted a coinage of leather, so that nobody might be tempted to come there with merchandise or any manufactured goods. Hence it was impossible for the inhabitants of that city ever to grow in number.

Since all our actions resemble those of nature, it is neither possible nor natural that a slender trunk should support a heavy branch. Hence a small republic cannot take possession of cities and kingdoms which are stronger and larger than itself: and, should it actually do so, it will happen as it does in the case of a tree which has a branch that is bigger than its trunk: it will support the branch with difficulty, and the least wind weakens it. This is just what happened to Sparta. It occupied all the cities of Greece. Then, when Thebes rebelled, all the other cities rebelled, and the trunk was left without branches. In Rome's case this could not happen, for it had so large a trunk that it could easily support any branch. This mode of procedure, therefore, together with others of which we shall presently speak, made Rome great and exceedingly powerful, as Titus Livy pithily points out when he says: 'Rome meanwhile grows on the ruins of Alba.'

4. Republics have adopted Three Methods of Expansion

THE student of ancient histories will find that there are three ways in which republics have expanded. The first was that which the Tuscans of old adopted, namely, that of forming a league consisting of several republics in which no one of them had preference, authority or [rank above the others; and in which, when other cities were acquired, they made them constituent members in the same way as the Swiss act in our times, and as in Greece the Achaeans and the Aetolians acted in olden times. Now, since the Romans made frequent war on the Tuscans, I shall pay special attention to them in order the better to show the nature of this first method.

Before the Romans established their imperium in Italy, the Tuscans were very powerful both by sea and by land. Though of their affairs history gives no exact account, there are one or two records and monuments which give some indication of their greatness. We know, for instance, that

they sent to the *mare superum*, a colony which they called
Adria, and that it was of such noble proportions that it gave
its name to that sea which is still called the 'Adriatic' by the
Latins. We likewise know that their arms held sway from
the Tiber right up to the foot of the Alps, which encircle here
the main portion of Italy, though they lost their *imperium* over
that country which is now called Lombardy two hundred
years before the Romans had acquired much power. For this
district was occupied by the Gauls, who, driven by necessity
or attracted by the sweetness of its fruit and especially of its
wine, invaded Italy under Bellovesus, their leader, defeated
and drove out the inhabitants, and settled in this region, where
they built many towns. They called this district 'Gaul', since
this was the name they then bore; and they held it till they
were conquered by the Romans. The Tuscans, therefore,
worked on the basis of equality, and, in expanding, followed
the first of the methods mentioned above. There were twelve
cities, and among others they included Chiusi, Veii, Arezzo,
Fiesole, Volterra and so forth, each of which, as a member of
the league, shared in the government of its empire. They never
succeeded, however, in extending their gains beyond Italy;
and of Italy, too, the greater part remained intact, for reasons
which will presently be given.

The second method consists in forming alliances in which
you reserve to yourself the headship, the seat in which the
central authority resides, and the right of initiative. This was
the method adopted by the Romans. The third method is to
make other states subjects instead of allies, as the Spartans and
the Athenians did. Of these three methods the last is quite
useless, as is seen in the case of the two republics just mentioned. For they came to disaster for the simple reason that
they had acquired a dominion which they could not hold.
For to undertake the responsibility of governing cities by
force, especially such as have been accustomed to self-

government, is a difficult and tiresome business. And unless
you have armed forces, and they are strong forces, you can
neither impose obedience on, nor rule, them. For, if this be
your plan, it is essential to have allies to assist you, and to
increase the population of your own city. Wherefore, since
these two cities did neither of these things, their mode of
procedure was futile. But, since Rome, which exemplifies the
second method, did both, she rose to exceedingly great power.
And, since she was the only state that thus behaved, she was
the only one that became so powerful. And, since she made
·many states her allies throughout the whole of Italy, which to
a large extent lived under the same laws, and since, on the
other hand, she reserved to herself, as has been said, the seat
of empire and the right to issue orders, these allies without
being aware of it, fell under her yoke and laboured and shed
their blood on her behalf. For when they began to go forth
with the armies of Italy and to transform kingdoms into
provinces and to make subjects of those who did not mind
being subjects since they were accustomed to live under
kings, and who, since they had Roman governors and had
been conquered by armies bearing the Roman insignia,
recognized no superior other than Rome, the result was that
Rome's allies inside Italy found themselves before long en-
circled by Roman subjects and with an immense city, such
as Rome had now become, towering above them; so that,
when they realized the mistake they had been making, it was
too late to put it right, so great was the authority Rome now
exercised over outside provinces and so great the force which
lay at her disposal within, since she had a city so enormous
and so extremely well armed. And though her allies, to
avenge their injuries, formed a league against her, they were
soon defeated in war, with the result that their position
became worse, for instead of being Rome's allies, they now
became Rome's subjects. This mode of procedure, as has been

said, has only been adopted by the Romans. Nor can a republic that wants to expand, adopt any other, for experience has shown that no other is so certain or so sure.

The alternative method of leagues, mentioned above and adopted by the Tuscans, the Achaeans, and the Aetolians, and today by the Swiss, is the next best to that of the Romans. For, though by this method it is impossible to expand indefinitely, it has two advantages. First, it does not readily involve you in war; secondly, you can easily hold as much as you take. The reason why such a republic cannot expand is that its members are distinct and each has its own capital; which makes it difficult for them to consult and to make decisions. It means also that they are less keen on acquiring dominion, for, since many communities share in that dominion, they do not appreciate further acquisitions in the same way as does a single republic which hopes to enjoy the whole. Furthermore, a league is governed by a council, which must needs be slower in arriving at any decision than are those who dwell within one and the same circle. Experience shows, too, that such a method of forming a confederation has a fixed limit, and that there is no case which indicates that this limit can be transcended. Twelve or fourteen communities join together, and beyond that they do not seek to go; for, having attained the stage at which it seems to them they can defend themselves against all comers, they do not try to extend their dominion, whether because necessity does not require them to have more power, or because they see no advantage in acquisitions for the reasons already given. For in that case they would have to do one of two things: either to proceed to get allies, which, owing to their number, would entail confusion; or to make others their subjects, which they do not care to do since in it they see difficulty and in having them no great advantage. Hence, when they have reached the number which appears to promise them security, they devote themselves to two things. (i) They accept and undertake the protection of those who apply for it, and by this means get from all around money which can easily be distributed among them. (ii) They also fight for others and take pay from a prince here and a prince there who is prepared to spend money on his enterprises.

This, as we see, is what the Swiss are doing today. It is also, as we read, what was done by the states mentioned above. Titus Livy bears witness to this when he tells us that, at a conference between Philip, king of Macedonia, and Titus Quintius Flaminius, they were talking together amicably in presence of a praetor from the Aetolians, and that, when this praetor came to speak with Philip, Philip upbraided him for the avarice and double-dealing of his people, alleging that the Aetolians had not been ashamed to fight on one side and then to let their men take service with its enemy; so that the insignia of the Aetolians were often seen in two armies which were opposed. We find, then, that this method of forming leagues has always been the same, and has led to the same results. We see, too, that this method of acquiring subjects has always entailed weakness and has produced but small advantages; and that those who went beyond the appropriate limit, were speedily ruined. Moreover, if this method of acquiring subjects is useless to republics that are armed, it is utterly useless to those that are without arms; as it has proved to be in the case of the Italian republics in our time.

It thus becomes clear that the proper method to adopt is that which the Romans adopted; which is so much the more remarkable in that it was never adopted before, and has never been imitated by anyone since Rome. As to leagues, they are only found among the Swiss, and in the Swabian league which has copied it. And, as will be said at the close of this topic a great many institutions observed in Rome, pertaining both to internal and to foreign affairs, are not only not imitated at the present time, but are deemed to be of no account, since some are looked on as fables, others as impracticable, others as irrelevant and useless; with the result that, owing to this ignorance, we [in Italy] have become the prey of anybody who has wanted to overrun this land. Yet, if to imitate the Roman way seems to be difficult, that of the Tuscans of old should not appear so difficult, especially to the Tuscans of today. For, though they were unable, for the reasons assigned, to form an empire like that of Rome, they did succeed in acquiring in Italy such power as this method of proceeding allowed. This method, too, was for a long time secure, resulting in the greatest glories of empire and of arms in the highest degree as well as customs and religious observances which are worthy of the highest praise. It was by the Gauls that this power and glory was first reduced, and by the Romans that it was extinguished; and so completely was it extinguished that great as was the power of the Tuscans two thousand years ago, of it at present there scarce remains a trace. Which leads me to consider how things come to be thus lost in oblivion, a point that will be discussed in the next chapter.[41]

5. Changes of Religion and of Language, together with such Misfortunes as Floods or Pestilences, obliterate the Records of the Past

To those philosophers who want to make out that the world is eternal, I think the answer might be that, if it really were as old as all this, it would be reasonable to expect there would be records going back further than five thousand years, did we not see how the records of times gone by are obliterated by diverse causes, of which some are due to men and some to heaven. Those which are due to men are changes in religious institutions and in language. For, when a new religious

institution comes into being, i.e. a new religion, its first care
is, for the sake of its own reputation, to wipe out the old one;
and, when the founders of a new religion happen to speak a
different tongue, the old one is easily abolished. This becomes
clear if we consider the measures which Christianity adopted
vis-à-vis Paganism; how it abolished all pagan institutions, all
pagan rites, and destroyed the records of the theology of the
ancients. It is true that Christianity did not succeed in wiping
out altogether the record of what outstanding men of the old
religion had done; which was due to the retention of the Latin
language, for this they had to retain so that they might use it
in writing down their new laws. Had they been able to write
them in a new tongue, there would, if we bear in mind the
way they persecuted in other matters, have been no record of
the past left at all.

Whoever reads of the measures taken by Saint Gregory and
other heads of the Christian religion, will see what a fuss they
made about getting rid of all records of the past, how they
burnt the works of poets and historians, destroyed images
and spoiled everything else that betokened in any way antiquity. So much so that, if to this persecution there had been
conjoined a new language, in a short time one would have
found all traces of the past wiped out. One can well believe,
therefore, that what Christianity did with regard to Paganism,[42] Paganism did to the religion that preceded it; and, as
there have been two or three changes of religion in five or
six thousand years, the record of what happened before that
has been lost; or, if of it there remains a trace, it is regarded
as a fable and no credence is given to it; as has happened with
regard to the *History of Diodorus Siculus*, which covers a
period of some forty or fifty thousand years, but is looked
upon as untrustworthy, as I believe it to be.

The causes due to heaven are those which wipe out a whole
generation and reduce the inhabitants in certain parts of the

world to but a few. This is brought about by pestilence or by famine or by a flood and of these the most important is the last alike because it is more widespread and because those who survive are all of them rude mountain-dwellers who have no knowledge of antiquity and so cannot hand it down to posterity; and should there be among the survivors anyone who has such knowledge he will conceal it or distort it in his own fashion so as to establish his own reputation and that of his family, with the result that there will remain to his successors just so much as he has chosen to record and nothing more.

That these floods, pestilences and famines happen, I do not think anyone can doubt, for plenty of them are recorded everywhere in history, their effect in obliterating the past is plain to see, and it seems reasonable that it should be so. For, as in the case of simple bodies, when nature has accumulated too much superfluous material, it frequently acts in the same way and by means of a purge restores health to the body. Similarly in the case of that body which comprises a mixture of human races, when every province is replete with inhabitants who can neither obtain a livelihood nor move elsewhere since all other places are occupied and full up, and when the craftiness and malignity of man has gone as far as it can go, the world must needs be purged in one of these three ways, so that mankind, being reduced to comparatively few and humbled by adversity, may adopt a more appropriate form of life and grow better.

There was, then, as we have said before, a time when Tuscany was a powerful country, full of religion and of virtue, with its own customs and its own language, all of which we know was wiped out by the power of Rome, so that of it, as has been said, there remains nought but the remembrance of its name.

Book Two

[DISCOURSES 6–10]

[COLONIZATION AND WAR:
ITS CAUSES AND COST]

---

6. How the Romans proceeded in the waging of War

HAVING discussed the procedure which the Romans adopted in expanding their dominions, I shall now discuss the procedure they adopted in conducting a war. As in all their actions it will be seen here how wise they were to depart from generally accepted methods in order to pave the way to greatness of the highest order. The aim of those who make war by choice or from ambition is to get something, and to keep what they acquire; and in this to proceed in such a way that the country, which is their fatherland, is thereby not impoverished but enriched. It is necessary, therefore, alike in acquiring and in keeping, to avoid expense, and, instead, to do everything so that the public may profit thereby.

In view of all this, it is expedient to keep to the Roman way of proceeding, which in the first place was, as the French would say, to make wars short and crushing. For, since the Romans put large armies in the field, the wars they waged with the Latins, the Samnites and the Tuscans were all over in a very short time. If one consults the records, indeed, it will be found that all their expeditions from the start up to the siege of Veii took but, in some cases six, in some ten, and in others twenty days. For their practice was, as soon as war had been declared, to lead forth their armies against the enemy and at once to engage him in battle. When they had won, the enemy, to prevent them devastating the surrounding country, came to terms; and the Romans confiscated some of his lands, which they handed over either for private use or to a colony which they placed on the enemy's frontiers for the protection of Rome's boundaries, with advantage both to the colonists who had the land and to the Roman public who had a garrison there at no expense to themselves. Nor, than this way of proceeding could any be safer, more forceful or more useful. For, so long as the enemy was not in the field, this garrison sufficed; while, should they go forth in strength to attack the colony, once again the Romans marched out in strength and gave them battle; and when the battle had been fought and won, and they had imposed yet heavier conditions, they went back home. They thus came step by step to acquire a reputation greater than the enemy's and to increase their own strength at home.

They kept strictly to this method of making war till after the siege of Veii, when they made a change in their procedure. That they might carry on a longer war, they decided to pay their soldiers, which at first had been unnecessary since the wars were short, so they were not then paid. But, though the idea of the Romans in paying their troops was that it would enable them to make longer wars and to meet the case of more distant wars which would keep the troops longer in the field, yet they never departed from their basic principle of getting wars over quickly as far as place and time allowed. Nor did they ever depart from the custom of sending out colonies.

For in regard to the first method, namely, that of making wars short, apart from this having become their natural practice, the ambition of the consuls kept them to it; since they held office only for a year, of this year spent six months at home, and were keen on ending the war in order to have a triumph. They continued to plant colonies because of their usefulness and of the great opportunities they provided. They did, indeed, change somewhat the arrangement in regard to booty, and in this were not so generous as they had been at first. For (i) it did not seem to them necessary now that the troops were paid, and (ii), since the booty was now greater, they thought it a good plan that the public should benefit by it, so that they would not have to tax the city to pay for their enterprises. In a very short time this practice made the treasury very rich.

These two methods, then, of distributing the spoils and of sending out colonies, caused Rome to become enriched by her wars, whereas other princes and republics, being less wise, are impoverished by them. Indeed it went so far that in the end a consul does not seem to have been able to obtain a triumph unless he brought plenty of silver and gold and other booty of all sorts for the treasury's benefit. Thus, the Romans by the aforesaid methods and by getting their wars over quickly – being able in the long run to tire out their enemies alike by defeating them, raiding them, and by means of treaties advantageous to themselves – became ever richer and more powerful.

7. How much Land the Romans gave to their Colonists

I FIND it difficult to discover the truth about how much land the Romans distributed when they started a colony; for it depended more or less, I think, on the places to which colonies were sent. It would seem, however, that in all cases and in all places no colonist got more than a small share. This was done, first that more men might be sent out as a garrison to defend some district; and secondly, because it was unreasonable that whereas at home people lived as poor men, they should want their colonists to have a superfluity. Titus Livy tells us how, when Veii was taken, they sent out a colony and to each colonist granted three *jugera* and seven *unciae* of land, which in our measure comes to. . . . For this they had a further reason. It was not, they held, having plenty of land but its good cultivation that would tell. But all colonies, of course, necessarily had also public land on which anyone's cattle might graze and where wood might be gathered for fires; without which no colony can support itself.

8. *The Causes which lead Peoples to quit their own Country and to inundate the Lands of Others*

SINCE we have just been discussing the procedure adopted by the Romans in their wars, and how the Tuscans were attacked by the Gauls, it will not be irrelevant here, I think, to point out that there are two ways in which wars come about. Sometimes they are due to the ambition of princes or of republics which are seeking to set up an empire; under which head fall the wars waged by Alexander the Great and those waged by the Romans, and those which are continually being waged between this power and that. Such wars are dangerous, but they do not entirely remove the inhabitants of the country invaded; for the victor is content provided its people became subject to his obedience, often lets them keep their own laws, and always leaves them their houses and their chattels. The other way in which war is brought about is when a whole people with all its families leaves a place, driven thence either by famine or by war, and sets out to look for a new home and a new country in which to live. In this case it does not, as in the previous case, merely govern there, but it takes possession of every single thing, and expels or kills the old inhabitants. This is war of the most cruel and terrifying

kind. It is to such wars that Sallust refers when, towards the
end of his *Jugurtha*, he says that, after Jugurtha's defeat, the
progress of the Gallic invasion of Italy began to be felt; and
of this invasion says also that, whereas the Roman people
fought with all other peoples merely for supremacy, with the
Gauls the fight was always as to which of them should
survive. For to a prince or to a republic that invades a foreign
province it suffices if he gets rid of those who rule there, but
to whole peoples it is essential to get rid of all the inhabitants
since they want to live on that on which the others used to
live.

The Romans sustained three of these extremely dangerous
wars. During the first Rome was captured and occupied by
those Gauls who, as we said, had taken Lombardy from the
Tuscans and established themselves there. For this war Livy
assigns two causes. First, as we said, they were attracted by
the delicious Italian fruit and wines which in Gaul were not
to be had. Secondly, the population of the kingdom of Gaul
had multiplied to such an extent that they could no longer
find enough food there, so the princes in those parts deemed
it necessary that some of them should go in search of new
lands, and, after discussing the matter, chose as the commanders of those who were to depart, Bellovesus and Sigo-
vesus, two Gallic kings, of whom the first went to Italy, and
the second crossed into Spain. The result of Bellovesus' going
to Italy was the occupation of Lombardy, and from this arose
the first war which the Gauls made on Rome. The next was
that which occurred after the first Punic war, when between
Piombino and Pisa the Romans killed more than two hundred
thousand Gauls. The third was that in which the Germans
and the Cimbri invaded Italy, where, after defeating several
Roman armies, they were beaten by Marius. The Romans,
then, won these three highly hazardous wars, and to win them
called for more than a modicum of virtue; for we see how,

when, later on, the virtue of Rome declined and its armies lost their former virtue, their empire was destroyed by peoples of the same type, namely, by Goths, Vandals and such-like peoples, who occupied the whole of the Western empire.

Peoples such as these quit their own lands when constrained to do so by necessity, as had been said above; and the necessity is due either to famine or to a war or to hardships undergone in their own country; for in such a case they are constrained to go in search of new lands. And such peoples when they are very numerous and then make a violent incursion into the lands of others, kill the inhabitants, seize their goods, and establish a new kingdom under a new name. This was done by Moses and by the peoples who overran the Roman empire. For the new names now used in Italy and other provinces are due simply to their having been so called by their new conquerors. Thus, Lombardy used to be called Cisalpine Gaul; France used to be called Trans-Alpine Gaul, but got its present name from the Franks, who gave it this name when they occupied it. Slavonia used to be called Illyria; Hungary, Pannonia; England, Britannia; and so of many other provinces with changed names which it would be tedious to recount. So, too, Moses gave the name Judea to that part of Syria which he occupied.

Since I said above that such peoples are sometimes forced to go and look for new lands because they are driven from those they inhabit by war, I propose, as an instance of this, to cite the Moors, peoples that originally dwelt in Syria. When these peoples heard that the Hebrews were coming, they thought resistance impossible, so decided that it would be better to leave their country and save themselves rather than to lose themselves in an attempt to save their country. So with their families they deserted it and went to Africa, where they established themselves, after expelling the inhabitants whom they found in those parts. Thus, a people which could not defend its own country, succeeded in taking somebody else's. Procopius, who writes of the war Belisarius waged with the Vandals, who occupied Africa, tells us he came across inscriptions on certain columns in places where the Moors used to live, which said: 'We are the Moors, who fled before the face of Joshua, the robber, the son of Nun.' This makes it clear why the Moors left Syria.

Peoples, therefore, who have been driven out by sheer necessity, are very formidable, and, unless confronted by good armies, can never be held back. But when those who are constrained to abandon their country are not numerous, they are not so dangerous as the peoples we have been discussing. For they have not the same force at their disposal, but must resort to artifice in order to get territory, and, having obtained it, must make alliances and form confederations in order to hold it; as we see that Aeneas, Dido, the Massilians, and such-like, did, all of whom maintained their footing in the place where they had settled by the consent of their neighbours.

The larger migrations, involving whole peoples, have come from Scythia, a country that is cold and poor. In it, when the population becomes large, the land is not fertile enough to sustain it, and they are forced to emigrate; for there are many causes to drive them out and none to keep them at home. And if for the last five hundred years there have been no inundations of these peoples, there are several causes that account for this. First, there was the great evacuation which occurred in that country during the decline of the Empire, when more than thirty peoples emigrated. Secondly, Germany and Hungary, from which emigrations of these peoples also took place, are now prosperous lands where people can live in comfort, so that there is no need to change their habitation. On the contrary, since these peoples are extremely warlike, they form a bastion which prevents the Scythians who live on their borders from attempting either to conquer them or to pass through them. There have also frequently been very great movements among the Tartars, which the Hungarians and the people of Poland have withstood; and it has often been their boast that, if it had not been for them, Italy and the Church would on many an occasion have felt the weight of Tartar armies. But of these peoples I think I have now said enough.

9. *What Causes commonly give rise to Wars between Different Powers*

THE cause of the war between the Romans and the Samnites, with whom for a long time they had been in alliance, is one which arises commonly between powerful states. It consists in some incident which is brought about either by chance or by those who are desirous of provoking a war. That which gave rise to war between the Romans and the Samnites was due to chance. For, when the Samnites made war on the Sidicines and then on the Campanians, they had no intention of making war on Rome. But, when the Campanians were attacked and appealed to Rome, which neither the Romans nor the Samnites had expected, the Romans, to whose suzerainty the Campanians had submitted, had to defend them, and so to take on a war which it did not seem to them that they could with honour escape. For, though it did not appear reasonable that they should defend their allies, the Campanians, against their allies, the Samnites, yet, when the former had become their subjects and had accepted their suzerainty, it seemed to them shameful not to defend them; for they thought that, if they did not undertake to defend them, it would put an obstacle in the way of any others who contemplated submitting to their dominion. Since, therefore,

Rome was aiming at empire and glory, not at tranquillity, they could not decline to take the matter up.

The same causes were operative at the beginning of the first Punic war, which was due to the Romans having undertaken the defence of the Messinians in Sicily, an undertaking which again was brought about by chance. This was not the case later in the second war which arose between them; for Hannibal, the Carthaginian commander, attacked the Saguntines, who were allies of the Romans, in Spain, not out of hostility to them, but to get the Roman armies to take action, so as to provide him with an opportunity of attacking them and of crossing into Italy.

This method of starting new wars has always been the practice with powerful states who have a certain respect both for treaties and for one another. For, if I want to make war on some prince and between us there is a treaty the articles of which have been observed for a considerable time, rather than attack him, I shall look for some justification and ground for attacking one of his allies, knowing full well that, if his ally be attacked, either he will resent it and I shall get what I want in that war will arise, or, if he takes no notice, he will disclose either his weakness or his unreliability in that he does not defend a dependent state. In either case he will lose his reputation and it will be easier for me to accomplish my designs.

With regard, then, to the provoking of a war, due note should be taken of what has just been said about the submission of the Campanians. It should be noted, too, that a city which does not suffice for its own defence, has a remedy, should it desire at all costs to defend itself against attack. The remedy consists in submitting voluntarily to the state whose protection you propose to invoke. Thus the Capuans submitted to the Romans, and the Florentines to king Robert of Naples, who, though not prepared to defend them on the basis of an alliance, when they became his subjects, defended them against all the forces which Castruccio da Lucca was employing against them.

10. *Money is not the Sinews of War, as it is commonly supposed to be*

SINCE it is open to anyone having the requisite authority to begin a war but not to end it, a ruler before committing himself to such an undertaking should calculate what forces he has at his disposal and act accordingly. Moreover, he should also take good care not to make any mistake about such forces, as he will do every time he bases his calculations on money or on the terrain or on the goodwill of men, but, on the other hand, lacks troops of his own. For though such things undoubtedly add to your strength, they certainly do not provide you with it; and, as such, are nought and of no avail without faithful troops. For, without these no amount of money will suffice you: the natural strength of the country will not help you; nor will the goodwill of men last, since they cannot remain faithful to you unless you are able to protect them. Every mountain, every lake, every inaccessible fastness, becomes but as a plain, when strong defenders are lacking. Money, too, not only affords you no protection, but makes you the sooner fall a prey. Nor can any opinion be more false than that which asserts that money is the sinews of war.

This view was advocated by Quintus Curtius in connection with the war which took place between Antipater, the Macedonian, and the king of Sparta; where he tells how, for want of money, the king of Sparta of necessity had to join battle, and was beaten; whereas, had he postponed the battle for a few days, he would have had news from Greece of the death of Alexander, and so would have remained the victor without putting up a fight. But, since he was without funds and feared lest for lack of them his army might desert, he was forced to try his luck in battle. On which ground Quintus Curtius maintains that money is the sinews of war.

The view adopted by Quintus Curtius is put forward daily, and is followed by rulers whose prudence is not up to the mark. Taking this as their basic principle, they think they can defend themselves if they have a well-filled treasury, and do not consider that, if treasures guaranteed victory, Darius would have conquered Alexander, the Greeks would have conquered the Romans, in our day Duke Charles would have conquered the Swiss; nor yet, but a few days ago, would the combined forces of the Pope and the Florentines have had any difficulty in overcoming Francesco Maria, the nephew of Julius II, in the war of Urbino. Yet all those mentioned were overcome by those who held that the sinews of war lay not in money, but in good soldiers.

Among the other things that Croesus, king of Lydia, showed to Solon, the Athenian, was a treasure too great to count. Solon was then asked what opinion he had formed of the king's power, to which he replied that he did not think him more powerful on this account, for war is made with steel, not with gold, and if anyone came along who had more steel than he had, he could deprive him of his power.

Again, when, after the death of Alexander the Great, a host of Gauls crossed into Greece, and then to Asia, and sent ambassadors to arrange a treaty with the king of Macedonia, the king, in order to display his power and to frighten them, showed them a lot of gold and silver; whereupon the Gauls who up till then had been intent on peace, broke off negotiations, so eager were they to relieve him of that gold. So the king was despoiled on account of the very thing he had accumulated for his defence.

The Venetians, a few years ago, also had a well-filled

treasury, yet lost all their dominions without being able to use their treasures to defend them.

I assert, then, that it is not gold, as is acclaimed by common opinion, that constitutes the sinews of war, but good soldiers; for gold does not find good soldiers, but good soldiers are quite capable of finding gold. If the Romans had chosen to wage war rather by means of money than by the sword, not all the treasure in the world would have sufficed in view of the great enterprises they undertook and the difficulties they had to encounter in them. But, since they made war with the sword, they did not suffer for want of gold, because those who were afraid of them brought it right into their camps. And if that Spartan king for lack of money had to try his luck in battle, what happened to him on the score of money has very often happened for other reasons; for it is obvious that, when an army is short of provisions and must needs either die of hunger or fight, it always chooses to fight, since this is the more honourable course, and one that gives fortune some chance to show you favour. Again, it often happens that when a general sees that the enemy's army is about to be reinforced, he must either engage it and try his fortune in battle, or wait till the enemy's force has increased, and then have to fight it anyhow to his own great disadvantage. One sees, too – as happened to Hasdrubal when he was attacked jointly by Claudius Nero and the other Roman consul in the March [of Ancona] – how a general who is obliged either to run away or to fight, always chooses to fight, since it seems to him that this course, even should the issue be extremely doubtful, gives him a chance to win, whereas the other would mean losing in any case. There are, then, many situations which compel a general to prefer the alternative of fighting even though he had no intention of so doing, of which lack of money may sometimes be one. But one ought not for this reason to infer that money is the sinews of war, any more

than are other situations which place men in a like predicament.

I repeat, therefore: gold is not the sinews of war, but good
soldiers are. Gold is necessary, but is of secondary importance,
and good soldiers can get it for themselves; for it is as impossible for good soldiers to fail to find gold as it is for gold
to find good soldiers. That in this we are speaking the truth
history shows again and again, in spite of the fact that Pericles
advised the Athenians to wage war with the whole of the
Peloponnese on the ground that their industry and their
pecuniary resources should enable them to win it. And,
though during the war the Athenians sometimes prospered,
in the end they lost, so that Sparta's wisdom and good soldiery
was worth more than Athens' industry and money. On this
point Titus Livy is a better witness than anybody else. I refer
to the passage in which he discusses whether, if Alexander the
Great had come to Italy, he would have beaten the Romans.
In it he points out that three things are necessary for war;
plenty of good soldiers, wise generals and good luck; and
then, having inquired whether the Romans or Alexander was
the better off in these things, he draws his conclusion without
any mention of money. The Capuans, when they were asked
by the Sidicines to take up arms for them against the Samnites,
must have calculated their strength on a monetary basis, and
not on the basis of troops, for, when they decided to help them,
after being twice routed, they were forced to become Rome's
tributaries if they wished to survive.[43]

Book Two

---

11. *It is not a Wise Course to make an Alliance with a Ruler[a] whose Reputation is greater than his Strength*

THE mistake the Sidicines made in trusting to the Campanians for help, and the mistake the Campanians made in thinking they could defend them could not be shown more vividly than it is by Titus Livy when he writes: 'The Campanians brought a name to the help of the Sidicines instead of forces to protect them.' It should be noted here that leagues made with rulers who lack either the means to help because they are too far away, or the power to help because they are disorganized or for other reasons, bring rather repute than assistance to those who trust in them.

It happened thus in our day to the Florentines when in 1479 the Pope and the king of Naples attacked them. They were allies of the king of France, but from this alliance gained 'rather a name than protection'. The same thing would happen to the ruler who should enter on some enterprise relying on the Emperor, Maximilian, for it would be one of those alliances that bring 'rather a name than protection',

[a] *uno principe* – this term, as the context shows, is used both in this and in the next chapter to denote the ruler of a principality or the rulers of a republic.

which is what Livy says the Capuans brought to the Sidicines. The Capuans, therefore, erred here in thinking their strength greater than it was.

So small is the prudence of men that they sometimes undertake to defend others when they neither know how, nor are able, to defend themselves. Thus, when the Roman army had taken the field against the Samnite army, the Tarentines sent ambassadors to the Roman consul to inform him that they wished there to be peace between these two peoples, and that they proposed to make war on whoever should disturb that peace. At this the consul laughed, and in the presence of the ambassadors had the trumpets sound for battle. He then told his army to go for the enemy, thereby showing, by actions, not by words, what answer he thought they deserved.

Having in this chapter discussed the means rulers take, to their own hurt, for the defence of others, in the next I propose to discuss the means they take to defend themselves.

12. *Whether it is better, when threatened with Attack, to assume the Offensive or to await the Outbreak of War*

I HAVE sometimes heard men with considerable experience in matters connected with war, discussing whether, if of two rulers of approximately equal strength the more aggressive has declared war on the other, it is the better course for that other to await the enemy within his own boundaries or to assume the offensive and attack him in his own country; and for each course I have heard arguments adduced. Those who maintain that he should assume the offensive, cite the advice Croesus gave to Cyrus when he reached the borders of the Messagetans' territory to make war on them, and Tomyris, their queen, sent him word that it was up to him to choose between two courses, either to enter her kingdom, where she was awaiting him, or to let her come and seek him out. When

the matter came up for discussion Croesus, contrary to the
views expressed by others, advised him to go and seek her
out, on the ground that, if he defeated her when she was
outside her own kingdom, he would not deprive her of it,
for she would have time to re-form her forces; but that, if he
defeated her on her own territory, he should be able to pursue
her when she fled, and, since this would give her no chance to
re-form, he would deprive her of her state.

They allege, too, the advice which Hannibal gave to Antiochus, when this monarch was contemplating a war with the
Romans. The Romans, he argued, could only be beaten in
Italy, for others might there be able to avail themselves of
their arms, their riches and their allies; whereas anyone who
fought with them outside Italy and left Italy unmolested,
would leave them with that inexhaustible source whence to
draw forces as need arose. He ended by saying that Antiochus
had better first try to take Rome before attacking the empire,
and Italy before attacking the other provinces.

They also point out that when Agathocles was unable to cope
with war at home, he took the offensive against the Carthaginians who were making war on him, and forced them to sue
for peace. They point out, too, that Scipio took the offensive
in Africa in order to stop the war in Italy.

Those who take the opposite view say that if one wants an
enemy to succeed ill one should get him away from his home.
They cite the Athenians who kept the upper hand so long as
they were waging war conveniently at home; but who, when
they left it and took their armies to Sicily, lost their freedom.
They also appeal to poetical fables which tell how Antaeus,
king of Libya, when attacked by Hercules Ergidius, was insuperable as long as he awaited him within the confines of his
own kingdom, but how, when induced by the craft of
Hercules to leave it, he lost both his throne and his life. This
gave rise to the fable depicting Antaeus on the ground drawing

strength from his mother, the Earth, and Hercules, on seeing
this, lifting him up and holding him away from the earth.

They also cite modern opinions. Everybody knows that
Ferdinand, king of Naples, was held in his time to be a very
wise prince, and that two years before his death it was ru-
moured that Charles VIII, king of France, intended to come
and attack him; for which Ferdinand made due preparation,
but then fell ill. When about to die he left to his son, Alfonso,
among other memoranda, one telling him to await the
enemy within his own domains; and to let nothing on earth
persuade him to lead his forces outside the state, but to keep
well within his own borders awaiting invasion with all his
forces intact. Of this advice he took no notice, but sent an
army into the Romagna, where without fighting a battle he
lost both his army and his throne.

Besides the reasons adduced above, others are adduced by
either side, such as that he who takes the offensive shows more
spirit than he who awaits an attack, and so inspires his army
with more confidence; and, in addition to this, deprives the
enemy of the power to utilize his own resources since he
cannot avail himself of those subjects who have been despoiled. Also, owing to his having the enemy within his own
domain, the ruler has to be more careful about imposing taxes
and other intolerable burdens on his subjects; so that, in the
end, as Hannibal said, the fount from which he can draw
supplies for the war, will run dry. Moreover, the invader's
troops being in a foreign country, there would be all the more
necessity for them to fight, and necessity engenders virtue, as
we have often remarked.

On behalf of the other view it is said that to await the
enemy's attack has many advantages; for, without any disadvantage to yourself, you can impose on him many disadvantages in the matter of provisions and of anything else of
which an army has need; you can also the better thwart his

plans owing to your having a better knowledge of the country than he has; and, again, you can oppose him with stronger forces owing to the ease with which you can bring them all together, which you could not do were they all at a distance from their homes; also, if you are routed, you can easily re-form, both because a considerable part of your army will survive since it has a refuge at hand, and because reinforcements have not to come from a distance: so that, though you may have to risk all your forces, you will not be risking your whole fortune, whereas, abroad, you would be risking your whole fortune, but not risking all your forces. There have, indeed, been some who, in order to weaken the enemy more, have allowed him to advance for several days into their country and take a number of towns, so that he may weaken his army owing to the garrisons he leaves in all of them, and thus it will be easier to face him in battle.

Let me now say what I think about this. I think a distinction must be made. For either I have my country well equipped with arms, as the Romans had and as the Swiss have; or I have a country ill equipped with arms, as the Carthaginians had, and as have the king of France and the Italians today. In the latter case the enemy should be kept at a distance, for, since your virtue lies in money, not in men, as soon as anything gets in the way of your obtaining it, you may be undone; nor does anything impede you so much as does war in your own domains. This is exemplified by the Carthaginians, who, so long as their country was unoccupied, could use the revenue to make war on the Romans, but, when it was attacked, could not withstand Agathocles. Nor had the Florentines any remedy against Castruccio, Lord of Lucca, because he waged war on them within their own lands, so that, to defend themselves, they had to submit to Robert of Naples. Yet, after Castruccio's death, these same Florentines summoned up courage to attack the duke of Milan in his own territory and strove to deprive him of his kingdom. Thus, they displayed great virtue in waging war away from home, but great cowardice when it was near at hand.

But when states are strongly armed, as Rome was and as the Swiss are, the more difficult it is to overcome them the nearer they are to their homes: for such bodies can bring more forces together to resist attack than they can to attack others. Nor on this point am I impressed by the authority of Hannibal, for it was resentment and self-interest that made him say what he did say to Antiochus. For, had the three disastrous defeats Hannibal inflicted on the Romans in Italy taken place in Gaul in the same space of time, the Romans would undoubtedly have been undone, since they would have been unable to make use of the forces that survived, as they were able to do in Italy; nor would it have been so easy for them to re-form; nor yet would they have been able with such forces to withstand the enemy, as they were able to do. One does not find that, in attacking a foreign country, they ever sent out armies of more than fifty thousand men; but for home defence they put under arms against the Gauls after the first Punic war eighteen hundred thousand. Nor would they have been able later on to vanquish them in Lombardy as they vanquished them in Tuscany because against so numerous an enemy they would not have been able to bring to that distance such strong forces, nor have fought them under the same advantageous conditions. The Cimbri broke up a Roman army in Germany, and the Romans had no way to repair their defeat. But, when the Cimbri arrived in Italy, and against them the Romans could bring all their forces to bear, they were undone. The Swiss are easy to beat when away from home, whither they cannot send more than thirty or forty thousand men; but to defeat them at home where they can muster a hundred thousand, is very difficult.

In conclusion, therefore, I say again that a ruler who has his people well armed and equipped for war, should always wait at home to wage war with a powerful and dangerous enemy, and should not go out to meet him; but that one who has ill-armed subjects and a country unused to war should always meet the enemy as far away from home as he can. Both of them will in this way defend themselves better, each in his degree.

13. Men rise from a Low to a Great Position by Means rather of Fraud than of Force [44]

IT is quite true, I think, that seldom, if ever, do men of low position[a] obtain high rank except by force and by fraud, though there are, of course, others to whom rank comes merely by way of gift or inheritance. Nor do I think that force by itself ever suffices, whereas instances can easily be found in which fraud alone has sufficed. Anyone who has read the life of Philip of Macedon or that of Agathocles the Sicilian, for instance, or others of that ilk, will see that, from an extremely low, or at any rate a low position, they rose either to a kingdom or to very great power. Xenophon, in his Life of Cyrus, calls attention to the necessity for deceit. For in view of the amount of fraud used in the first expedition Cyrus made against the King of Armenia, and of the fact that it was by means of deceit, not by means of force, that he acquired his kingdom, one cannot but conclude from such actions that a prince who wishes to do great things must learn to practise deceit. Besides this, Xenophon also makes him deceive Cyaxares, king of the Medes, his maternal uncle, in various ways, and shows that without such frauds Cyrus could not have attained the greatness he did attain.

Nor do I think that anyone can be found whose position at

[a] *di piccola fortuna* in contrast with *gran fortuna*, the terms used in the heading.

the outset was humble, but who subsequently acquired vast power simply by the use of open and undisguised force: but it can quite well be done by using only fraud, as was done by Giovanni Galeazzo in order to deprive his uncle, Bernabo, of his position as ruler of Lombardy. And what princes have to do at the outset of their career, republics also must do until such time as they become powerful and can rely on force alone.

Since in all her decisions, whether by chance or by choice, Rome took all steps necessary to make herself great, she did not overlook fraud. She could not at the start have been more deceitful than she was in the means she took, as we were saying just now, to acquire allies, since under this title she made them her servants, as was the case with the Latins and other peoples round about. For she first availed herself of their arms in order to subjugate neighbouring peoples and to build up her reputation as a state, and then, having subdued them, she increased to such an extent that she could beat anyone. Nor would the Latins ever have realized that in reality they were mere slaves, if they had not seen the Samnites twice defeated and forced to accept Rome's terms. Since this victory increased the already great reputation of the Romans with more distant rulers, who thus felt the impact of her name though not of her arms, envy and suspicion were aroused in those who did see and feel the weight of her arms, among them the Latins. So strong became this envy and this dread that not only the Latins, but also the colonies Rome had in Latium, together with the Campanians who a short while before had been defended by Rome, joined in a conspiracy against her. The Latins provoked this war in the way in which most wars are provoked, as has been pointed out above, namely, not by attacking the Romans, but by protecting the Sidicines against the Samnites, who had made war on them with Rome's sanction. That the Latins were moved to do this because they recognized the deceit Rome had practised, is shown by the words Titus Livy puts into the mouth of Annius Setinus, the Latin praetor, when speaking before the allied council: 'For if under cover of a treaty between equals it has been possible to reduce us to servitude', and so forth.[45]

It is clear, therefore, that, when the power of the Romans was first beginning to grow, they did not fail to use fraud; of which it is always necessary that those should make use who from small beginnings wish to rise to sublime heights, and the better they conceal it, as the Romans did, the less blameworthy it is.

14. *Men often make the Mistake of supposing that Pride is overcome by Humility*

THERE are to be found numerous cases in which humility is not only no help, but is a hindrance, especially when used in dealing with arrogant men who, either out of envy or for some other cause, have come to hate you. This, our historian assures us, was the cause of the war between the Romans and the Latins. For, when the Samnites complained to the Romans that the Latins had attacked them, the Romans were unwilling to forbid the Latins to make war on them, because they did not wish to annoy them. Yet, by so doing, they not only annoyed them, but intensified their animosity and caused them the sooner to become open enemies. This is borne out by what the prefect, Annius, the Latin praetor, said to the aforementioned council of the allies: 'You have tried their patience, by refusing them troops. Who can doubt that this has made them angry? Yet they have put up with it. They have heard that we have an army ready to attack their allies, the Samnites, yet they have not stirred from the city. To what is this marked modesty due if it be not that they are aware of the strength of our respective forces, ours and their own?' This shows very clearly how much the patience of the Romans intensified the arrogance of the Latins.

A ruler, therefore, should never forget his dignity, nor, if he cares for his honour, should he ever waive a point agreed upon unless he can enforce it, or thinks he can enforce it. For it is almost always better, when your position is such that you cannot in this way make the concession, to let it be extracted by force rather than by the threat of force; because, if you yield to a threat, you do so in order to avoid war, and more often than not, you do not avoid war. For those before whom you have thus openly demeaned yourself by yielding, will not stop there, but will seek to extort further concessions, and the less they esteem you the more incensed will they become against you. On the other hand, you will find your supporters growing cooler towards you, since they will look upon you as weak or pusillanimous. But if, as soon as you become aware of your adversary's intentions, you prepare to use force, even though your forces be inferior to his, he will begin to respect you, and, since those with which you were allied will now esteem you, they will be ready to help when you begin to arm, which they would never have done had you given up.

This applies where you have but one enemy. If you have more, the wiser course is to hand over some of your possessions to one of them so as to win him to your side even after war has been declared, and that you may detach a member of the confederation which is hostile to you.

15. The Decisions of Weak States are always fraught with Ambiguity, and the Slowness with which they arrive at them is Harmful

IN regard to the topic we have been discussing in connection with the outbreak of war between the Romans and the Latins, it may be remarked that in all consultations it is well to come to the point which is under discussion, not to remain ever hesitant and uncertain in regard to the real issue. This is brought out very clearly in the consultation the Latins held when they were considering whether to leave the Roman confederation. For, when the Romans came to be aware of the ill humour with which the Latin peoples had become imbued, in order to clear up the situation and to see whether they could not regain the loyalty of these peoples without having recourse to arms, they suggested to them that they should send eight citizens to Rome to discuss the matter. On hearing this, the Latins, conscious that they had in many things acted contrary to the wishes of the Romans, held a council to decide who should go to Rome and to instruct them what to say. During the discussion of the question in council, Annius, their praetor, got up and said: 'It seems to me to be of the utmost importance in this business that you should consider what is to be done rather than what is to be said. It will be easy, when you have arrived at a decision, to accommodate words to acts.'

This assertion is undoubtedly true, and every prince and every republic should ponder it well. For, where there is ambiguity and uncertainty as to what others want to do, it is impossible to choose the right words; but, once one's mind is made up and it has been decided how to implement one's decision, it is easy to find the right words. I am the more ready to call attention to this, since I have often noticed what harm such ambiguity has done in public affairs, to the detriment and to the discredit of this republic of ours. Where there is doubt as to which course to choose and it requires courage to decide, this ambiguity will always be found if on the point under discussion the decision rests with weak men.

Slow and tardy decisions are no less harmful than are ambiguous decisions, especially when the point at issue is whether support is to be given to an ally; for by such slowness nobody benefits and to oneself it does harm. Slowness in arriving at decisions proceeds either from lack of courage and of strength, or from malevolence on the part of those with whom the decision rests. In the latter case men who are moved by their own appetites to seek either the downfall of the government or the fulfilment of some other aim of theirs, do not let the discussion follow its normal course, but impede it and raise difficulties; whereas good citizens even though they see that popular indignation is bent on taking a pernicious course, never place obstacles in the way of a decision, especially if the matter be urgent.

After the death of Hieronymus, the tyrant of Syracuse, when the great war between Carthaginians and Romans was still going on, a dispute arose among the Syracusans as to whether they should ally themselves with Rome or with Carthage. So great was the ardour displayed by each side that the issue remained doubtful and no decision was taken until Apollonides, one of the chief men in Syracuse, delivered an extremely prudent speech in which he showed that, though no blame attached to those who were in favour of an alliance with the Romans, nor to those who wanted to throw in their lot with the Carthaginians, yet ambiguity and slowness in reaching a decision was to be deprecated, for it was clear to him that this wavering would bring about the ruin of the republic, whereas, should they arrive at a decision, whichever way it went, they might expect good to come of it.

Nor could Titus Livy have shown more clearly than does this passage the harm that comes from indecision. He shows it, too, in an incident involving the Latins, for, when the Lavinians were asked to help them against the Romans, the former put off deciding so long that, when they were actually marching out through the city gate with an army to give succour to the Latins, news came that the Latins had been defeated. Whereupon Milionius, their praetor, said: 'For this short journey the Romans will make us pay dear.' For, had they decided at first either to help or not to help the Latins, they would by not helping them have avoided annoying the

Romans, and by helping them in good time, might by means of their combined forces have enabled them to win; but by their procrastination they stood to lose either way, as happened in point of fact.

Nor, had the Florentines noted the significance of this incident, would they have suffered such losses nor such vexations at the hands of the French as they did when the French king, Louis XII, moved into Italy on his way to attack Ludovico Sforza, Duke of Milan. For, when the king was considering this expedition, he sought to come to terms with the Florentines; and their representatives, who were then at his court, agreed that they should remain neutral, and that, in return, when the king came to Italy, their form of government should be maintained, and Florence should receive his protection. The city was given a month to ratify this agreement. Its ratification, however, was put off, owing to the imprudence of those who sympathized with the cause of Ludovico; so that, when the King was already on the point of victory and the Florentines then wanted to ratify the agreement, their proposal was not accepted, since the King knew that they were forced to take this line, and were not doing it voluntarily out of friendship for him. This cost the city of Florence no small sum of money, and came near to causing a revolution, which on another occasion was actually brought about in this way. The course they took was the more harmful in that it in no way helped the Duke, who, had he won, would have displayed much more hostility towards the Florentines than did the King.

Though the evils to which this weakness gives rise in republics I have already discussed under another heading, I decided to avail myself of the opportunity provided by a fresh incident to repeat what I had said, since it seems to me to be a matter of which republics, especially those that resemble ours, should take careful note.

Book Two

---

16. How far the Discipline of Troops in our Day falls short of that maintained in Days gone by[46]

THE most important battle ever fought by the Romans in any war with another nation was the battle they fought with the Latin peoples in the consulate of Torquatus and Decius. For everything shows that, just as the Latins by losing became a subject people, so the Romans would have become a subject people, had they not won. This is the view held by Titus Livy, for in all respects the two armies were alike in discipline, virtue, truculence and in numbers; the only difference was that the commanders of the Roman army had more virtuosity than those of the Latin army.

One notes, too, how in the conduct of this battle there occurred two unprecedented incidents of which there have been but few examples since; namely, to strengthen the resolution of the soldiers and to make them obey orders, of the two consuls one killed himself and the other killed his son. The parity which Titus Livy says held between the two armies was due to their having for a long time waged war together, and consisted in their having the same language, the same discipline, and the same kind of arms, for in drawing up

317

troops for battle they used the same formation, and both units and officers bore the same names. It was essential, therefore, since both in strength and in *virtù* they were equal, that something extraordinary should take place whereby to strengthen the ardour and truculence of the one rather than the other, for, as we have remarked on other occasions, it is on determination that victory depends, since, so long as it lasts in the breasts of those who are fighting, an army will never turn tail. And in order that it might last longer in the breasts of the Romans than with the Latins it came about, owing partly to chance and partly to the virtue of the consuls, that Torquatus had to kill his son and Decius to kill himself.

When pointing out this parity in strength Titus Livy describes in detail how the Romans drew up their armies and how they disposed them for battle. He has done this at considerable length, so I shall not repeat it all, but shall discuss the points which I deem worthy of note, points which are ignored by all present-day commanders, with the result that there is a grave lack of proper order alike in drawing up armies and in battle. From Livy we gather that in the Roman army there were three main divisions for which the Tuscan term three 'ranks' may be used. They called the first *Hastati*, the second *Principes*, the third *Triarii*. Each had its own cavalry attached. In drawing them up for battle, they put the *Hastati* in front; in the second place, immediately behind the *Hastati*, they put the *Principes*; in the third, all covering precisely the same space, they placed the *Triarii*. The cavalry pertaining to each of these divisions they put on the right and on the left of the three formations. These mounted troops, on account of their formation and their position, were called *alae*, because they looked like two wings attached to the body. They drew up the first rank, consisting of the *Hastati* who were in front, in close formation, so that they might thrust forward and hold up the enemy. The second rank, consisting of *Principes*, since they were not to be engaged at the outset, but were to come to the aid of the first should they be beaten or hard pressed, they did not draw up in such close formation, but kept their lines thinner so that this rank could receive the first rank, without disturbing its formation, should the latter be overcome by the enemy and have to fall back. The third rank consisting of *Triarii*, were drawn up in yet thinner lines than the second, so as to receive the two first ranks, comprising *Principes* and *Hastati*, should need arise. When their ranks had thus been drawn up in this formation, they went into battle; and, should the *Hastati* be forced back or defeated, they fell straight back upon the thinner ranks of the *Principes*, and the two ranks, thus united to form one compact body, resumed the fight. Should these ranks be beaten and forced to retreat, they retired upon the thinner ranks of the *Triarii*, and all three ranks, together forming one body, renewed the fight. But should they be overcome, the day was lost, since they had no further chance to re-form. Wherefore, since every time this last rank of *Triarii* became engaged, it meant danger to the army, there arose the proverb: 'It all depends on the *Triarii*', or, as we say in the Tuscan idiom: 'We have played the last stake'.

As generals in our days have abandoned all other traditions and pay no attention to any point in ancient military discipline, so they have abandoned it in regard to this point, which is of no small importance. For where an army is so drawn up as to be able to re-form three times during a battle, to lose the day luck must go against it three times and the valour of those attacking it must be sufficient to beat it three times over. But an army that can withstand but one attack, as is the case with all Christian armies, may easily lose, for, if it become in any way disorganized or its valour be but indifferent, its chance of victory goes. The inability of our armies thrice to re-form is due to their having dropped the custom of receiving one rank into the other. This in turn is due to there being in present-day battle-formations one of two defects: either they station their ranks one alongside the other, and make their formations broad in extent but thin in the line of attack, which makes them weaker owing to their lack of depth; or when, to make them stronger, they actually draw up the ranks in Roman fashion, then, since no arrangement is made for the first to be received by the second, when the first is routed, all get mixed up together and defeat themselves. For if the rank in front gets the worst of it, it collides with the second; and, if the second wants to advance, it is impeded by the first. Hence when the first falls back on the second, and the second on the third, so much confusion arises that the whole army is frequently ruined should the least misadventure befall.

At the battle of Ravenna, in which Monsieur de Foix who commanded the armies of France was killed – a well-fought battle as things go today – both the Spanish and the French armies were drawn up in one of the ways just described, i.e. each of the two armies advanced with all its troops drawn up shoulder to shoulder so that both presented but a single front which was much greater in extent than it was in depth. This is always their procedure when they are operating on a large plain such as they had at Ravenna; for, realizing the disorder a retreat causes when troops are arranged in files, they avoid this, when they can, by making their front broad, as has been said. But should the available space be narrow they put up with the aforesaid bad arrangement without providing any remedy. And in the same bad formation they ride through the enemy's country, whether to loot it or to perform any other military manoeuvre.

Again, at San. Regolo in the territory of Pisa, as also at other places in which the Florentines were routed by the Pisans during the war which took place between the Florentines and that city owing to its having rebelled after Charles, king of France, passed through Italy, the disaster was entirely due to the allied cavalry which, being in front and having been repulsed by the enemy, fell back on the Florentine infantry and broke it up, so that the rest of the troops all turned tail. Messer Ciriaco dal Borgo, once a captain of Florentine infantry has also often stated in my presence that he had never been routed except by the cavalry of his allies. The Swiss, who are masters of modern warfare, when fighting on the French side, make it their first care to station themselves on the flanks, so that, should the allied cavalry be driven back, it will not clash with them. Yet, though such things are both easy to understand and very easy to carry out, none the less there has not appeared as yet any of our contemporary generals who has adopted the ancient formations and emended the modern ones. And though they may again have the three-fold army formation, called respectively the vanguard, the main body and the rearguard, it serves no purpose other than that of disposing men in billets. Moreover, when they make use of it, as was said above, it rarely happens that the self-same fortune does not befall all these bodies.

Since many, to cover their ignorance, assert that the destructive power of artillery does not in these days permit the use of many ancient practices, I propose to discuss this question in the following chapter, and to inquire whether artillery renders it impossible to display the valour of days gone by.

17. In what Esteem Artillery should be held by Armies at the Present Time, and whether the Opinion universally held in its Regard is Sound

WHEN in addition to what I have just written, I consider how many open battles which in our time the French call 'days' and the Italians call 'feats of arms', were fought by the Romans at different times, there comes to my mind the common opinion so many hold, an opinion which would have it that, had there been artillery in those days, it would not have been possible for the Romans to have conquered provinces and to have made peoples become their tributaries so easily as they did; nor would they have been able in any way to make such bold acquisitions. They allege, too, that the use of these destructive weapons prevents men from employing and displaying their virtue as they used to do of old. And as a third point they add that it is more difficult than it was then to come to an engagement, and that it is impossible to keep to the ancient usages. In fact, war before long will be reduced to the question of artillery.

I do not think it beside the point to discuss whether this view is sound, or to inquire whether artillery has increased or has lessened the strength of armies, and whether it has deprived good generals of, or has provided them with, an opportunity for acting 'virtuously'. So let me begin by dealing with the first of these claims, namely, that Roman armies of old would not have made the acquisitions they did make, if in those days there had been artillery.

In reply to this I would point out that wars are either offensive or defensive. Hence we must first ask to which of these two kinds of warfare artillery is the more useful or the more dangerous. Though there is something to be said for either view, yet I am convinced that artillery is incomparably more harmful to defenders than to those who attack. The reason why I say this is that the defenders are either in a walled town or are encamped behind a stockade. If they are within a walled town, either it is small, as are most fortresses, or it is large. In the first case, it is all up with the defenders, for the force of artillery is such that no wall can stand it, not even the thickest, for more than a few days. Hence if those within have not a goodly space into which to retire and dig trenches and build ramparts they are doomed. Nor can they

withstand the attack of an enemy determined to force his way
through a gap in the walls, even if they have artillery to help
them, for it is an accepted maxim that against a heavy massed
attack artillery is powerless. For this reason the defending of
towns against the fury of ultramontane attacks has not been
successful but against the assaults of Italians they have been
highly successful, for the latter do not attack *en masse* but in
detachments, a form of attack for which much the best name
is skirmishing. To advance thus coolly in such weak formation
towards a breach in the walls where there is artillery, is to
advance to certain death, and against such attacks artillery is
of service. But when the attackers form a dense mass and
come on one after the other to a breach in the walls, they get
through anywhere unless held up by trenches and ramparts.
Artillery will not hold them, for, though some get killed,
there will not be so many killed as to prevent a victory.

That this is so is shown by the many towns stormed by the
ultramontanes in Italy, and especially by that of Brescia. For
when this town rebelled against the French who still held the
citadel on behalf of the king of France, in order to prevent
raids being made on the town from the citadel, the Venetians
fortified the whole of the street leading down from the citadel
to the city with artillery, placing it both in front and on the
flanks and in any other convenient place. But of this Monsieur de Foix made no account. On the contrary, with a
squadron of his cavalry, who dismounted, he got right through
the artillery and took the city; nor do we hear that the
artillery caused him any appreciable loss. So that the defenders
of a small town, as we have said, when they find their walls
laid low and have no space into which to retire behind
ramparts and in trenches, but have to rely on their artillery,
are speedily undone.

If you are defending a large town where you have all you
need for a withdrawal, artillery is still of far greater use to

those who are outside than to those who are within. First, because, if artillery is to do any damage to those who are outside, you must needs raise it above the level of the ground, for, if on the level, every little trench the enemy digs and every rampart he puts up will afford him security, and you can do him no harm. So much so that, having raised your artillery and dragged it into some recess in the walls or having in some other way elevated it above the ground, you will then meet with two difficulties. First, you cannot bring into action artillery of the same size and power as those outside can avail themselves of, since in a small space it is impossible to manipulate large pieces. Secondly, should you succeed in getting it there, you will not be able to construct reliable and safe ramparts whereby to protect the said artillery, which can be done quite easily outside, on *terra firma*, where there are all the conveniences and as much space as anyone can want. Hence it is impossible for the defenders of a town to have their artillery in high positions when those who are outside have enough artillery and that of a powerful kind; and if they are driven to place it in a low position, it is in large part useless, as has been said. Consequently, the defence of a city has to be carried on by hand-to-hand fighting, as was done of old, supported by artillery of very light calibre. Wherefore, though some slight benefit may accrue from this light artillery, it brings with it a disadvantage which counterbalances the advantage due to artillery, because, owing to the heavy artillery, the walls of towns are demolished and lie flat, buried, as it were, in ditches, so that, when it comes to hand-to-hand fighting, the defenders have a worse time of it than they had before, since their walls have been battered down or their trenches filled up. These engines of war, therefore, as was said above, are of more use to the besiegers of towns than they are to the besieged.

As to the third point, if your camp has been placed behind a stockade so as to avoid open battle unless it suit your conveni-

ence and is to your advantage, I claim that in this case you are
ordinarily no better off in regard to preventing an engagement
than was the case in the old days, and that there are times
when, on account of artillery, you may be at a greater disadvantage. For, should the enemy come upon you and have
a slight advantage in position, as may easily happen should he
find himself on higher ground than yours; or should you on
his arriving not yet have made your trenches and dug yourself
well in; straightway, and without your being able to do
anything about it, he will dislodge you and you will have to
quit your fortified position and join battle. This happened to
the Spaniards at the battle of Ravenna. They had fortified
themselves on the banks of the Ronco, but the earthworks
they had thrown up were not sufficiently high and the French
had a slight advantage in position, so that they were compelled
by artillery to quit their fortifications and join battle. But
suppose, as should usually be the case, that the site you have
chosen for the camp is above that occupied by the enemy and
that its earthworks are good and strong, so that, owing to
your position and the other preparations you have made, the
enemy does not dare to attack, it will be found that in such a
case recourse will be had to the methods that were used in
ancient times when someone had his army in a position in
which it could not be attacked, namely, to scouring the
country, taking or laying siege to towns that are friendly to
you, and cutting off your supplies, so that you will be forced
under such conditions to leave your camp and come out into
the open, where artillery, as I shall presently point out, cannot
do much. In view, therefore, of the reasons for which the
Romans made war, and seeing that almost all their wars were
of the offensive and not of the defensive type, it would seem
that what we have said above holds good, namely, that it
would have been to their advantage and would have speeded
up their conquests, had there been artillery in those days.

As to the second charge, which alleges that men cannot

display their valour as they used to do of old, on account of artillery, I admit it is true that, where men in small detachments have to expose themselves, there is greater danger now than then, should they have to scale the walls of a town or to make an assault of this kind not with a compact body of troops but individually, first one appearing and then another. It is also true that the officers and generals of an army are more exposed to the danger of death now than then, since anywhere they may come under artillery fire. Nor does it help them to be in the last squadron or to be supported by very brave men. One finds, none the less, that rarely does either of these two dangers occasion any out-of-the-way loss. For the walls of well-fortified towns cannot be scaled, nor are attacks on them made with weak troops. If a town is to be taken, it has to be besieged, just as it was of old. Nor, even when it is taken by assault are the dangers much greater now than they were then, for the defenders of towns even in those days did not lack equipment for launching projectiles, which, if not so terrifying, were no less effective in the matter of killing men. As to the death of officers and army commanders, in the last twenty-four years during which there have been wars in Italy, there have been fewer cases than there were during ten years of war in olden times. For, except for Count Ludovico della Mirandola, who was killed at Ferrara when the Venetians attacked that state a few years ago, and for the Duke of Nemours, who was killed abroad at Cerignuola, artillery has not killed anybody; for Monsieur de Foix was killed with a sword, not by a cannon-ball. Hence if men do not, as individuals, display their valour, it is not due to artillery, but to bad methods and to the weakness of [modern] armies, for since they lack valour as a whole, they cannot display it in the part.

To their third allegation which is that it is impossible to bring about a hand-to-hand fight and that war will eventually become a matter of artillery, I reply that this statement is

altogether false, and will always be looked on as false by those
who want their armies to display in their operations the virtue
of ancient times. For it behoves him who wants to form a
good army, to accustom his men by means of sham fights or
real fights to engage the enemy at close quarters, sword in
hand. Hence he should rely more on infantry than on cavalry,
for reasons which will presently be given. And, if he does rely
on infantry, trained as we have said, artillery becomes quite
useless, since it is easier for infantry when engaging the enemy
to avoid cannon-balls than it was of old for them to avoid an
attack by elephants or by chariots armed with scythes, or
other unfamiliar weapons such as the Roman infantry had to
encounter. Against such devices they always found a remedy;
and against artillery would the more easily have found a
remedy in that the time during which it may harm you is
shorter than that during which elephants and scythed chariots
could do you harm. For the latter throw you into disorder
during a battle, whereas the former is a nuisance only before
the fight begins; and this nuisance infantry easily avoid either
by availing themselves of such cover as the site offers or by
lying flat on the ground when a volley comes. Experience,
however, has shown that this is unnecessary, especially as a
defence against heavy artillery; for with heavy artillery the
range cannot be so nicely adjusted. Hence either the fire is too
high, and does not get you, or it is too low and falls short of
you.

Again, when armies come to hand-to-hand conflict, it is as
clear as the day that neither heavy nor light artillery can hurt
you. For if the enemy place it in front, you capture it; and, if
he puts it behind, it hits his own folk before it hits you; while
on the flanks it cannot do you so much damage but that you
can go and get it, so that in the end it all comes to much the
same thing. Nor is there much question about this. For it is
clear from the case of the Swiss, who at Novara in 1513 were

without either artillery or cavalry, yet went for the French army, which was supported by artillery in a fortified position, and found no difficulty on this account in breaking it up.

The reason for this, besides what I said above, is that, if artillery is to function, it must be protected either by walls or trenches or earthworks, and, if either form of protection is lacking, it either gets taken or becomes useless, just as happens when men have to defend it in pitched battles and open engagements. Nor can it be used on the flanks except in the way the ancients used projectile launching devices. Such instruments were then placed outside the main body, in order that they might function outside the ranks, and, should those who used them be overcome at any time by cavalry or other forces, they took refuge behind the regular troops. Those who expect anything more from artillery do not understand it properly and place their trust in what can easily let them down. And if by using artillery the Turk gained a victory over Sophy and the Sultan, it was solely in virtue of the panic caused among their cavalry by its unfamiliar noise.

On coming, then, to the end of this discourse, my conclusion is that artillery is useful to an army provided it be backed by valour such as was displayed of old; but, without this, it is of not the least use against a valorous army.[47]

18. *That Infantry should be more highly esteemed than Cavalry is shown by the Authority of the Romans and by the Example of Ancient Military Practice*

IT is possible to give many reasons and to cite many cases showing clearly how much greater esteem the Romans had for foot-soldiers than for cavalry in all military operations, and how upon this basis they drew up all plans for their forces. Numerous instances illustrate this; among others the battle fought with the Latins near Lake Regillus, where, when the

Roman army began to give way, to support them some troops on horseback were ordered to dismount and fight on foot, by which means the battle was renewed and a victory gained. From which it is obvious that the Romans had more confidence in their men when on foot than when mounted. They used this expedient in many other battles, and always found it the best remedy in dangerous situations.

Nor can this be countered by the opinion expressed by Hannibal when during the battle of Cannae he noticed that the consuls had made their cavalry dismount, and joked about it, saying: '*Quam mallem vinctos mihi traderent equites,*' i.e. 'I should have liked it better had they handed the horsemen over to me bound.' Though this opinion is voiced by a first-class man, yet, if it be a question of authority, one should put more credence in a Roman republic and in the many first-class generals who were in it than in Hannibal alone. Furthermore, apart from an appeal to authority, sound reasons can be adduced; for a foot-soldier can get to many places to which a mounted man cannot go; infantry can be taught to keep their ranks, and, when broken, know how to re-form them, whereas it is difficult for cavalry to keep their ranks, and impossible for them to re-form when their ranks are disorganized. Besides which, one finds that horses, like men, sometimes have little spirit and sometimes a great deal, and quite often it happens that a spirited horse is ridden by a timid man and a timid horse by a man of spirit; and of whichever kind the disparity be, the result is subversive of utility and order.

Infantry when well drawn up, can easily break cavalry, but with difficulty are routed by them. This view is corroborated not only by many instances, both ancient and modern, but also by authors who prescribe rules for the conduct of civic affairs and in them show that wars were first fought with cavalry, since there were then no rules for drawing up infantry; but when these were made, it was at once recognized that infantry are more useful than cavalry. But it does not follow from this that cavalry is not essential to an army alike for the purpose of scouting, of raiding and pillaging the country, of pursuing the enemy when in flight, and again as a partial counterpoise to the cavalry of the adversary: but it is infantry that should constitute the basis and sinews of an army and that should be held in the higher esteem.

Among the sins committed by Italian princes who have made Italy the slave of the foreigner, there is none more grave than that of having held this arm of small account and of having devoted all their attention to mounted troops. This mismanagement is due to the perversity of captains[a] and to the ignorance of those who hold office. For the Italian militia having lost all official status during the last twenty-five years had become like soldiers of fortune. It occurred to the militia that their reputation would be made if they had the armed forces while the rulers had none. Since, then, they could not maintain a large number of infantry continually in their pay and they had no subjects of whom they could avail themselves, and since a small number would not make their reputation, they turned to cavalry; for with two or three hundred cavalry in his pay, the reputation of a *condottiere* was safe, and the pay was not such as to prevent him getting it from ministers of state. So the more easily to attain their end and to keep up their reputation they made light of all the esteem and repute in which infantry was held, and applied it instead to their own cavalry: an abuse which has grown to such an extent that even of the largest armies the infantry constitute but a fraction. It is this practice, conjoined with numerous other abuses associated with it, that has made the Italian militia so weak that Italy has become an easy prey, downtrodden by all the ultramontanes.

To show yet more clearly what a mistake it is to prefer

[a] *capi*, heads, bosses.

cavalry to infantry, I shall take another example from Rome. The Romans were encamped before Sora. From the town there came forth a troop of cavalry to attack their camp. The Roman master of horse advanced to meet them with his cavalry. When they met, luck would have it that at their first encounter the officers commanding both bodies of troops were killed. Though without their leaders, the fight none the less went on, and that they might the more easily get the better of their foes, the Romans dismounted, and forced the enemy's cavalry in order to defend themselves, to do the same; by which means the Romans gained the victory. Than this example none shows better how much more virtue there is in infantry than in cavalry; for in other actions the consuls made the Roman cavalry dismount that they might help the infantry who were hard pressed and were in need of support; but in this case they dismounted, not to help the infantry, nor yet to engage the enemy's foot-soldiers, but because, while fighting as cavalry against cavalry, it occurred to them that, since as cavalry they could not prevail, they might win more easily by dismounting. Whence I infer that it is only with the greatest difficult that infantry when properly drawn up, can be overcome except by other infantry.

Crassus and Mark Antony, two Romans, overran the domains of the Parthians for many days with very few cavalry but plenty of infantry, though against them they had vast numbers of Parthian cavalry. Crassus with part of the army got killed, but Mark Antony fought valiantly [a] and escaped. None the less, in the misfortunes the Romans suffered, we see how much more value infantry were than cavalry, for the country was vast, mountains scarce, streams very scarce, the sea far away, and no conveniences at hand; yet Mark Antony, as the Parthians themselves admitted, saved himself by his outstanding virtue; nor did the Parthian cavalry, numerous as it was,

[a] *virtuosamente.*

ever dare to try conclusions with his army. And, if Crassus was left behind, he who studies closely the record of his doings, will see that it was by deceit rather than by force that he was undone, for, in spite of all his troubles, the Parthians never ventured to attack him. On the contrary, they always went roaming about, intercepting his convoys, making promises which they did not keep, till they had reduced him to dire extremity.

I should have been at more pains, I think, to prove that the 'virtue' of infantry is more potent than that of cavalry if there had not been so many recent examples which provide abundant evidence of this. There were the nine thousand Swiss we have already mentioned, who at Novara proceeded to attack ten thousand cavalry and as many infantry, and beat them; for the cavalry could not get at them, and they thought little of the infantry, since it consisted for the most part of Gascons and was badly organized. Then there were the twenty-six thousand Swiss who went as far as Milan to look for Francis, king of France, who had with him twenty thousand cavalry, forty thousand infantry, and a hundred pieces of artillery; and if they did not win the day as they had done at Novara, they fought valiantly [a] for two days, and, though routed, got away with half their forces. Marcus Regulus Atilius had the courage to oppose not only cavalry, but elephants, with infantry; and, if his project did not succeed, it was not because his infantry were so lacking in virtue, that he had not sufficient confidence in them to believe that they would overcome the difficulty. I repeat, then, that to get the better of well-disciplined infantry it is necessary to bring against them better disciplined infantry; otherwise the case is plainly hopeless.[48]

In the days of Philip Visconti, Duke of Milan, there descended on Lombardy about sixteen thousand Swiss. Whereupon the Duke, whose forces were then commanded

[a] *virtuosamente.*

332

by Carmignuola, sent him with about a thousand cavalry and a few infantry to meet them. Carmignuola, unacquainted with their way of fighting, attacked them with his cavalry, assuming that he would be able to break them at once. But they stood firm, and, having lost many of his men, he retired. Being, however, a very brave man, who knew how to take fresh chances when circumstances changed, as soon as reinforcements came along to make up his strength, he went to meet them, told all his men-at-arms to dismount, and, putting them at the head of his infantry, set out to attack the Swiss. For whom there was no escape, because Carmignuola's men-at-arms having dismounted and being well protected by armour, they could easily pierce the ranks of the Swiss without suffering any harm, and, having got through, could easily overcome them. The result was that of all the Swiss there remained alive only those whom the humanity of Carmignuola chose to spare.

I believe many are aware of the difference in virtue that exists between these two kinds of troops, but so unhappy are these our times that neither ancient nor modern examples nor its being admittedly a mistake is sufficient to make modern rulers revise their point of view and realize that, if a province or a state is to keep up its military reputation, it is essential to resuscitate these services, to have them at hand, to restore their credit, to put fresh life into them, so that they may bring to the ruler both life and reputation. But, as rulers have departed from these ways, so they have departed from others mentioned above, and in consequence acquisitions do harm to a state instead of contributing to its greatness, as will presently be pointed out.

Book Two

[THE ADMINISTRATION OF CONQUERED TERRITORY AND OTHER PROBLEMS WHICH ADMIT OF NO MIDDLE COURSE]

---

19. *Acquisitions made by Republics, when not well governed nor handled with the Virtue the Romans displayed, contribute to the Downfall, not to the Advancement, of such Republics*

THE erroneous views, based on ill-chosen examples, which have been introduced by our corrupt age, prevent men from considering whether to depart from the customary methods. Who could have persuaded an Italian, thirty years ago, that ten thousand infantry could attack ten thousand cavalry and as many infantry in an open plain and not only engage them in battle but defeat them, as happened at Novara – to cite a case already mentioned more than once? Even though history is full of such examples, nobody would have credited them; and, had they been credited, it would have been objected that in these days there are better arms, and that a squadron of men-at-arms should be able to hurl itself against a rock, not merely against an infantry battalion. With such false pretexts men impaired their judgement; nor would they have taken into account that Lucullus with a small force of infantry routed a hundred and fifty thousand cavalry under Tigranes,

334

and that among these horsemen was a type of cavalry precisely similar to our own men-at-arms; nor yet again how this fallacy has been exposed by the example of ultramontane peoples.

And since what history teaches about infantry is thus seen to be true, in the same way one should give credit to, and profit by, all other ancient practices. Were this done, republics and princes would make fewer mistakes, would be stronger in repelling an attack which should catch them unawares, and would not set their hopes on flight. Those who have to handle a body politic would know better how to direct its policy, whether with a view to its expanding or to holding its own; would realize that the right way to make a republic great and for it to acquire an empire is to increase the number of its inhabitants, to make other states its allies, not its subjects, to send out colonies for the security of conquered territory, to fund the spoils of war, to subdue the enemy by raids and battles, not by sieges, to enrich the public but to keep individuals poor, to attend with the utmost care to military training. And, should this method of providing for expansion not meet with their approval, they should reflect that acquisitions made in any other way spell ruin to a republic and so should bridle all ambition, provide well for the internal administration of their city-state by means of laws and customs, forbid it to make acquisitions, and look only to its defence, for which good preparation should be made. This is how the republics of Germany act, and, because they have taken such steps, they enjoy freedom, and have enjoyed it for quite a spell.

None the less, as I have said elsewhere[49] when discussing the difference between constituting a state with a view to expansion and with a view to its maintaining the *status quo*, it is impossible for a state to remain for ever in the peaceful enjoyment of its liberties and its narrow confines; for, though it may not molest other states, it will be molested by them, and, when thus molested, there will arise in it the desire, and the need, for conquest. It will find, too, that, when it has no external foe, there will be one at home, for this seems necessarily to happen in all large cities.

That the republics of Germany have been able to live in this way [i.e. to maintain their *status quo*], and have lasted a considerable time, is due to the conditions which prevail in that country and are not found elsewhere, conditions without which it is impossible to maintain this type of polity. The part of Germany of which I am speaking was, like France and Spain, subject to the Roman empire; but, when later the Empire declined and the Imperial title was transferred to Germany, its more powerful towns, owing either to the weakness or to the exigences of the emperors, began to free themselves, recompensing the emperor by the payment of a small annual tribute, so that little by little all the towns which had been directly dependent on the emperor and were not subject to any other prince, purchased their freedom in like manner. It also happened that, whilst these towns were in process of recovering their freedom, other communes which were subject to the Duke of Austria, rebelled against him – among them Fribourg, the Swiss communes, and others like them. These communes prospered from the start, and grew little by little to such dimensions that not only did they never fall under the Austrian yoke again, but they became the terror of all their neighbours. I mean the communes now called Switzerland.

Germany, then, is divided among the Swiss, republics called free states, princes and the emperor. And the reason why amidst such diverse forms of constitution wars do not arise, or, if they do arise, do not last long, is the Imperial title, for, though the emperor has no power to enforce his will, yet he has such standing among them that he acts as an arbitrator, and by interposing his authority, mediates between them and at once puts an end to any dissension. The more important and the longest wars that have occurred there, have been those between the Swiss and the Duke of Austria; and, though for many years the Emperor and the Duke of Austria have been identical, this has not enabled the Duke to overcome the boldness of the Swiss, among whose communes there would never have been an *entente* if they had not been driven to it. Nor has the rest of Germany given the Emperor much help; for, on the one hand, the communes do not want to harm those who desired, like themselves, to be free, and, on the other, the princes are in some cases unable to help on account of their poverty, and in others do not care to help, since they envy the Imperial power.

These communities, therefore, are able to live, content with their small dominions, since with respect to the Imperial authority they have no cause to desire more. Within their walls they live united because in the offing there is an enemy who, should there be internal disorder, would take the opportunity to subjugate them. Were conditions in Germany other than these, they would have to seek expansion and disrupt their present tranquillity. And, since elsewhere such conditions are not present, other states cannot adopt this type of polity, but must needs expand either by means of confederations or in the way the Romans did. To adopt any other policy is to seek not life but death and ruin; since conquests are harmful in a thousand ways and for many reasons. For it is easy to acquire dominion but not at the same time military strength, and yet it must needs be that those who acquire dominion and not at the same time military strength are ruined. Nor can one who has been impoverished by wars acquire forces even if he be victorious, because he spends on them more than he gets from what he has acquired. This is what the Venetians and the Florentines did, and, when the one held Lombardy and the other Tuscany, they were both much weaker than when the one was content with the sea and the other with boundaries six miles long.

The trouble in all such cases is that with the will to acquire there does not go the wisdom to adopt the right method. This is the more blameworthy in that today there is less excuse for it; for the way the Romans behaved is there for all to see, and their example can be followed, whereas the Romans had no example before them, and had to use their own intelligence in order to discover what to do.

In addition to this, conquests sometimes do no small harm even to a well-ordered republic when the province or city it has acquired is given to luxurious habits which can be taken up by those who have intercourse with it; as happened first to Rome when she acquired Capua, and then to Hannibal. Indeed, had Capua been so remote from Rome as to have had no remedy at hand for the mistake the soldiers made, or had Rome then been in any way corrupt, the acquisition of Capua would undoubtedly have been the end of the Roman republic. Titus Livy bears witness to this when he says: 'Capua was by no means good for military discipline, for it afforded all manner of opportunities for indulgence which obliterated the memory of their fatherland in the debilitated minds of the troops.' In this way cities and provinces avenge themselves on their conquerors without either battle or bloodshed, for, when the latter have become imbued with their deplorable habits, they are liable to be beaten by anyone who attacks them. This could not be put better than it is by Juvenal in his *Satires*, where, in dealing with this question, he says that the acquiring of foreign lands familiarized the minds of the Romans with foreign customs, so that, in place of frugality and its other high virtues, 'gluttony and self-indulgence took possession of it and avenged the world it had conquered'.

If, then, the acquisition of territory did so much harm to the

Romans at a time when their conduct was conspicuous for prudence and virtue, what effect will it have upon states whose conduct is very far removed from this? Upon states which, in addition to the other mistakes they make, of which enough has been said above, in their wars use either mercenary or auxiliary troops? From which there results harm of diverse kinds which will be mentioned in the next chapter.

20. On the Dangers which accrue to the Prince or the Republic that employs Auxiliary or Mercenary Troops

IF I had not in another of my works[50] discoursed at length on the futility of mercenary and auxiliary troops and on the advantage of one's own, I should make this discourse of greater length than I shall do; but having spoken at length elsewhere, I shall here be brief. Yet I cannot well omit to mention an important example which I have found in Titus Livy concerning auxiliary troops, where by 'auxiliary troops' I mean those that a prince or a republic sends to help you under commanders appointed and paid by that prince or that republic.

Coming then to Livy's evidence, I would point out that, after the Romans in two different places had routed two Samnite armies with the armies which they had sent to help the Capuans, and had thus freed the Capuans from the war the Samnites had been waging against them, they decided to return to Rome. But lest the Capuans, when deprived of their help, should again fall a prey to the Samnites, they left two legions in the neighbourhood of Capua to defend them. These legions began to enjoy an idleness which was bad for them; so much so that, though it would mean being false to their fatherland and to the respect they owed the senate, they thought of taking up arms and making themselves lords of the country which by their valour they had defended, for it seemed to them that the inhabitants were unworthy to possess good things which they knew not how to protect. When this became known it was stopped by the Romans and matters were put right, as we shall explain at length when we come to speak of conspiracies.

I repeat, then, that of all kinds of soldiers auxiliaries are the most hurtful, for over them the prince or the republic who accepts their aid, has no authority at all: the only person who has authority over them is the person who has sent them. For auxiliary troops are, as I have said, troops sent to you by a ruler under their own commanders, with their own standards, and in his pay, as was the army which the Romans sent to Capua. Such soldiers, when they have won, often prey on those who have commissioned them in the same way as they prey on those against whom they have been commissioned to fight, moved thereunto either by the malignity of the prince who sends them, or by their own ambition. Though the Romans had no intention of breaking the alliance and agreement they had made with the Capuans, yet so easy did the conquest of Capua seem to these soldiers that they were readily induced to consider depriving the Capuans of their lands and of their independence.

Of this numerous examples might be given, but I shall be content with this one and with that afforded by Rhegium, which was robbed of its independent life and of its territory by a legion which the Romans had sent to guard it. A prince or a republic, therefore, ought first to adopt any course rather than bring into the state for its defence auxiliary forces, when it means that they will be entirely dependent on them; for any treaty or convention, however hard, that they can make with any enemy will be light as compared with such an alternative. Those who study closely the past and discuss the present will find that for each case that has led to good results there are any number that turned out to be mistakes. Nor can an ambitious prince or republic have a better chance of getting hold of a city or a province than to be asked to send his armies there to protect it. Hence he who is so ambitious as to invoke such help, not merely to defend himself but to attack others, is seeking to acquire what he cannot keep, for by what he has used to get it, it can easily be taken away. Yet so great is man's ambition that, in striving to slake his present desire, he gives no thought to the evils that in a short time will follow in its wake. Nor is he stirred by the lessons of the past, as I have shown in regard to this and to other matters; for, if he were moved by them, he would see that the greater the liberality he displays towards his neighbours, and the more averse he is to seizing their lands, the more ready they will be to throw themselves into his lap; as will be shown below from what happened in the case of the Capuans.

21. The First Praetor the Romans sent out was to Capua, Four Hundred Years after they had first begun to make War

How much the methods used by the Romans in acquiring territory differed from those at present used to extend the dominion of a state, has been sufficiently explained in a previous discourse, and also how the Romans let the towns which they did not destroy, live under their own laws, even in the case of those which did not become their allies, but, when they surrendered, were made subjects; for in such a case the only token of the *imperium* exercised by the Roman people was the imposing of certain conditions, the which being observed, they allowed them to retain their own form of government and their prestige. These methods we know were kept up until they had gone beyond Italy, and begun to reduce kingdoms and states to provinces.

Of this the best example is that of the first praetor the

Romans ever sent to a place [outside Rome], namely, to Capua, for it was not ambition that induced them to send him, but because the Capuans had asked for one, since they were at loggerheads with one another and thought it necessary to have a Roman citizen in their city who should put matters right and reunite them. Moved by this example the people of Antium, when in like case, were constrained to ask that a prefect should be sent to them. Apropos of which incident and of this new way of exercising authority, Titus Livy says that 'not only the arms of the Romans, but Roman law began now to prevail'.

We see, therefore, how much this procedure contributed to the increase of Rome's power. For cities, especially those accustomed to freedom or to being ruled by a native of the place, rest more tranquil and content under a government they do not see, though it may bear on them somewhat hardly, than under a government with which they are brought into daily contact and which thus reminds them daily of their servitude. There is also a further advantage gained by the ruler. It is this. Since the judges and magistrates who exercise civil and criminal jurisdiction over the citizens are not his ministers, their judgements cannot cause difficulty or bring discredit on the ruler, so that many grounds for hating and calumniating him are thus avoided.

In addition to other examples one might adduce from antiquity to prove the truth of this, there has recently occurred one in Italy. For Genoa, as everybody knows, has more than once been occupied by the French, and in all cases except the present one the king sent a French governor to rule it in his name. But on the present occasion, not by choice but because he could not help it, the king let the city govern itself, and the governor appointed was a Genoese. Nor can it be doubted that, should anyone inquire as to which of these two methods brought greater security to the king and to the king's authority there, or greater contentment to the people, he would certainly favour the last method.

Besides which, men are more inclined to throw themselves on your lap the more averse you appear to be to have them there; and for their liberties fear less, the more humane and the more easy-going is your treatment of them. It was the easy-going ways and the generosity of the Romans that made the Capuans hasten to call in a Roman praetor; whereas had the Romans shown the least desire to send one there, they would at once have become suspicious and kept clear of them.

But what need is there to go to Capua and Rome for instances of this when they are to hand in Florence and Tuscany? Everyone knows how long it is since the city of Pistoia came of her own accord under the dominion of Florence. Everybody is also aware what hostility there has been between the Florentines and the Pisans, the Lucchesi and the Siennese. The diverse attitude here adopted did not proceed from the small value the Pistoians set on their liberty as compared with the others, nor from their thinking less of themselves than the others did; but from the Florentines having always treated the Pistoians as brothers, and the others as enemies. It was this that made the Pistoians so quick and so willing to accept Florentine suzerainty, and that made, and still makes, the others exert all their efforts not to come to this. Had the Florentines, whether by means of confederations or by helping them, been easy-going with their neighbours instead of treating them roughly, they would unquestionably be the lords of Tuscany today. I do not mean to say that armed forces should not be used, but that they should be used only as a last resort, when other means prove inadequate.

22. How frequently Erroneous are the Views Men adopt in regard to Matters of Moment

HOW frequently men form false opinions has been observed and is still observed by those who happen to be witnesses of their decisions, the which, unless made by men of first-class ability, are very often the reverse of being sound. And because in corrupt republics, especially in untroubled times, men of first-class ability are ousted by the envy and ambitious scheming of others, men fall back on what by a common error is judged to be good, or else by those who are seeking popularity rather than the common good. Such mistakes are discovered afterwards when things go wrong, and recourse is then had of necessity to those who in peaceful times had been, as it were, forgotten, as in its proper place in this connection we shall endeavour to show. There sometimes occur also events about which men who have had no great experience of affairs, are easily mistaken, since such happenings have plausible features which make men believe that the outcome in such a case will be what they have persuaded themselves it will be. These remarks are made with reference to what Numicius, the praetor, persuaded the Latins to do after they had been beaten by the Romans, and to what many believed a few years ago when Francis I, king of France, set out to acquire Milan, which the Swiss were defending.

I would point out, then, that, after the death of Louis XII, Francis of Angoulême succeeded to the crown of France and was anxious to recover the Duchy of Milan, which, a few years before, had been occupied by the Swiss, supported by Pope Julius II. To facilitate his attack, he desired to find help in Italy, so, besides the Venetians whom Louis had won over, he approached the Florentines and Pope Leo X, under the impression that his task would be easier if he could first win them over, since the King of Spain's troops were in Lombardy and other forces belonging to the Emperor were in Verona. Pope Leo declined to accede to the king's wish, but was persuaded by his advisers – so it was said – to remain neutral, for they pointed out that by adopting this course he would be certain to emerge victorious, for it did not suit the Church to have as powers in Italy either the king or the Swiss; but, being anxious to restore Italy to its former freedom, it was essential to free it from servitude to either. And since it was impossible to overcome both of them, either singly or both together, the best course was to let one of them overcome the other, and then for the Church with her allies to fall on the victor. Nor could there be a better opportunity than the present, since both armies were in the field, and the Pope had his forces in readiness and could send them to the confines of Lombardy, near to both the armies, under the pretext of protecting his own territory, where they could remain until the battle took place. This might reasonably be expected to be sanguinary on both sides, since both armies were good ones,[a] and hence should leave the victor so weak that it would be easy for the Pope to attack and break him, which would be a glorious thing since it would leave him master of Lombardy and the arbiter of all Italy.

How false this opinion was is seen by the event; for, when the Swiss were overcome after a long fight, the forces of the Pope and of the king of Spain did not dare to attack the victor, but made ready for flight, and even this would not have helped them, had it not been that the king, for humanity's sake or because indifferent, did not look to a second victory, but was content to make peace with the Church.

Though, when viewed from a distance, there were grounds which made the view here adopted seem sound, it was in fact utterly false. For it rarely happens that a victor loses very many of his troops; since they are killed in battle, not in flight, and

[a] virtuoso.

345

in the ardour of the combat when men are face to face, but few get killed, especially if the battle lasts but for a short time, as usually it does. While even if it lasts long, and many of the victor's men get killed, the repute gained by the victory and the terror he now inspires, much more than compensates for the loss suffered by the death of his men. Hence anyone who sets out to attack an army, which in his opinion has been weakened by a fight, will find himself mistaken unless his own army be such that at any time, even before the victory, he could afford to fight. In that case he might win or he might lose, according to his luck and to his 'virtue'; but an army which has just fought and gained a victory would be at an advantage rather than at a disadvantage in his regard.

This is put beyond question by the experience the Latins underwent and the mistake the praetor, Numicius, made, and by what happened to those who believed him. For when the Romans had defeated the Latins, Numicius went about shouting all over Latium that now was the time to attack the Romans since they were weakened by the battle they had fought with them, and all they had gained was a nominal victory, which in reality was a defeat owing to the losses they had suffered, so that any small force which should make a fresh attack on them, would finish them off. So the peoples who believed him, raised a fresh army, and were routed forthwith, wherein they suffered a loss which is always suffered by those who lend ear to such advice.

23. *When Events required that the Romans should pass Judgement on Subject Peoples they avoided a Middle Course*[51]

'THE state of things in Latium was now such that it could stand neither peace nor war.' The most unhappy of all unhappy positions is that of a prince or of a republic which is reduced to such extremities that it can neither accept peace nor sustain war. Such a position arises when the conditions of peace are too severe, and war means that either they become the prey of their allies or that they remain a prey to their enemies. All such extremities are brought about by bad counsels and bad decisions, made without first estimating carefully the forces at one's disposal, as has been said above. For the republic or the prince who measures his forces well, will with difficulty be brought to the pass to which the Latins were led. For they came to terms with the Romans when they ought not to have done so, and declared war on them when they ought not to have declared war; and by so doing created a situation in which the enmity and the friendship of the Romans was from their point of view equally harmful. The Latins, therefore, were conquered and brought into complete subjection, first by Manlius Torquatus and then by Camillus, who, having forced them to surrender unconditionally, and having put garrisons in all the Latin towns and everywhere taken hostages, returned to Rome and announced to the senate that all Latium was in the hands of the Roman people.

Since what Camillus said is important and deserves the attention of all rulers who would emulate his example should occasion arise, I shall here quote the words which Livy puts into the mouth of Camillus, for they bear witness to the way in which the Romans extended their dominions, and also to the fact that in judgements pronounced by their government they always avoided a middle course, and preferred the extremes. For government consists in nothing else but so controlling subjects that they shall neither be able to, nor have cause to, do you harm; which may be done either by making quite sure of them by depriving them of all means of doing you harm, or by treating them so well that it would be unreasonable for them to desire a change of fortune. All this is made quite clear, first by Camillus's statement and then by the judgement the senate came to in its regard. These are Livy's words: 'The immortal gods have vouchsafed to you the power to decide whether Latium is to be or not to be. Its future lies in your hands. In so far as the Latins are concerned, it rests with you to make a peace which shall be perpetual, either by punishing them cruelly or by pardoning them. Do you think it advisable to be brutal towards those who have surrendered and been conquered? If so, you can wipe out the whole of Latium. Do you want, after the manner of our forefathers, to augment the Roman state by admitting the conquered to citizenship? The material whereby to increase it to its great glorification lies ready to hand. Of a surety that empire is most secure in which obedience is conjoined with happiness. It behoves you then to subjugate them while their minds are so stunned that they know not what to expect, either by punishing them or by becoming their benefactor.' Having heard this proposal, the senate came to a decision which followed the lines the consul had laid down, which was that, after duly considering one by one each town, they should either treat all citizens of importance generously or wipe them out; by conferring on those they treated generously exemptions and privileges, granting them citizenship, and using every endeavour to make them loyal; and by demolishing the towns of the others, sending colonies there, and taking the inhabitants back to Rome or so dispersing them that they could no longer do harm either by appeal to arms or by their machinations. Nor did they ever adopt a middle course as I have said, of importance, towards men and other rulers should imitate them in this.

This is what the Florentines should have done when in 1502 Arezzo and the whole of the Val di Chiana revolted. If they had done this, they would have made their dominion secure, Florence would have become a great city, and they would have acquired that *lebensraum* [a] which they lacked. But they adopted that middle course, which is the most prejudicial that men can take. Some of the Aretines they banished, some they condemned [to death], and from all they took away the honours and positions sanctioned by the ancient customs of that city. But the city they left intact. And if in their discussions any citizen advised that Arezzo be destroyed, the reply given by those who seemed to be more wise was that to destroy it would do little credit to the republic, since it would appear that Florence had not the forces to hold it. Such arguments are based on appearances, not on the truth. For on this showing no parricide or criminal or notorious person would be put to death for fear lest, by so doing, a ruler should show that he had not the power to curb a particular individual. Those who are of this opinion do not see that, whenever men individually or a whole city offends against a state, its ruler has, both as an example to others and for his own security, no alternative but to wipe them out. Honour consists here in being able, and knowing how, to castigate it, not in being able to hold it, thereby incurring a thousand risks. For the ruler who does not punish an offender in such a way that he cannot offend again, is deemed either an ignoramus or a coward.

The policy of the Romans in this matter is again confirmed, if there be need to confirm it, by the judgement they passed on the Privernates. In what Livy says of it two things should be noted: first, as has been said above, that subject peoples should either be generously treated or be wiped out; secondly, how helpful a generous disposition may be, and how helpful it is to tell the truth when one is called on to give evidence before prudent men. The Roman senate had met to pronounce judgement on the Privernates, who had rebelled, but had subsequently been forced to return to the Roman obedience. The people of Privernum had sent many of their citizens to

[a] *quegli campi che per vivere.*

ask the senate to pardon them. When they came before the senate, one of them was asked by a senator: 'What punishment he thought the Privernates deserved?' To which the man from Privernum replied: 'That which men deserve who think themselves worthy of freedom.' To which the consul answered: 'Supposing that we remit the penalty, what kind of peace can we expect to have with you?' His answer was: 'If you are good to us, a loyal perpetual peace; if you treat us badly, not a long one.' Though many dissented, the wiser among the senators then said: 'We have been listening to those who are both men and free men; nor do I think it possible for any people or any man to remain longer than he can help in a situation which he deplores. Peace treaties can be relied upon when they are made voluntarily. Loyalty is not to be expected from those who are ready to become slaves.' In consequence of this speech, it was decreed that the Privernates should become Roman citizens, and should share in the privileges and honours which citizenship conferred. 'Those whose minds are set on liberty, and nothing but liberty', it was said, 'are worthy to be made true Romans.'

Such was the pleasure which this straightforward and generous answer gave to generous minds. To have given any other would have been deceitful and base. Those who believe that men are not like this, especially when they have been accustomed either to being free men or to looking on themselves as free men, are mistaken, and decisions based on this mistake are neither good for those that make them, nor satisfactory to others. Hence come frequently rebellions and the ruin of states.

But to return to our main topic. From the two judgements passed on these Latin peoples, I conclude that, when sentence has to be passed on cities which are powerful and accustomed to a life of freedom, either they should be eliminated or they should be caressed. Any other decision is futile. At all costs should the middle course be avoided; for it is hurtful, as it was to the Samnites when they caught the Romans in the Caudine Forks and were unwilling to follow the advice of the old man who told them either to treat the Romans as honourable men and to set them free, or to kill the lot. For they took the middle course, disarmed them, marched them under the yoke, and then set them free, burning with shame and indignation. With the result that, later on, they learned to their cost that the old man's advice was sound and their own decision harmful, as will be shown more at length in its proper place.

Book Two

---

24. *Fortresses in General are much more Harmful than Useful*

To the wiseacres of our times it may perhaps seem a foolish thing that when the Romans wanted to ensure the loyalty of the people of Latium and the city of Privernum it did not occur to them to build any sort of fortress to curb them and keep them loyal, especially as in Florence it is an accepted principle, so our wiseacres say, that Pisa and other such cities should be held by means of fortresses. Had the Romans been of their calibre, it would undoubtedly have occurred to them to build fortresses, but since their virtue, judgement, and power was of different order they did not do so. So long as Rome enjoyed freedom and was loyal to her institutions and to her efficient^a constitution she never held either cities or provinces by means of fortresses save where they were already built. In view, then, of the way the Romans acted in this matter and of the way rulers^b act today, it seems to me worth while considering whether it is good to build fortresses and whether they are harmful or useful to those who build them.

^a virtuose.   ^b principi – and so throughout the chapter.

It must be borne in mind, then, that fortresses are constructed as a defence either against enemies or against subjects.
In the first case they are unnecessary, and in the second case
harmful. Let us begin by explaining why in the second case
they are harmful. I maintain that when a prince or a republic
is afraid of its subjects and fears they may rebel, the root cause
of this fear must lie in the hatred which such subjects have for
their rulers: a hatred which is due to their misbehaviour; and
a misbehaviour which is due to their fancying they can hold
them by force, or to their foolish way of governing them.
And one of the things that makes rulers believe in force is the
fact that they have fortresses to fall back on. For when mismanagement gives rise to hatred it is mainly due to a prince
or a republic having fortresses; and, when this is the case,
fortresses are far more harmful than useful. For, in the first
place, they make you more foolhardy and violent in dealing
with your subjects, as has been said. Next, they do not afford
you internally that security you fancy they do. For no force
and no violence is of the least use in controlling your people
except under one of two conditions: either you have a good
army which you can put in the field, as the Romans had; or
your people are so exhausted, spent, disorganized and divided,
that they cannot unite to do you hurt. For if you reduce them
to poverty, 'though despoiled, they still have arms', and, if
you disarm them, 'their fury will provide them with arms'.
If you kill their leaders and suppress all other signs of insur-
rection, like the heads of the Hydra other leaders will
arise. If you erect fortresses, they are useful in time of peace
because they give you more courage in ill-treating your
subjects, but in time of war they are quite useless, for they will
be attacked both by your enemies and by your subjects, and
against both it is impossible for them to stand. And if there
ever was a time when they were useless, it is now on account
of artillery, for against its fire it is impossible to defend such

small places where there are no embankments behind which men can retire, as we have shown above.

In discussing this question I am going to particularize. Do you, my prince, with your fortresses want to keep a firm hand on the people in your city? Do you, be you a prince or a republic, want to tighten your grip on a city you have taken during a war? I tell you, if you be a prince, that as a means of controlling your citizens, nothing can be more futile than a fortress for the reasons I have given: it makes you quicker to use, and less careful in using, harsh measures, and by such measures you make them long for your downfall, and they become so furious that, for this very reason, your fortress will afford you no protection. So obvious is this, that a wise and good prince never constructs fortresses if he wants to remain good and to avoid providing his sons with a reason for wanting to become bad, for he would have them rely not on fortresses, but on their subjects' goodwill.

And if Count Francesco Sforza, having become Duke of Milan, was reputed a wise man, and yet built a fortress in Milan, I maintain that in this he was not wise, and the result has proved that this fortress did harm to his heirs instead of affording them security. For with a fortress they thought they were safe and could oppress their citizens and subjects, so lost no opportunity of doing them violence; with the result that they came to be detested beyond all measure, and lost their state to the first enemy who attacked them. Nor was this fortress any protection or of any service to them in time of war, while in time of peace it did them much harm, since, if they had not had it, yet had been so unwise as to treat their citizens harshly, they would have realized their danger sooner and would have withdrawn from it. In which case they would have been able to put up a more spirited resistance to the French attack with loyal subjects but without a fortress than with a fortress and disloyal subjects.

In no way, then, do fortresses help you, for you will lose them either through the treachery of their keepers, or by some violent attack, or, by their being starved out. While, if you do want them to help you, and to enable you to recover a state you have lost, in which there remains to you only a fortress, you must have an army with which to attack those who have driven you out, and when you have such an army, you will recover your state anyhow, even if there be no fortress there; and this the more easily when your men are friendly and have not been badly treated owing to the arrogance a fortress instils. Experience then shows that this Milanese fortress was not the least use either to the Sforzas or to the French when with either of them things went wrong. On the contrary, to both it brought disaster and ruin in that it prevented them from considering whether there might not be a more honest way of maintaining their position.

Guidobaldo, Duke of Urbino, the son of Frederick, who was highly esteemed in his day as an army commander, was expelled from his state by Caesar Borgia, the son of Pope Alexander VI. When later, owing to an accident, he got back, he had all the fortresses in that district razed to the ground since he thought them mischievous. For with respect to his people who were fond of him, he did not need fortresses and, so far as his enemies were concerned, he realized he could not protect the fortresses, since he would require to have an army in the field to defend them. So he resolved to get rid of them.

Pope Julius, when he had expelled the Bentivogli from Bologna, erected a fortress in that city, and afterwards caused its inhabitants to be cruelly oppressed by one of his governors so that they rebelled; and straightaway he lost the fortress, which thus did not help him, but harmed him in as much as, had he acted otherwise, it would have helped him.

Niccolò da Castello, father of the Vitelli, on returning to his country from which he had been exiled, at once pulled down two fortresses which had been built there by Pope Sixtus IV, for he held that it was not the fortress, but the affection of his people which would preserve his state for him.

But of all such cases the most recent and the most noteworthy in every way as illustrating the futility of building fortresses and the utility of demolishing them, is what happened at Genoa not long ago. Everybody knows that in 1507 Genoa rebelled against Louis XII, King of France, who came in person with all his forces to reconquer it, and that, on recovering it, he constructed a fortress stronger than any at present known, since, situated on the point of a hill which juts into the sea, called by the Genoese Codefà, it was, owing to its position and to a number of other circumstances, impregnable, and commanded the port and a large part of the city of Genoa. It none the less came about that in 1512, when the French were driven from Italy, Genoa rebelled, despite the fortress; Ottaviano Fregoso seized the government; and, after a siege of sixteen months in which he used all possible devices, he starved the fortress out. Everyone then expected, and many advised, that it should be kept as a refuge in case of emergency, but Fregoso, like a prudent man, destroyed it, for he recognized that it is not fortresses but the wills of men that keep rulers in power. Thus, instead of relying on a fortress, he relied on virtue and sound sense, and so held his position and holds it still. And, whereas to change the government of Genoa, a thousand infantry used to suffice, its adversaries have since attacked it with ten thousand and have done it no harm. Hence one sees that dismantling a fortress did not hurt Ottaviano, and erecting one did not help the king. For so long as he could come with an army into Italy, he could recover Genoa without having a fortress there; but, when he could not come into Italy with an army, he could not hold Genoa, though he had the fortress. Thus, constructing the fortress was expensive to the king, and losing it shameful;

whereas to Ottaviano the reconquering of the fortress brought glory and the demolishing of it advantage.

We come now to republics which erect fortresses not in their native land but in towns which they have acquired. If the instances already given, of France and of Genoa, do not suffice to show the fallacy involved, it should be enough if I cite those of Florence and Pisa. The Florentines erected fortresses to hold the city of Pisa, not considering that, since the Pisans had always been hostile to Florentine power, had enjoyed freedom and regarded rebellion as a means to freedom, it was necessary, if they were to retain Pisa, to adopt the Roman method, i.e. either to make it an ally or to destroy it. For the virtue of the fortresses became evident on the arrival of King Charles, to whom they surrendered owing either to the bad faith of their custodians or for fear of worse to come. Whereas if there had been no fortresses, the Florentines would not have based on them their power to hold Pisa; nor would the king have been able by means of them to deprive the Florentines of that city; for the means they had taken thus far might perchance have enabled them to keep it, and unquestionably would not have proved more disastrous than the fortresses.

I conclude, therefore, that for the purpose of holding one's own country fortresses are hurtful, and that for the purpose of holding acquired towns they are futile. The authority of the Romans is enough for me here, for round the towns they wanted to hold by force they did not build walls but pulled them down. And, if against this my view anyone should cite in ancient times the case of Tarentum, and in modern times Brescia, both of which places were regained, thanks to fortresses, after their subjects had revolted, I answer thus. To recover Tarentum Fabius Maximus at the beginning of his year of office, was sent with a whole army, which would have sufficed for its recovery even if there had been no fortress there; and though Fabius made use of it, if it had not been there he would have adopted other means which would have produced the same effect. What use there is in a fortress I do not know, if, to recover a town, one needs a consular army and a Fabius Maximus to command it. Moreover, that the Romans would have recovered it in any case, is seen from the example of Capua, where there was no fortress, but which the Romans retook by the valour of the army.

But let us turn to Brescia. I maintain that what happened in that rebellion is a rare occurrence. Rarely when a town rebels does it happen that the fortress remains in your hands and that you have a large army in the neighbourhood, as the French then had. For Monsieur de Foix, the king's commander, had an army at Bologna, and when he heard that Brescia was lost, he went without delay to deal with the revolt, in three days reached Brescia, and with assistance from the fortress recovered the town. Here again, then, for the fortress at Brescia to be of any use, it needed a Monsieur de Foix and a French army to relieve it after three days march. The case of Brescia, therefore, is not enough to refute examples of the opposite kind; for in wars recently waged, numbers of fortresses have been taken and retaken with the same fortune that has attended the taking and retaking of open country, not only in Lombardy, but in the Romagna, in the kingdom of Naples, and in every part of Italy.

As to building fortresses for defence against external foes, I maintain that they are unnecessary where peoples or kingdoms have good armies and that to those who have no such armies they are useless; for good armies without fortresses suffice for defence, and fortresses without good armies are no defence. This is borne out by the experience of men of high repute as rulers and in other matters, for instance, the Romans and the Spartans; for if the Romans did not build fortresses, the Spartans not only abstained from doing this, but did not per-

mit their cities to have walls, because they chose to rely for
defence on the virtue of the individual, and wanted no other.
Hence, when a Spartan was asked by an Athenian whether the
walls of Athens did not look fine, he answered: 'Quite!
provided it be ladies who live there.'

The ruler, then, who has good armies, may sometimes find
it useful, though not essential, to have fortresses on the coast
and on the frontiers of his domains to hold off the attack of an
enemy till he gets properly going. But, if he has not a good
army, to have fortresses within his state or on its frontiers is
either harmful or useless: harmful because he so easily loses
them and, when lost, they make war on him; or, if they
should chance to be so strong that the enemy cannot capture
them, they get left behind by the hostile army and so come
to be useless. For, when good armies do not meet with very
strong opposition, on entering a country they pay no attention
to cities and fortresses, which they may leave behind them.
We see this in ancient history just as we have seen it done by
Francesco Maria, who in quite recent times, when on his way
to attack Urbino, left behind him ten of the enemy's cities,
without bothering about them.

The ruler, then, who can muster a good army, can do without fortresses, and the ruler who has not a good army had
better not build them. The best thing he can do is to fortify
the city where he dwells, to keep it provisioned and its
inhabitants well disposed, so as to hold off an enemy's attack
till he can either come to terms or get outside help to relieve
him. All other plans are expensive in time of peace and useless
in time of war. In view, then, of all I have said, it will be seen
that, as the Romans were wise in their other institutions, so,
too, were they prudent when they decided in the case of the
Latins and the Privernates to dispense with fortresses and took
more virtuous and wiser means of securing their loyalty.

25. To attack a Divided City in the Hope that its Divisions will facilitate the Conquest of it is Bad Policy

THERE was so much discord between the plebs and the nobility in the Roman republic that the Veientes, in conjunction with the Etruscans, thought this disunion would enable them to destroy the power of Rome. Having, therefore, formed an army and invaded Roman territory, the senate sent Gaius Manlius and Marcus Fabius to engage them. When the army they were leading drew near to the army of the Veientes, the latter kept on attacking and vilifying the Roman name with insults and abuse. And so great was their rashness and insolence that the Romans became united instead of disunited, and, when it came to a fight, broke and defeated the enemy. Thus one sees, as we have said above, how mistaken men are when in coming to decisions they rely on discord, and how often, when they think they have a sure thing they lose. The Veientes thought that if they attacked the Romans, when disunited, they would overcome them; but their attack caused the Romans to unite and brought about their own ruin. For discord in a republic is usually due to idleness and peace, and unity to fear and to war. Had the Veientes been wise, then, the more disunited they found the Romans to be, the more studiously should they have refrained from going to war with them, and have striven to get the better of them by the artifices men use in time of peace.

The way to set about this is to win the confidence of the city which is disunited; and, so long as they do not come to blows, to act as arbitrator between the parties, and, when they do come to blows, to give tardy support to the weaker party, both with a view to keeping them at it and wearing them out; and, again, because stronger measures would leave no room for any to doubt that you were out to subjugate them and make yourself their ruler. When this scheme is well carried

SCORN AND ABUSE   II.25-6

out, it will happen, as always, that the end you have in view
will be attained. The city of Pistoia, as I have said in another
discourse and apropos of another topic, was acquired by the
republic of Florence by just such an artifice; for it was divided
and the Florentines supported now one, now the other, party
and, without making themselves obnoxious to either, led
them on until they got sick of their turbulent way of living
and in the end came to throw themselves voluntarily into the
arms of Florence.

The city of Siena has never changed its form of government
with the help of the Florentines except when their help was
weak and infrequent; for, when it was frequent and strong, its
effect was to make that city united in defence of the government in power.

I wish to add to the above-mentioned examples a further
example. Filippo Visconti, Duke of Milan, several times made
war on the Florentines, relying on their disunion, and in all
cases came out the loser, so that when he was bewailing these
attacks, he used to say that the follies of the Florentines had
involved him in an expenditure of two millions in gold to no
purpose.

It remained, then, that the Veientes and the Tuscans were
mistaken on this point, as was said above, so that in the end
there came a battle when the Romans conquered them. And
in like manner will others find themselves mistaken, should
they imagine that by such means and in such circumstances
they can bring a people into subjection.

26. Scorn and Abuse arouse Hatred against those who indulge in them without bringing them any Advantage

I HOLD it to be a sign of great prudence in men to refrain
alike from threats and from the use of insulting language, for
neither of these things deprives the enemy of his power, but

the first puts him more on his guard, while the other intensifies his hatred of you and makes him more industrious in devising means to harm you. This is seen in the case of the Veientes, whom we were discussing in the previous chapter. Besides the injury done by the war, they abused the Romans by word of mouth, a thing which every sensible general should prevent his soldiers from doing, for such language does but exasperate the enemy and move him to vengeance, nor, as has been said, does it in any way interfere with his attack: so that in fact they are weapons which turn against you.

Of this a notable instance occurred in Asia. When Cobades, the Persian commander, had been besieging Amida for a considerable time, he grew weary of the tiresome business and decided to withdraw. While he was striking camp the townsmen, exhilarated by their victory, all climbed on the walls and used every sort of abuse, calumniating and accusing and upbraiding the enemy for his cowardice and poltroonery. This so annoyed Cobades that he changed his mind, and, indignant at the injustice, returned to the siege and in a few days had taken and sacked the city.

The same thing happened to the Veientes, who, as I have said, were not content to make war on the Romans, but also spoke of them contemptuously, going up to the stockade surrounding their camp and shouting abuse at them. This annoyed the troops much more than the fighting did; so that, whereas they had at first fought unwillingly, they now pressed the consuls to join battle, with the result that the Veientes, like those mentioned above, were punished for their contumacy as they deserved. Good army commanders and good republican rulers should take all appropriate measures to prevent the use of abusive language and taunts, whether in the city or in their army, and whether used one towards another or towards the enemy. For, if used towards the enemy, there ensue the aforesaid inconveniences, and still worse inconveniences if used one towards the other, unless precautions be taken, as they always have been by prudent men.

When the Roman legions, left in Capua, conspired against the Capuans, as will be narrated in due course, and in connection with this conspiracy a mutiny arose, subsequently quelled by Valerius Corvinus, among other points in the convention he drew up, it prescribed the severest penalties on those who should reproach any of the troops for having taken part in the mutiny.

Tiberius Gracchus, who, during the war with Hannibal, had been put in command of a certain number of slaves, whom, owing to the shortage of men, the Romans had armed, made a special point of the capital punishment he prescribed for anyone who should reproach any slave with his servitude.

We see, then, how harmful the Romans thought it to calumniate others or to reproach them for a shameful deed, as has been said, for than this there is nothing that inflames the mind more, or arouses greater indignation, whether the taunt be true or be said in jest, 'For smart sayings, when they border on the truth, leave a bitter taste behind them.'

27. *Prudent Princes and Republics should be content with Victory, for, when they are not content with it, they usually lose*

SPEAKING to the disparagement of an enemy is usually due to the arrogance aroused in you by victory or by the false hope of victory. False hopes of this kind not only cause men to make mistakes in what they say, but also in what they do. For, when such hopes enter men's breasts they cause them to dispense with caution, and often to miss the chance of obtaining a sure thing in the hope, but by no means the certainty, of improving on it. This matter is worth considering, since very often men make mistakes in regard to it, detrimental to their country. Wherefore, since it cannot be so clearly proved by an appeal to reason, I shall cite examples both ancient and modern in support of it.

After routing the Romans at Cannae, Hannibal sent messengers to Carthage to announce his victory, and to ask for reinforcements and supplies. During the discussion in the senate as to what should be done, Hanno, an old and prudent Carthaginian citizen, urged that it would be wise to use the victory as a lever for securing peace with the Romans which they should be able to obtain with honour since they had beaten them, instead of waiting till their own defeat caused them to make it. The aim of the Carthaginians should be to make it clear to the Romans that to have fought with them sufficed. Having won, they should not now go and spoil their chances in the hope of improving on them. This course was not adopted by the Carthaginian senate, though it recognized later the wisdom of it when the opportunity had been lost.

When Alexander the Great had conquered the whole of the East, the republic of Tyre, which in those days ranked high and was powerful, since, like Venice, it was on the coast, recognized Alexander's greatness, and so sent ambassadors to say that they were ready to become his loyal subjects and to obey his behests, but that they were not prepared to receive either him or his troops in their town. Alexander was indignant that a city should want to shut in his face a door that the whole world had thrown open, declined to accept their conditions, and set out to besiege the city. But this sea-girt and fortunate town was so well stocked with provisions and other supplies needed for its defence, that after four months Alexander saw that it was taking him longer to win glory in the case of this city than it had taken him to acquire many other places, and hence decided to make peace overtures and to concede the point that Tyre had asked. But the men of

Tyre, elated with success, not only refused to accept his terms, but killed the envoy who came to arrange matters. Whereupon Alexander, becoming indignant, put such life into the siege that he took and demolished the city, and either killed or made slaves of its inhabitants.

In 1512 a Spanish army invaded the dominions of Florence with a view to restoring the Medici and levying a tax on the city, acting on behalf of fifth columnists who had led them to expect that, once they had crossed the border, they would take up arms in their favour. On entering the plain [of the Arno] they found none of them, and, as they were short of provisions, they made overtures of peace. The people of Florence were too proud to accept them. Hence the loss of Prato, and the ruin of that state.

Rulers of states, when attacked, therefore, cannot make a greater mistake than to refuse to come to terms when the forces attacking them are a good deal stronger than their own, especially if the overtures are made by the enemy: for the terms will never be so hard but that in them some benefit will accrue to those who accept them, so that in a way they will share in the victory. The people of Tyre, for instance, should have been content that Alexander had accepted the conditions which he had at first refused, and the victory thus gained would have been considerable, since with their armed forces they had compelled a great man to condescend to their wishes. It should, in like manner, have sufficed the people of Florence that the Spanish army had yielded to any of their demands instead of fulfilling all their own, for this, too, would have been a considerable victory. For what the Spanish army wanted was to change the form of government in Florence, to put an end to its attachment to France, and to levy tribute. If of these three things the Spaniards had gained the last two, and the people of Florence had gained the first, that is the retention of their form of government, each would have acquired a certain honour and a certain satisfaction; nor would the people have been likely to trouble much about the other two things, so long as their lives were safe. Nay, even had they seen there was a good, and almost certain, chance of a greater victory, they should not have placed themselves wholly at the discretion of fortune and ventured their last stake, which it is never wise to risk unless driven to it.

When Hannibal, who had enjoyed great glory in Italy for sixteen years, left it on being recalled by the Carthaginians to help his own country, he found Hasdrubal and Syphax routed, the kingdom of Numidia lost, and the Carthaginians cooped up within their own walls, destitute of hope except what he and his army should bring. Realizing that his country was reduced to its last stake, he was determined not to risk that till he had tried all other remedies, and so was not ashamed to sue for peace, since he was convinced that, if there was any hope at all for his country, it lay in this and not in war. When peace was refused, he did not decline to fight though bound to lose, since he felt that he could still win, but if he had to lose, he could at least lose gloriously. If, then, Hannibal, who was so full of virtuosity, and had his army still intact, preferred peace to war when he saw that, by losing, his country would be enslaved, what should a man do who has neither the efficiency nor the experience of Hannibal? Yet there are men who make this mistake, in that to their hopes they set no bound, and are ruined because they rely on such hopes and take no account of other things.

Book Two

[ROME'S DEALINGS WITH NEIGHBOURING STATES AND CITIES IN PEACE AND WAR]

---

28. *How Dangerous it is for a Republic or a Prince not to avenge an Injury done either to the Public or to a Private Person*

WHAT is likely to make men indignant with others may easily be learnt from what happened to the Romans when they sent the three Fabii as ambassadors to the Gauls, who were about to attack Tuscany and, in particular, Clusium. The people of Clusium had appealed to Rome for help against the Gauls. Hence the Romans sent the three Fabii as ambassadors to the Gauls to insist in the name of the Roman republic on their abstaining from a war with the Tuscans. When they arrived at their destination the ambassadors, who were better at acting than speaking, found the Gauls and the Tuscans about to join battle, whereupon they were the foremost to enter the fray. It thus came about that when the Gauls became aware of this, their annoyance with the Tuscans was turned against the Romans. And their indignation was intensified when the Gauls having complained to the Roman senate through their ambassadors of this unfairness and demanded that the aforesaid Fabii be handed over to them to

367

compensate for the harm they had done, they were not only
not handed over or punished in some other way, but an
election was held in which they were made tribunes with
consular power. Consequently when the Gauls saw those being honoured who ought to have been punished, they took
it as an affront and an indignity offered to themselves, and,
inflamed with indignation and anger, marched on Rome and
took it, except for the Capitol. A disaster which the Romans
brought on themselves through their disregard of justice, for
since their ambassadors had offended 'against the Law of
Nations',[52] they should have been punished, instead of being
honoured.

This leads one to consider how important it is for every
republic and every prince to take account of such offences,
not only when an injury is done to a whole people, but also
when it affects an individual. For if an individual is grievously
offended either by the public or by a private person, and does
not receive due satisfaction, he will, if he lives in a republic,
seek to avenge himself, even if it lead to the ruin of that
republic; and, if he live under a prince and has a spark of
manliness, will never rest content till he has in some way or
other wreaked vengeance on him even though he see that, in
doing so, he will bring disaster on himself.

In verification of this there is no finer or more relevant
instance than that of Philip, king of Macedon, the father of
Alexander, in whose court there was a handsome and noble
young man, Pausanias. With him Attalus, one of the chief
men in Philip's entourage, was enamoured, and had on several
occasions sought to get him to assent, but found that he had
no liking for such things; so, seeing that he could not get
what he wanted otherwise, he decided to set a trap for him
and to use force. He gave, therefore, a great banquet, which
Pausanias and other noble barons attended, and, when they
had had their fill of food and wine, he had him seized and

bound; then he not only used force in order to gratify his lust, but, to his greater shame, got others to treat him in the same disgusting way. Of this affront Pausanias complained several times to Philip, who, having kept him for a time in expectation of vengeance, not only did not avenge him, but made Attalus governor of a Grecian province. Pausanias, therefore, seeing his enemy honoured instead of being punished, gave full vent to his indignation not only against the perpetrator of the deed, but against Philip who had not avenged it. So, one morning, the day of the solemn wedding of Philip's daughter, who was being married to Alexander of Epirus, he killed Philip as he was going to the temple for the celebration standing between the two Alexanders, his son and his son-in-law. Of this incident, which is akin to that which happened to the Romans, all who rule should take note, so that they may never esteem any man so lightly as to think that, if injury be added to injury, the injured person will not consider how to vindicate himself, even though it involve him in all manner of dangers and entail his own downfall.

29. Fortune blinds Men's Minds when she does not wish them to obstruct her Designs

IF one ponders well the course of human affairs, it will be seen that many events happen and many misfortunes come about, against which the heavens have not been willing that any provision at all should be made. Since this statement holds good in the case of Rome, which was conspicuous alike for virtue, religion and orderly conduct, it is no wonder that the same thing happens yet more often in cities and provinces which are lacking in these respects. There is a well-known passage in which Titus Livy shows at length and with great force the power that heaven exercises over human affairs. He says that, with a view to making the Romans recognize its power, heaven first caused the Fabii to act wrongly when sent as ambassadors to the Gauls, and by means of what they did excited the Gauls to make war on Rome; then ordained that in Rome nothing worthy of the Roman people should be done to meet their attack; for first it brought about that Camillus, who was the only hope they had in those evil days, should be sent as an exile to Ardea; then that, when the Gauls were marching on Rome, they did not appoint a dictator, as they had done many times to meet the attack of the Volsci and other enemies in the neighbourhood. It also caused them to be weak and to take no particular care in calling up troops, who were so slow in taking up arms that they scarce had time to confront the Gauls on the banks of the Allia, which was but ten miles from Rome. There the tribunes set up their camp without their accustomed diligence, since they did not inspect the site beforehand, nor surround it with trenches and stockades, nor take any other precautions, either human or divine; while in preparing for battle they made their ranks thin and weak, and neither troops nor officers behaved as Roman discipline required. No blood was shed during the battle because at the first onslaught the Romans ran away, the greater number going to Veii, and the rest retiring on Rome, where they sought refuge in the Capitol without first going home; whereupon the senate took so little thought for Rome's defence that, for one thing, they omitted to close the gates; and some of its members fled, while others went with the rest into the Capitol. Granted, in their defence of the Capitol they used some sort of discipline, for they did not pack all the useless people inside, and they got in all the corn they could, so as to be able to stand the siege; while of the useless crowd of old men, women and children, most fled to the country round about, and the rest stayed in Rome at the mercy of the Gauls. So that no one who had read of what was done so often in years gone by and were to read what was now being done, would think they were one and the same people.

Having described all the disorders mentioned above, Titus Livy concludes with the remark: 'To such an extent does fortune blind the minds of men when she does not want them to oppose the force she is using.'

Nor can anything be more true than the conclusion Livy draws. Hence men who in this life normally either suffer great adversity or enjoy great prosperity, deserve neither praise nor blame; for one usually finds that they have been driven either to ruin or to greatness by the prospect of some great advantage which the heavens have held out, whereby they have been given the chance, or have been deprived of the chance, of being able to act virtuously. Fortune arranges this quite nicely. For, when it wants a man to take the lead in doing great things, it chooses a man of high spirits and great virtue who will seize the occasion it offers him. And in like manner, when it wants a man to bring about a great disaster, it gives precedence to men who will help to promote it; and, if anyone gets in the way, it either kills him off or deprives him of all power of doing good.

It plainly appears from Livy's evidence that, in order to make Rome greater and to lead it on to its future greatness, fortune decided it was necessary first to chastize it in a way that will be described at length in the beginning of the next book, but did not want to ruin it altogether. Hence we see that it made an exile of Camillus, but did not cause him to die; that it caused Rome to be taken, but not the Capitol; that it arranged matters so that nothing useful was thought of to help Rome, nor anything overlooked that could help in the defence of the Capitol. It brought it about that, since Rome was to be taken, the greater part of the troops which were routed at Allia, should go on to Veii, thus leaving the city without any men to defend it. But in arranging things thus, it also prepared the way for Rome's recovery; for since there was a Roman army at Veii, and Camillus was at Ardea, it became possible to make a more vigorous attempt to deliver the fatherland under a general whose career was free from the stain of defeat and whose reputation was untarnished.

In confirmation of this one might adduce further examples from modern times, but I do not think this necessary, so pass them over, since that I have given should be enough to satisfy anybody. I assert once again as a truth to which history as a whole bears witness that men may second their fortune, but cannot oppose it; that they may weave its warp, but cannot break it. Yet they should never give up, because there is always hope, though they know not the end and move towards it along roads which cross one another and as yet are unexplored; and since there is hope, they should not despair, no matter what fortune brings or in what travail they find themselves.

30. *Really Powerful Republics and Princes do not purchase Alliances with Money, but obtain them by means of the Virtue and the Reputation of their Forces*

THE Romans were being besieged in the Capitol, and, though they expected help from Veii and from Camillus, were in such bad case owing to famine that they came to terms with the Gauls and agreed to pay them so much gold. They were weighing out the gold agreed upon when Camillus arrived with his army; whereupon fortune, says the historian, decided that 'the Romans should not by purchase save their lives'.

This kind of thing is not only noticeable in this case but characterizes the behaviour of this republic throughout. We never find the Romans purchasing towns, or paying in order to obtain peace. They always acquired both by virtue of their arms. Nor do I think that this has ever happened in the case

of any other republic. Among other indications of the power
of a strong state one looks to the terms on which it lives with
its neighbours. When it is so governed that, to obtain its
friendship, its neighbours become its tributaries, it is a sure
sign that the state is powerful; but when the said neighbours,
though inferior in strength, extract payment from it, it is a
sure sign of its weakness.

As one runs through Roman history, one sees how the
Massilians, the Aedui, the Rhodians, Hiero of Syracuse, king
Eumenes and king Masinissa, who were neighbours with
estates bordering on the empire of Rome, were ready to incur
expense and pay tribute in order to obtain the friendship of
Rome, and in return ask only for her protection. In weak
states one finds just the opposite. To begin with, in our own
state, Florence, in times past when its reputation stood at its
highest, there was no lord in the Romagna who did not receive
payment from it. It also made grants to the Perugians, the
Castellani and all its other neighbours. Had this city been
armed and strong, everything would have been just the contrary, for to secure its protection many states would have paid
money to it, and would have sought to purchase its friendship,
not to sell their own.

Nor are the Florentines the only people who have thus
demeaned themselves since the Venetians and the King of
France do the same thing; for the latter, great as his kingdom
is, habitually pays tribute to the Swiss and to the King of
England. This all comes from depriving the people of arms,
and from the fact that this king and the other states mentioned
have chosen rather to enjoy the present advantage of being
able to despoil their people and of being able to avoid an
imaginary rather than a real danger, instead of so acting as to
secure their people's goodwill and to make their state happy
for ever. A malpractice such as this, though it may bring a
little temporary quiet, in time becomes the cause of crises,

disaster and irremediable ruin. It would take too long to relate how often the Florentines, the Venetians, and this kingdom, have bought off wars and submitted to an ignominy which the Romans submitted to but once. It would take too long to recount how many towns the Florentines and the Venetians have purchased in which one afterwards saw disorder, and how they failed to protect with steel what gold had purchased. The Romans kept up their standards so long as they remained free; but when they fell under the yoke of the emperors, and the emperors began to behave badly and to prefer the shadow to the sun, they, too, began to make grants sometimes to the Parthians, sometimes to Germany, sometimes to other neighbouring peoples; which was the first step towards that great empire's downfall.

Such are the inconveniences, then, that arise from depriving your people of arms.[53] And there is a worse trouble, too, for the greater the force of the enemy's attack, the weaker do you find yourself; for he who lives in the aforesaid way treats ill the subjects who reside within his domain, but treats well those who live on its confines in order to have people well disposed to keep the enemy off. It thus comes about that, in order the better to keep the enemy off, he subsidizes the lords and peoples who are his next-door neighbours, with the result that the states which he has thus kept going, offer a modicum of resistance on the frontiers, but, when the enemy has crossed them, no further remedy is available. Such states do not see that their way of proceeding is incompatible with any kind of good order. For it is the heart and the vital parts of the body that have to be strengthened, not its extremities, since without them the body can survive, but, if the former be injured, it dies; yet such states keep unarmed the heart, but arm the hands and the feet.

What this lack of order has done for Florence is clear, and may be seen any day; for when an army crosses its frontiers and gets near its heart, it finds itself without further remedy. Of it the Venetians also gave proof a few years ago, and, if their city had not been girt about by water, it would have been the end of it. In France this experience is not found so frequently, for it is so large a kingdom that it has but few enemies superior to it. None the less, when the English attacked this kingdom in 1513, the whole realm was in trepidation, and the king and everybody else thought that a single defeat would spell ruin to the king and to the state. Very different was it in the case of the Romans, for the nearer the enemy approached to Rome the greater he found the city's power of resistance to be. When Hannibal invaded Italy, one sees how, after three defeats and the death of so many generals and soldiers, it was still able, not merely to withstand the enemy, but to win the war. All this comes from having fortified well the heart, but of the extremities made less account. For of basic importance in this state were the people of Rome, the people known as Latins, the other parts of Italy associated with it, and its colonies. Thence came the vast number of soldiers which enabled it to fight and to hold the whole world. That this is so may be seen from the question asked by Hanno, the Carthaginian, of the messengers who came from Hannibal after the rout at Cannae. Having made much of Hannibal's exploits, they were asked by Hanno whether the Roman people had sent to ask for peace, and whether among the Latins and in its colonies any town had revolted against the Romans. To both questions the answer was in the negative, whereupon Hanno remarked: 'This war, then, is still in as full swing as it was at the start.'

We see from this discourse and from what I have said in other places, how great is the difference between the procedure of present-day republics and that of ancient republics. We see, too, how, because of this, astonishing acquisitions are made and astonishing losses occur daily. For where men have but little virtue, fortune makes a great display of its power; and, since fortune changes, republics and governments frequently change; and will go on changing till someone comes along, so imbued with the love of antiquity that he regulates things in such fashion that fortune does not every time the sun turns round get a chance of showing what it can do.

31. *How Dangerous it is to put Confidence in Refugees*

IT may not be amiss among other topics to show how dangerous it is to trust those who have been driven from their country, since this is a matter with which everyone who holds office has to deal.[54] In support it is possible to adduce a noteworthy case which Titus Livy cites in his histories, though it lies outside his main topic. When Alexander the Great crossed with his army into Asia, Alexander of Epirus, a relative – in fact his uncle – went with some troops to Italy, having been invited by some Lucanian refugees who had led him to expect that through their mediation he would gain the whole of that country. Relying on their word and on the hopes they aroused, he came to Italy and was put to death by them; for their fellow-citizens had promised that, if they would kill him, they might return to their own country. One should reflect, therefore, on the unreliability of agreements and promises made by men who find themselves shut out from their country, because in determining what such men's word is worth it must be borne in mind that, once they get a chance of returning to their country without your help, they will desert you and turn to others in spite of any promises they may have made you. While in regard to the vain promises and hopes, so intense is their desire to get back home that they naturally believe much that is false and artfully add much more: so that between what they believe and what they say they believe they fill you with a hope which is such that, if

THE TAKING OF TOWNS

you rely on it, either you incur expense in vain or take up what will ruin you.

I propose to let this example of Alexander suffice, conjoined with that of Themistocles the Athenian, who, having been proclaimed a rebel, sought refuge with Darius in Asia; to whom he promised so much if he would but attack Greece that Darius resolved to do so. When later he was unable to fulfil these promises whether out of shame or for fear of punishment, Themistocles poisoned himself. Wherefore, if so eminent a man as Themistocles made this mistake, how much more likely are those to err who are less virtuous and let themselves be swayed by their desires and their passions. A ruler, therefore, should be slow to take up an enterprise because of what some exile has told him, for more often than not all he will get out of it is shame or most grievous harm.

And because the taking of towns by stealth and owing to information supplied by their inhabitants rarely succeeds, it does not seem to me irrelevant to discuss this in the next chapter, as also in how many ways the Romans acquired them.

32. On the Various Methods used by the Romans in taking Towns

SINCE the Romans were all keen on war, they always and on all occasions took advantage of anything, alike in the matter of expense and of any other matter, that promised to help. It was for this reason that they took care not to besiege the towns they took, for they thought this method so costly and so clumsy that its disadvantages would much more than counterbalance the advantages likely to accrue from the conquest. Hence they deemed it better and more useful to subjugate towns by any other means rather than lay siege to them, so that in all their wars and in all the years they took, there are very few instances of their having used sieges.

In order to get hold of a city, therefore, the Romans either took it by assault or got it to surrender. Their assaults were either carried out openly in strength and with violence, or by force conjoined with fraud. When storming a town openly they used two methods. Either they attacked it on all sides without first demolishing the walls, which is called 'putting a crown round the city' since the whole army surrounds it and engages it at all points; and in this way they often succeeded in taking a city, even a very large one, at the first assault, as Scipio took New Carthage in Spain. Or, when an attack failed, they set about breaking down the walls with rams and other siege implements, or made a sap by which they obtained entrance to the city, as was done when Veii was taken; or to get on a level with those defending the walls, they constructed wooden towers, or raised earthworks against the walls from without, so as to be at the same height as the defenders.

Against such assaults the city's defenders in the first case, where the attack came from all sides, were more quickly exposed to danger and had more dubious remedies. For, since many defenders were needed everywhere, either those they had were not enough to provide them all with reserves and reliefs; or, if they could, not all were equally courageous in resisting, and, if a section shirked the battle, all was lost. Hence it often happened, as I have said, that this method proved successful. But when the first assault was not successful, they did not keep it going long, because this was too dangerous for the army; for, since it covered so much ground, it could as a whole resist but feebly a sortie made by those within. The troops, too, got out of hand and grew weary; but for just once, when it was unexpected, they would try this method. When a breach was made in the walls, it was countered by means of ramparts as at the present time. And to counteract a sap, they made a countersap through which they got at the enemy either with their weapons or by other devices; of which one consisted of barrels filled with feathers to which they applied a light, and, when burning, put them in the sap so that the smoke and the stench might prevent the enemy getting through. While, if attacked from towers, they tried to destroy them by fire; and, if from earthworks, they made a hole in the lower part of the wall on which the earthwork was lean-ing, and drew in the earth which those outside had put there, so that, since the earth was being piled up outside and being taken away from the inside, the earthwork did not grow.

Such methods of storming a town could not be kept up for long, so they had either to raise their camp or to devise other methods of winning the war, as Scipio did when he got to Africa; for when he attacked Utica, but did not succeed in taking it, he raised his camp and sought to engage the Carth-aginian armies and break them. Or they would have recourse to a siege, as they did at Veii, Capua, Carthage, Jerusalem and other towns which they took by means of sieges.

The acquiring of towns by furtive violence is illustrated in the case of Palaeopolis, which the Romans took by arrange-ment with fifth columnists[a] inside. This form of attack has often been tried by the Romans and by other peoples, but has seldom succeeded. The reason is that at the smallest set back the plan breaks down, and such setbacks easily happen. For in the first place the conspiracy may be discovered before it comes to a head, and in discovering it there is not much difficulty, owing sometimes to the treachery of those who have been told of it, sometimes to practical difficulties. For you must get in touch with the enemy, with whom it is not permitted to speak unless you can find some excuse. And, should the plot not be discovered while arrangements are being made, a host of difficulties occur when the time comes for action. For if you arrive before the time appointed, or get there late, anything may upset the plot. So, too, if there occurs some unexpected noise, such as the geese made at the Capitol,

[a] *per trattato di quelli di dentro.*

or if the normal course of events is interrupted. Given the least blunder or the smallest mistake, the attack is bound to fail. In addition to which there is the darkness of the night to add to the fear of those engaged in such dangerous tasks; and the fact that most of the men who are taken on such expeditions, having had no experience of the country or of the place to which they are being led, may get muddled and faint-hearted, or upset by some tiny and accidental mishap; and any false impression is enough to make them turn tail.

Anyone more lucky in such stealthy nocturnal ventures than Aratus the Sicyonian is not to be found, yet, bold as he was in these, he was equally nervous about ventures in day-light and in the open. This we may put down to some occult virtue with which he was endowed, rather than to anything in the nature of nocturnal expeditions which makes them more fortunate than others. Though such means are frequently planned, therefore, but few arrive at fruition, and very few succeed.

When towns are acquired by surrender, the surrender may either be voluntary or compulsory. When voluntary, it is due either to some external circumstance which compels a town to seek protection under another's wing, as Capua sought Rome's; or to the desire to be well ruled, a desire evoked by the good government exercised by the prince in question over those who of their own accord have placed themselves in his hands, as was the case with the Rhodians, the Massilians and other such cities which surrendered to the Roman people. When the surrender is compulsory, it is either brought about by a long siege, as we have said above; or it is due to the continued vexation produced by raids, depredations and other annoyances, to escape which a city surrenders.

Of all the methods mentioned above, the Romans used the last more than any. For more than four hundred and fifty years they sought to tire out their neighbours by defeats in the field and by raids, and by means of treaties managed to acquire greater repute than their rivals did, as we have pointed out elsewhere. It was on this method that they always relied most, though they tried them all, but found the others fraught with danger or of no use. For sieges are long and costly, assaults of doubtful issue and risky; and conspiracies are unreliable. They also realized that, if the enemy's army was routed, they acquired a kingdom in a day; whereas, if they besieged an obstinate city, it might take years to get it.

33. *The Romans gave to Army Commanders Discretionary Powers*

IF one is to profit from the perusal of Livy's history one ought, I think, to take account of all the modes of procedure used by the people and senate of Rome and among other points worthy of notice there is the authority we find them giving to their consuls, dictators and other army commanders when in the field. It was of a very high order, for the senate reserved to itself only the power to initiate fresh wars and to confirm peace treaties. All else was left to the discretion and power of the consul. For, when the people and senate had decided to go to war, against the Latins, for instance, they left everything else to the discretion of the consul, who could either give battle or not give it, and attack this or that town as he thought fit.

This is confirmed by numerous examples, but especially by what occurred in an expedition against the Tuscans. The consul, Fabius, had defeated those who were near Sutrium, and was planning next to lead his army through the Ciminian forest *en route* for Tuscany. About this, not only did he not consult the senate, but he did not even inform them, though the war was to be carried on in a new, unexplored and dangerous country. Further confirmation is afforded by the

action the senate here took, which was of the opposite kind;
for, when they heard of the victory which Fabius had gained
and wondered whether his next step would be to pass through
the said forest into Tuscany, they thought it best not to run
the risk this war would entail, and so sent two legates to
Fabius to stop him from going on to Tuscany. But, when they
arrived, he had already got there and had won a victory, so
that, instead of preventing a war, the legates came home
bringing news of a conquest and of glory won.

Whoever considers carefully this technique will see that it
was very wise to make use of it. For, if the senate had required
a consul in conducting a war to proceed step by step according
as they directed, it would have made him less circumspect and
slower to act, for it would have seemed to him that the glory
of victory would not be wholly his, but that the senate would
share in it, since it would have been carried out under its
directions. Furthermore, the senate would have had to advise
on matters of which it had no immediate cognizance; for,
though the senators were all men of considerable experience
in military matters, yet, as they were not on the spot, they
would not be acquainted with the multitudinous details which
it is essential to know before one can give sound advice, and
so would have made numerous mistakes. This being so, they
preferred that the consul should decide what to do, and that
the glory should be wholly his, for they thought his actions
would be so restrained and regulated by his love of glory that
he would do his utmost.

To this I have the more willingly called attention, because I
notice that the republics of today, such as the Venetian and
the Florentine republics, act differently, for if their generals,
administrators or commissioners, have to set up a piece of
artillery, they want to know of it and to advise about it, – a
procedure as praiseworthy as are others of that ilk, which
together have brought us to our present pass.

Book Three

[THE EXAMPLE
OF ROME'S GREAT MEN]

The purpose of Book Three is to show 'how much the action
of particular men contributed to the greatness of Rome and
produced in that city so many beneficial results' [D. III. 1.11].
The examples from Roman History are taken mainly from
Livy, Books II to X.

   As in Books One and Two the grouping of discourses
under headings has been introduced for the convenience of
the reader.

L.J.W.

Book Three

[REFORM, SECURITY AND THE
ELIMINATION OF RIVALS]

---

1. *In Order that a Religious Institution or a State should long survive it is essential that it should frequently be Restored to its original principles* [a]

I T is a well-established fact that the life of all mundane things is of finite duration. But things which complete the whole of the course appointed them by heaven are in general those whose bodies do not disintegrate, but maintain themselves in orderly fashion so that if there is no change; or, if there be change, it tends rather to their conservation than to their destruction. Here I am concerned with composite bodies, such as are states and religious institutions, and in their regard I affirm that those changes make for their conservation which lead them back to their origins. [b] Hence those are better constituted and have a longer life whose institutions make frequent renovations possible, or which are brought to such a renovation by some event which has nothing to do with their constitution. For it is clearer than daylight that, without renovation, these bodies do not last.

The way to renovate them, as has been said, is to reduce

[a] *ritirarla spesso verso il suo principio.* [Walker says, 'to its start'.]
[b] *le riducano inverso i principii loro.* [Walker says, 'to their start'.]

them to their starting-points. For at the start religious institutions, republics and kingdoms have in all cases some good in them, to which their early reputation and progress is due. But since in process of time this goodness is corrupted, such a body must of necessity die unless something happens which brings it up to the mark. Thus, our medical men, speaking of the human body, say that 'every day it absorbs something which from time to time requires treatment'.

This return to its original principles in the case of a republic, is brought about either by some external event or by its own intrinsic good sense. Thus, as an example of the former, we see how it was necessary that Rome should be taken by the Gauls in order that it should be re-born and in its re-birth take on alike a new vitality and a new virtue, and also take up again the observance of religion and justice, both of which had begun to show blemishes. This plainly appears from Livy's account where he shows how, when the Romans led out their army against the Gauls and created tribunes with consular power, they observed no religious ceremony. And, in like manner, not only did they not punish the three Fabii who had attacked the Gauls 'in contravention of the Law of Nations', but they made them tribunes. Whence it is easy to infer that of the good constitutions established by Romulus and by those other wise princes they had begun to take less account than was reasonable and necessary for the maintenance of a free state. This defeat in a war with outsiders, therefore, came about so that the institutions of this city should be renovated and to show this people that not only is it essential to uphold religion and justice, but also to hold in high esteem good citizens and to look upon their virtue as of greater value than those comforts of which there appeared to them to be a lack owing to what these men had done. This actually came about. For as soon as Rome had been recovered they renewed all the ordinances of their ancient religion and punished the Fabii who had fought 'in contravention of the Law of Nations'. They also set such esteem on the virtue and goodness of Camillus that the senate and the rest, putting envy aside, laid on his shoulders the whole burden of this republic.

It is, therefore, as I have said, essential that men who live together under any constitution should frequently have their attention called to themselves either by some external or by some internal occurrence. When internal, such occurrences are usually due to some law which from time to time causes the members of this body to review their position; or again to some good man who arises in their midst and by his example and his virtuous deeds produces the same effect as does the constitution.

Such benefits, therefore, are conferred on a republic either by the virtue of some individual or by the virtue of an institution. In regard to the latter, the institutions which caused the Roman republic to return to its start were the introduction of plebeian tribunes, of the censorship, and of all the other laws which put a check on human ambition and arrogance; to which institutions life must needs be given by some virtuous citizen who cooperates strenuously in giving them effect despite the power of those who contravene them. Notable among such drastic actions, before the taking of Rome by the Gauls, were the death of Brutus' sons, the death of the ten citizens, and that of Maelius, the corn-dealer. After the taking of Rome there was the death of Manlius Capitolinus, the death of Manlius Torquatus' son, the action taken by Papirius Cursor against Fabius, his master of horse, and the charge brought against the Scipios. Such events, because of their unwonted severity and their notoriety, brought men back to the mark every time one of them happened; and when they began to occur less frequently, they also began to provide occasion for men to practise corruption, and were attended with more danger and more commotion. For between one case of disciplinary action of this type and the next there ought to elapse at most ten years, because by this time men begin to change their habits and to break the laws; and, unless something happens which recalls to their minds the penalty involved and reawakens fear in them, there will soon be so many delinquents that it will be impossible to punish them without danger.

In regard to this, those who governed the state of Florence from 1434 to 1494 used to say that it was necessary to reconstitute the government every five years; otherwise it was difficult to maintain it; where by 'reconstituting the government' they meant instilling men with that terror and that fear with which they had instilled them when instituting it – in that at this time they had chastised those who, looked at from the established way of life, had misbehaved. As, however, the remembrance of this chastisement disappears, men are emboldened to try something fresh and to talk sedition. Hence provision has of necessity to be made against this by restoring that government to what it was at its origins.

Such a return to their original principles in republics is sometimes due to the simple virtue of one man alone, independently of any laws spurring you to action. For of such effect is a good reputation and good example that men seek to imitate it, and the bad are ashamed to lead lives which go contrary to it. Those who in Rome are outstanding examples of this good influence, are Horatius Cocles, Scaevola, Fabricius, the two Decii, Regulus Attilius, and several others, whose rare and virtuous examples wrought the same effects in Rome as laws and institutions would have done. If then effective action of the kind described above, together with this setting of good example, had occurred in that city at least every ten years, it necessarily follows that it would never have become corrupt. But when both the one and the other began to occur more rarely, corruption began to spread. For, after

the time of Marcus Regulus, there appeared no examples of
this kind, and, though in Rome there arose the two Catos,
between them and any prior instance there was so great an
interval, and again between the Catos themselves, and they
stood so alone that their good example could have no good
effect; especially in the case of the younger Cato who found
the greater part of the city so corrupt that he could not by his
example effect any improvement among the citizens. So
much then for republics.

As to religious institutions one sees here again how necessary
these renovations are from the example of our own religion,
which, if it had not been restored to its starting-point by St
Francis and St Dominic, would have become quite extinct.
For these men by their poverty and by their exemplification of
the life of Christ revived religion in the minds of men in whom
it was already dead, and so powerful were these new religious
orders that they prevented the depravity of prelates and of
religious heads from bringing ruin on religion. They also
lived so frugally and had such prestige with the populace as
confessors and preachers that they convinced them it is an
evil thing to talk evilly of evil doing, and a good thing to live
under obedience to such prelates, and that, if they did wrong,
it must be left to God to chastise them. And, this being so, the
latter behave as badly as they can, because they are not afraid
of punishments which they do not see and in which they do
not believe. It is, then, this revival which has maintained and
continues to maintain this religion.

Kingdoms also need to be renovated and to have their laws
brought back to their starting-points. The salutary effect this
produces is seen in the kingdom of France, for the conduct of
affairs in this kingdom is controlled by more laws and more
institutions than it is in any other. These laws and these institutions are maintained by *parlements*, notably by that of
Paris, and by it they are renovated whenever it takes action

against a prince of this realm or in its judgements condemns the king. Up to now it has maintained its position by the pertinacity with which it has withstood the nobility of this realm. But should it at any time let an offence remain unpunished and should offences begin to multiply, the result would unquestionably be either that they would have to be corrected to the accompaniment of grievous disorders or that the kingdom would disintegrate.

The conclusion we reach, then, is that there is nothing more necessary to a community, whether it be a religious establishment, a kingdom or a republic, than to restore to it the prestige it had at the outset, and to take care that either good institutions or good men shall bring this about rather than that external force should give rise to it. For though this on occasion may be the best remedy, as it was in Rome's case, it is so dangerous that in no case is it what one should desire.

In order to make it clear to all how much the action of particular men contributed to the greatness of Rome and produced in that city so many beneficial results, I shall proceed to narrate and to discuss their doings, and shall confine myself to this topic in this third and last book on this first Decad [of Livy's history]. And, though the actions of the kings were great and noteworthy, since history deals with them at length I shall not mention them here, except where they may have done things with a view to their personal advantage. I begin, then, with Brutus, the father of Rome's liberties.

2. *That it is a Very Good Notion at Times to pretend to be a Fool*

No one ever acted so prudently nor acquired such a reputation for wisdom owing to any remarkable deed as that which Junius Brutus earned by pretending to be stupid. And although Titus Livy assigns but one cause as the ground which induced

him to practise this dissimulation, namely, that he might live
in greater security and preserve his estates, none the less, in
view of his conduct, one can well believe that he practised it
also in order to escape observation and that he might get a
better opportunity of downing the kings and liberating his
country, whenever they gave him a chance. That it was of
this he was thinking is clear first from the interpretation he
put on the oracle of Apollo when he pretended to fall down
so that he might kiss the ground, and from this inferred that
the gods looked with favour on what he had in mind; and,
later, when on the death of Lucretia he was the first to pull the
dagger out of the wound in the presence of her father, her
husband and other of her relatives, and to make the bystanders
swear that they would never tolerate for the future any king
reigning in Rome.

From the example this man set, all those who are ill content
with a prince should take note that they ought first to measure
and to weigh their strength. Should they be so powerful that
they can afford to declare themselves his enemies and openly
to make war on him, this is the course they should adopt, since
it is less dangerous and more honourable. But if their position
is such that they have not sufficient forces to make war openly,
they should use every endeavour to acquire the prince's
friendship; and to this end should avail themselves of every
opening which they think necessary to attain it, by becoming
obsequious to his wishes and by taking pleasure in everything
in which they see that he takes pleasure. Such familiar intercourse in the first place assures that your life will be safe, and,
without entailing any danger, allows you to enjoy the prince's
good fortune just as he does himself. It also provides you with
ample opportunity for fulfilling your intentions.

True, there are those who say that you ought not to live in
such close proximity to princes as to be included in their
downfall, nor yet so far away from them that, when their

downfall occurs, you cannot take advantage of it; and doubt-less the middle course would be the best, were it possible to adopt it. As, however, I am convinced that this middle course is impracticable, it behoves one to have recourse to the aforesaid two methods, i.e. either to act openly or to get tied up with them. He who acts otherwise, if he be a man who by his endowments has gained eminence, lives in perpetual danger. Nor is it enough for him to say: 'There is nothing I am out to obtain. I want neither honours nor advantages. All that I ask for is to live quietly and without embarrass-ment!' For such excuses are heard but gain no credence. Nor can men who are distinguished take this line, even though they sincerely desire to do so and have no further ambition, since no one will believe them; so that, though they prefer to be left alone, others will not leave them alone. It behoves them, therefore, to play the fool, as Brutus did, and to act more or less like lunatics, admiring, talking about, attending to, and doing things in which they have not the slightest interest in order to ingratiate themselves with the prince.

We have been discussing the prudence displayed by Brutus in his endeavour to restore freedom to Rome, so let us now say something about the severity he displayed in maintaining it.

3. When Liberty has been newly acquired it is Necessary in Order to maintain it to 'Kill the Sons of Brutus'

THE severity used by Brutus was no less necessary than it was useful in maintaining the liberty which Rome had just acquired by his aid. Of such severity one rarely comes across a case in history in which a father not only sits on a tribunal and condemns his own sons to death, but is present at their death. Those, however, who are familiar with ancient history are well aware that, when the form of government has been changed, whether from a republic to a tyranny or a tyranny to a republic, it is in all cases essential that exemplary action be taken against those who are hostile to the new state of affairs. He who establishes a tyranny and does not kill 'Brutus', and he who establishes a free state and does not kill 'the Sons of Brutus', will not last long.

Since this question has already been discussed at length elsewhere[55] I refer the reader back to what was there said, and shall here give but one example, a modern one, which took place in our own day and in our own country. It is that of Piero Soderini who thought that by patience and goodness he could quell the desire of 'Brutus's sons' to return to another form of government, but in this he was mistaken. Though, being a prudent man, he recognized the need for action, and thought the type of ambitious men who were against him gave him ground for getting rid of them, yet he could never make up his mind to do this. For, in addition to thinking that he could by patience and goodness extinguish their malevolence, and by distributing rewards put an end to some of their hostility, he was of opinion – and often told his friends so in confidence – that, if he were to take vigorous action against his opponents and to fight his adversaries, he would need to assume extraordinary authority and introduce laws disruptive of civic equality; and that such a course and such authority, even though he did not henceforth use it tyrannically, would so alarm the general public that, after his death, they would never again agree to appoint a gonfalonier for life, an office which he thought it would be well to strengthen and to keep up.

Such a point of view was wise and good. None the less, an evil should never be allowed to continue out of respect for a good when that good may easily be overwhelmed by that evil. Soderini ought to have considered that, when his actions and his intentions came to be judged by their end and in the light of the good fortune and the life that had accompanied them, he would be able to convince everyone that what he had done, was done for the security of his country, and not for ambitious reasons. He could, moreover, so have regulated things that none of his successors could do with evil intent what he had done with good intent. But the view which he first adopted misled him, for he failed to realize that malevolence is not vanquished by time, nor placated by any gifts. With the result that, through his inability to emulate Brutus, he lost both his position and his reputation, a loss in which his country shared.

And just as it is a difficult thing to give security to a self-governing state, so, too, is it difficult to give security to a kingdom, as will be shown in the next chapter.

4. *A Prince cannot Live Securely in a Principality while those are Alive who have been despoiled of it*

THE death of Tarquinius Priscus at the hands of the sons of Ancus, and the death of Servius Tullius at the hands of Tarquin the Proud, show how difficult and dangerous it is to deprive anyone of his kingdom and to leave him alive even though one try to win him over by benefits. Tarquinius Priscus was clearly led astray because, aware that he had a juridical right to the kingdom which he had obtained through the gift of the people confirmed by the senate, he did not believe that the sons of Ancus could be so indignant as not to rest content with that with which all Rome was content. And Servius Tullius was mistaken, because he thought he could be conferring on them fresh benefits win over the sons of Tarquin.

The first case is, therefore, a warning to all princes that they can never live secure in their principality so long as those live who have been despoiled of it. The second is a reminder to all potentates that old injuries are never cancelled by new benefits, least of all when the benefits are of less importance

than the injuries previously inflicted. Undoubtedly Servius
Tullius was far from prudent in thinking that the sons of
Tarquin would be content to be his sons-in-law when in their
opinion they ought to have been his king. The passion for
ruling is, moreover, so great that it not only enters the breasts
of those who have a claim to the kingdom but also into the
breasts of those who have not. This was so in the case of the
wife of the younger Tarquin, Servius' daughter, who, impelled by this mad passion, thought so little of her duty to her
father that she incited her husband to take both his life and his
kingdom, so much more highly did she fancy herself as a
queen than as the daughter of a king.

If, then, Tarquinius Priscus and Servius Tullius lost their
kingdoms through not knowing how to secure themselves
against those whose kingdom they had usurped, Tarquin the
Proud lost his through not observing the institutions made by
its former kings, as will be shown in the next chapter.

5. What it is that causes a Hereditary Prince to lose his Kingdom

SINCE Servius Tullius left no heirs, Tarquin the Proud, who
had killed him, entered into secure possession of the kingdom,
for he had nothing to fear from the kind of thing that had
injured his predecessors. Though this way of obtaining a kingdom is abnormal and odious, yet, had Tarquin respected the
ancient institutions of former kings, he would have been in a
strong position, and would not have antagonized the senate
and the populace so that they sought to deprive him of it.
The reason for his expulsion, then, was not that his son, Sextus, had ravished Lucretia, but that he had violated the laws of
the kingdom and ruled tyrannically. He deprived the senate
of all authority and took it into his own hands. Business which
used to be transacted in public assemblies to the senate's

satisfaction, he carried on in his palace, accepting the responsibility and its consequences. The result was that before long
Rome had lost all the liberties she had enjoyed under previous
kings. Nor did it suffice to have made the patricians his
enemies; he aroused also the animosity of the plebs by setting
them mechanical tasks to do, quite different from those which
his predecessors had set them to do; so that by filling Rome
with instances of his cruelty and pride, he had already aroused
in the minds of all Romans a spirit of revolt, ready to break out
should occasion arise. Hence, if the Lucretia incident had not
occurred, something else would have happened and would
have led to the same result. Whereas, if Tarquin had behaved
like the other kings, when his son, Sextus, committed his
crime, Brutus and Collatinus would have appealed to Tarquin
to avenge it, and not to the Roman people.

From this princes should learn, therefore, that they begin to
lose their state the moment they begin to break the laws and to
disregard the ancient traditions and customs under which men
have long lived. And if, when they have been deprived of their
state, they should ever become so prudent as to realize with
what ease principalities may be held by those who think
wisely, their loss will inevitably become much more bitter and
will condemn them to a punishment greater than that to which
they have been condemned by other men. For it is much
easier to acquire the affection of good men than of bad, and to
obey laws rather than to override them.

If they would discover how to behave in order to do this, all
they have to do is to glance at the looking-glass in which the
lives of good men are reflected: Timoleon the Corinthian,
for instance, Aratus the Sicyonian and such-like; in whose
lives they will find both governors and governed enjoying
such security and contentment that it should make them
desire to imitate them, which they can do easily for the reasons
aforesaid. For when men are well governed, they do not go

about looking for further liberty; as was the case with the peoples governed by the two persons mentioned above, for they insisted on their remaining princes so long as they lived, though more than once both of them sought to retire to private life.

Since in this and in the two preceding chapters we have dealt with the disaffection aroused against princes and with the conspiracy organized by the sons of Brutus against their country, and with those made against Tarquinius Priscus and Servius Tullius, it will not be beside the point, I think, to discuss conspiracies at length in the next chapter, since they constitute a topic of which both princes and private persons should take due note.

Book Three

[DISCOURSE 6]
[ON CONSPIRACIES]

---

6. On Conspiracies

[*In view of the abnormal length of this Discourse, insets indicating the subjects discussed have been inserted (by Fr. Walker) at the beginning of each paragraph or set of paragraphs*]

SINCE conspiracies are of such dangerous consequence alike to princes and to private persons, I cannot well omit to discuss their nature, for it is plain that many more princes have lost their lives and their states in this way than by open war, because it is given to but few to make open war on a prince, whereas anyone can conspire against him.[56] There is, on *Introductory* the other hand, no enterprise in which private persons can engage, more dangerous or more rash than is this, for it is both difficult and extremely dangerous in all its stages. Whence it comes about that, though many conspiracies have been attempted, very few have attained the desired end. Hence, in order that princes may learn how to guard against these dangers, and that private persons may think twice before undertaking them and may learn, instead, to be content with life under the regime which fate has placed over them, I shall speak of conspiracies at length, omitting nothing of importance that is relevant either to a prince or to a private person. There is, in fact, a golden saying voiced by Cornelius Tacitus, who says that men have to respect the past but to submit to the present, and, while they should be desirous of having good princes, should put up with them of whatever sort they may turn out to be. And unquestionably those who act otherwise usually bring disaster both upon themselves and upon their country.

In starting to deal with this topic the first thing to be considered is against whom conspiracies are formed. It will be found that they are formed either against one's fatherland or against a prince. I propose here to discuss both these types, for of conspiracies formed with a view to handing over a town to the enemy besieging it or conspiracies which for one reason or another resemble this, enough has been said elsewhere.

We shall deal in the first part of this discourse with conspiracies against a prince, and shall inquire first as to their
Causes causes, which are many. There is, however, one which is much more important than all the rest. This consists in the universal hatred a prince may evoke, for when a prince has aroused such universal hatred it is to be expected that there will be certain persons to whom he has given greater offence and that they will seek vengeance. This desire will be intensified by the universal ill will which they notice has been aroused against him. A prince, therefore, should avoid incurring these personal reproaches, and since what he has to do in order to avoid them has been discussed elsewhere I shall refrain from discussing it here: I mention it because, if he does guard against this, the mere giving of offence to individuals will evoke less hostility. The reason is, first, that one rarely comes across men so indignant at an unjust act as to endanger themselves to such an extent by seeking vengeance; and secondly, that, should they actually be inclined to do this and have the requisite power, they are restrained by the universal goodwill which they see that the prince enjoys.

Injuries may affect either a man's property, his life or his honour. The threat of bloodshed is more dangerous than is the shedding of blood. To threaten to shed blood is, in fact, extremely dangerous: whereas to shed it is attended with no danger at all, for a dead man cannot contemplate vengeance, and those that remain alive usually leave you to do the contemplating. But a man who has been threatened and sees that he must of necessity either do something or be for it, has been turned into a real menace for the prince, as we shall cite cases presently to show.

Prescinding from the case in which action is imposed by necessity, injuries affecting a man's property or honour are the two things which give men greater offence than anything else, and against them the prince should be on his guard, for he can never so despoil anyone but that there will remain to him a knife with which to wreak vengeance. Nor can he deprive a man of his honour to such an extent that his mind will cease to be set on vengeance. And of the honours of which men may be deprived, that which imports most is a woman's honour, and, after that, contempt for a man's person. It was this that caused Pausanias to take up arms against Philip of Macedon; and this that has caused many others to take up arms against many other princes. In our day Lucio Belanti would not have been moved to conspire against Pandolfo, the tyrant of Siena, if he had not given him his daughter to wife and then taken her away again, as we shall relate in due course. The chief cause which led the Pazzi to conspire against the Medici was the inheritance of Giovanni Bonromei of which they had been deprived by the Medici's orders.

Another cause, and this a very powerful one, that makes men conspire against a prince, is the desire to liberate their fatherland of which a prince has seized possession. It was this that caused Brutus and Cassius to turn against Caesar; this that led to many other conspiracies, against Phalaris, Dionysius and against other usurpers of their country's rights. Nor can any tyrant prevail over this spirit, except by discarding his tyranny. And since one does not find tyrants doing this, one finds few who have not come to a miserable end. Hence the verse of Juvenal:

> To Pluto's realm few kings unscathed descend,
> Nor tyrants oft escape a sticky end.

The dangers involved in conspiracies, as I have said above, are considerable, and go on all the time, for in a conspiracy *One-man* dangers crop up alike in forming the plot, in *conspiracies* carrying it out, and as a result of its having been carried out. Plots may be formed by one conspirator, or by several. If by one person only, it cannot rightly be called a conspiracy. Rather it is a firm resolve on the part of some individual to kill the prince. Of the three dangers conspiracies entail, a one-man conspiracy lacks the first. For no danger can arise before the time for action comes, since no one else being privy to the secret, there is no danger of the plot being carried to the ears of the prince. To make a resolve of this kind lies within the competence of anybody whatsoever, be he great, small, noble or insignificant,[a] intimate or not intimate with the prince. For anyone is allowed at some time or other to speak to the prince, and anyone who gets the chance of speaking to him, gets a chance to relieve his feelings. Pausanias, of whom we have already spoken several times, killed Philip of Macedon as he was on his way to the temple with a lot of armed men about him and his son on one side and his son-in-law on the other. The former, however, was a nobleman and an acquaintance of the prince. [But there are others.] A poor, miserable Spaniard stuck a dagger in the neck of Ferdinand, king of Spain, and, though

[a] *nobile, ignobile* – Terms used in *Discourses* I.30 to indicate the upper and the lower classes.

the wound was not fatal, it shows us that a man of this type
may have both the intention and the opportunity of doing
such a thing. A dervish, or Turkish priest, struck at Bajazet,
the father of the present Turk, with a scimitar. He did not
kill him, but he certainly had the intention and the opportunity of so doing. One finds plenty of people, I think, who would
like to do such things, for the intention is attended neither
with penalty nor danger of any kind. Yet there are but few
who actually do such things, and of those who do, there are
very few, if any, who do not themselves get killed in the very
act. Hence one does not find men keen on going to certain
death. But let us leave these one-man plots and turn to conspiracies involving several people.

I maintain that one finds in history that all conspiracies have
been made by men of standing or else by men in immediate
attendance on a prince,[a] for other people, unless
they be sheer lunatics, cannot form a conspiracy;
since men without power and those who are not
in touch with a prince are devoid alike of any
hope and of any opportunity of carrying out a conspiracy
successfully. For, first of all, men without power cannot get
hold of anyone who will keep faith with them, since no
one can consent to do what they want under any of those
prospects which induce men to take great risks, so that, once
the plot has been communicated to two or three people,
an informer will turn up and they are ruined. Moreover,
should they actually be lucky enough to avoid informers, the
carrying out of the plot will involve them in such difficulties,
owing to the lack of easy access to the prince, that it will be
impossible for them to escape disaster in carrying out their
scheme. For, if men of standing and those who have easy
access succumb to these difficulties, which will be dealt with

Conspiracies formed by the weak

[a] *fatte da uomini grandi o familiarissimi del principe*; the phrase 'men of
standing' has been used throughout in translating '*grandi*'.

presently, it is to be expected that in the case of these others such difficulties will be magnified without end. Consequently, since when their lives and property are not at stake, men do not entirely lose their heads, they become cautious when they recognize their weakness, and when they get sick of a prince confine themselves to cursing him, and wait for those of higher standing than they have, to avenge them. So that, should one in fact come across somebody of this kind who has attempted such a thing, one should praise his intention but not his prudence.

It would seem, then, that conspirators have all been men of standing or intimates of the prince, and, of these, those who have been moved to conspire by too many benefits are as numerous as those moved to conspire by too many injuries, as was the case with Perennis *versus* Commodus, Plautianus *versus* Severus, and Sejanus *versus* Tiberius. For to all these men their emperors had granted such wealth and so many honours and titles that there seemed to be nothing wanting to complete their power, save the imperial title; so, since with the lack of this they were unwilling to put up, they were moved to conspire against their prince, and their conspiracy in each case was attended with the results which their ingratitude merited.

Conspiracies formed by the strong

Of similar conspiracies which have occurred in more recent times there is, however, one that met with success, that of Jacopo di Appiano against Messer Piero Gambacorti, prince of Pisa; for this Jacopo had been brought up by, reared by, and owed his reputation to, the very person whom later on he deprived of his power. There is also in our own times the conspiracy of Coppola against king Ferdinand of Aragon; the said Coppola having attained a greatness such that the only thing that seemed to him to be lacking was a kingdom, and since he made up his mind to acquire this, he lost his life. And yet, if any conspiracies against a prince, made by men of standing, ought to have succeeded it should surely have been this, since it was made by another king, so to speak, who had every convenience requisite to satisfying his desire. But that lust for domination, which blinds men, blinds them yet again in the way they set about the business: for, if they knew but how to do their evil deeds with prudence, it would be impossible for them not to succeed.

A prince, therefore, who wants to guard against conspiracies, should fear those on whom he has conferred ex-
A warning cessive favours more than those to whom he has
to princes done excessive injury. For the latter lack op-
portunity, whereas the former abound in it, and the desire is the same in both cases; for the desire to rule is as great as, or greater than, is the desire for vengeance. Consequently princes should confer on their friends an authority of such magnitude that between it and that of the prince there remains a certain interval, and between the two a something else to be desired. Otherwise it will be a strange thing if that does not happen to them which happened to the princes we have been talking about. But to return to the lines of our discourse.

Having said that conspirators must be men of standing and have easy access to the prince, I must now discuss the success of
The danger these, their undertaking, and inquire as to why
due to some have succeeded and others have failed. As I
informers have remarked above, in conspiracies there are
three stages at which danger may be found to occur: at the start, while carrying them out, and afterwards. One finds that few conspiracies prove successful because it is impossible, or almost impossible, to pass through all three stages successfully. Let us begin by discussing the dangers incurred at the outset. These are the more important, I maintain, since there is need of great discretion and one must have considerable luck if, in making one's plans, the plot is not to be discovered. Plots are discovered either from in-

formation received or by conjecture. Leakage of information is due either to lack of loyalty or to lack of discretion among those to whom you communicate the plot. Lack of loyalty may easily occur, because you can only communicate your plan to those in whom you have such confidence that you think they will risk death for your sake, or else to men who are discontented with the prince. Now there may be one or two persons whom you can trust, but it is impossible to find such men if you reveal your plans to many people, for the goodwill they bear you must indeed be great if the danger and the fear of punishment is not to outweigh it in their estimation. Men, too, quite frequently make mistakes about the affection another man has for them, nor can you be sure of it unless of it you have previously had experience, and to acquire experience in such a matter is a very risky business. Even should you have had experience of some other dangerous affair in which they have been loyal to you, you cannot infer from their loyalty in this case that they will be equally loyal in another which far exceeds it in dangers of all kinds. While if you judge of a person's loyalty by the degree of disaffection he has for the prince, here, too, you may easily be mistaken; for by the very fact of your having opened your mind to such a malcontent, you provide him with material with which to obtain contentment, so that, if he is to keep faith with you, either his hatred must be great or your influence over him must be very great indeed.

It thus comes about that conspiracies are frequently revealed and are crushed at the very start. Indeed, it is looked on as a marvel if a plot which has been communicated to many people, remains secret for any length of time, as was the case with that formed by Piso against Nero, and in our day with that formed by the Pazzi against Lorenzo and Juliano de' Medici, to which there were privy more than fifty persons and yet it was not discovered till it came to the point of execution.

As to discovery due to lack of discretion, this comes about

when a conspiracy is spoken of without due caution and a
The danger servant or some third person gets to hear of it, as
due to happened to the sons of Brutus who were over-
indiscretion heard discussing their plans with Tarquin's messengers by a servant who informed against them.
Or it may be due to your having lightly communicated it
to a lady friend or to a boy friend or to some other frivolous
person, as did Dymnus, who with Philotas and others conspired against Alexander the Great, and talked of the conspiracy to Nicomachus, a boy of whom he was fond, who at
once told his brother, Cebalinus, about it, and Cebalinus told
it to the king.

As to discovery due to conjecture, we have an example of
this in the Pisonian conspiracy formed against Nero, in which
Discovery Scaevinus, one of the conspirators, made his will on
due to the day before he had to kill Nero, ordered
conjecture Milichus, his freedman, to have his old and rusty
dagger sharpened up, freed all his slaves and gave
them money, and had bandages got ready for binding up the
wounded; from which facts Milichus conjectured that there
was a plot and told Nero. Scaevinus was arrested, together
with Natales, another conspirator, who had been seen talking
together for a long time and in secret the day before; and, as
their explanations did not agree, they were forced to tell the
truth; so that the conspiracy was discovered, with disastrous
results for all concerned in it.

Against discovery due to such causes it is impossible so to
guard as to prevent the plot being revealed, whether owing to
The difficulty malice, to indiscretion or to frivolous con-
of preventing versation, in all cases in which the number of
discovery those who are cognizant of it exceeds three or
four. For, should more than one of the conspirators be arrested, it is impossible to prevent its coming
out, because two cannot possibly agree as to every detail in
the explanations they give. If only one man is arrested and

he be a man of resolution, he may have sufficient strength of mind to be silent about his fellow conspirators. It is essential, however, that the other conspirators have no less courage than he has in standing their ground and not running away, for the conspiracy will be revealed by either party in which courage is lacking, whether by the man who has been arrested or those who are still at large.

There is, indeed, a rare case given by Titus Livy, namely, the conspiracy formed against Hieronymus, king of Syracuse, in which, when Theodotus, one of the conspirators, was arrested, he showed great virtue in concealing all the other conspirators, and accused the king's own friends; and the other conspirators, on their part, had such confidence in Theodotus' virtue, that not one of them left Syracuse or showed any other sign of fear.

These, then, are the dangers to which a conspiracy is exposed in the course of its formation before the time comes for it to be carried out; and, if they are to be avoided, these are the remedies. The first, the safest and, to tell the truth, the

Precautions against discovery
only one, is not to allow the conspirators time to give information against you, and to tell them of your plan only when you are ready to act, and not before. Those who have so acted, at any rate escape the dangers involved in contriving the plot, and more often than not, the others also. All of them, in fact, have been successful, and any prudent man should find it possible to conduct things in this fashion. I shall cite two cases, and leave it at that.

Nelematus, being unable to stand the tyranny of Aristotimus, tyrant of Epirus, collected in his house many of his relations and friends, and exhorted them to set their country free. Some of them asked for time to consider the matter and to put their affairs in order. Whereupon Nelematus told his servants to lock the doors of the house, and to those whom he had called together said: 'Either you swear to go and do the deed now, or I shall hand you all over as prisoners to Aristotimus.' These words got them going; they took the oath, and, having set out without delay, they successfully carried out Nelematus's instructions. When one of the Magi by subterfuge got possession of the Persian throne, and Otanes, one of the leading men in the kingdom, heard of it and discovered the fraud, he conferred with six other leading men in the state, and told them that it was for them to rid the kingdom of the tyranny of this Magus. When one of them asked for time, Darius, one of the six who had been called together by Otanes, got up and said: 'Either we go at once and put this business through, or I shall go and lay information against the lot of you.' So with one accord they got up, and succeeded in carrying out their plan before anyone had time to repent. Similar to these two cases also was the method the Aetolians adopted in order to kill Nabis, the Spartan tyrant; for they commissioned their fellow-citizen, Alexamenes, to go with thirty horse and two hundred foot ostensibly to the assistance of Nabis, communicated the secret only to Alexamenes, and told the rest to obey him on each and every point under pain of banishment. So Alexamenes went to Sparta and never mentioned the commission entrusted to him till he was ready to carry it out; with the result that he succeeded in killing Nabis. These folk, then, by adopting these methods, have avoided the dangers which attend the planning of a conspiracy; and those who follow their example will always avoid them.

That anyone can do as they did, I propose now to prove by citing the case of Piso, of whom mention has already been *Their practicability* made. Piso was a man of very high standing and great repute, and was intimate with Nero, who had considerable confidence in him. Nero used frequently to dine with him in his gardens. Piso, therefore, could have made friends with men who in mentality, courage and inclination were of the right kind to carry out such a scheme, for to a man of standing this is quite an easy matter; and while Nero was in his gardens, he could have told them of the business and with suitable words got them to do what there would have been no time for them to refuse and what could not but have succeeded. Hence if we inquire into conspiracies in general, but few will be found that could not have been carried out in the same way. Ordinarily, however, men pay but little attention to the affairs of the world and so make frequently the gravest blunders, especially in matters which lie outside the ordinary run of things, as this does.

A plot, then, should never be divulged unless one is driven to it and it is ripe for execution, and if you, perforce, have to *Further precautions* divulge it, it should be told to but one other person, and this a man of whom you have had very considerable experience, or else one who is actuated by the same motives as you are. To find such a man is far easier than to find several, and for this very reason is less dangerous. Moreover, should you, in fact, make a mistake, you have here a chance of protecting yourself, which is not the case where many conspirators are involved. For I have heard a wise man say that you can talk about anything to one person alone, since, unless you allow yourself to be persuaded to commit yourself in writing, one man's 'yes' will be worth just as much as the other man's 'no'. And against writing anything down everybody should be on his guard as against a rock, for nothing is more likely to convict you than is your own handwriting. Plautianus, having made up his mind to kill the emperor, Severus, and his son, Antoninus, entrusted the secret to Saturninus, the tribune, who wanted to inform against him instead of doing what he wished, but was afraid that, when he brought the charge, more credence might be given to Plautianus than to himself. So he asked for something in writing that might serve as evidence of the commission entrusted to him. Blinded by ambition, Plautianus gave it him, with the result that the tribune brought the accusation and he was convicted. Yet without this commitment in writing and certain other evidence against him, Plautianus would have got the better of him, so brazen was he in denying the charge. There is then some chance of getting off when a charge is brought by but one person provided you cannot be convicted by a written document or other evidence telling against you, which one should take care not to provide.

In the Pisonian conspiracy there was a woman called Epicharis, who had formerly been Nero's mistress. Since she thought it would help to get a captain of some triremes which served as Nero's guard to join the conspirators, she told him of the plot, but not who the conspirators were. Subsequently, when the captain broke his word and charged her with it to Nero, Epicharis denied the charge with such vehemence that Nero could not make up his mind and let her off. There are, then, in communicating a plot to a single other person two dangers: the first is that he may accuse you of his own accord; and the second is that he may get arrested on suspicion or because there is some evidence against him, and accuse you when convicted and constrained by torture to do so. In both these cases the danger is not irremediable; for in the first case you can deny the charge and allege that he made it because he hated you; and in the second you can deny it, alleging that under force he has been compelled to tell a lie.

The wisest thing, therefore, is not to tell anybody what you are about, but to act in accordance with the examples given above; or, if you have to tell somebody, not to tell more than one, in which case, though the danger will be somewhat greater, it will not be so great as if you had told it to many. The case is some-what the same when necessity constrains you to do that to a

Unpremeditated assassination

prince which you see that the prince is about to do to you, for your need is then so great that it does not give you time to think of precautions. A necessity of this kind almost always leads to the end desired; and, to prove it, I propose to give just two examples.

Among the chief friends and intimates which the emperor, Commodus, had, were Laetus and Eclectus, who were in charge of his praetorian troops, and for one of his principal concubines or lady friends he had Marcia; and because they sometimes reproached him for sullying alike his person and his imperial position by his behaviour, he decided to put them to death, and made out a list on which he wrote the names of Marcia, Laetus and Eclectus, and several others whom he proposed on the following night to put to death. This list he put under the pillow of his bed. Having gone to wash himself, a favourite little boy of his was romping about the room and on the bed when he came across the list, and, having gone outside with it in his hand, met Marcia, who took it from him, and, having read it and noted its contents, sent at once for Laetus and Eclectus. All three of them realizing the danger in which they stood, decided to forestall it; so, without wasting any unnecessary time, they killed Commodus the following night.

Again, the emperor Antoninus Caracalla, when with his army in Mesopotamia, had as his prefect, Macrinus, who was more of a civilian than a soldier; and, as is usually the case with princes who are not good, he was for ever afraid that others should not act towards him as he thought he deserved. So Antoninus wrote to Maternianus, a friend of his in Rome, to request him to inquire of the astrologers whether anybody was aspiring to become emperor, and to advise him accordingly. Maternianus, therefore, wrote him that Macrinus was the man who had this idea in mind, but the letter fell into the hands of Macrinus before it got to the emperor, and, in consequence, Macrinus saw that it was necessary either to kill him before a further letter came from Rome, or to be killed; so he instructed Martialis, a centurion who was devoted to him and whose brother Antoninus had killed a few days before, to assassinate the emperor, a commission which he carried out successfully.

Hence we see that when necessity becomes so urgent that it leaves no time for delay, it produces much the same effect as does the method adopted by Nelematus of Epirus, which I have described above. We see, too, that what I have said almost at the beginning of this discourse, also holds good, namely, that threats do more harm to princes and are more likely to result in conspiracies than the actual infliction of injuries. Against threats, therefore, a prince should be on his guard; for either he should make a fuss of men or should make sure they will do him no harm, but in no case should he put them in such a position that the only courses which appear open to them are either to get killed or to kill somebody else.

As to the dangers which occur during the carrying out of a plot, these are due either to a change of plan, or to lack of courage on the part of the person who is to carry it out, or to the operative's making some mistake owing to carelessness, or to failure to complete the job in that there remain alive some of those who were to have been killed. I would here point out, therefore, that nothing so perturbs and interferes with anything undertaken by men as does their having suddenly and without due notice to change their plan and to give up that laid down at the start. And, if such a change of plan anywhere gives rise to disorder, it is in military operations and in affairs such as those of which we are speaking; because in a business of this kind what it is essential to do first and foremost is to get clearly into the heads of those concerned the part which each of them has to play, and, if men have for several days been picturing to themselves a certain

Dangers arising from a change of plan

course of action and a certain plan, and this is suddenly changed, it is impossible but that it should throw everything out of gear and spoil the whole scheme. So that it is much better to carry out the original plan, even if one sees in it certain inconveniences, than it is to cancel it and thereby to involve oneself in a host of inconveniences. This applies to cases in which there is no time to draw up a new plan, for, if there is time, a man can arrange matters as he pleases.

The conspiracy of the Pazzi against Lorenzo and Giuliano de' Medici is familiar to all. According to the plan that had been given out, they were to be invited to dinner with the Cardinal of St George, and at the dinner were to be assassinated. Those who were to kill them, those who were to seize the palace and those who were to run about the city calling on the people to free themselves, had all been detailed. It happened that, when the Pazzi, the Medici and the Cardinal were attending a solemn function in the cathedral church of Florence, it became known that Giuliano was not going to dine with them that day; so the conspirators got together and decided that what they had been going to do in the house of the Medici should be done in the church. This upset the whole plan, for Giovambatista da Montesecco declined to take part in the murder, since he was not going to do it in church, he said. So they had to find new operatives and to redistribute the parts assigned, and, since there was no time for them to get clear as to their parts, they made such blunders in carrying it out that they were overcome.

Irresolution on the part of operatives in doing their job, is due either to human respect or to personal cowardice. Such is the majesty and the respect inspired by the presence of a prince that it may easily damp the resolution of an operative or terrify him. When Marius was taken prisoner by the Minturnians a slave was sent to kill him, but, so overawed was he by the presence of such a man and by the recollection of what his

Failure due to irresolution

name stood for, that he lost courage and hadn't the strength to kill him. If, then, such power appertains to a man who is chained up in prison and overwhelmed with misfortune, how much greater must be that of a prince who is not thus encumbered, but is there in his majesty, wearing his robes and decorations, surrounded by pomp and by his courtiers. Such pomp as this may well affright you, or again the graciousness of his welcome may soften you. Certain persons were conspiring against Sitalces, king of Thrace, had settled the day on which the deed was to be done, and had got to the place assigned at which the prince then was; yet none of them ventured to attack him, so that at length they went away without trying to do anything and without quite knowing what had prevented them, each laying the blame on the other. They made the same mistake more than once, so that in the end the conspiracy was discovered and they were punished for a crime which they could have committed but were reluctant to· commit. Two of his brothers conspired against Alfonso, Duke of Ferrara, and used as an intermediary Giannes, a priest and a cantor in the duke's employ. Several times at their request he got the duke to meet them, so that it lay in their power to kill him; in spite of which not one of them dared to do it, so that, the plot being discovered, they suffered the penalty of their wickedness and their want of prudence. Such negligence could not have been due to anything except their being frightened by the presence of the prince or humbled by some gracious act of his.

Inconveniences in the carrying out of a conspiracy are due to mistakes caused either by lack of prudence or by lack of courage, for both these two things may befall you and cause you such confusion of mind that you say and do what you oughtn't to say or do. That men do get thus overwhelmed and confused cannot be better illustrated than by what Titus Livy tells us of Alexamenes, the Aetolian, who had made up his

*Failure
due to
perturbation
of mind* mind to kill Nabis the Spartan, of whom we have already spoken. When the time came to do it, he explained to his men what it was they had to do, and, says Livy, 'pulled himself together, for his mind had become confused by thinking of so great a matter'. It is, indeed, impossible, that any man, even though he be strongminded, familiar with death and accustomed to using the sword, should not become confused. Hence men should be chosen who have had experience in doing such deeds, and one should entrust them to no one else, brave as he may be thought to be. For when it comes to doing big things of which a man has had no previous experience, no one can say for certain what will happen. This confusion, for instance, might be such as to cause you to let the weapon fall from your hand, or to let slip some word which would have precisely the same effect. Lucilla, the sister of Commodus, arranged with Quintianus to kill him. Quintianus lay in wait for Commodus at the entrance to the amphitheatre, and, going up to him with a naked dagger, greeted him with the words: 'The senate sends you this!', words which led to his being arrested before he had lowered his arm to strike. Messer Antonio de Volterra was deputed, as we have already said, to kill Lorenzo de' Medici. On coming up to him he said: 'Ah, traitor!', an exclamation which saved Lorenzo's life and ruined the conspiracy.

It is not easy to do the thing perfectly when a conspiracy is directed against one ruler, for the reasons alleged, and still less *Conspiracies
directed
against
more than
one prince* is it easy to do it perfectly when a conspiracy is directed against two. On the contrary, it is so difficult that it is almost impossible for the conspiracy to succeed. For it is almost impossible to do similar actions in different places at one and the same time, and you cannot perform them at different times if you do not want one to

spoil the other. Hence, if to conspire against one prince is a doubtful, dangerous and imprudent undertaking, to conspire against two is altogether foolish and frivolous. Were it not for my respect for the historian I should never have thought that what Herodian says of Plautianus were possible, namely, that he should have commissioned the same person, Saturninus the centurion, to kill both Severus and Antoninus who dwelt in different places, for the thing is so utterly unreasonable that nothing short of his authority would make me believe it.

Certain Athenian youths conspired against Diocles and Hippias, tyrants ruling in Athens. They killed Diocles, but Hippias escaped and avenged him. Chion and Leonides of Heraclea, disciples of Plato, conspired against the tyrants, Clearchus and Satyrus. They killed Clearchus, but Satyrus remained alive to avenge him. The Pazzi, whom we have mentioned more than once, only succeeded in killing Giuliano. Hence no one should engage in conspiracies against more than one ruler since he will do not good either to himself or to his country or to anybody at all. On the contrary, those who survive, will become more insupportable and more bitter, as Florence, Athens and Heraclea, to which I have already alluded, found out. True, the conspiracy which Pelopidas formed for the liberation of Thebes, his fatherland, involved all these difficulties, and yet was successful; for Pelopidas conspired not only against two tyrants, but against ten, and not only was he an outsider to whom access to the tyrants presented a difficulty, but he was a rebel. None the less, he was able to get into Thebes, to kill the tyrants and to liberate his country. Actually, however, it was with the assistance of Charon, counsellor to the tyrants, that he did all this, for it was through him that he gained easy access to do the deed. Nor should anyone nevertheless emulate his example; for it was an impossible undertaking and a marvellous thing that it succeeded. It was also, as all writers are agreed who have mentioned it, a rare and almost unparalleled thing.[57]

The carrying out of a plot may be ruined by a false impression or by an unforeseen accident which occurs in the course of it. On the very morning on which Brutus and the other conspirators had decided to kill Caesar, it happened that he held a long conversation with Gaius Pompilius Lenas, who was one of the conspirators, and when the others saw him talking for so long, they wondered whether the said Pompilius was not telling Caesar of the conspiracy, and were on the point of killing him there and then, without waiting for him to come into the senate. They would, indeed, have done this, had the argument not come to an end and had they not then been reassured when they saw Caesar gave no sign of unusual emotion. False impressions of this kind should be taken into account and due attention be paid to them, if one would be prudent; the more so in that it is easy to get such false impressions. For, when a man has a bad conscience, he readily believes that people are talking about him, and a remark which is irrelevant may disturb your equanimity and make you think that it has bearing on your business, and this causes you either to give the conspiracy away by running off, or to muddle it by acting before the proper time. And the more there are who are in the know, the more likely is this to happen.

Failure due to false impressions

As to accidents, since they cannot be foreseen, the only thing one can do is to give examples showing how cautious men ought to be in regard to them. Lucio Belanti of Siena, of whom mention has already been made, was so indignant with Pandolfo, who had taken away the daughter he had previously given him in marriage, that he decided to kill him, and chose the occasion as follows. Pandolfo used to go daily to visit

Failure due to unforeseen accidents

a sick relative, and, in doing so, passed by Lucio's house.
Lucio, having noticed this, arranged for his conspirators to
be ready in his house to kill Pandolfo as he was going by.
He placed them inside the doorway with their arms, and
stationed one of them at the window ready to give the signal
when Pandolfo was to pass by the doorway, whereupon they
were at once to issue forth. It so happened that, when Pandolfo
came along and the signal had been given, Pandolfo met a
friend who stopped him, and some of those who were with
him went on ahead, saw what was happening, heard the clatter
of arms and so discovered the trap; with the result that
Pandolfo escaped and Lucio and his accomplices had to fly
from Siena. Thus this accidental meeting interfered with
the business in hand and caused Lucio's scheme to end in
disaster. Since accidents, such as these, are of rare occurrence,
it is impossible to prescribe any remedy. What one must do is
to consider everything that is likely to happen, and to provide
accordingly.

It remains now for us to discuss the dangers that may occur
after a conspiracy has been successfully carried out. There is
but one. It is that someone may be left alive who
will avenge the death of the prince. There may,
for instance, remain brothers or sons or other
supporters to whom the principality was expected to come. Survival of those who may wreak vengeance
may be due either to your negligence or to the causes mentioned above. Thus, when Giovanni Andrea da Lampognano
and his accomplices had killed the Duke of Milan, there remained one of his sons and two of his brothers, who in due
course came to avenge his death. In cases such as these the
conspirators have an excuse, for there is nothing they can do
about it; but when it is owing to lack of prudence or to their
negligence that someone is left alive, they have in that case
no excuse. Some conspirators who were citizens of Forli,

*Dangers
subsequent to
a conspiracy*

killed Count Girolamo, their Lord, and took prisoner his
wife and his children, who were little ones. It seemed to them,
however, that their lives would scarce be safe unless they
could get hold of the citadel, which its governor declined to
hand over. So Mistress Catherine, as the countess was called,
promised the conspirators that, if they would let her go to the
citadel, she would arrange for it to be handed over to them.
Meanwhile they were to keep her children as hostages. On
this understanding the conspirators let her go to the citadel,
from the walls of which, when she got inside, she reproached
them with killing her husband and threatened them with
vengeance in every shape and form. And to convince them
that she did not mind about her children she exposed her
sexual parts to them and said she was still capable of bearing
more. The conspirators, dumbfounded, realized their mistake
too late, and paid the penalty for their lack of prudence by
suffering perpetual banishment.

But of all the dangers that may ensue after a successful conspiracy there is none more inevitable or more to be dreaded
than when the people are well disposed to the prince you
have killed; for in such a case, since there is no remedy to
which the conspirators can have recourse, there is no chance
of their ever obtaining security. Caesar is a case in point, for
he was avenged by the people of Rome who were friendlily
disposed towards him; and of the conspirators, after they had
been driven out of Rome, one and all were killed at various
times and in various places.

Conspiracies against one's country Conspiracies against one's country are less dangerous to those who take part in them than are
conspiracies against princes, since fewer dangers
occur in the planning of them than in the latter
case; in carrying them out they are the same; and afterwards there are none. There are not many dangers in planning the conspiracy because a citizen can scheme to obtain

power without revealing his mind or his plan to anybody else, and, if his schemes are not interfered with, success will attend his undertaking; while if they should be interfered with by some law or other, he must bide his time and look for some other opening. This applies to a republic which is to some extent corrupt, for, since in one that is not corrupt no starting on evil courses there finds a place, no citizen is likely to harbour such thoughts. There are, then, all manner of ways and means of which citizens who aspire to a principality can avail themselves without running any risk of getting into trouble, alike because a republic is slower to take action than is a prince, is less suspicious, and for this reason less cautious, and because it has more respect for citizens of standing, and, in consequence, the latter are more daring and more inclined to act contrary to its interests. Everybody has read Sallust's account of the conspiracy of Catiline, and is aware that Catiline not only remained in Rome after the conspiracy was discovered, but attended the senate, where he made opprobrious remarks about the senate and about the consuls, so great was the respect which this city had for its citizens. Nor, when he had left Rome and was already in touch with the armies, would Lentulus and others have been arrested if they had not had in their possession letters in their own hand which plainly showed their complicity.

Again, when Hanno, one of the leading citizens in Carthage, who hoped to set up a tyranny, had arranged to poison the whole senate at the marriage-feast of one of his daughters, and afterwards to make himself prince, all the senate did, when it got to hear of the business, was to pass a law restricting the amount to be spent on banquets and marriages, so great was the respect they had for a man in his position.

On the other hand, it may well be that in carrying out a conspiracy against one's country there is more difficulty and the dangers are greater, for in a conspiracy aimed at so many

people your own forces will scarce suffice; and not everybody
has an army at his disposal, as had Caesar, Agathocles, Cleomenes and such-like, who have at one stroke subjugated their
country by means of the forces they commanded. For to
such folk the way is easy enough and safe enough; but others
who have not such forces at their disposal, must give effect to
their designs either by means of deceit and artifice or with the
help of foreign troops. The use of deceit and artifice is illustrated in the case of Pisistratus, the Athenian, who by his
victory over the Megarians gained favour with the people.
One morning he appeared in public, wounded, said that the
nobility out of envy had attacked him, and asked that he
might go about with an armed force for the protection of his
person. This being authorized, he had no difficulty in arro-
gating to himself such great power that he became tyrant of
Athens. Pandolfo Petrucci, on his return to Siena with other
exiles, was given command of the guard in the Piazza, a
routine business which others had refused; yet this armed force
in course of time acquired for him such repute that he became
before long a prince. Many others have adopted other
devices and other methods and in course of time and without
danger have achieved their aim.

Those who have conspired to get control of their country
by means of their own forces or with foreign armies have met
with varied success according as fortune has favoured them or
not. Catiline, whom we mentioned above, perished in the
attempt. Hanno, of whom also we made mention, having
failed to succeed by using poison, armed several thousands of
his partisans, and both he and they were slain. Some of the
principal citizens of Thebes called in a Spartan army to help
them, and set up a tyranny in that city. If, then, we inquire
into all the conspiracies men have made against their country,
it will be found that none of them, or but few, have been
suppressed while the plot was being contrived, but that all of

them have either succeeded or been ruined when it came to carrying them out. Nor, when successful, do they entail any subsequent dangers other than those which pertain to a principality by its very nature. For, given that a man has become a tyrant, he is faced with the dangers which tyranny naturally and normally involves, and to avert them has no remedies other than those that we have already discussed.

This is all that needs to be said about conspiracies, and if I have taken account of those in which the sword and not

The use of poison

poison has been used, it is because they are all of one and the same pattern. It is true that the use of poison is more dangerous owing to its being more uncertain, for not everybody has the commodity, so that those who have it must needs be consulted and the necessity of consulting others means danger to yourself. Again, for a variety of reasons, a poisoned drink may not prove fatal, as those discovered who were to kill Commodus, for, on his throwing up the poison they had given him, they were forced to strangle him if they wanted him to die.

There is nothing, then, more inimical to princes than a conspiracy. For, when a conspiracy is formed against them,

Tactics to be used in suppressing a conspiracy

either they get killed or they incur infamy; since, if it succeeds, they die, and if it is discovered and they kill the conspirators, the conspiracy is apt to be regarded as a device on the part of the prince whereby to cloak his avarice and his cruelty *vis-à-vis* the lives and property of those he has put to death. I must not, therefore, neglect to warn that prince or that republic who knows that a conspiracy has been planned, to endeavour to discover its precise character before they take punitive action, and to compare carefully the strength and standing of the conspirators with their own; and, should they find it large and powerful, to take no notice of it until they have at their disposal enough forces

to crush it. To act otherwise is but to court disaster. Hence
they should practise dissimulation as best they can, lest the
conspirators, finding themselves discovered, be driven of
necessity to take immediate action regardless of the result.

The Romans afford us an example of this. Two legions of
soldiers were left to guard Capua against the Samnites, as we
have pointed out elsewhere. Those who were in command of
these legions conspired together to reduce the Capuans to
subjection. When this came to be known in Rome, Rutilus, a
new consul, was commissioned to look into the matter. To
keep the conspirators quiet, he made public the senate confirmation of the Capuan legions' lodging quarters. The troops
believed this, and, since there seemed to them to be plenty of
time to carry out their plan, they made no attempt to hurry
things. So matters stood until they came to realize that the
consul had separated one legion from the other, which
caused them to grow suspicious, to come out into the open
and to give orders for their scheme to be put into execution.
Nor can there be a better example than this from whichever
point of view we look at it, for we see how slow men are to
act when they think they have time, and how quick to act
when the need becomes urgent. Nor yet can a prince or a
republic that wants to postpone the discovery of a conspiracy
in its own interests do better than artfully to provide the
conspirators with an opportunity at some future date, so that,
while they await it in the belief that there is no hurry, that
prince or that republic may have time to arrange for their
punishment.

Those who have acted otherwise have but hastened their
own downfall, as the Duke of Athens did, and Guglielmo
de' Pazzi. When the duke became tyrant of Florence and
heard that a conspiracy had been formed against him, he had
one of the conspirators arrested but did not inquire further
into the matter, with the result that the rest at once flew to

arms and deprived him of the government. When Guglielmo was commissioner in the Val di Chiana in 1501 and learned that a conspiracy in favour of the Virelli had been formed in Arezzo whereby the Florentines were to be deprived of that town, he went at once to that city, and without considering either the strength of the conspirators or his own and without having any forces in readiness, on the advice of the bishop, his son, he had one of the conspirators arrested. After the arrest, the remaining conspirators at once took up arms, took the town from the Florentines and Guglielmo became a prisoner instead of a commissioner.

But when conspiracies are weak they both can, and ought, to be suppressed without further ado. Nor should either of the two following expedients be adopted, though one is almost the exact opposite of the other. One was used by the aforesaid Duke of Athens, who to show that he believed the Florentines to be well disposed towards him, put to death a man who had told him of a conspiracy. The other was adopted by Dion, the Syracusan, who, to discover the intentions of someone of whom he was suspicious, allowed Callippus, whom he trusted, to pretend to be forming a conspiracy. Both these expedients led to disaster, for the first discouraged informers and encouraged would-be conspirators, and the second made it an easy matter to compass Dion's death by means of the very conspiracy of which he was the real head, as he learned by experience, for Callippus was now able without further ado to plot against Dion, and he plotted so well that he deprived him both of his state and of his life.

Book Three

[THE NEED OF ADAPTATION
TO ENVIRONMENT]

---

7. *How it comes about that Changes from Liberty to Servitude and from Servitude to Liberty sometimes occur without Bloodshed and sometimes abound in it*

SOME perchance may wonder how it comes about that of many revolutions involving a change from freedom to tyranny or the other way about, some are accompanied by bloodshed and others not. For it is plain from history that in such revolutions sometimes vast numbers of men get killed, and that in others nobody at all gets hurt, as happened in the change which Rome made from kingship to rule by consuls, for in it no one was banished except the Tarquins, and nobody else at all got hurt.

The answer is that it all depends upon whether the change in form of government is or is not brought about by violence; for when it is accompanied by violence it is inevitable that many should get hurt, and then of necessity those who in their downfall have been injured seek revenge, and this desire for vengeance gives rise to bloodshed and loss of life; but when that form of government has been brought into being by the common consent of a whole people*a* which has made it great,

a da uno comune consenso d'una universalità.

425

there is no reason why, when the said people as a whole meets its downfall, they should harm anyone except its head. This was the case with Rome's government and with the expulsion of the Tarquins. It was also the case with the government of the Medici in Florence, which, when it fell in 1494, harmed nobody but the Medici themselves.

Revolutions of this kind, therefore, are not attended with much danger. Those, on the other hand, are extremely dangerous which are brought about by men who are out for vengeance, and have invariably been of such a kind as to appal those who read of them, to say the least. Since of such revolutions there are plenty of instances in history, I propose to leave it at that.

8. *He who would transform a Republic should take Due Note of the Governed*

THAT a bad citizen cannot do much harm in a republic that is not corrupt has been shown in a previous discourse, and, in addition to the reasons there adduced,[58] this conclusion is confirmed by the case of Spurius Cassius and that of Manlius Capitolinus. The former, an ambitious man, desirous of acquiring extraordinary authority in Rome, ingratiated himself with the plebs by conferring on them many benefits, such as dividing among them the lands which the Romans had taken from the Hernici. When the city fathers discovered his ambitious projects and made them known, he became so suspect that, on his addressing the populace and offering to give them the money accruing from the sale of the corn which the public had caused to be brought from Sicily, they refused it outright, since it seemed to them that Spurius was offering it them as the price of their liberty. Whereas, had the populace been corrupt, they would have accepted the money, and would have laid open the way to tyranny instead of closing it.

The example of Manlius Capitolinus is even more remarkable; for from his case it may be seen how the inordinate
desire to rule afterwards cancels out virtues of mind and body
and services rendered to one's country, however great they
may be. This desire, it is clear, was in his case aroused by the
envy he felt for Camillus on whom great honours had been
bestowed, and in him it begat so great a mental blindness that
without pausing to reflect on the mode of life prevailing in
the city, or to inquire with what kind of subjects he had to
deal and whether they were yet averse to accept a bad form
of government, he set about raising tumults in Rome alike
against the senate and against his country's laws. This incident
shows how perfect the city then was and how good the
material of which it was composed; for in his case none of the
nobles, who were usually very keen to defend one another,
rose to support him, nor did any of his relations make a move
on his behalf; nor yet, though it was customary in the case of
an accused person for his relations to appear in mourning, clad
in black, and all of them sorrowing, so as to evoke sympathy in
favour of the accused, did anyone at all appear in Manlius's
case. The tribunes of the plebs, who were wont always to look
favourably on causes which appeared likely to benefit the
populace, and to promote them the more vigorously the more
inimical they were to the nobles, in this case joined with the
nobles in suppressing a common pest. The Roman populace,
looking eagerly to its own interests and sympathetic to
projects which might thwart the nobility, in spite of its having
been so favourable to Manlius, none the less when the tribunes
cited him to appear, and referred his case to the judgement of
the populace, this same populace, become now the judge of its
defender, paid no attention to this, but condemned him to
death.

Hence I do not think that there is any example in the history
we are considering, capable of showing more clearly than this,

how sound were all the institutions of that republic, in view of the fact that not a soul in that city was disposed to defend a citizen who was replete with virtue of every kind and alike in public and in private had done very many things worthy of commendation. For with all of them love of country weighed more than any other consideration, and they looked upon the present dangers for which he was responsible as of much greater importance than his former merits; with the result that they chose he should die in order that they might remain free. 'Such,' says Titus Livy, 'was the fate of a man who would have been illustrious if he had not been born in a free city.'

There are two things here which should be borne in mind. One is that, in order to obtain glory, a man must use different methods in a city that is corrupt from what he would use in one in which political life is still vigorous. The other, which is almost the same as the first, is that in the way they behave, and especially where deeds of moment are concerned, men should take account of the times, and act accordingly.

Those who owing to bad judgement or to their natural inclinations are out of touch with the times are in most cases unfortunate in their life and unsuccessful in their undertakings. But it is otherwise with those who are in accord with the times. From the words of the historian cited above, it may without hesitation be inferred that, had Manlius been born in the days of Marius or Sulla, when the material was corrupt and it would have been possible to impress on it the form to which his ambition looked, he would have met with the same success that attended the actions of Marius and Sulla and others who, after them, aspired to tyranny. And in the same way, had Sulla and Marius lived in the time of Manlius, they would have been crushed at the very outset of their careers. For a man can easily by his behaviour and his evil devices begin to corrupt the populace in a city, but it is impossible for him to live long enough to corrupt it to such an extent that he himself shall reap the fruits. And, even if it were possible for him to live long enough to do this, it would still be impossible for him to succeed, for men are so impatient in the way they carry on that they cannot restrain their passions for very long. Consequently they make mistakes in handling their affairs, especially when they are too eager; with the result that, either through impatience or through mistakes, they are likely to take premature action and to meet with disaster.

If anyone, then, wants to seize supreme power in a republic and to impose on it a bad form of government, it is essential that he should find there a material which has in course of time become disordered, and that this disorder shall have been introduced little by little and in one generation after another. And this, as we have remarked in a previous discourse, must of necessity come about unless that republic be given fresh life by the example of good men or by fresh legislation be brought back to what it was at the start.

Manlius, therefore, would have been an exceptional and a remarkable man, had he been born in a corrupt city. Hence citizens who in republics take up any enterprise, whether in favour of liberty or with a view to tyranny, should take account of the subjects with which they have to deal and on this should base their estimate of the difficulties their undertaking involves; for it is just as difficult and dangerous to try to free a people that wants to remain servile as it is to enslave a people that wants to remain free.

Since I have remarked above that in human affairs men should study the nature of the times and act accordingly, of this we shall speak at length in the next chapter.

9. *That it behoves one to adapt Oneself to the Times if one wants to enjoy Continued Good Fortune*

I HAVE often thought that the reason why men are some-times unfortunate, sometimes fortunate, depends upon whether their behaviour is in conformity with the times.[a] For one sees that in what they do some men are impetuous, others look about them and are cautious; and that, since in both cases they go to extremes and are unable to go about things in the right way, in both cases they make mistakes. On the other hand, he is likely to make fewer mistakes and to prosper in his fortune when circumstances accord with his conduct, as I have said, and one always proceeds as the force of nature compels one.

Everybody knows how Fabius Maximus, when in com-mand of the army, proceeded circumspectly and with a caution far removed from the impetuosity and boldness characteristic of the Roman; and by good luck this sort of thing just fitted the circumstances. For Hannibal had arrived in Italy, a young man flushed with success, and had twice routed the Roman people, so that this republic had lost almost all its best troops and was alarmed. Hence it could not have been more fortunate than to have had a general who by his slowness and his caution held the enemy at bay. Nor could Fabius have met with circumstances more suited to his ways; and it is to this that his fame was due.

That in so doing Fabius behaved naturally and not by choice is shown by the fact that, when Scipio wanted to go to Africa with his armies to bring the war to an end, Fabius was much against this, since he could not get out of his ways and habits; so that, if it had been left to him, Hannibal would still be in

[a] *i tempi* – the 'times' or the 'circumstances'; in the translation sometimes one and sometimes the other of these terms has been used.

Italy, for he did not see that times had changed, and that new methods of warfare were called for. So that, if Fabius had been king of Rome, he might easily have lost this war, since he was incapable of altering his methods according as circumstances changed. Since, however, he was born in a republic where there were diverse citizens with diverse dispositions, it came about that, just as it had a Fabius, who was the best man to keep the war going when circumstances required this, so later it had a Scipio at a time suited to its victorious consummation.

For this reason a republic has a fuller life and enjoys good fortune for a longer time than a principality, since it is better able to adapt itself to diverse circumstances owing to the diversity found among its citizens than a prince can do. For a man who is accustomed to act in one particular way, never changes, as we have said. Hence, when times change and no longer suit his ways, he is inevitably ruined.

Piero Soderini, whom we have mentioned several times,[59] conducted all his affairs in his good-natured and patient way. So long as circumstances suited the way in which he carried on, both he and his country prospered. But when afterwards there came a time which required him to drop his patience and his humility, he could not bring himself to it; so that both he and his country were ruined. Pope Julius II during the whole course of his pontificate acted with impetuosity and dash, and, since the times suited him well, he succeeded in all his undertakings; but had other times come which called for other counsels, he would of necessity have been undone, for he could not have changed his ways or his method of handling affairs.

There are two reasons why we cannot change our ways. First, it is impossible to go against what nature inclines us to. Secondly, having got on well by adopting a certain line of conduct, it is impossible to persuade men that they can get on well by acting otherwise. It thus comes about that a man's fortune changes, for she changes his circumstances but he does not change his ways. The downfall of cities also comes about because institutions in republics do not change with the times, as we have shown at length already,[60] but change very slowly because it is more painful to change them since it is necessary to wait until the whole republic is in a state of upheaval; and for this it is not enough that one man alone should change his own procedure.

Since we have mentioned Fabius Maximus who held Hannibal at bay, it seems to me appropriate in the next chapter to discuss whether a general who is determined at all costs to force the enemy to fight, can be prevented by the enemy from doing this.

Book Three

[SUNDRY REMARKS ON STRATEGY,
TACTICS, NEW DEVICES AND
DISCIPLINE]

---

10. *That a General cannot avoid an Engagement if the
Enemy is determined to force him to it at All Costs*

'GAIUS SULPICIUS, the dictator, when waging war with the
Gauls, was unwilling to try his fortune in an engagement with
an enemy whose position time and an awkward situation
was steadily making worse.' When there occurs an error
which all men, or most men, are liable to make, it is not a bad
thing, I think, to warn them often against it. Since, therefore,
as I have frequently pointed out, the way in which important
matters are dealt with today does not come up to the standard
of the ancients, it does not seem to me superfluous at this
juncture to point it out once again. For, if there be any way in
which there has been a departure from ancient customs, it is
especially so in military matters, in which none of the things
the ancients esteemed so highly are now done. This inconvenience is due to republics and princes having entrusted such
matters to other people. To avoid danger they themselves keep
clear of military operations and, though one does sometimes
find a king in these days sallying forth in person, I do not on
this account think that it leads him to do much else that is

433

worthy of commendation. For when they actually do engage in military operations, they do it for the sake of display and not for any praiseworthy reason. True, in that they occasionally review their troops and reserve to themselves the title of commander, they make mistakes of less moment than do republics, especially Italian republics, which rely on others and understand nothing which has to do with war, and yet in their desire to look like a prince in the eyes of the army, make decisions, and, in doing so, commit innumerable blunders.

And although some of these blunders I have discussed elsewhere, I cannot here be silent about one which is very important. When these idle princes or effeminate republics are sending one of their generals on an expedition, it seems to them that the wisest thing they can commission him to do, is on no account to engage in open battle, but, on the contrary, above all else to be on his guard against an engagement; for they think that in so doing they are emulating the prudence of Fabius Maximus who, by putting off an engagement, saved the Roman state from destruction; wherein they overlook the fact that, more often than not, such a commission is nonsensical or dangerous. The point one has to bear in mind here is that a general who proposes to remain in the field cannot avoid battle if the enemy is determined to force one on him at all costs. Hence what such a commission amounts to is just this: 'Join battle at the enemy's behest, not at your own.' For, if one wants to remain in the field and not join battle, the only safe thing to do is to put at least fifty miles between oneself and the enemy, and then to have good scouts so that, should he come your way, you may have time to get farther off. Another alternative in this case is to shut yourself up in a city. But both courses are extremely harmful. For the first leaves your country at the mercy of the enemy, and a valiant prince would sooner try his fortune in battle than prolong a war at such cost to his subjects. While the second alternative is manifestly that of a lost cause, for what it comes to is that, when you have got your army into a city, you may be besieged, and before long to be reduced by the pangs of hunger to surrender. Hence to avoid battle in either of these two ways is extremely hurtful. The plan adopted by Fabius Maximus of occupying strong positions is good so long as you have so valiant[a] an army that the enemy does not dare come and seek you out in your position of vantage. Nor can it be said that Fabius avoided battle, but rather that he preferred to fight when he had the advantage. For, if Hannibal had gone to seek him out, he would have awaited him and made a day of it. But Hannibal did not dare to fight with him on these terms. So that it was as much Hannibal who avoided battle as Fabius; but, if either had determined at all costs to fight, the other would have had to adopt one of three courses, i.e. either to adopt one of the two courses mentioned above, or else to run away.

That what I am saying is true can be clearly seen from a host of cases, and especially in the war the Romans had with Philip of Macedon, the father of Perseus. For, when Philip was attacked by the Romans, he decided not to join battle, and, to avoid it, did at first what Fabius Maximus did in Italy: posted himself with his army on top of a mountain where he erected fortifications, thinking that the Romans would not dare to go and seek him out. But they did go, and, having fought with him, drove him from the mountain, and he, being powerless to resist, fled with the greater part of his forces. What saved him from being utterly undone was the impossible country, which prevented the Romans from following him up. Philip, therefore, still desirous of avoiding battle and being encamped in the neighbourhood of the Romans, had to get away; and, having learned by experience that, to avoid battle, it is not enough to take up a position on top of a mountain, and being averse to shutting himself up in towns, decided to take the remaining course and to put many miles between himself and

[a] *virtuoso.*

the Roman camp. Hence, when the Romans were in one province, he moved to another, and, in like manner, whenever the Romans moved out, he moved in. But when at length he came to see that by prolonging the war in this way his situation was getting worse, and that, now by him, now by the enemy, his subjects were being harassed, he decided to try his fortune in battle. He thus came to an engagement with the Romans, as was proper.

It is useful then not to fight under the conditions in which Fabius' army found itself, or again in those in which Gaius Sulpicius found himself, i.e. when you have so good an army that the enemy does not dare to come and oust you from your fortified position; or when the enemy is in your country, but without having the footing there that would guarantee provisions. In this case the course adopted is useful for the reasons Livy gives when he says: 'he was unwilling to try his fortune in an engagement with the enemy so long as time and his adverse situation were daily making the enemy's position worse'. But under all other conditions battle cannot be avoided without incurring dishonour and danger, for if you run away, as Philip did, it is as bad as being routed, and is the more shameful in that you afford less proof of your virtue. And if he thus succeeded in getting away, another who is not helped by the country may not be so successful as he was.

That Hannibal was a past master in warfare no one will deny. Hence, when he was up against Scipio in Africa, if he had seen any advantage in prolonging the war he would have done so; and peradventure, being a good general and having a good army, he might have done as Fabius did in Italy. But, as he did not do it, it must be supposed that strong grounds impelled him to act thus. For a commander who has an army massed together and sees that for lack of funds or of allies he cannot keep it long in the field, is quite mad if he does not put his fortune to the test before his army has to be disbanded;

because, if he waits, he is surely lost; but if he tries, he may succeed.

Another point of importance to be considered here is that one ought, if one is going to lose, to try to acquire glory, and there is more glory in being overcome by force than there is when it is through some other inconvenience that you come to lose. Hannibal must have been constrained by these necessities. On the other hand, should Hannibal have put off giving battle and Scipio had not enough courage to go and attack him in his strong positions, Scipio would have been none the worse for this, since he had already beaten Syphax - and acquired so many towns in Africa that his position there was as safe and as comfortable as if he were in Italy. This was not the case with Hannibal when he was up against Fabius, nor with the Gauls when they were up against Sulpicius.

Still less, again, is it possible for him to avoid battle who with his army is attacking a foreign country, for if he wants to get into the enemy's country, it behoves him when the enemy shows fight, to give battle, and if he takes up his position before a town, he is so much the more obliged to give battle. This happened in our times in the case of Charles, Duke of Burgundy, who, when encamped before Morat, a Swiss town, was attacked and routed by the Swiss; and in the case of the French army which was besieging Novara and was in like manner routed by the Swiss.

11. *That he who has to deal with several Foes, even*
though he be Weaker than they are, can actually Win,
provided he can sustain their First Attack

THE power of the tribunes of the plebs in the city of Rome was considerable, which was necessary since otherwise they could not have checked the ambition of the nobility, as we have frequently pointed out;[61] and the nobility would in that case have corrupted the republic long before they did. Nevertheless, because inherent in everything is its own peculiar malady, as has been said elsewhere, and this gives rise to fresh misfortunes, it is necessary to provide against them by fresh enactments. Hence, when the tribunes grew arrogant in the use of their authority and became a menace alike to the nobility and to the whole of Rome, there would have arisen an inconvenience harmful to Roman liberty if Appius Claudius had not shown how the ambition of the tribunes might be counteracted. This consisted in looking among them for someone who was either timorous or corruptible or devoted to the common good, and who could thus be induced to oppose the will of the rest when they were proposing to do something contrary to the will of the senate. This remedy acted in no small measure as a restraint on the excessive authority of the tribunes and was often of service to Rome.

This leads me on to consider how it sometimes happens that, when many powers are united against a single power, though in combination they are much more powerful than it is, yet more is always to be expected from the single power, though less strong, than from the many even though very strong, for apart from the many advantages which a single power has over the many – and they are countless – there is always this: it will be able by using a little industry to break up the many, and to make what was a strong body, weak. I shall not adduce examples from ancient history, for they would be many, but shall content myself with modern examples which have happened in our own times.

In 1483 all Italy formed a confederation against the Venetians, who, since they had lost everything and their army could no longer hold its own in the field, suborned Signor Ludovico who was ruling in Milan and by means of this managed to obtain terms by which they not only recovered their lost lands, but obtained part of the state of Ferrara. Thus, though they were losing the war, when peace came, they were better off than before.

A few years ago the whole world formed a confederation against France, yet, before the war came to an end, Spain had fallen out with the confederation and made peace on its own account, with the result that the remaining confederates shortly afterwards also had to come to terms with France.

The conclusion to be drawn from this is obvious. If the many make war on the one, the one will come out of it best provided her virtue be such that she can sustain the first attack and await her opportunity by procrastinating. For, should she not be able to do this, a host of dangers may ensue, as happened to Venice in '08 when, could she have temporized with the French army and have found time to win over one of the states confederated against her, she might have avoided disaster. But since in arms she was not sufficiently strong[a] to be able to temporize with the enemy, and so had not time to persuade any power to leave the confederation, she was undone. Yet one finds that the Pope, once he had recovered his lost territory, became her ally, and so did Spain; and either of these two princes would have been very glad to help her to save Lombardy so as to prevent the French becoming too powerful in Italy, had they been able to do so. Hence the Venetians, by giving up part of their territories, might have saved the rest; and this would have been a very wise course had it been done in time before the war broke out so that they should not appear to have been driven to it. But after the war had begun it would have been reprehensible, and probably of but little use. Yet, before war broke out, few Venetian citizens saw the danger, and still fewer the remedy; and there was no one to advise them.

But to come back to where we started. The conclusion I draw from this discourse is that, just as the Roman senate

[a] *non avendo virtuose armi.*

found means to save their country from the ambition of the tribunes because there were many tribunes, so any prince who is assailed by many, has a remedy to hand, if he be wise enough to take appropriate steps to break up the confederation.

12. *That a Prudent General should make it absolutely necessary for his own Troops to Fight, but should avoid forcing the Enemy to do so*

WE have in other discourses shown how useful a part necessity plays in human affairs, and to what glorious deeds it may lead men. As some moral philosophers in their writings have remarked, neither of the two most noble instruments to which man's nobility is due, his hands and his tongue, would have attained such perfection in their work or have carried man's works to the height which one can see they have reached, if they had not been driven to it by necessity.[62] Since, therefore, army commanders of old were aware of the virtue that lies in necessity, and how steadfast, when necessity drives, the minds of soldiers can become in their resolve to fight, they used every endeavour to put their troops under such constraint and, on the other hand, employed any device that would free the enemy from such constraint. To this end they often left open to the enemy a route they might have closed, and closed a route to their own soldiers which they might have left open. If, then, anyone wants a city to be obstinately defended or an army in the field to fight obstinately, he should, first and foremost, seek to instil this necessity into the minds of those who have to do the fighting.

It follows that a prudent general who has to go and lay siege to a city should base his estimate of how easy or how difficult it is going to be to take it on the knowledge and consideration of the extent to which necessity will constrain the inhabitants to defend it; and, if he find the necessity con-

straining them to defend it, considerable, should account the
siege difficult, but, if otherwise, should account it easy. It is for
this reason that towns which have rebelled are more difficult
to acquire than they are to acquire in the first instance; for in
the first instance they have no cause to expect punishment for
having given offence, and so surrender easily; but, since they
are aware, when in revolt, of having given offence, and in
consequence fear punishment, they become difficult to take.
Again, obstinacy of this kind is also aroused by the natural
hatred which neighbouring princes and neighbouring republics have for one another; which, in turn, is occasioned by
the ambition which moves states to dominate one another,
and by their jealousy, especially if they are republics, as was
the case in Tuscany, and this rivalry and competition have
made it difficult, and will continue to make it difficult, for one
to seize the other. If, therefore, one considers carefully what
neighbours the city of Florence has and what neighbours the
city of Venice has, it is not so extraordinary as many make out
that Florence should have spent more on wars and have
acquired less than Venice, since it is all due to the towns in the
neighbourhood of Venice not being so obstinate in defending
themselves as are those in the neighbourhood of Florence.
This comes about because the cities abutting on Venetian
territory are accustomed to live under a prince, and are not
free cities; and cities accustomed to subjection are usually not
so particular about changing masters: on the contrary, they
are often glad to do so. Hence, though Venice's neighbours
are more powerful than those of Florence, yet, on account of
its having found the towns less obstinate, Venice has been able
to subdue them more quickly than has Florence, which is
surrounded entirely by free cities.

But to return to the main topic of this discourse. When a
general is attacking a town he should endeavour with all
diligence to relieve its defenders of the necessity we have been

discussing, and so of their obstinacy; by promising them pardon if they are afraid of punishment, and, if they fear for their liberty, by explaining that no attack is being made on the common good, but only on a few ambitious citizens. This has often facilitated the attack on, and the taking of, towns. And, though such false colours are easily seen through, especially by men of prudence, the populace is none the less often deceived; for, in its eagerness for a speedy peace it shuts its eyes to any trap which may underlie generous promises. Innumerable cities have by this means been reduced to servile states. It was so with Florence, for instance, quite recently; and it happened to Crassus and his army; for, though he realized the emptiness of Parthian promises, made merely to deprive his troops of the need to defend themselves, this did not enable him to sustain their steadfastness, blinded as they were, by the offers of peace which the enemy had made: a point one sees clearly if one reads his life.

In this connection I might mention that when the Samnites, in contravention of their treaty and owing to the ambition of the few, raided and pillaged the lands of Rome's allies; and then sent ambassadors to Rome to sue for peace, offering to restore what they had taken and to hand over those responsible for the disturbances and for the booty taken, their offer was turned down by the Romans. On their returning to Samnium without hope of an agreement, Claudius Pontius, then in command of the Samnite army, in one of his remarkable speeches, pointed out that the Romans had anyhow wanted war, and that, though on their part they were anxious for peace, necessity constrained them to go to war. He then used these words: 'War is justified, if necessity forces one to it, and to arm is a duty, if in arms lies one's hope' and upon this necessity he based the hope of victory for his troops.

That I may not have to return later to this topic, it will be best for me to mention the more noteworthy instances in

Rome's case. There was that of Gaius Manlius who led his army against the Veientes, and, when a section of the Veientine army broke through his stockades, hurried with a detachment to defend them and, to prevent the Veientes escaping, put a guard on all the exits from the camp. Hence, finding themselves shut in, the Veientes began to fight so furiously that they killed Manlius, and would have got the better of all the rest of the Romans if one of the tribunes had not had the sense to let them out. Thus we see that, so long as necessity constrained the Veientes to fight, they fought with great ferocity, but, when they saw the way was open, thought more of getting away than of fighting.

The armies of the Volsci and the Aequi had crossed the Roman frontiers. Against them the consuls were sent. In the course of the battle the Volscian army, commanded by Vettius Messius, found itself at one moment shut up between its stockades which the Romans had taken, and the other Roman army. Seeing that he must needs die or use his sword to fight for his life, Vettius Messius said to his soldiers: 'Follow me. There is neither wall nor rampart in the way, but just armed forces to oppose armed forces. In valour we are equal, but in necessity which is the last weapon and the best of all, you have the advantage.' Thus Livy calls necessity 'the last and best of all weapons'.

Camillus, the most prudent of all Rome's generals, having already got into the city of Veii with his army, in order to facilitate the taking of it and to deprive the enemy of a last necessity to defend it, gave orders within the hearing of the Veientes to the effect that no one should touch those who were without arms. The result was that they threw down their arms and the city was taken almost without bloodshed. This device was afterwards adopted by many generals.

13. *Which is it best to trust, a Good General with a Weak Army or a Good Army with a Weak General?*

CORIOLANUS, being banished from Rome, went to the Volsci, where, having got together an army wherewith to avenge himself on his fellow citizens, he set out for Rome, but turned back rather out of devotion to his mother than to the Roman forces. Commenting on this incident, Livy remarks that from it we may learn that the Roman republic grew more through the virtue of her generals than through that of her soldiers for, in view of the fact that the Volsci had thus far always been beaten, they could have won on this occasion only because Coriolanus was their general. But, though Livy advances this opinion, many passages in his history show that soldiers without a general have given remarkable proof of their virtue, and that they have been better disciplined and more determined after the death of their consuls than before they got killed. It happened thus with the army the Romans had in Spain under the Scipios, for, when both these generals had been killed, its virtue was such that not only did it successfully defend itself, but it beat the enemy and thus saved this province for the republic. Hence all things considered, there are many cases in which the virtue of the soldiers alone has won the day, and many others in which the virtue of generals has had the same effect, so that, one can say that each has need of the other.

In this connection it will be well to consider first which is more to be feared: a good army badly generalled, or a good general who has poor troops. If we follow here the opinion of Caesar, neither one nor the other is worth much. For when he went to Spain against Afranius and Petreius, who had a first-class army, he showed how little esteem he had for them by remarking that 'he was going to fight an army without a general', thereby indicating the weakness of the generals. On the other hand, when he went to Thessaly to fight Pompey, he said: 'I am going to meet a general without an army.'

We can now turn to the further question: whether it is easier for a good general to make a good army, or for a good army to make a good general. I submit that on this point there can be no dispute; for it is easier for many, if good, to select or make a good man of someone, than it is for one good man to do it for many. Lucullus, when he was sent against Mithradates, was wholly without experience of warfare; yet the army, which was good and had excellent officers, soon made him a good general. Again, the Romans, who were short of men, armed a number of slaves, and handed them over to Sempronius Gracchus to train, and in a short time he made of them a good army. Pelopidas and Epaminondas, as I have remarked elsewhere, when they had delivered Thebes, their fatherland, from servitude to the Spartans, in a short time made such excellent soldiers of the Theban peasants that they could not only stand up against the Spartan militia but beat it.

The arguments are evenly balanced, because, if one is good, it can make the other like it. A good army, none the less, if it lacks a good head is apt to become mutinous and dangerous, as happened with the Macedonian army after the death of Alexander, and with the veterans in the civil war. Hence I am of opinion that more confidence should be placed in a good general who has time to train his men and a chance to arm them, than in a mutinous army with a turbulent fellow it has chosen as its head. Twice the glory and praise is due, then, to those generals who have not only had an enemy to beat, but, before coming to grips with him, have had to drill their troops and make a good army of them; for in this they display a twofold virtue, which is so rare that if it were given to many to be such strict disciplinarians, they would be much less esteemed and lauded than they are.

14. *What Effects are produced by the Appearance of New Inventions in the course of a Battle and by the hearing of Unfamiliar Cries*

OF what importance in strife and battle may be an unprecedented incident due to something seen or heard for the first time can be shown by numerous incidents and especially by that which occurred during the battle the Romans fought with the Volsci, when Quintius, seeing that one wing of his army was giving way, began to call to it in a loud voice to stand firm since the other wing was winning; for by these words he put courage into his own men and alarmed the enemy, and so won the day. And if on a well-disciplined army such remarks have a great effect, on a disorderly and ill-disciplined army they have a still greater effect, for the whole is swayed, as it were, by a wind.

Let me give you a remarkable instance which occurred in our own times. A few years ago, the city of Perugia was divided between two factions, the Oddi and the Baglioni. The latter were in power, the former having been banished. But, with the help of their friends, they got together an army and assembled it in one of their towns close to Perugia. Then, with the connivance of their partisans they got one night into the city and were on their way to take the piazza without having been discovered. Since at every street corner in the city chains had been placed to block the way, the troops of the Oddi put at their head a man with an iron mace to break the locks fastening the chains so that the cavalry could get through. It remained for him to break only that which barred the way into the piazza when the cry 'To arms!' was raised, and on the fellow who was doing the breaking the crowd pressed so hard that he could not raise his arm to strike, so, in order to manage it, he called out 'Get back there!',

words which, as they passed from rank to rank, became 'Get
back!'. Whereupon those in the rear began to run away, and
one after another, the rest followed suit with such frenzy that
their own men were thrown into confusion. So that the
plans of the Oddi came to nought owing to this insignificant
incident.

This leads me to observe that good discipline is needed in an
army not merely to enable it to fight in orderly fashion, but
also that you may not be perturbed should some tiny misadventure befall. For this reason alone the masses are useless in
war, since any rumour, any cry, any commotion may change
their mood and make them run away. Hence it is essential to
discipline that a good general should depute men to take note
of his verbal instructions and to pass them on to others; that
he should accustom his troops to pay no heed to anyone else,
and his officers not to depart from what they have been commissioned by him to say; for we find that failure to observe
these points carefully has often led to the greatest confusion.

In regard to strange sights, every general should try to
present something of the sort while his army is in action so as
to give courage to his own men and to dispel that of the
enemy; for among the events which are incidental to
victory this is especially effective. In illustration of this the
case of Gaius Sulpicius, the Roman dictator, may be adduced,
who, when engaged in battle with the Gauls, armed all his
baggage-men and a low lot of camp-followers, put them on
mules and other mounts so that with their arms and standards
they looked like a troop of horse, and stationed them with
flags flying behind a hill, with orders that, at a given signal
when the fighting grew hotter, they should appear and show
themselves to the enemy. This being done, as arranged, it so
terrified the Gauls that they lost the day. There are two things,
then, that a good general should do: first, he should see
whether by employing some such novel device he can scare the

enemy; and, secondly, he should be on the look-out so that, should the same trick be played on him by the enemy, he may discover it and nullify its effect.

It was thus that the King of India acted when Semiramis, noticing that the king had a good number of elephants, in the hope of intimidating him and showing him that she, too, had plenty of them, constructed a number of them out of the hides of buffaloes and cows and put them on camels which she sent ahead; but, the trick having been discovered by the king, her plan not only proved useless but turned out to her disadvantage. So, too, when the dictator, Mamercus, was at war with the Fidenates, to frighten the Roman army they ordered that in the heat of battle a number of troops should sally forth from Fidenae with torches on their lances in the hope that, distracted by the novelty of the thing, the Romans would break their ranks.

It should be noted here that, when such devices involve more truth than fiction, they can in that case be used on men with advantage, for if they have sufficient boldness, their weakness cannot be discovered so quickly. But when they involve more fiction than truth it is well either not to use them at all, or, if employed, to hold the performance some way off so that the fraud cannot be so quickly detected, as Gaius Sulpicius did with his muleteers. For if fraught with internal weakness, and they be near, they will soon be seen through, and will do you harm instead of good; as the elephants did to Semiramis and the torches to the Fidenates; for, though at the start they upset the army a little, yet, when the dictator came along and began to shout at the men, telling them not to be such cowards as to run away from the smoke like bees but to turn back and go for them, crying: 'Use the flames to destroy Fidenae since you have failed to pacify them with kindness', the device proved of no avail to the Fidenates, who were left the losers of the battle.

15. That at the Head of an Army there should be One, not Several, Commanders, and that to have a Plurality is a Nuisance

W HEN the Fidenates rebelled and put to the sword the colony the Romans had sent to Fidenae, to right the insult the Romans appointed four tribunes with consular power, of whom one was left to guard Rome, and the other three were sent against the Fidenates and the Veientes. Owing to the divided command and to the tribunes being at loggerheads one with the other, they returned discredited, though there had been no disaster. For the discredit they were responsible, but that there had been no disaster was due to the valour of the troops. Hence when the Romans saw what was wrong, they had recourse to the appointment of a dictator so that one man should be responsible for putting right the disorder that three had caused. This shows us the futility of having several persons in command of the same army or in charge of the defence of the same town. Nor can the case be put more clearly than it is by Titus Livy when he writes: 'The three tribunes with consular power afforded an illustration of how futile it is for many to share the imperium in a war, for each inclined to follow his own counsel, and since the others thought otherwise, they gave the enemy their chance.'[63]

And though this example is sufficient to show the disorders that a plurality of commanders causes in a war, I propose to give two more, one modern and the other ancient, the better to establish this point.

In 1500, after the King of France, Louis XII, had retaken Milan, he sent his troops to Pisa to recover it for the Florentines. The commissaries, Giovambatista Ridolfi and Luca di Antonio degli Albizi, were in command. Since Giovambatista was a man with a reputation and had seen more service,

Luca left the management of everything to him, but though he did not display his own ambition by opposing him, he displayed it by his silence, by his negligence and by criticizing everything, with the result that he helped the siege operations neither by action nor advice, but behaved like a man of no account. Later on, however, when something occurred which necessitated Giovambatista's returning to Florence, one finds everything quite different; for, when Luca was left in sole charge, he showed his worth alike by his courage, his industry and his sound sense, all of which characteristics had failed to show themselves so long as he had a colleague.

In confirmation of this remark of Titus Livy's I would cite another example: the expedition which the Romans sent against the Aequi under Quintius and his colleague, Agrippa. Agrippa who wanted the whole conduct of the war to be undertaken by Quintius, says: 'In the administration of affairs of moment it is highly advisable that the supreme command should be in the hands of one man.'

This is just the opposite of what our republics and princes do today, for to improve the administration they now send to a place more than one commissioner and more than one head, and this leads to indescribable confusion. Indeed, were one to seek the causes of the disasters that have befallen Italian and French armies in our own times, it would be found that this is the most potent. In conclusion, then, one may be quite certain that it is better to entrust an expedition to one man of average prudence than to give to two men of outstanding ability the same authority.

Book Three

---

*16. Genuine Virtue counts in Difficult Times, but,
when Things are going well, it is rather to those whose
Popularity is due to Wealth or Parentage that Men look*

IT always has been, and always will be, the lot of great and
outstanding men to be passed over by a republic in times of
peace, for the reputation acquired by their virtue arouses envy,
and in peaceful times there are plenty of citizens who seek not
merely to become their equals but even their superiors. On
this point there is a good passage by Thucydides, the Greek
historian, who shows how, when the Athenians had got the
upper hand in the Peloponnesian war, and had curbed the
pride of the Spartans and brought the rest of Greece into
subjection, their reputation was almost so great that they
planned to occupy Sicily. When the invasion was under
discussion in Athens, Alcibiades and some other citizens urged
that it should be undertaken, since they were men who cared
little for the public good, but were looking to the honours
they would gain, should they command the expedition as they
proposed to do. But Nicias, whose reputation stood higher
than anyone else's, dissuaded Athens from the course; and, in
addressing the people, the chief reason he gave to show that he

was in good faith was that, in advising against the war, he was advising them to do what could not be in his own interests, for, so long as Athens was at peace, he knew that a whole crowd of citizens would try to get ahead of him, but, in case of war, he knew that no citizen would be recognized as his superior or as his equal.

We see, therefore, in this incident a disorder to which republics are liable, namely that of showing but little esteem in time of peace for men of worth. This arouses their indignation on two accounts. First, they are themselves deprived of their position. Secondly, they find unworthy men who lack their competence, being made their associates and superiors. This disorder has brought about the ruin of many republics, for citizens who see that their merits are not appreciated and that this is because the times are untroubled and without danger, set about causing trouble and stirring up wars, prejudicial to the republic.

If one inquires what remedies may be applied, two suggest themselves. First, to keep the citizens poor, so that by wealth without worth they may be able to corrupt neither themselves nor other people. Secondly, to be so prepared that it may be possible at any time to go to war, in which case there will always be a demand for citizens of repute, as there was in Rome in its early days. For, since Rome always had armies in the field, there was always room for men of virtue. Nor could an office be taken from a man who deserved it and be given to one who did not; for though actually this was sometimes done by mistake or in order to test them, there soon followed such disorder and danger that there was a speedy return to the right road. But other republics which are not organized as Rome was, and which go to war only when necessity forces them to it, are unable to protect themselves against these inconveniences. On the contrary, they are ever likely to occur therein, and will always give rise to disorder should a citizen who has been passed over but is efficient, have some standing in the city and some adherents.

And if the city of Rome for a time remained immune, to her also, as we have pointed out elsewhere, when she had vanquished Carthage and Antiochus, and no longer feared war, it seemed permissible to entrust her armies to anyone she pleased on account not so much of virtue as of other qualities which appealed to the people. For we find that Paulus Aemilius was more than once refused the consulate, nor was he made consul till the Macedonian war began, when it was granted to him unanimously since the situation was thought to be dangerous.

There were many wars in which this, our city of Florence, was engaged after 1494, and in them the Florentine citizens all showed up badly, till the city chanced upon someone who taught it how an army should be commanded. This was Antonio Giacomini. So long as the city was engaged in a dangerous war, all the other citizens dropped their ambitions, and in the election of a commissioner and head of the army Antonio had no competitor. But when they were engaged in a war about the issue of which there was no doubt and there were plenty of honours and offices to be had, there were so many candidates that, when three commissioners had to be chosen for the campaign against Pisa, Antonio was passed over. And, though it is impossible to estimate precisely how much harm the public suffered through its having failed to appoint Antonio, yet it can quite easily be conjectured. For, as the Pisans no longer had the means to defend themselves or to obtain food, if Antonio had been in command they would soon have been in such straits that they would have had to surrender to the Florentines unconditionally. But as the siege was being conducted by commanders who did not know how to tighten it up and to apply pressure, they were so long about the business that the Florentines had to purchase what they could have obtained by force. Antonio must have been so disgusted at this as to have needed great patience and goodness not to have sought revenge as he might have done, to the ruin of the city or to the injury of some particular citizen. Against this a republic should be on its guard, as we shall show in the next chapter.[64]

17. That to a Person to whom Offence has been given, no Administrative Post of Importance should subsequently be assigned

A REPUBLIC should take good care not to give any administrative post of importance to anyone to whom some notable wrong has been done. Claudius Nero left the army with which he was confronting Hannibal, and went with part of it to the March[a] to look for the other consul so that they might engage Hasdrubal before he could join Hannibal. On a previous occasion he had found himself in Spain facing Hasdrubal, whom he had so penned up with his army that he must needs either fight at a disadvantage or perish of hunger. Hasdrubal, however, had cleverly deceived him by making proposals of peace, and had then slipped away, thus depriving Claudius of the chance of defeating him. When this came to be known in Rome it brought on him the grave reproaches alike of the senate and of the people, and he was spoken of disparagingly throughout the city to his discredit and to his disgust. So, when later on he became consul and was sent to fight Hannibal, he took the other course described above; which was so exceedingly dangerous a thing to do that it caused in

[a] *Andò nella marca.* – The term 'marca', frontier, when used with a capital of a district in Italy usually signifies the 'March of Ancona' on the Adriatic coast. Actually, it was at Sena Gallica, just north of Ancona, that the 'other consul' had taken up his position, and thither that Claudius Nero went to join him.

Rome grave doubts and great anxiety till the news of the
routing of Hasdrubal at length arrived. When asked afterwards why he had adopted so dangerous a course whereby
without any grave necessity he had come near to risking the
freedom of Rome, Claudius replied that he had done so
because he thought that, if he succeeded, he would regain the
glory he had lost in Spain, and that, if he did not succeed but
the course he had adopted led to disaster, he would feel that he
had avenged himself on a city whose citizens had treated him
so ungratefully and so unwisely.

If the passions aroused by such offences could have so great
an effect on a Roman citizen at a time when Rome was as yet
free from corruption, one can well imagine how great an
effect injuries are likely to have on a citizen of some other city
which is not constituted as Rome then was. Moreover, since
no sure remedy can be prescribed for such disorders, to which
republics are liable, it follows that it is impossible to constitute
a republic that shall last for ever, since there are a thousand
unpredictable ways in which its downfall may be brought
about.

18. Nothing becomes a General more than to anticipate the Enemy's Plans

EPAMINONDAS, the Theban, used to say that nothing is
more essential or more useful to a general than to discover
what the enemy has decided and is planning to do. And since
it is difficult to discover this, the more praiseworthy does he
become who conjectures it aright. Nor is the difficulty confined to understanding the enemy's plans, it is sometimes
difficult also to understand his actions, and this not only
when they are remote, but when they are done here and now
in the neighbourhood. For it has often happened that, when a
battle has gone on into the night, the winner thinks he has lost,

and the loser thinks he has won. This kind of mistake has made people adopt courses which did not contribute to the safety of those adopting them, as happened to Brutus and Cassius, who through a mistake of this kind lost the war; for, whereas Brutus had been victorious on his own flank, Cassius, who had lost, thought that the whole army must have been routed, a mistake which led him to despair of its safety, so that he killed himself.

In our time in the battle which Francis, King of France, fought with the Swiss at Santa Cecilia in Lombardy, that portion of the Swiss army which had remained intact, thought they had won when night came, for they knew nothing of those who had been routed and killed. In consequence of this mistake they did not save themselves, but remained to fight again in the morning to their very great disadvantage. Their mistake also caused the Papal and Spanish army to make a mistake, and on account of it almost to get wiped out; for, on receiving false news of the victory, they crossed the Po and, had they advanced too far, would have been taken prisoners by the victorious French.

Such mistakes as these occurred in the camps of the Romans and of the Aequi. For instance, when the consul, Sempronius, led an army out to meet the enemy and engaged them in battle, the fight lasted till the evening with varying fortune on either side, and, when night came on, both had lost half their men, so that neither of them returned to their camps, but, instead, withdrew to neighbouring hills where they thought they would be more secure. The Roman army was divided in two parts, of which one went with the consul and the other with one, Tempanius, a centurion, to whose valour it was due that the Roman army had not been entirely routed during the battle. When morning came, the Roman consul, who was without further news of the enemy, retired towards Rome. The army of the Aequi withdrew in like manner; for each of them thought the enemy had won, and in consequence, each retired without troubling about the booty that had been left in their camps. It so happened, however, that Tempanius, who was also retiring with the rest of the Roman army, heard from certain wounded Aequi that their generals had departed and had abandoned their camp. So, on receipt of the news, he went to the Roman camp and salvaged it, then sacked that of the Aequi and returned to Rome victorious. This victory, as we see, depended simply upon which came first to hear of the enemy's panic. It should be noted, therefore, that it may often happen that two armies confronting one another have each been thrown into disorder and are pressed by the same necessity, in which case that army will come out victorious which first hears of the necessity in which the other is placed.

I shall now give of this an example which concerns ourselves and occurred recently. In 1498, when the Florentines had a large army enveloping Pisa and were pressing that city hard, the Venetians, who had undertaken to protect Pisa, since they did not see any other way of saving it, decided to create a diversion by sending another expedition to attack the Florentine dominions. So, with a powerful army they entered the Val di Lamona, took the town of Marradi and laid siege to the citadel of Castiglione, which stands on a hill above it. When the Florentines got to know of this, they decided to send help to Marradi, but not to weaken the forces they had before Pisa. So they made new levies of infantry and enrolled fresh troops of cavalry, and sent them there under the command of Jacopo IV d'Appiano, Lord of Piombino, and Count Rinuccio da Marciano. When, therefore, these troops reached the hill above Marradi, the enemy raised the siege of Castiglione and all withdrew into the town. After the two armies had been facing one another for several days, both of them began to suffer considerably from lack of provisions and other necessities; and neither of them daring to attack the other, nor aware of the other's difficulties, each of them decided one fine evening to raise their camp the following morning, and to retire, the Venetians on Bersighella and Faenza, the Florentines on Casaglia and the Mugello. When morning came and each of the camps had begun to send away its baggage, it so happened that a woman came out of the town of Marradi and approached the Florentine camp, for on account of her age and poverty she felt safe and was anxious to see some of her relations who were in that camp. From her the commanders of the Florentine forces heard that the Venetians had struck camp, so, on this news, they plucked up courage, changed their plans to those they would have adopted had they dislodged the enemy, went after them and wrote to Florence announcing that they had repelled the enemy and won the war. This victory was due solely to their having been the first to hear of the enemy's departure, and had this knowledge come first to the other side, they would have done against our men precisely the same thing.

Book Three

[ADMINISTRATIVE METHODS: THE RIVAL CLAIMS OF SEVERITY AND GOOD FELLOWSHIP]

19. Whether in controlling the Masses Considerateness[a] is more Necessary than Punishment

THOUGH the Roman republic was distraught owing to the hostility between the nobles and the plebs, none the less, when war came, it commissioned Quintius and Appius Claudius to lead the armies forth. Appius, who was a brutal and harsh commander, was so badly obeyed by his troops that he had to quit his province as though he had been defeated. Quintius, who was of a kindly and humane disposition, was obeyed by his troops and returned victorious. It would seem better, therefore, in controlling a large number of men, to be humane rather than arrogant, compassionate rather than cruel.

[a] *ossequio.* – The Latin term '*obsequium*' is used frequently by Tacitus both in his *Annals* and his *Histories*. It is derived from the verb '*obsequor*', which means to accommodate oneself to, to gratify, humour, show complacency. Hence, when applied to a ruler, as it is here, it means to show consideration towards the ruled – considerateness, and, when displayed in an exaggerated form, is equivalent to what in slang is called 'soft soap'. The correlative attitude on the part of the ruled is subservience and in its exaggerated form obsequiousness. [Surely 'condescension' is then the better word? B.R.C.]

Cornelius Tacitus, however, – and many other writers agree
with him – arrives at the opposite conclusion, which he
expresses in these words: 'In ruling the masses punishment is of
more avail than considerateness.'

With a view to reconciling these two opinions I would point
out that either the men you have to rule are in ordinary
circumstances your associates, or they have always been your
subjects. When they are your associates, you cannot in your
dealings with them use penalties, nor yet that severity which
Cornelius advocates. Wherefore, since in Rome the plebs had
an equal share in the government with the nobility, neither
could, on becoming the ruler for the time being, treat the
other brutally and harshly. Very often, too, one sees that
Roman generals succeeded better when they made their
armies love them and treated them with consideration than
did those who made themselves excessively feared, unless
such behaviour was accompanied by outstanding virtue, as it
was in the case of Manlius Torquatus. On the other hand, in
governing one's subjects, which is what Cornelius has in
mind, lest they should become insolent and trample on you
should you be too easy with them, it is better to rely on
punishment rather than on considerateness. But this also
should be used with moderation, so as to avoid cause for
hatred; for no ruler benefits by making himself odious. To
avoid this he should leave his subjects' property alone; for,
except as a cover for pillage, no prince is keen on shedding
blood unless he be driven to it, and need for this seldom arises.
But in connection with pillage bloodshed is always happening,
nor is either the occasion or the desire to shed it ever lacking, as
in another treatise discussing this topic has been shown at
length.[65] More praise is due, then, to Quintius than to
Appius, and Cornelius's view, under the conditions he supposes but not in those observed in the case of Appius, deserves
approbation.

And while we are on this topic of punishment and considerateness it will not be irrelevant, I think, to cite a case in which an act of common decency availed more with the Falisci than did the use of arms.

20. *A Single Act of Common Humanity made a Greater Impression on the Falisci than did all the Forces of Rome*[66]

WHEN Camillus and his army lay before the Faliscan city, which he was besieging, a schoolmaster who taught the most noble youths in the city, thinking to ingratiate himself with Camillus and the Roman people, went with his pupils outside the town ostensibly to give them exercise, led them to where Camillus was encamped, and offered to hand them over, saying that, if they were used as a lever, the town would place itself in his hands. Camillus not only rejected the offer, but had the teacher stripped, his hands tied behind his back, and to each of the boys gave a rod with which to beat him often and hard on his way back to the town. When the citizens saw this, they were so pleased with the humanity and integrity of Camillus that they no longer wanted to go on with the defence, but decided to hand over the town. This authentic incident affords us an excellent example of how a humane and kindly act sometimes makes a much greater impression than an act of ferocity or violence; and how districts and cities into which neither arms nor the accoutrements of war, nor any other kind of human force would have been able to obtain entry, it has been possible to enter by displaying common humanity and kindness, continence or generosity.

Of this there are in history many other examples besides the above. One sees, for instance, how Roman forces failed to drive Pyrrhus from Italy, which he quitted, none the less, owing to the generosity of Fabricius who told him of an offer which had been made to the Romans by one of his servants, to poison him. One sees, too, how Scipio Africanus did not gain so much renown in Spain for taking New Carthage as he did by the continence he showed in sending back to her husband his young and beautiful wife, inviolate. The repute he gained by this action made the whole of Spain his friend.

We see, again, how keen peoples are on their great men doing this kind of thing, and how much it is praised by writers, both by the biographers of princes and by those who have laid down rules for their behaviour. Xenophon, for instance, is at considerable pains to show what great honours, what great victories, and how much good repute Cyrus gained by his humanity and his affability, and how entirely free he was from pride, cruelty, licentiousness and other vices by which the lives of men are marred. Since, however, Hannibal gained great fame and great victories by the opposite method, it is fitting that in the next chapter I should inquire how this came about.

21. *How it comes about that Hannibal, whose Procedure differed radically from Scipio's, yet produced the same Effect in Italy as Scipio did in Spain*

SOME people, I fancy, would be astonished were they to notice how certain generals, in spite of their having adopted a contrary line of conduct, produced the same effects as those who behaved in the way we have just described. Hence it would seem that the causes of victory did not rest on the grounds alleged, but, on the contrary, that such methods bring you neither greater strength nor better luck, since glory and reputation can be gained by the opposite methods. Let me keep to the two men mentioned above, and try to make my meaning more clear. Scipio, we find, entered Spain and by his humane and kindly conduct at once made that country his friend, and won the respect and admiration of its people. We find, on the other hand, that Hannibal entered Italy and by totally different methods, i.e. by cruelty, violence, rapine and every sort of perfidy, produced there the same effect as Scipio had produced in Spain; for all the Italian cities revolted to him, and all its peoples became his followers.

If one asks how this came about, there would appear to be several reasons. First, men are fond of novelty; so much so that those who are prosperous desire it as much as those who are poor. For, as has been said before, and rightly, in prosperity men get fed up, and in adversity cast down. Now, this desire for novelty throws open the door to anyone in the neighbourhood who puts himself at the head of a new movement. If he be a foreigner, men run after him; and, if he be a local man, they crowd round him, boost him and push him forward; with the result that, whatever line he takes, he succeeds in making great headway in this locality. Besides which, men are moved in the main by two things; either by love or by fear. Hence it comes about that a person in authority may be either one who makes himself loved or one who makes himself feared. Indeed, a man who makes himself feared is usually better followed and better obeyed than is one who makes himself loved.

It matters then little to a general along which road he travels, provided he has virtuosity, and his virtue gives him standing with men. For when there is great efficiency as there was in Hannibal and Scipio, it counterbalances all the mistakes due to their having made themselves too much loved or too much feared. For from both of these two lines of conduct there may arise serious inconveniences, likely to bring about the downfall of a ruler; because he who is too anxious to gain affection, should there be any little departure from the straight path, may become despised: while the other, who is anxious to be feared, should there be any excess in his behaviour, may become odious. And to keep precisely on the middle path cannot be done, for it is alien to our nature. Hence it is necessary that any excesses in action should be compensated by exceeding efficiency, as they were in Hannibal and Scipio. None the less, though it was by behaving thus that they made their name, it is clear that in both cases their conduct did them harm.

How each of them came to make his name has already been explained. The harm done, so far as Scipio is concerned, was that in Spain his soldiers mutinied, and were joined by some of his allies. This was due entirely to their not being afraid of him; for men are so restless that should the least thing open the door to their ambition, they at once belie the love which their ruler may have evoked by his decency, as did the aforesaid soldiers and allies. Consequently Scipio, to remove this inconvenience, had to resort to some measure of that cruelty which he had thus far avoided. As to Hannibal, there is no particular instance of his cruelty or his faithlessness doing him harm. One can well imagine, however, that Naples and many other towns which remained loyal to the Roman people, did so through fear of him. It is certain, too, that his impious behaviour made him more odious to the Roman people than any other enemy which that republic ever had. For, whereas to Pyrrhus, when he and his army were in Italy, they revealed a plot to poison him, they never forgave Hannibal, even when his troops were disarmed and disbanded, until they had compassed his death. Owing to Hannibal's reputation for impiety, faithlessness and cruelty, then, this inconvenience arose; but, on the other hand, he derived from it a very great advantage, of which all writers have spoken with admiration. For, though his army was composed of men from different races, there never arose any dissension either among the men themselves or between them and him. This can only have been due to the terror his person inspired, which was so great that, in conjunction with the reputation he acquired for efficiency, it kept his troops quiet and united.

I conclude, therefore, that it does not matter much in what way a general behaves, provided his efficiency be so great that it flavours the way in which he behaves, whether it be in this way or that. For, as we have said, in both there are defects and dangers unless they be corrected by outstanding virtue. Hence, if Hannibal and Scipio produced the same effect, the one by praiseworthy and the other by reprehensible methods, it will not be amiss, I think, for me to discuss two Roman citizens who acquired the same glory by different methods, both of which were praiseworthy.

22. How the Severity of Manlius Torquatus and the Sociability[a] of Valerius Corvinus won for Each the same Degree of Fame[b]

THERE were living in Rome at the same time two first-class generals, Manlius Torquatus and Valerius Corvinus, equal in virtue, equal in the number of their triumphs and equal in fame. In dealing with the enemy the virtue they each displayed in the conquests they made was also on a par, but in the way they handled the army and in their treatment of the troops they behaved very differently. For Manlius was a commander who used every type of severity, and never let his soldiers off either fatigues or punishments. Valerius, on the other hand, treated them with the utmost consideration in every way, and in his bearing was familiar and homely. Consequently one finds one of them killing his own son in order to secure the obedience of the troops, and the other harming nobody. None the less, from their diverse methods they reaped the same fruit, alike in contest with the enemy and

[a] la comità.   [b] la medesima gloria.

in the honour brought both to the republic and to themselves. For no soldier ever shirked battle, or mutinied or failed to comply with the wishes of either of them; though so peremptory were Manlius's commands that all orders which exceeded the bounds of moderation came to be called 'Manlian orders'. Hence we must first inquire how it came about that Manlius was constrained to behave with such rigidity: secondly, what enabled Valerius to behave with such consideration; thirdly, what caused these different methods to produce the same effect; and, finally, which is the better way and which the most useful to imitate.

If anyone considers carefully the character of Manlius from the time when Titus Livy first mentions him, he will realize that he was a very brave man, devoted to his father and to his country, and very respectful towards his superiors. This is shown in his killing of that Gaul, by his defence of his father against the tribune, and from what he said to the consul before he went to fight the Gaul, namely: 'Without an order from you I will never fight against any enemy, even though I am sure of victory.' When, therefore, a man of this kind obtains the rank of commander he expects to find everybody else like himself, and the boldness which characterizes him makes him order bold actions, and what he orders he expects to be carried out in precisely the way he prescribes. It is indeed a very sound rule that, when harsh commands are given, one should be harsh in seeing them carried out; otherwise you will find yourself let down. It should also be noted that, if one wants to be obeyed, one should know how to command, and that one can know how to command only if one has compared one's own character with the character of those who have to obey, and gives orders only when one sees that they harmonize and, when they clash, abstains.

It has been said by a wise man that, if one is to hold a state by violent means, the force employed should be proportionate to the resistance offered. So long as this proportion obtains, it is to be expected that the violence will last; but should the violated be stronger than the violator, it is probable that the violence will some day cease.

But to return to our discourse. I maintain that, if bold things are to be ordered, one must be a bold man; and that, given a man has the strength and that he issues bold orders, then he cannot be soft in seeing that his orders are obeyed; whereas a man who has not this strength of character, should be careful not to give such out-of-the-way orders, but in giving orders can afford to act in accordance with his common humanity, because ordinary punishments are not ascribed to the ruler, but to the laws and institutions. It must be supposed, therefore, that Manlius was constrained to act thus rigidly owing to the extraordinary orders he gave, to which he was inclined by his nature. And that such orders should be given is useful in a republic, since they restore its discipline to its pristine state and revive its ancient virtue. And, as we have said before, should a republic be so fortunate as frequently to have men who by their example give fresh life to its laws, and do not merely stop them going to rack and ruin, but restore their former vigour, such a republic would last for ever.

Such a one was Manlius, for by the harshness of his commands he maintained military discipline in Rome, whereunto he was constrained first by his nature and then by his desire to see those orders carried out which his natural appetite had prompted him to issue. Valerius, on the other hand, could go gently, as one to whom it sufficed to see done what it was customary to do in the Roman armies. These customs, since they were sound, were enough to keep up his reputation, and since they were not hard to observe, there was no need for Valerius to punish delinquents, because there weren't any, but had there been any they would have ascribed their punishment, as was said, to the ordinances, not to the brutality of their prince. So that Valerius could indulge his natural bent for kindliness of all sorts, and by these means acquire gratitude from the troops and be able to keep them contented. It thus came about that, since the same obedience was shown to both, both were able to produce the same effect though by different means. Those who desire to imitate them may, however, fall into the vices I mentioned in connection with Hannibal and Scipio, namely, the evoking of contempt or of hatred, vices which you can avoid only if in you there be more than ordinary virtue, but not otherwise.

It remains to consider which of these two ways of behaving is the more praiseworthy. This is open to question, I think, for some authors praise one and some the other. Yet writers who describe how a prince should govern, incline rather to Valerius than to Manlius, and Xenophon, whom I have cited already, gives many instances illustrative of Cyrus's consideration for others, and thus agrees closely with what Titus Livy says of Valerius. For, when he was consul in the Samnite war, and the day came on which they had to give battle, he addressed his troops with the same consideration he usually displayed in dealing with them. Having given the speech, Titus Livy adds these remarks: 'No commander was ever more familiar with his soldiers, for he deemed it no burden to share their duties with the meanest of them. He would take part especially in their military sports, in which men contend with one another in speed and strength as equals, and in this easy comradeship never changed his countenance whether he won or was beaten. He was never contemptuous towards anyone who challenged him as an equal. In his actions he was kind when circumstances permitted, and in his conversation was scarce less mindful of the liberty of others than he was of his own dignity. And – what is more popular than aught else – he behaved towards them just as he had behaved when a candidate for office.'

Titus Livy speaks with the same respect of Manlius, pointing out that the severity he showed in killing his son, made the army obey him when he was consul, which was the cause of the victory gained by the Roman people over the Latins. Indeed, in praising him he goes further than this, for, after mentioning this victory, he describes in detail how he drew the troops up for this battle, points out the dangers which the Roman people ran in it, and the difficulty they had in winning it, and ends with the remark that it was the virtue of Manlius alone that gave the Romans the victory. He compares, too, their respective forces, and asserts that whichever side had had Manlius as consul would have won. Hence, in view of what historians have said, it is difficult to judge between Manlius and Valerius.

I do not want to leave the matter undecided, however, so shall say this. For a citizen who is living under the laws of a republic I think it is more praiseworthy and less dangerous to adopt the procedure of Manlius, since this way of behaving was entirely in the public interest, and was in no way affected by private ambition, for it is impossible to gain partisans if one is harsh in one's dealing with everybody and is wholly devoted to the common good, because by doing this one does not acquire particular friends or – as I have just called them – partisans. Wherefore, than such a procedure none can be more advantageous or more desirable in a republic, since it neither fails to take account of the interests of the public nor does it suggest that personal power is in any way being sought. But of Valerius's procedure the contrary is true, for, though so far as the public is concerned, it has the same effects, yet, if a man should win the special goodwill of the troops and should retain his command for long, there is grave reason to fear that the result may be prejudicial to liberty.

If such prejudicial effects were lacking in the case of Publicola, the reason was that the minds of the Romans were not as yet corrupt, and that he did not hold office for a long time without intermission. But if one takes the case of a prince, which is the case Xenophon is considering, we should have to side wholly with Valerius and to discard Manlius. For a prince should seek to gain the obedience and affection of his soldiers and of his subjects; their obedience by his fidelity to the constitution and by the reputation he has for virtue; their affection by his affability, kindliness, compassion, and the other qualities for which Valerius was conspicuous; and Cyrus also, so Xenophon tells us. For that a prince should be well liked by each of his subjects and should have a devoted army, is in conformity with other features appertaining to his princely status. But for the army to be devoted to the cause of a private citizen is not consistent with his position, since he is bound by the laws and should obey the magistrates.

We read in the annals of ancient Venice, that when the galleys of this republic had returned to port, a quarrel arose between the sailors and the populace resulting in disturbances in which arms were used; nor could the tumult be quelled either by the police force or by highly respected citizens, or by fear of the magistrates, until a gentleman who had been in command of the sailors the year before, suddenly appeared before them and they stopped fighting out of the affection they had for him. This subservience aroused such suspicions in the senate that the Venetians shortly afterwards made sure of him either by imprisonment or death.

I conclude, therefore, that Valerius' method is advantageous in the case of a prince but harmful in the case of a private citizen, alike to his country and to himself; to his country because such behaviour prepares the way for tyranny; to himself because the suspicion his behaviour arouses forces his city to protect itself against him to his own undoing. On the other hand, I claim that in a prince the behaviour of Manlius is harmful and in a private citizen of advantage, especially to his country. Nor will it hurt the private citizen unless the hatred you incur by your severity is intensified by the suspicion to which the great reputation your virtue has brought you, may give rise; as we shall now show that it did in the case of Camillus.

23. *Upon what Account Camillus was banished from Rome*

W E have just reached the conclusion that anyone who behaves like Valerius does harm both to his country and to himself, but that if he behaves as Manlius did he helps his country and sometimes harms himself. This is borne out to a large extent by the case of Camillus, whose behaviour was more like that of Manlius than Valerius. Hence Titus Livy says of him that 'the soldiers both hated and admired his virtue'.

It was his solicitude, his prudence, his magnanimity and the good discipline he maintained in his administration and command of the army, that caused him to be so much admired. It was because he was more severe in chastizing than generous in rewarding that he came to be hated. For this hatred Titus Livy ascribes the following reasons. First, he assigned the money which had been obtained from the sale of goods taken from the Veientes, to the public use, instead of distributing it with the booty. Secondly, at his triumph he caused his triumphal chariot to be drawn by four white horses, which they said was due to his pride and to his desire to emulate the Sun. Thirdly, he made a vow to give a tenth part of the Veientian booty to Apollo, and, in order to fulfil this vow, had to deprive the soldiers of booty on which they had already laid their hands.

From this it may clearly and easily be seen what kind of thing makes a prince odious to his people. Of such things the chief is to deprive them of what they value. This is a matter of considerable importance because, when a man is deprived of something which possesses intrinsic value, he never forgets it, and you are reminded of it every time you in any way need it; and, since such need is of daily occurrence, you are reminded of it every day. The other thing is to be proud and puffed up in your bearing; than which nothing is more odious to the populace, especially when that populace is free. And even should this pride and ostentation cause them no inconvenience, they none the less hate him who displays it. Hence a ruler should avoid this as he would a rock, for to draw hatred down on your head without deriving thence any profit is an extremely rash and in no wise a prudent policy.

Book Three

---

24. The Prolongation of Military Commands[a] made Rome a Servile State

A CAREFUL study of the procedure of the Roman republic will show that two causes contributed to the dissolution of that republic. The first was the disputes which arose concerning the Agrarian law. The second was the prolongation of military commands.[a] Had their consequences been recognized from the beginning and due remedies applied, freedom[b] would have lasted longer in Rome, and life there would have been perhaps more tranquil. And although there is no record of any tumults having arisen in Rome owing to the prolongation of a military command, it is clear that in fact great harm was done to the city by the authority its citizens acquired in this way.

Had other citizens whose period of office was extended, been as wise and good as Lucius Quintius, this inconvenience would not have arisen. His goodness was exemplary; for when by agreement between the plebs and the senate, the plebs prolonged the tribunes' commission for a year in the hope of thus strengthening their resistance to the ambition of the nobles, the senate out of jealousy of the plebs, not wanting to be outdone, wished to prolong the consulate of Lucius Quintius. But he would have none of it, for bad examples

a imperii.   b il vivere libero.

ought to be ignored, he said, not strengthened by the addition of another even worse example; so he desired them to make new consuls. Had such goodness and prudence characterized all Rome's citizens, they could not have allowed this custom of prolonging public offices to be introduced, nor from these would they have passed on to the prolonging of military commands, which in due course led to the downfall of the republic.

The first to have his military command prolonged, was Publius Philo. He was besieging the city of Palaeopolis when his consulate came to an end. Since it seemed to the senate that he was on the point of winning a victory, they did not appoint a successor, but made him proconsul. He was thus the first proconsul. Though, in doing this, the senate was looking to the public interest, it was this that eventually made Rome a servile state. For, the further the Romans went afield with their armies, the more necessary did this prolonging of commands seem to be, and the more use they made of it. From which there resulted two inconveniences. First, but a small number of men acquired experience as military commanders, and in consequence but few acquired a reputation for it. Secondly, when a citizen had been for long in command of an army, he won the army over and made it his partisan; so that it came in time to forget of the senate and to recognize its commander alone as its head. It thus came about that Sulla and Marius were able to find troops to support them in actions contrary to the public good, and it thus came about that Caesar was able to reduce his country to subjection. Had the Romans not prolonged offices and military commands, they would not have attained such great power in so short a time, and, had they been slower in making conquests, they would also have been slower to arrive at servitude.[67]

25. Concerning the Poverty of Cincinnatus and of many other Roman Citizens

W e have maintained elsewhere that the most useful institution to have in a state which enjoys freedom[a] is one that keeps the citizens poor. Though in Rome it is not clear which institution had this effect, since the Agrarian law, especially, encountered a good deal of opposition, yet we have evidence that for four hundred years from the time the city was built, there was a very great deal of poverty there. Nor can one think of any institution which tended more to produce this effect than the knowledge that poverty did not bar you from any office or from any honour, and that virtue was sought out no matter in whose house it dwelt. This way of life made riches less desirable.

This is obvious. For, when Minucius was consul, and his army was beset on all sides by the Aequi, Rome was so terror-stricken lest the army should be lost, that it had recourse to the appointment of a dictator, its last resource in times of great distress. The appointment was given to Lucius Quintius Cincinnatus, who was found in his little farm ploughing with his own hands. This incident is enshrined in a golden saying of Titus Livy, who says: 'It is worth while recording it for the sake of those who in comparison with riches despise all human values, and have not much use for honour or virtue unless it brings them wealth.' Cincinnatus was ploughing his little farm which was not more than four half-acres in extent, when messengers from the senate in Rome came to tell him of his appointment to the dictatorship, and to point out in what danger the Roman republic stood. Whereupon he put on his toga, came to Rome, got together an army, and went to the rescue of Minucius. Having defeated and despoiled the

[a] uno vivere libero.

475

enemy and relieved Minucius, he was unwilling that an army
which had let itself be surrounded should share in the spoils;
for, he said, 'I do not propose that you should share in booty
taken from those who almost made booty of you.' He then
deprived Minucius of the consulship, made him legate, and
said to him, 'You will keep this rank till you have learnt how
to be a consul.' He had also made Lucius Tarquinius his
master of horse, though he was so poor that he fought on foot.

Honour, then, was paid to poverty in Rome, as has been
said; for a man as wise and valiant as Cincinnatus thought four
half-acres of land sufficient to live on. There was still the
same degree of poverty at the time of Marcus Regulus, for,
when he was with his army in Africa, he asked leave of the
senate to return to look after his farm, which his labourers
were neglecting. And here two things especially are noteworthy; first, poverty, and how content people were with it,
and how the citizens thought it sufficient to win honours in a
war, and to leave all the profits to the public; for, if Regulus
had been contemplating enrichment as the result of the war,
he would not have bothered about his fields being neglected.
The second point to be considered is the magnanimity of these
citizens whose greatness of spirit when in command of an
army rose above that of any prince who had respect neither
for kings nor republics, and were alarmed and frightened at
nothing; but, when they returned to private life, they became
frugal, humble, careful of their little properties, obedient to
the magistrates, and respectful to their superiors. So much so
that it seems incredible that one and the same mind should
have undergone so great a change.

This poverty lasted to the days of Paulus Aemilius, which
were the last happy days this republic enjoyed, days wherein a
citizen would by his triumph bring riches to Rome, yet himself remain a poor man. And, in such high esteem was poverty
still held in Paulus' day that, when he wanted to do honour to
those who had done well in the war, he gave his son-in-law

a silver cup, which was the first piece of silver that had ever been in his house. I might indeed discourse at length on the advantages of poverty over riches, and how poverty brings honour to cities, provinces and religious institutions, whereas the other thing has ruined them; if it had not already been done so often by others.

26. How Women have brought about the Downfall of States

A RIOT was caused in the city of Ardea owing to a quarrel between the patricians and the plebs about a marriage. A rich woman was anxious to get married, and a plebeian and a noble both asked for her hand. She had no father, and whereas her guardians wanted her to marry the plebeian, her mother preferred the noble. This caused such a disturbance that people took up arms, the nobles in support of the noble, and the plebs in support of the plebeian. The plebs were beaten, left Ardea, and sent to the Volsci for help. The nobles appealed to Rome. The Volsci were first in the field, reached Ardea, and laid siege to the city. The Romans then came along, hemmed the Volsci in between the city and their own army; with the result that, straitened by famine, they were forced to surrender at discretion. The Romans then entered the city, killed the promoters of the disturbance and restored order.

There are several points to be noticed here. First, we see how women have been the cause of many troubles, have done great harm to those who govern cities, and have caused in them many divisions. In like manner we read in Livy's history that the outrage done to Lucretia deprived the Tarquins of their rule, and that done to Virginia deprived the Decemviri of their power. Among the primary causes of the downfall of tyrants, Aristotle puts the injuries they do on account of women, whether by rape, violation or the breaking up of marriages. But this we have discussed at length in the chapter dealing with conspiracies. I say here, then, that absolute princes and the rulers of republics should not treat such matters as of small moment, but should bear in mind the disorders that such events many occasion and look to the matter in good time, so that the remedy applied may not be accompanied by damage done to, or revolts against, their state or their republic; as happened to the people of Ardea who allowed the quarrel between their citizens to grow and to split them into factions, and then, to unite them again, had to appeal to foreigners for assistance, which is an excellent prelude to slavery.

Let us turn now to the other point to be noted, which is how in a city unity can be restored. Of this I shall speak in the next chapter.

27. *How Unity may be restored to a Divided City, and how mistaken are those who hold that to retain Possession of Cities one must needs keep them divided*

FROM the example set by the Roman consuls who reconciled the people of Ardea we may learn how to deal with a divided city. The only way to cure it is to kill the ringleaders responsible for the disturbances. For there are but three ways of dealing with them: either to kill them as the consuls did; or to expel them from the city; or to force them to make peace with one another and to undertake not to attack one another. Of these three methods the last is the most hurtful, the least reliable and the most futile. For, where there has been considerable bloodshed or other such-like outrages, it is impossible that a forced peace should last where people are meeting one another every day, and it is difficult to prevent them attacking one another since in their daily intercourse fresh occasions for quarrelling are liable to arise.

Of this no better example can be given than what happened

in the city of Pistoia. Fifteen years ago that city was divided, as it is still, into the Panciatichi and the Cancellieri, but in those days they were armed, whereas today they have given this up. Between them there had been many disputes, which led to bloodshed, the destruction of houses, the plundering of property, and other hostile acts of all kinds. The Florentines, whose job it was to compose this strife, always used the third method in doing this, and always there arose worse tumults and greater troubles. So that they got tired of it and tried the second method, which consists in removing the party leaders. Some they put in prison; others they banished to various places; so that the concord thus established might last, as it has lasted, until now.

Yet it would unquestionably have been safer to use the first method. Since, however, in executions of this kind there is something great and grand, a weak republic cannot do such things. So alien, indeed, are they to its character that it is with difficulty that it brings itself to use the second remedy.

These are some of the mistakes which, as I said at the beginning, rulers in our day make when they have to deal with affairs of importance, for they should be ready to hear of how those acted who in olden days had to deal with such problems, whereas, instead, so feeble are men today owing to their defective education and to the little knowledge they have of affairs, that they look upon the judgements of their forefathers as inhuman in some cases and in others as impossible. Yet the modern views they held to are quite unsound; for instance, that advocated a while ago by wise folk in our city who said that Pistoia should be held by means of factions and Pisa by means of fortresses. They fail to see how futile such means are in both cases.

I shall say nothing here about fortresses because I have elsewhere discussed them at length. What I propose to discuss here is the futility of trying to keep the towns you have to

govern, divided. First of all, whether it be a prince or a
republic that is governing them, it is impossible for you to
remain friends with both of two factions. For it is natural and
inevitable that men should take sides in any dispute, and should
be more drawn to this side than to that. So that, if one party
in the town you hold is discontented, it will cause you to lose
it as soon as war comes along, for it is impossible to hold a city
which has enemies without as well as within. If it is a republic
that governs the city, there is no surer way of making its
citizens bad subjects and of provoking divisions in your own
city than to have to govern a divided city; for each party will
seek to win favour, and each will use corrupt practices in
order to gain supporters. From which two very serious
inconveniences arise. First you will never make them your
friends owing to your inability to govern them well so long as
their government changes frequently according as now one
and now another humour prevails. Secondly, the encouragement of parties in the city must needs provoke divisions in
your republic. To this Biondo bears witness when he says of
the Florentines and the Pistoians that: 'In their endeavour to
restore unity to Pistoia, the Florentines themselves became
divided.' Hence it is easy to see to what evils a divided city
gives rise.

When in 1502 Arezzo was lost, together with the whole of
the Val di Tevere and the Val di Chiana, which were occupied
by the Vitelli and by the Duke of Valentino, a Monsieur de
Lanques was sent by the French king to restore to the Florentines all the towns they had lost. Since in every city which
Lanques visited, he found men who said they belonged to
Marzocco's party,[a] he strongly criticized these divisions. If in
France, he said, a man were to claim to belong to the king's
party, he would be punished, for such a statement would
imply that in that town there were people hostile to the king,

_____
[a] della parte di Marzocco – the heraldic lion of Florence.

whereas it was the king's wish that all the towns should support him, and should be united, not split into parties.

All such behaviour and such distorted views are due to the weakness of the overlords, who, because they cannot hold their dominions by force and by virtue, have recourse to such devices, which in quiet times may occasionally be of use, but which, when adversity comes and the times are troubled, show how fallacious they are.

28. *That a Strict Watch should be kept on the Doings of Citizens since under cover of Good Works there often arises the Beginning of Tyranny*

WHEN the city of Rome was suffering from famine and the public resources had come to an end, a certain Spurius Maelius, a very rich man in those days, took it into his head to lay in a private supply of corn and to dole it out to the plebs to acquire gratitude. He thereby gained such favour with the crowd that the senate, foreseeing the inconvenience to which this liberality of his might give rise, in order to put a stop to it before he should acquire more power, appointed forthwith a dictator and put Maelius to death. Our attention is thus drawn to the fact that actions which appear to be done from a sense of duty and cannot reasonably be found fault with, may lead to victimization and prove very dangerous to a republic unless they are corrected in good time.

Let me further elaborate this point. I agree that a republic cannot survive nor be governed at all well unless in it there are citizens of good repute. On the other hand, the reputation citizens acquire in a republic may bring about a tyranny; and to provide against this, it is essential to exercise control in such wise that the reputation of a citizen shall be helpful, not harmful to the city and to its liberties. Hence the means whereby a reputation is obtained, must be inquired into. Such means are of two kinds in point of fact: public or private. The means taken are public when a person, by the soundness of his advice and the even greater efficiency of his performance, benefits the public, and so acquires a reputation. To acquire such a reputation should be open to citizens, and rewards should be offered both to those who advise and to those who act, so that they may thus acquire honour and satisfaction. And provided reputations gained by such means be honest and above board, they should never be dangerous to the state; but when acquired in the other way we mentioned, i.e. by private means, they are very dangerous and extremely harmful. The private way consists in conferring benefits on this or that individual, such as lending him money, marrying off his daughters for him, protecting him from the magistrates and doing other favours of a personal nature which cause men to become partisans, and encourage those who are thus favoured, to become corrupters of public morals and law breakers.

A well-ordered republic, therefore, should, as we have said, make it open to anyone to gain favour by his services to the public, but should prevent him from gaining it by his services to private individuals. And this is what we find Rome did; for she rewarded those who laboured well in the public cause, by giving them triumphs and all the other honours she was wont to bestow on her citizens, while she condemned those who under various pretexts sought by private means to acquire greatness, and ordered them to be prosecuted; and, should this not suffice owing to the populace being dazzled by a kind of spurious goodness, she appointed a dictator who by using his royal prerogative should constrain them to return to the fold they had deserted, as she did to punish Spurius Maelius. For should anything of this kind be left unpunished, it is liable to ruin a republic, since to restore it to normal life is difficult after such an example has been set.

29. *That the Faults of Peoples are due to Princes*[68]

PRINCES ought not to complain of any fault committed by the peoples whom they govern, because such faults are due either to their negligence or to their being themselves sullied by similar defects. Those who talk about the peoples of our day being given up to robbery and similar vices, will find that they are all due to the fact that those who ruled them behaved in like manner. The Romagna, before Pope Alexander VI got rid of the lords who ruled it, exemplified the very worst types of behaviour, for it was apparent to every one that every least occasion was followed by killings and wholesale rapine. It was the wickedness of the princes that gave rise to this, not the wicked nature of man, as people said. For the princes who were poor, yet desired to live like rich men, of necessity had frequent recourse to robberies of one kind or another. One of the dishonourable means they adopted, was to make laws forbidding this action or that. They were then the first to provide occasion for the non-observance of these laws, but never punished the delinquents until they saw that a considerable number were involved in the same predicament. They then had recourse to punishment, not out of zeal for the laws they had made, but out of cupidity, that they might collect the fines imposed.

This gave rise to numerous inconveniences, of which the worst was that it impoverished the people without amending them, and that those who were impoverished sought to get the better of their weaker brethren. It was in this way that there arose all the evils mentioned above, and it was the prince who was responsible for them. That this is so Titus Livy shows in the account he gives of the Roman legates who took the gifts of booty from Veii to the temple of Apollo. They were captured by corsairs of Lipari in Sicily, whither they were taken. When Timasitheus, their leader, heard what the gifts were for, whither they were going and who had sent them, though a native of Lipari, he behaved as if he was a Roman, pointing out to the populace that it was impious to seize such gifts; with the result that, with everybody's consent, he let the legates go with all they had with them. The comment made by the historian is this: 'Timasitheus instilled religion into the masses, who always resemble their ruler.' This is confirmed by a remark of Lorenzo de' Medici, who says:

> What the prince does the many also soon do,
> For to their eyes the Prince is ever in view.

30. (i) *It is necessary for a Citizen who proposes to use his Authority to do any Good Work in a Republic first to extinguish all Envy; and (ii) what Provisions are to be made for the Defence of a City which the Enemy is about to attack*

WHEN the Roman senate heard that all Tuscany had made a new levy for the invasion and destruction of Rome and that the Latins and the Hernici, who had hitherto been allies of the Roman people, had come to terms with the Volsci, Rome's perpetual enemies, it was of opinion that the war would be a hazardous affair. Moreover, since Camillus happened then to be a tribune with consular power, the senate thought it should be possible to manage without appointing a dictator, provided the other tribunes, his colleagues, would entrust him with the supreme command. This the said tribunes did willingly. 'Nor,' says Titus Livy, 'did anybody deem it derogatory to his authority, to subordinate it to his.' Camillus, therefore, on receiving their promise of obedience, ordered that three armies should be enrolled. Of the first he decided himself to take command and to march against the Tuscans.

He appointed Quintus Servilius to the command of the second, which was to remain near Rome to impede the Latins and the Hernici, should they make a move. Over the third army he put Lucius Quintius with orders to protect the city, and to defend the gates and the senate-house in any eventuality that should arise. In addition to this, he gave Horatius, one of his colleagues, charge of providing the arms and the corn and other things requisite in time of war. And yet another of his colleagues, Cornelius, he appointed president of the senate and of the public council to advise it on the actions which had to be taken and carried out day by day. Thus the tribunes in those days with a view to the safety of their country were prepared both to command and to obey.

We see in this incident what a good and wise man may do, how much good he may occasion, and what great advantages he can bring to his country when, thanks to his goodness and his virtue, he has got rid of envy, which is so often the cause why men cannot do good since it prevents them from acquiring that authority which they must needs have if they are to deal with important matters. Envy may be got rid of in two ways. Either by some serious misfortune, difficult to deal with, in which everybody sees disaster ahead and so, dropping any ambition, hastens to obey one whose virtue promises him freedom. This happened in the case of Camillus, for, since he had given such proof of his excellence and, having thrice been dictator, had always administered that office to the benefit of the public, not in his own interests, no one feared his having great power, nor, in view of his deservedly great reputation, thought it an indignity to serve under him. Hence the remark which Titus Livy shrewdly makes: 'Nor did anybody' . . . etc.

The other way in which envy is removed is when, either by violence or in the natural course, those are removed who were your rivals in the contest for fame and power; for, as long as such men see that your reputation is greater than theirs, they will never remain quiet and bear it with patience. Moreover, should such men have been used to living in a corrupt city in which education had not done them any good, it is impossible for any misfortune to convert them to a better state of mind. Rather would they see their country ruined than fail to obtain their ends and satisfy their perverse mentality. To overcome envy of this kind the only remedy lies in the death of those who are imbued with it. When fortune so favours the virtuous man as to bring about their death in the ordinary course, there is no scandal, and he becomes famous by being able to display his virtue without obstacle or offence. But when this does not happen, it behoves him to devise some way of getting rid of the persons in question, and he should take steps to overcome the difficulty before doing anything else.

He who reads the Bible with discernment will see that, in order that Moses might set about making laws and institutions, he had to kill a very great number of men who, out of envy and nothing else, were opposed to his plans. The need for this was clearly recognized by Friar Girolamo Savonarola and also by Piero Soderini, the Gonfalonier of Florence. But one of them, namely, the Friar, was unable to overcome the difficulty, for he lacked the requisite authority, and those of his followers who might have had the authority for it, did not get his meaning right. It was not, however, his fault that this did not happen and his sermons were full of indictments against the wise of this world, and of invectives against them; and by 'the wise of this world' he meant those who were envious and were opposed to his ordinances. The other believed that his goodness, the favour of fortune, and his beneficence towards all, in time would extinguish envy. For in view of his being as yet fairly young and of how much favour he had recently gained by his method of governing, he thought he would be able to get the better of those who through envy were opposing him, without either scandal, violence or disturbance. What he failed to realize was that time waits for no man, that goodness alone does not suffice, that fortune is changeable and that malice is not to be placated by gifts. So that both these men were ruined, and in both cases their downfall was due to their not knowing how, or not being able, to overcome envy.

Another noteworthy point about Camillus is the arrangements he made for the defence of Rome, both within and without. It is, indeed, not without reason that good historians, such as our author, give a particularly detailed account of certain incidents that posterity may learn how to defend itself in like situations. And in this it should be observed that no defence is more dangerous or more futile than one that is tumultuous and without order. This is shown by the third army which Camillus caused to be enrolled and left in Rome to guard the city. For many might have thought, and still may think, that his action here was superfluous, since the people were in any case armed and were warlike. Hence it would seem that there was no need of a further enrolment, but that it would have sufficed to hand out the arms when the need arose. But Camillus thought otherwise, and so will anyone else who is as wise as he; for the masses ought never to be allowed to take up arms except under definite instructions and conditions.

From the example of Camillus, therefore, one learns that he to whom the guardianship of a city has been entrusted, should avoid as he would a rock the giving of arms to a tumultuous crowd. Instead, he should first select and enrol those whom he wishes to bear arms, and whom they obey in all things; and those whom he has not enrolled he should order to stay at home and look after their houses. He who orders things in this way can easily defend a city that is attacked; but he who acts otherwise, and declines to emulate Camillus, will not be able to defend it.

Book Three

[EQUANIMITY, INSURRECTION, CONFIDENCE, ELECTIONEERING AND THE TENDERING OF ADVICE]

---

31. *Strong Republics and Outstanding Men retain their Equanimity and their Dignity under all Circumstances*

AMONG the other splendid things which our historian makes Camillus say and do in order to show how an outstanding man should behave he puts into Camillus' mouth these words: 'The dictatorship did not elate me, nor did exile depress me.' One sees here how great men remain the same whatever befalls. If fortune changes, sometimes raising them, sometimes casting them down, they do not change, but remain ever resolute, so resolute in mind and in conduct throughout life that it is easy for anyone to see that fortune holds no sway over them. Not so do weak men behave; for by good fortune they are buoyed up and intoxicated, and ascribe such success as they meet with, to a virtue they never possessed, so that they become insupportable and odious to all who have anything to do with them. This then brings about a sudden change in their lot, the prospect of which causes them to go to the other extreme and to become base and abject. Hence it comes about that rulers so built prefer to run away rather than to defend themselves in adversity, just as do men who find themselves defenceless because they have misused the good fortune they had.

These virtues and these vices, which are found as I have been saying in a particular man, are also found in a republic; of which the Romans and the Venetians provide us with examples. No bad luck ever made the first become abject, nor did good fortune ever make them arrogant. This is manifest from their behaviour after the defeat at Cannae, and after the victory they gained over Antiochus. For though the defeat was very serious since it was their third, they never became disheartened; but kept their armies in the field; declined to redeem those who had allowed themselves to be taken prisoners, contrary to their practice, did not send emissaries to Hannibal or to Carthage to sue for peace; but, dispensing with any such abject steps as these, devoted their whole attention to the war, and, owing to shortage of men, armed both the old and their slaves. When Hanno, the Carthaginian, came to hear of this, he pointed out to the Carthaginian senate – as we have remarked above, what small account the Romans made of the defeat at Cannae. Hence it is clear that in trying times the Romans were not despondent, nor were they humbled. Nor, on the other hand, did prosperous times make them arrogant; for when Antiochus sent envoys to Scipio to ask for terms prior to the battle in which he was finally defeated, Scipio laid down the following as his conditions for peace: that Antiochus should withdraw into Syria and that the rest should be left to the decision of the Roman people. These terms Antiochus having rejected, a battle took place, and having lost it, he sent to Scipio envoys commissioned to accept all the conditions which the victors should lay down. Whereupon Scipio proposed precisely the same terms as those he had offered before he won, and then remarked 'that the Romans, when beaten, do not lose courage, nor, when they win, do they become arrogant'.

The Venetians we find doing just the opposite of this. To them it seemed that their good fortune was due to a virtue which they did not in fact possess. Moreover, so arrogant did they become that they called the king of France a 'son of St Mark', showed no respect for the Church, had their eye by no means on Italy alone, but had already made up their minds to set up a monarchy similar to that of Rome. Then, when good luck deserted them and a partial defeat was inflicted on them at Vaila by the king of France, they lost the whole of their dominions, not merely through rebellions, but a goodly portion of them they gave to the Pope and to the king of Spain out of sheer dejection and despondency of mind. So dispirited, indeed, were they that they sent ambassadors to the Emperor offering to become his tributaries, and wrote grovelling and abject letters to the Pope to stir up his compassion. To reach which unhappy state it took them four days, and yet it was but a partial defeat they had suffered; for, after the engagement, in the fighting which took place during the retreat of their army only about half their forces were engaged, so that one of their commissioners who escaped, reached Verona with more than twenty-five thousand troops, comprising both foot and cavalry. Hence, if in Venice and in Venetian institutions there had been any sort of virtue they could easily have pulled themselves together and tried their luck again, this time either to win or to lose with greater glory, or to come to an agreement on more honourable terms. But their pusillanimity, which arose from their institutions being ill adapted for war, made them lose at one stroke alike their dominions and their courage.

It will always happen thus to any state governed as was theirs. For this arrogance in prosperity and dejection in adversity is due to the way you behave and to the education you have received; which, if it be feeble and futile, makes you the same, and if it be of the other kind, makes you another sort of person, i.e. makes you know the world better and so be less exhilarated in good times and less depressed in bad. And what I say of the individual here may be said also of the many who live together in one and the same republic, for they are fashioned to the same state of perfection as characterizes that republic's mode of life.

Although I have said elsewhere that the security of all states is based on good military discipline, and that where it does not exist, there can neither be good laws nor anything else that is good, to repeat this does not seem to me superfluous; for the need for this discipline is apparent on every page in Livy's history, where one sees that the soldiery cannot be good unless they are in training, and that it is impossible to train them unless they are your own subjects. For, since no soldiery is always at war, nor yet can be, it is important to train it in time of peace; but this training is impossible on account of the cost except in the case of your own subjects.

When Camillus led forth an army to fight the Tuscans, as we have said above, and his soldiers saw how large was the army of the enemy, they were terrified, for so inferior did they feel themselves to be that it looked to them as if they could not possibly withstand their attack. When it came to the ears of Camillus that the men in camp were so ill disposed to fight, he appeared among them and, going about the camp talking to this group of soldiers and that, drove this notion out of their heads. Finally, without issuing any further orders to those in camp, he merely said: 'Let each man do what he has been taught to do or has been accustomed to do.' If we consider carefully this plan of action and the words used to encourage the men to go and fight the enemy, it is clear that neither could such words have been used nor the army have been induced to do any such thing unless that army had already been trained and drilled both in peace-time and in war. For on soldiers who have not learned how to do anything, no general can rely, confident that anything they may do will be well done. Even should a second Hannibal command such troops he would in that case go under. For, since during a battle a general cannot be everywhere, he will inevitably meet with disaster unless he has already so drilled every unit that it has imbibed his spirit and is well acquainted with his practice and mode of procedure.

If then a city be armed and disciplined as Rome was, and all its citizens, alike in their private and official capacity, have a chance to put alike their virtue and the power of fortune to the test of experience, it will be found that always and in all circumstances they will be of the same mind and will maintain their dignity in the same way. But, when they are not familiar with arms and trust merely to the whim of fortune, not to their own virtue, they will change with the changes of fortune and will display in all cases the characteristics exemplified by the Venetians.

32. *What Means some have adopted to prevent a Peace*

THERE were two Roman colonies, Circei and Velitrae, which had rebelled against the Roman people in the hope that the Latins might support them. When the Latins were beaten and this hope disappeared, many citizens urged that envoys should be sent to Rome to plead their cause with the senate. This advice was strenuously opposed by those responsible for the rebellion, since they feared that all the blame would fall on their heads. To remove any discussion of peace, they incited the masses to take up arms and to cross the Roman frontiers. And it is, indeed, true that, should anyone want to remove from the mind of a people or a prince all idea of coming to terms, there is no more certain or more reliable way than to get them to commit a grave outrage of this kind against the party with which you do not want them to come to terms; for in all such cases the fear of the punishment which the offender will think his fault merits, will keep him away from the other.

After the first war the Carthaginians had with the Romans, the troops which had been employed by the Carthaginians during the war in Sicily and Sardinia, went to Africa when peace had been declared. Where, being dissatisfied with their pay, they induced the troops to revolt against the Carthaginians: appointed two of themselves as commanders, Matho and Spendius; seized a considerable number of Carthaginian towns, and sacked many of them. The Carthaginians, desiring at first to try other expedients in preference to war, sent to them one of their citizens, Hasdrubal, as ambassador, for they thought he would have some influence with them since formerly he had been their general. When the latter arrived, Spendius and Matho determined to deprive all the soldiers of any hope of ever coming to terms with the Carthaginians that thus they might be forced to fight. So they persuaded them that the best thing to do was to kill Hasdrubal together with all the Carthaginian citizens who were with them as their prisoners. In consequence they not only killed them, but first inflicted on them all manner of tortures; and to this outrage added an edict to the effect that all Carthaginians would be killed in the same way, should they happen to take them. This edict and the enforcement of it made that army cruel and steadfast in its opposition to the Carthaginians.

33. *To win a Battle it is essential to inspire the Army with Confidence both in Itself and in its General*

IF an army is to win the day it is essential to give it confidence so as to make it feel sure that it must win, whatever happens. The conditions on which such confidence depends are that the troops should be well armed, well disciplined and well acquainted with each other. Nor can there be this confidence or this discipline unless among soldiers who are natives of the same country and have lived together. It is important, too, that the general should be so esteemed for his qualities that the men have confidence in him, and this they will always do when they see that he is always on the alert, is solicitous and courageous, and that he knows well how to uphold the dignity of his position and to maintain his reputation; which he can always do if he punishes men for their mistakes, does not impose on them unnecessary burdens, keeps the promises he has made them, and points out how easy it is to win, concealing or making light of things, which when viewed from afar, might suggest danger. Such things, when duly observed, are the principal causes of an army's morale, and – through its morale – of its victory.

The Romans used to inspire their armies with this confidence by means of religion. Hence it came about that they used auguries and auspices in appointing consuls, in enrolling troops, and when their armies were setting forth or were about to join battle. And, if he had omitted any of these things a good and wise general would never undertake any action of moment, since he thought he might easily lose unless his troops had first been assured that the gods were on their side. So, too, if any consul or other general had engaged in battle contrary to the auspices, they would punish him, as they punished Claudius Pulcher. There is abundant evidence of this throughout the whole of Roman history, but to clinch the matter we have the words which Livy puts into the mouth of Appius Claudius. When he was complaining to the people of the insolence of the plebeian tribunes, and showing how it was through their fault that the auspices and other things pertaining to their religion were growing corrupt, he spoke thus: 'Nowadays they are allowed to mock at religious rites; what does it matter if the chickens don't eat, if they are too slow in coming out of their pens, or if one of the birds clucks? They are small things, but it was by not despising small things that our ancestors made this republic as great as it is.' For it is in such small things that resides the power of keeping soldiers united and confident – which is the primary cause of victory. It is important, none the less, that such things should be accompanied by *virtù*, otherwise they are of no avail.

The Praenestines who had sent out an army to attack the Romans, went to the Allia and set up their camp on its banks in the place where the Romans had been beaten by the Gauls. They did this to give their troops confidence and that the Romans might be discouraged by the misfortune associated with the place. But, though this course was to be approved of for the reasons set forth above, the upshot of the affair none the less showed that true valour is not set at nought by every trifling circumstance. This is expressed very neatly in the words the historian puts into the mouth of the dictator, who said to his master of horse: 'You notice that those fellows yonder, trusting to fortune, have taken up a position on the Allia! You put your trust in your arms and in your courage and go straight for them!' For true *virtù*, good discipline and a sense of security born of many victories, cannot be dissipated by things of little moment, nor can vain imaginings make men of such calibre afraid, nor yet a mishap do them harm. This is clearly seen in the case of the two Manlii: for, when as consuls they were at war with the Volsci, and had rashly sent a detachment from their camp on a foraging expedition, it came about that those who had gone and those who remained found themselves besieged at the same time, and it was not the skill of the consuls but the valour of the troops themselves that extricated them from the danger. Upon which Titus Livy makes this remark: 'Tried *virtù* is safe even when troops are without a leader.'

Nor must I omit to mention an expedient used by Fabius to

inspire confidence when leading his army for the first time into Tuscany. Since the country into which he had led it was new and he was attacking new foes, it was all the more necessary, he thought, that the troops should feel confidence; so before the battle he addressed them, pointing out that there were many reasons why they should expect a victory, and adding that he could tell them also of something specially good from which they would see that victory was certain, were it not dangerous to mention it. This was a clever expedient to adopt and is well worth imitating.

34. *What Kind of Reputation or Gossip or Opinion causes the Populace to begin to favour a Particular Citizen; and whether the Populace appoints to Offices with Greater Prudence than does a Prince*

WE have spoken elsewhere of how Titus Manlius, afterwards called Torquatus, procured the acquittal of his father, Lucius Manlius, from a charge brought against him by Marcus Pomponius, the tribune of the plebs. Though the means he took to save him were somewhat violent and extraordinary, yet his filial devotion was so pleasing to the people at large that, not only was he not condemned, but at a subsequent election of tribunes for the legions Titus Manlius obtained the second appointment. In regard to his success, I think it well to reflect on the way in which the populace estimates the merits of candidates for election, and to consider how far the conclusion drawn above is true, namely that the populace is a better judge in appointing to office than is a prince.

I claim, then, that the populace in choosing between candidates relies on common gossip and on their reputation when it has otherwise no knowledge of them based on noteworthy deeds; or else on some preconceived opinion it has formed of them. In both cases reliance is placed on the fact that their fathers were men of standing who did much for the city, it being assumed that their sons should be like them unless their actions indicate the contrary; or else reliance is placed upon what is said about the way they behave. The points which count most in their behaviour are that they should be known to associate with seriously minded persons, of good habits, and whom everybody esteems as prudent men. For nothing indicates more plainly what a man is than the company he keeps. The man who associates with honest people deservedly acquires a good name, for it is impossible but that he be of the same kidney. Or, again, a reputation with the public may be gained by some out-of-the-way and conspicuous action which, though of a private character, has brought you honourable notice. Of all three ways in which good repute may at the start be obtained, none is more effectual than this last. For the first, in which reputation is based on the doings of relatives and ancestors, is so unreliable that men are slow to accept it and it evaporates unless accompanied by virtue on the part of the person concerned. The second way, in which you become known by way of the company you keep, is better than the first, but not nearly so good as the third. For until you give some indication of what you can do, your reputation is based only on opinion, which may quite easily prove to be wrong. But the third way, since it originates in, and is based on, facts and on what you have actually done, gives you at the start so great a name that you would have to do much that belied your character before your reputation vanished.

Men who are born in a republic, therefore, ought to adopt this course, and to try, by doing things out of the ordinary, to rise above the rank and file. In Rome many did this in their youth by promulgating some law promoting the public good; or by attacking some powerful citizen for violating the laws; or by doing some other such new and remarkable thing as might occasion talk. Not only are such things necessary at the outset to gain a reputation; they are also necessary to maintain it and to augment it. To do this, such actions must be repeated, as they were by Titus Manlius throughout the whole of his life. For he obtained his early reputation by defending his father so virtuously and in so odd a way. Some years later he fought with that Gaul, and, after killing him, took off him that golden collar which gave him the name Torquatus. Nor was this all, for later, when he grew up, he killed his son for having engaged in battle without permission, though he had beaten the enemy. These three deeds gave him a greater name at the time, and made him more celebrated for all time, than any triumph did, or any other victory, though he was as successful in this respect as any other Roman. The reason is that in respect of these other victories very many resembled Manlius, but with respect to his particular actions very few or none.

All his triumphs did not win such glory for Scipio the Elder as did his youthful act of defending his father on the Ticinus, or the oath which with drawn sword he in his fervour made several young men take not to desert Italy after the defeat at Cannae, as some of them had already resolved to do. The beginning of his reputation rested on these two actions, which served as stepping-stones to the triumphs of Spain and of Africa. And his repute was still further increased when in Spain he sent back a daughter to her father and a wife to her husband. This type of conduct is not only necessary to such citizens as desire to acquire fame with a view to obtaining positions of honour in their republic; it is also necessary to princes who wish to keep up their reputation in a principality; for nothing makes a prince so esteemed as when by some singular deed or saying bearing on the common good, he himself sets a striking example which shows his lordship to be either magnanimous or liberal or just, and which is such that it can be circulated in the form of a proverb among his subjects.

But to return to the point first mentioned in this discourse. I maintain that when the populace first assigns some office to one of its citizens, their choice has not a bad basis if it rests on the three grounds aforesaid. But it has a better one, if numerous instances of good conduct have made the person noteworthy, for in that case it is hardly ever possible to make a mistake. I am speaking only of those offices which are given to men early on, before definite experience has been gained as to their character, or they have done something which has changed it for the worse. And here, in regard to forming a false opinion, or judging as to the likelihood of deterioration, the populace always makes fewer mistakes than do princes. Yet, because it is possible for the populace to be deceived in regard to a man's fame or repute or actions, esteeming them to be greater than they are – a mistake that a prince does not make since he should be told of them and warned by his advisers – and so that a populace also may not lack such counsel, good legislators in founding republics have provided that, when an appointment has to be made to the higher offices in the city to which it would be dangerous to appoint incompetent men, and when it looks as if the popular fancy were inclined to appoint an incompetent person, it shall be lawful, and indeed glorious, for any citizen to broadcast the candidate's defects so that the people, knowing them, may be better advised.

That this was the custom in Rome the speech of Fabius Maximus attests. He delivered it before the people during the second Punic war, when there was question of appointing consuls and Titus Otacilius was a prime favourite for the post. Fabius thought him not the man to hold the consulate in those times, spoke against him, and pointed out his incompetence with such effect that he kept him out of it and induced the

populace to favour one who deserved it more. In appointing
to offices, therefore, the populace judges according to the best
advice available better substantiated, and, where it can get
advice as a prince can, it makes few mistakes than does a prince.
So the citizen who contemplates winning popular favour
should make sure of it by doing something remarkable, as
Titus Manlius did.

35. What Dangers are run by one who takes the Lead in advising some Course of Action; and how much greater are the Dangers incurred when the Course of Action is Unusual

How dangerous it is to take the lead in a new enterprise in
which many may be concerned, and how difficult it is to handle
and direct it, and once directed on its way, to keep it going,
would be too long and too deep a topic for us to discuss here.
Reserving it, therefore, for a more convenient place,[69] I shall
here speak only of the dangers incurred by citizens or by those
advising a prince to take the lead in some grave and important
matter in such a way that for the whole of this advice they
may be held responsible. For men judge of actions by the
result. Hence for all the ill that results from an enterprise the
man who advised it is blamed, and, should the result be good,
commended; but the reward by no means weighs the same as
the loss.

The present Sultan, Selim, called the Great Turk, had –
according to those who have lately returned from his dominions – made preparations to invade Syria and Egypt, when he
was strongly advised by one of his pashas whom he had posted
on the frontiers of Persia, to attack the Sophy. Acting on this
advice, he set forth on the enterprise with a very large force.
On reaching a broad expanse of open country where there
were many deserts but few streams, he found himself in the

very difficulty that had proved fatal to many a Roman army;
so much so that, though he was victorious in the war, he lost
through famine and pestilence the greater part of his troops.
Hence he was angry with the person who had advised him,
and put him to death.

We read of many citizens who, having promoted some
undertaking that turned out badly, were sent into exile. It
was owing to some Roman citizens who took the lead that a
plebeian consul was first appointed in Rome. It then happened
that the first time he led forth the armies he was beaten.
Consequently those who had advised the appointment would
have been in trouble, had they not been protected by the
party in whose interests the appointment had been made.

The advisers of a republic and the counsellors of a prince are
undoubtedly in a difficult position; for, unless they recommend the course which in their honest opinion will prove
advantageous to that city or to that prince regardless of
consequences, they fail to fulfil the duties of their office, while,
if they recommend it, they are risking their lives and endanger-
ing their position, since all men in such matters are blind and
judge advice to be good or bad according to its result. Nor
do I see any way of avoiding either the infamy or the danger
other than by putting the case with moderation instead of
assuming responsibility for it, and by stating one's views
dispassionately and defending them alike dispassionately and
modestly; so that, if the city or the prince accepts your advice,
he does so of his own accord, and will not seem to have been
driven to it by your importunity. If you act thus, it is unreasonable for a prince or a people to wish you ill on account
of your advice, since it has not been adopted against the will
of the majority. Danger is incurred only when many have
opposed you, and, the result being unfortunate, they combine
to bring about your downfall. And, though, in the case we
have taken, there is lacking the glory which comes to the man

who in opposition to the many, alone advocates a certain course which turns out well, it has two advantages. First, it does not entail danger. Secondly, if you tender your advice with modesty, and the opposition prevents its adoption, and, owing to someone else's advice being adopted, disaster follows, you will acquire very great glory. And, though you cannot rejoice in the glory that comes from disasters which befall your city or your prince, it at any rate counts for something.

I do not think any further recommendations can be made on this point, for, if one recommended men to be silent and not to express their views, this would be no use to the republic or to their prince; nor would danger thereby be eliminated, for before long they would become suspect, and that might happen which happened to some friends of Perseus, king of Macedonia. He had been defeated by Paulus Aemilius, and had escaped with a few of his friends. While they were reviewing what had taken place, it happened that one of them began to tell Perseus of the many mistakes he had made, and how they had been the cause of his undoing. At which Perseus was so annoyed that he said: 'Traitor, for you have delayed until now to speak of what I cannot undo!' On saying which, he killed him with his own hands. Thus was a man punished for keeping silent when he ought to have spoken, and for speaking when he ought to have been silent; so that he didn't avoid danger by not giving his advice. Hence it is best, I think, to keep to, and to act on, the lines laid down above.

Book Three

[ADVICE TO GENERALS IN
THE FIELD]

---

36. *Reasons why the French have been, and still are, looked upon in the Beginning of a Battle as more than Men, and afterwards as less than Women*

THE ardour[a] of the Gaul who challenged any Roman on the banks of the river Anio to single combat, which led to a fight between him and Titus Manlius, reminds me of what Titus Livy several times says of the Gauls, namely, that in the beginning of a battle they are more than men, but in the fighting that follows they turn out worse than women. As to how this comes about, many think that nature has made them so, which is no doubt true, but it does not follow from this that the nature which makes them ardent at the start could not be so regulated by rules as to keep them ardent right up to the end.

In proof of this let me point out that armies are of three types. In the first there is both ardour[b] and order. Now order promotes both ardour and *virtù* as it did in the case of the Romans; for, during the whole course of their history one finds that there was good order in their armies, which military discipline

a ferocità. *b furore.*

of long standing had introduced. In a well-disciplined army, no one should perform any action except in accordance with regulations. Hence in the Roman army – which, since it conquered the world, should be taken as a model by all other armies – we find that no one ate or slept or went wenching or performed any other action, military or domestic, without instructions from the consul. Armies which act otherwise are not true armies; and if they do anything of note they do it through ardour and impetuosity, not through valour. But when disciplined *virtù* uses its ardour in the right way and at the right time, no difficulties dismay an army or cause it to lose courage. For good discipline stimulates courage and ardour, in that it strengthens the hope of victory, which is never wanting so long as discipline remains.

The opposite of all this happens in those armies in which there is ardour but no discipline, as was the case with the Gauls, who in their fighting were wholly lacking in method; for if their first attack did not succeed, they faltered, since the ardour on which they relied was not sustained by disciplined valour, and there was nothing else on which they could rely when their ardour cooled. The Romans, on the other hand, made light of dangers since their discipline was good; and, since they did not despair of victory, they remained firm and dogged, and fought with the same courage and the same *virtù* at the end as at the start; nay, when stimulated by a fight, they always grew more ardent.

The third type of army is one in which there exists neither a natural ardour, nor yet discipline to supplement it; as is the case with Italian armies in our day, which are quite useless and never win unless they come across an army which happens for some reason to run away. There is no need to cite further instances, since every day they afford evidence of how utterly lacking they are in valour. So that, however, what Titus Livy says may make it plain to all how good soldiery should be

made and how worthless soldiery are made, I propose to cite
the speech which Papirius Cursor made when he wanted to
reprove Fabius, his master of horse. What he said was: 'No
one would have respect either for men or for the gods; they
would obey neither the edicts of generals nor the auspices;
soldiers without provisions, would wander about here and
there alike in peaceful and in hostile territory; forgetful of
their oath, they would discharge themselves from the army
without authority and when it pleased them; they would
leave the colours almost unguarded, and neither assemble nor
dismiss at the word of command; they would fight by day or
night whether the place were suitable or unsuitable, and with
or without orders from the general; they would keep neither
to their regiments nor to their ranks; but, like a band of robbers, were a blind and tumultuous, rather than a disciplined
and dutiful, soldiery.' And in this passage applied, it will at
once be seen whether the soldiery of our day is blind and
tumultuous or disciplined and dutiful, and how far it falls
short of what we commonly call soldiery, and how far
removed it is from being either ardent and disciplined, like the
Romans, or just simply ardent, like the Gauls.

37. Whether Skirmishes are Necessary before a Battle, and how, if one decides to do without them, the Presence of Fresh Enemy Troops is to be discovered

IT would appear that in human affairs, as we have remarked
in other discourses, there is, in addition to others, this
difficulty: that, when one wants to bring things to the pitch of
perfection, one always finds that, bound up with what is
good, there is some evil which is so easily brought about in
doing good that it would seem to be impossible to have the
one without the other. This is the case in everything that man

does. And it is because of it that the good is with difficulty attained unless you are so aided by fortune that fortune itself eliminates this normal and natural inconvenience. What moves me to say this is the fight Manlius had with the Gaul, of which Titus Livy says: 'This conflict was of great moment to the outcome of the whole war, for the army of the Gauls in trepidation deserted their camp and moved first into Tiburtine territory, and then into Campania'; for I hold, on the one hand, that a good general ought to avoid at all costs doing anything which, though in itself of small moment, can produce a bad effect on his army; because to engage in a battle in which all one's forces are not employed and thereby to risk one's whole fortune, is extremely rash, as I said above when I was talking about guarding passes.

On the other hand, I hold that when wise generals find they are up against a new enemy who has acquired a reputation, it is essential that, before engaging in a pitched battle, they let their troops find out by means of skirmishes what he is worth; so that, having acquired some knowledge of him and of how to deal with him, it may dispel the fears to which rumour and his standing had given rise. For a general to do this is of the utmost importance; for there is in this course a quasi-necessity that constrains you to adopt it, since you can scarce fail to see that you are plainly exposing yourself to disaster if you engage the enemy without having first provided your troops with some little experiment whereby to rid them of that fear which the enemy's reputation had aroused in their minds.

Valerius Corvinus was in command of the armies which the Romans had dispatched to deal with the Samnites, new enemies, of whose fighting capacities the Romans had thus far had no experience in actual combat one with the other. Hence Titus Livy says that Valerius caused the Romans to engage in some skirmishes with the Samnites 'so that they might be afraid neither of the new war nor of the new enemy'. None the less, there is a very great danger that, if your soldiers get the worst of the skirmishing it will increase their fear and their cowardice, and so will produce the opposite effect to that you had in mind; i.e. you will have alarmed them, whereas you wanted to make them feel safe. So that this is just one of those things in which evil is so closely associated with good, and so bound up are they one with the other, that it may easily happen that he who thinks he will get one, gets the other.

In regard, then, to this, I maintain that a good general should take every precaution to prevent the occurrence of any untoward event likely to diminish the courage of his army. But to begin by losing is just the thing that is likely to diminish its courage. Hence he should act cautiously in regard to skirmishes, and should not permit them unless he has a great advantage and he feels sure he will be victorious. Nor should he attempt to guard passes where he cannot bring the whole of his army into operation. Nor yet should he defend towns unless their loss will inevitably entail his ruin. And, if he does defend them, he should arrange for his army to cooperate with the garrison in repelling an attack, so that in dealing with the siege all his forces may be brought into play; otherwise he should leave the town undefended. For in losing what may be abandoned, provided his army is still intact, he will not in such a case lose either his reputation in the war or the hope of winning it; but when you lose what you have planned to defend and everybody knows that you were defending it, the loss is serious and may be disastrous; in fact, you may, like the Gauls, on account of something of small moment have lost the war.

Philip of Macedon, the father of Perseus, a soldier of high standing in his day, when attacked by the Romans, abandoned and laid waste a large part of his country which he judged it impossible to defend, for, being a prudent man, he thought it

more disastrous to lose his reputation by failing to defend
what he had set out to defend, than to let it fall into the hands
of the enemy as if it were a thing he did not mind losing.
When after the defeat at Cannae the affairs of the Romans
were in a bad way, they declined to help many of their de-
pendents and subjects, bidding them defend themselves as best
they could. Such courses are much better than taking up the
defence of allies and then letting them down, for in that case
one loses both one's allies and one's forces; but in the other the
allies alone are lost.

But to return to skirmishing, I maintain that if a general is
absolutely compelled to have recourse to skirmishes because
his enemy is a new one, he should only undertake them when
he has so considerable an advantage that there will be no danger
of his losing thereby. He should, otherwise, – and it is the
better course – do as Marius did when he went to fight the
Cimbri, a fierce tribe which had come to prey upon Italy and
which he was approaching with considerable trepidation owing to their ferocity and their numbers, and because they had
already defeated a Roman army. Judging it necessary before
engaging in battle to do something which would dispel the
panic into which fear of the enemy had thrown his army, like
a prudent general, he more than once stationed his army in a
position near to which the army of the Cimbri must pass,
with the intention that from behind the fortifications of their
camp, his troops should look at and accustom their eyes to the
enemy's appearance, so that when they saw what a disorderly
crowd they were, encumbered with baggage, their arms useless and some without arms, they might be reassured and
become eager for the fight. This course so wisely adopted by
Marius, others should diligently imitate, so as not to incur the
dangers I have described above, and not to have to act as the
Gauls did, 'who, in trepidation on account of an event of small
moment, moved first into Tiburtine territory and then into
Campania'.

Since we have in this discourse mentioned Valerius Corvinus, I propose in the next chapter to use his speech to show how a general should behave.

38. *What ought to be done by a General so that his Army may have Confidence in him*

VALERIUS CORVINUS, as we have said above, had gone with the army to fight the Samnites, enemies new to the Roman people; so, to give his troops assurance and some acquaintance with the foe, he caused them to make a few skirmishes, and, since this was not enough, he decided to address them before the battle, and to point out as forcefully as he could how little esteem they should have for such a foe, appealing in his speech alike to the valour of his soldiers and to his own. From the speech which Livy makes him deliver, one may learn how a general should act if his army is to have confidence in him. What he says is this: 'Look at the man under whose leadership and auspices you are going to fight! Ask yourselves whether the person to whom you are about to listen is but a brilliant orator, valiant in words, but inexperienced in military matters, or whether he knows how to handle weapons, to advance before the colours, and to plunge right into the thick of the fight! I want you, my good men, to go by my actions, not my words, and to look to me not merely for orders, but for an example, for with this my right hand I have as a consul thrice won the highest praise.' Anyone may learn from a speech such as this, if he ponder it well, how to act if he wants to occupy the rank of a general; and he who acts otherwise will find that his rank, whether it be by luck or by ambition that he has attained it, in due course will destroy, instead of making, his reputation; for it is not titles that make men illustrious, but men who make titles illustrious.

One ought again in what was said at the outset of this

discourse to observe that if great generals have used extraordinary means to strengthen the courage of a veteran army when confronted with an enemy with which it is unfamiliar, much greater industry will have to be used when in command of a new army which has never been in sight of the enemy. For if an enemy with which an old army is unfamiliar fills it with terror, so much the more must this be the case when a new army faces any enemy at all. Actually, however, one finds that all these difficulties are usually overcome by good generals with consummate prudence, as they were overcome by Gracchus the Roman, and by Epaminondas the Theban, of whom we have spoken on other occasions, for with new armies they defeated veteran armies with plenty of experience.

The methods they adopted were to exercise the troops for several months and to accustom them to obey orders by means of sham fights, after which they had so much confidence in them that they took them to a real fight. No military man, therefore, should be diffident as to his ability to form a good army, when there is no lack of men; so that the prince who has an abundance of men, but lacks soldiers, should bewail not the cowardice of his men, but merely his own laziness and folly.

39. *That a General ought to be acquainted with the Lie of the Land*

AMONG other things essential to the commander of an army is a knowledge of terrains and of countries, for, unless he has this knowledge, alike general and detailed, no army commander can perform any operation well. Wherefore, just as all sciences demand practice if we desire to attain perfection in them, so this is one that calls for a good deal of practice. And this practice and this detailed knowledge is acquired more by hunting, than by any other exercises. Hence ancient

writers tell us that the heroes who ruled the world in their day
were brought up in the forests and on the chase. For the chase
not only provides one with the requisite knowledge, but
teaches one a host of other things that are essential in warfare.
Thus, Xenophon, in his Life of Cyrus tells us how, when he
was about to attack the king of Armenia, in appointing tasks
he reminded those about him that it would be just like one of
those hunting expeditions on which they had often accompanied him; and to those whom he sent to form an ambush
in the mountains he said that they would be like men going to
lay snares on the ridges; and to those who had to scour the
countryside that they would be like men who went to rouse a
wild beast from its lair so as, after hunting it, to drive it into
the nets.

This I mention to show that Xenophon supports the view
that a hunting expedition is very like a war, and that, consequently, great men look on this sport as honourable and
necessary. Nor yet can a knowledge of the country be
acquired in a more convenient way than by hunting, for the
chase gives those who engage in it an exact knowledge of the
lie of the land in which the sport takes place. It also enables one
who has familiarized himself with one district, to grasp with
ease the details of any new region. For all countries and all
their parts have about them a certain uniformity, so that from
the knowledge of one it is easy to pass to the knowledge of
another; whereas he who has not acquired a good experience
of any one, can with difficulty acquire a knowledge of another,
and cannot acquire it at all unless he is there for a long time.
A person who has had practice, for instance, will see at a
glance how far this plain extends, to what height that mountain rises, where this valley goes, and everything else of this
kind, for of it all he has already acquired a sound knowledge.[70]

That this is so Titus Livy shows us in the case of Publius
Decius. When he was a tribune in charge of troops belonging
to the army which the consul, Cornelius, commanded in the

Samnite war, and the consul had led the Roman army into a valley where it could have been shut in by the Samnites, Decius saw the great danger to which it was exposed, and said to the consul: 'Do you see, Aulus Cornelius, that peak above the enemy? It is in that height that lies our hope of safety if we take it quickly, the Samnites having stupidly neglected it.' Also, before telling us what Decius said Titus Livy says: 'Publius Decius, a military tribune, observed a hill which rose above a wooded ravine and threatened the enemy's position, difficult of access to an army in marching order, but not difficult to light troops.' Whereupon he was sent there by the consul with three thousand soldiers and so saved the Roman army. Then, when night came on, and he was thinking of departing so as to save both himself and his troops, Livy makes him use these words: 'Come with me while the light holds, and let us reconnoitre the places in which the enemy has placed guards to see whether there is any way out.' All of which he carried out clad in a small military cloak, lest the enemy should notice an officer wandering about.

This evidence all goes to show how useful and necessary it is for a general to know the nature of the country; for, if Decius had not been a prudent man and acquired such knowledge, he would not have been able to see how useful it was to the Roman army to take that hill, nor would he have been able to tell from a distance whether the hill was accessible or not; nor yet, when he had been sent to the top of it and wanted to get back to the consul, would he, with the enemy on all sides, have been able to spot from a distance the way to go and the places which the enemy was guarding. One is bound then to infer that Decius had such expert knowledge, and that it was this that enabled him to save the Roman army by taking the hill, and afterwards when he was surrounded there, to discover a route whereby both he and the troops that were with him could reach safety.

Book Three

---

40. *That it is a Glorious Thing to use Fraud in the Conduct of a War*

ALTHOUGH to use fraud[71] in any action is detestable, yet in the conduct of a war it is praiseworthy and glorious. And a man who uses fraud to overcome his enemy is praised, just as much as is he who overcomes his enemy by force. This is seen in the judgement pronounced on great men by biographers, who praise Hannibal and others well known for this kind of behaviour. Of this one comes across so many examples that I shall not cite any, I will say but this, I do not mean that a fraud which involves breaking your word or the contracts you have made, is glorious; for, although on occasion it may win for you a state or a kingdom, as has been said in an earlier discourse, it will never bring you glory. I am speaking of fraud used in dealing with an enemy who has not kept faith with you, i.e., of the fraud which is involved in the conduct of a war; such as that which Hannibal used when at the Perugian lake he pretended flight in order to entrap the consul and the Roman army, and when, to escape from the hands of Fabius Maximus he lit up the horns of a herd of cattle.

To this class of fraud belongs that which was practised by

Pontius, the general of the Samnites, that he might entrap the Roman army in the Caudine Forks. Having placed his army up against the mountains, he sent some of his soldiers, dressed as shepherds, with a flock of sheep across the plain. They were captured by the Romans, who asked where the Samnite army was. All agreed in saying what Pontius had told them to say, i.e., that it had gone to lay siege to Nocera. The credence given by the consuls to this report led to their being caught between the Caudine cliffs, where, when they got there, they were at once hemmed in by the Samnites. This victory, which Pontius gained by fraud, would have redounded greatly to his credit had he followed his father's advice, which was that he should either let the Romans go scot-free or should slaughter them all, and that he should not take the middle course which 'neither makes you friends, nor removes your enemies'; and this middle course has always been harmful in affairs of state, as I have already pointed out in another discourse.

41. *That one's Country should be defended whether it entail Ignominy or Glory, and that it is Good to defend it in any way whatsoever*

THE consul and the Roman army were surrounded by the Samnites, as has just been said. The Samnites had imposed on the Romans ignominious conditions. They were to pass under the yoke and to be sent back to Rome without their arms and equipment. At this the consuls being astonished and the whole army being in despair, Lucius Lentulus, the Roman legate, told them that it did not seem to him that they should reject any alternative in order to save their country; for, since the survival of Rome depended on the survival of this very army, it should be saved in any way that offered; and that it is good to defend one's country in whatever way it be done, whether it entail ignominy or glory; for, if this army was saved, Rome might in time wipe out the ignominy; but that, if it were not saved and even if it should die gloriously, Rome and its freedom would be lost. So Lentulus's advice was followed.

This counsel merits the attention of, and ought to be observed by, every citizen who has to give advice to his country. For when the safety of one's country wholly depends on the decision to be taken, no attention should be paid either to justice or injustice, to kindness or cruelty, or to its being praiseworthy or ignominious. On the contrary, every other consideration being set aside, that alternative should be wholeheartedly adopted which will save the life and preserve the freedom of one's country.

This is the course the French adopt – both in what they say and what they do – in order to defend the majesty of their king or the power of their kingdom; for no voice is heard with greater impatience than one that should say: 'Such an alternative it would be ignominious for the king to adopt.' No decision the king makes can be shameful, they say, whether it leads to good or to adverse fortune, for, whether he wins or loses is entirely his business, they claim.

42. *That Promises extracted by Force ought not to be kept*

WHEN with an army that had been stripped of its arms and had suffered such ignominious treatment, the consuls returned to Rome, the first person to speak in the senate said that the peace made at Caudium ought not to be observed. This was the consul, Spurius Postumius. He said that the Roman people were not bound by it, but that he and the others who had promised peace, were bound by it. Hence, if the people wanted to be free from any obligation, they should send him and all those who had made the promise, back to the Samnites as prisoners. He defended this view with such tenacity that the senate yielded; sent him and the others as prisoners to Samnium, and protested to the Samnites that the peace was invalid. Fortune favoured Postumius in this case, for the Samnites did not keep him, and on his return to Rome he gained more glory in the eyes of the Romans by having surrendered than Pontius gained in the eyes of the Samnites by his victory.

Two things should here be noted. One is that glory can be gained by either kind of action, for it is acquired by victory in the ordinary course, and in defeat it is acquired if you can either show that the defeat was not your fault, or can at once perform some virtuous action which cancels it out. The other is that it is not shameful to fail to keep a promise which you have been forced to make. Forced promises affecting the public will, in fact, always be broken when the force in question is removed, and this without shame to those who break them. Everywhere in history one comes across examples of this of one kind or another, and everyone is aware that it happens also at the present day. And not only are forced promises not observed by princes when the force in question is no longer operative; but we also find that all other promises are broken when the reasons which caused such promises to be made no longer hold good. Whether this is praiseworthy or not, and whether a prince should or should not behave in this way, we have discussed at length in our treatise on *The Prince*. Here, therefore, nothing will be said about it.

Book Three

[FURTHER REFLECTIONS BASED ON THE SAMNITE WARS]

---

43. *That Men who are born in the same Country display throughout the Ages much the same Characteristics*

PRUDENT men are wont to say – and this not rashly or without good ground – that he who would foresee what has to be, should reflect on what has been, for everything that happens in the world at any time has a genuine resemblance to what happened in ancient times. This is due to the fact that the agents who bring such things about are men, and that men have, and always have had, the same passions, whence it necessarily comes about that the same effects are produced.[72] It is true that men's deeds are sometimes more virtuous in this country than in that, and in that than in some other, according to the type of education from which their inhabitants have derived their mode of life.

Knowledge of the future based on the past is also facilitated when we find a nation which for a long time has had the same customs, which has been, for instance, consistently grasping or consistently deceitful, or which has had any other such vice or virtue. Thus, whoever studies the past history of this our city of Florence and compares what happened then with what has happened in quite recent times will find the German and

French peoples imbued with avarice, pride, ferocity and unreliability, for all these four characteristics of theirs have at
different times done much harm to our city. In regard to
untrustworthiness, for instance, everybody knows how often
money was given to King Charles VIII, and how he promised
to restore the fortresses of Pisa and never did so; whereby this
king displayed alike his untrustworthiness and no small avarice.

But let us pass over these recent events. Everybody will
have heard of what happened in the war which the Florentines
waged against the Visconti, Dukes of Milan. Since the Florentines had no other expedient available, they considered bringing the Emperor into Italy that his standing and his forces
might be of avail in the attack on Lombardy. The Emperor
promised to come with a strong army to join them in their
war with the Visconti, and to protect Florence against that
power, on condition that the Florentines gave him a hundred
thousand ducats on his starting out and another hundred
thousand when he should arrive in Italy; to which terms the
Florentines agreed. Having been paid the first instalment, and
then the second, when he got to Verona he turned back
without doing anything, pleading that he was held up by
those who had not fulfilled the agreements he had made with
them. So that, had Florence neither been driven to it by
necessity nor overcome by passion, but had read about and
become acquainted with the habits of barbarians in ancient
times, she would not have been misled by them on this
occasion and on many others, since they have always been
the same and have behaved everywhere and to everybody in
the same way.

This may be seen from what they did of old to the Tuscans.
The latter were much harassed by the Romans by whom they
had often been put to flight and routed. It became clear to
them that with their own forces they could not resist such
attacks, so they made an agreement with the Gauls who had

settled on the Italian side of the Alps whereby in return for a sum of money they were to join forces with them and to march against the Romans. The result was that, having accepted the money, the Gauls refused to take up arms on their behalf, alleging that they had accepted it not on the understanding that they should make war on the enemies of Tuscany but that they should abstain from pillaging Tuscan territory. So that, owing to the avarice and untrustworthiness of the Gauls, the Tuscan peoples at once lost their money and the help they had hoped to get from them.

Thus we see that in the case of the ancient Tuscans and in that of the Florentines, the Gauls adopted the same policy; from which it is easy to judge how much reliance rulers can place in them.

44. Results are often obtained by Impetuosity and Daring which could never have been obtained by Ordinary Methods

WHEN the Samnites were attacked by the Roman army, and their own army was unable to keep the field against them, they decided to leave garrisons in the towns of Samnium and to move with all their forces into Tuscany which had made a truce with the Romans, in the hope that, by so doing, the presence of the army might induce the Tuscans to take up arms again, which they had declined to do when ambassadors were sent to them. In the speech which the Samnites made to the Tuscans, in the course of which they pointed out the causes which had induced them to take up arms, they made a remark worthy of attention, for they said that 'they had rebelled because when peace means servitude it is more intolerable to free men than is war'. And thus, partly by argument and partly owing to the presence of their army, they induced the Tuscans again to take up arms. Here it is to be noted that if one ruler desires to get something from another, he should, when circumstances permit, not give him time for consideration, but should act in such a way that he will see the need of a prompt decision, which he will do if he sees that to refuse what is asked or to postpone the matter will at once arouse resentment that may be dangerous.

We find that such means have been effectively employed in our own times by Pope Julius in his dealings with the French, and by Monsieur de Foix, the French king's general, in dealing with the Marquess of Mantua. For when Pope Julius wanted to expel the Bentivogli from Bologna, he realized that he would require French forces for this, and that the Venetians must remain neutral. So he approached them both, but, on receiving ambiguous and discrepant answers, he decided to bring both of them round to his point of view by giving them no time to do ought else. So he set out from Rome with such forces as he could muster, and approached Bologna, sending at the same time messages telling the Venetians to remain neutral and the King of France to send troops. Whereupon, since there was left to them but a brief space of time, and since the Pope would obviously become highly indignant if they hesitated or refused, they yielded to his wishes, and the king sent help and the Venetians remained neutral.

Similarly, when Monsieur de Foix, then at Bologna with his army, heard that Brescia had rebelled and wanted to go and recover it, he had two ways to go: one through territory belonging to the king, a long and tedious route; the other a short route through Mantuan territory. The latter route would not only mean that he had to pass through the dominion of the Marquess, but that he would also have to enter it by certain routes which lay between marshes and lakes wherein that region abounds, and which were locked and guarded by the Marquess with castles and other defences. Wherefore, de Foix, having decided to go by the short route, to obviate any difficult he did not give the Marquess time to consider, but at once marched with his troops along this road, and notified the Marquess that he should hand him the keys to pass through. Whereupon the Marquess, bewildered by this sudden decision, sent him the keys. This he would never have done if de Foix had been more hesitant in his behaviour, for the Marquess was in league both with the Pope and with the Venetians, and had a son in the Pope's charge, which would have afforded him plenty of honest excuses for refusing. But, overwhelmed by the sudden decision, he gave way, for the reasons given above. Just so did the Tuscans behave towards the Samnites, when, owing to the presence of an army in Samnium, they took up arms, which on previous occasions they had refused to do.

45. Whether it is the Better Course in Battle to await the Enemy's Attack and, having held it, to take the Offensive, or to make on the Enemy a Furious Onslaught at the Start

THE Roman consuls, Decius and Fabius, with two armies were about to engage the armies of the Samnites and the Tuscans, and happened to be engaged together in the same battle at the same time. Hence it is worth while asking which of the two diverse modes of procedure adopted by the two consuls was the better. For Decius attacked the enemy with the utmost impetuosity and with all his forces, whereas Fabius was content to hold them, since he was of opinion that it is more useful to be slow to attack, and to restrain one's impetuosity till a time comes when the enemy at length has lost the ardour for fighting he had at the start, and his fury, as one might say.

From the way things went, it may be seen that Fabius's plan was much better than that of Decius; for the latter tired himself out with the vehemence of his first onslaught, with the result that, when he perceived that his men would otherwise soon turn tail, he did what his father had done before him, sacrificed himself for the sake of the Roman legions, that by his death he might attain that glory which he had been unable to acquire by a victory. When Fabius heard of this, in order not to remain alive and yet gain less honour than his colleague had gained by his death, he pushed forward with all the forces he had reserved for such an eventuality, and gained a most glorious victory. So that obviously the way in which Fabius behaved is the safer and the more worthy of imitation.

46. *How it comes about that in a City a Family retains for a Long Time the same Customs*

IT would seem not only that one city differs from another in its customs and in its institutions, and produces men who are more stern or more effeminate; but one finds a like difference in the same city between this and that family. One meets with this in every city, and in the city of Rome one reads of many such cases; for one finds that the Manlii have ever been stern and obstinate, the Publicoli kindly and devoted to the people, the Appii ambitious and hostile to the plebs; and so of many other families, each of which has characteristics which distinguish it from the others.

This can scarce be wholly due to heredity, for intermarriage between different families would bring about variation; so it must needs be set down to the different way in which this family and that educates its children. For when a child of tender years begins to understand, it makes a great difference that he should hear some things spoken of with approval and some things with disapproval, since this must needs make an impression on him, by which later on his own conduct will be regulated in all the walks of life. If it were not so, it would have been impossible for the Appii to have had the same desires, and to have been moved by the same passions, as Titus Livy says many of them were. Thus, to take the last, who was appointed censor. When his colleague resigned his post – at the end of eighteen months, as the law required, Appius refused to resign, alleging that he was entitled to hold the post for five years, according to the first law which the censors had introduced; and, though numerous meetings were held to discuss the question and numerous disturbances arose, in spite of this and of his action being contrary to the will of the people and of the majority in the senate, there was no way of making him resign. So, too, whoever reads the speech he made against Publius Sempronius, the tribune of the plebs, will see that it is full of that arrogance which characterized the Appii, and, on the other hand, will note what goodness and humanity was shown by the great bulk of the citizens, and how ready they were to obey the laws of their country and the auspices.

47. That a Good Citizen out of Love for his Country ought to ignore Personal Affronts

WHEN Marcius, the consul, and his army were making war on the Samnites, he was wounded in a battle, and since this meant danger to his troops, the senate deemed it necessary to send Papirius Cursor as dictator to make up for the loss of the consul. It was essential that the dictator should be nominated by the consul, Fabius, who was with the armies in Tuscany. As he and Papirius were enemies, it was doubtful whether he would be willing to nominate him. So the senators sent two ambassadors to beg him to set aside private enmities, and in the public interest to make the nomination. This Fabius did, moved thereunto by love for his country, though by his silence and in many other ways he made it clear that the nomination hit him hard.

All those who desire to be looked upon as good citizens should emulate his example.

48. When an Enemy is seen to be making a Big Mistake, it should be assumed that it is but an Artifice

WHEN the legate, Fulvius, was left with the army which the Romans had in Tuscany, the consul having gone to Rome to attend some ceremonies, the Tuscans, in order to see whether they could catch him on the hop, set an ambush near the Roman camp, and sent some soldiers, dressed as shepherds, with a largish flock, telling them to let themselves be seen by the Roman army. Thus disguised, they went right up to the palisades surrounding the camp. The legate, wondering at their presumption which did not seem to him reasonable, took steps to discover the fraud, so that the Tuscans' plan was frustrated.

Here it is well to observe that the general of an army ought not to rely on an obvious mistake which an enemy is seen to make, for it will always be a fraud, since it is not reasonable that men should so lack caution. Yet very often the desire for victory so blinds men's eyes that they notice only what they want to see.

The Gauls, having defeated the Romans on the Allia, came to Rome, and, finding the gates open and unguarded, waited for a whole day and night without entering, since they were afraid of a fraud and could not believe that the Romans at heart were so cowardly or so stupid as to have abandoned their homeland.

When in 1508 the Florentines were besieging Pisa, Alfonso del Mutolo, a citizen of Pisa, finding himself a prisoner in the hands of the Florentines, promised that, if they would set him free, he would place one of the gates of that city at the disposal of the Florentine army. The man was set free. He then, on the plea of arranging practical details, came several times to talk with the delegates of the commissioners. Nor did he come secretly, but openly, and in the company of Pisans whom he left outside while he was talking with the Florentines. From this it might have been conjectured that he had double dealing in mind, for, if he had been acting in accordance with his promise it was unreasonable that he should have acted so openly. But so determined were the Florentines to have Pisa that, blinded by their desire for it, they went on his instructions to the Lucca gate, and left there, to their discredit, a number of officers and men owing to the double dealing of the said Alfonso.

Book Three

---

49. A Republic that would preserve its Freedom, ought daily to make Fresh Provisions to this End, and what Quintus Fabius did to earn for himself the title Maximus[73]

As we have remarked several times, in every large city there inevitably occur unfortunate incidents which call for the physician, and the more important the incidents the wiser should be the physician one looks for. If there was any city in which such incidents occurred, it was in Rome, where they were both curious and unexpected. For instance, on one occasion all the ladies of Rome had conspired to kill their husbands. Quite a number were found actually to have been poisoned, and for quite a number poison had been prepared.

Another instance was the conspiracy of the Bacchanals, which was discovered during the Macedonian war. In it so many thousands of men and women were involved that, if it had not been discovered, or if it had not actually been the custom in Rome to punish multitudes when they erred, it would have spelt danger for the city. For even if the greatness of that republic and its power of administration were not betokened in a thousand other ways, it is to be seen in the nature of the punishment inflicted on the evil-doer. Thus Rome did not hesitate to pronounce judicial sentence of death on a whole legion at a time, or on a city; not yet to banish eight or ten thousand men and to impose on them extra-ordinary conditions, which had to be observed not by one man alone but by so many; as she did in the case of the soldiers who had fought unsuccessfully at Cannae, and who were banished to Sicily, where they were forbidden to reside in towns and had to eat standing up.

But of all her administrative acts the most terrible was the practice of 'decimating' an army, i.e. of choosing by lot every tenth man, and putting him to death. No more terrify-ing punishment than this could possibly be devised for the purpose of chastising a multitude. For when a great number of people have done wrong, and it is not clear who is respon-sible, it is impossible to punish them all, since there are too many of them; and to punish some, and leave others un-punished, would be unfair to those who are punished, and the unpunished would take heart and do wrong at some other time. But by killing the tenth part, chosen by lot, when all are guilty, he who is punished bewails his lot, and he who is not punished is afraid to do wrong lest on some other occasion the lot should not spare him.

The poisoners and the Bacchanals, therefore, were punished for their sins as they deserved. And, although maladies of this kind do great harm to a republic, they are not fatal, for there is generally time to correct them. But there is no time as a rule when they affect the state, and, unless some wise man corrects them, the city is ruined.

Owing to the generous way in which the Romans used to grant citizenship to foreigners, there came to be in Rome such a cosmopolitan crowd of newcomers that they began to play an important part in the voting, with the result that the government began to change and to depart from those ways and from those men it had been accustomed to follow. Quintus Fabius, when he was censor, noticing this, allocated this cosmopolitan collection of newcomers to whose presence the trouble was due, to four 'tribes', and by restricting in this way the scope of their activities, prevented them from corrupting all Rome. Thus, having taken due cognizance of the trouble, Fabius, without altering the constitutions, applied an appropriate remedy and so acceptable was this to that city that he came deservedly to be called 'Maximus'.

NOTES

1. This makes it clear that Machiavelli only intended to comment on Livy's first ten books, which were on the causes of Rome's rise to power by virtue, as he saw it, of her republican constitution. Machiavelli's republican bias in the *Discourses* is thus both moral and methodological.
2. Here Machiavelli follows Polybius very closely, and in so doing virtually repeats Aristotle's classification of Book III of the *Politics* (see Walker, Vol. II, pp. 7–8).
3. Note that Machiavelli does not say that all men are wicked, but simply that legislators are wise to act as if this were true, i.e. 'Always drive your car as if both the man in front of you and the man behind are lunatics.'
4. The brothers Gracchus, Tiberius (163–133 B.C.) and Gaius (153–121 B.C.) were Tribunes who led popular demonstrations and riots, verging on rebellions, aimed at land reform in favour of the poor; both were assassinated or killed in street fights with aristocratic factions. Machiavelli refers to them several times, but always in a very neutral tone, neither praising nor condemning; rather he implies that such disruptive things will happen if the people are pushed too far.
5. Here *gentiluomini* are regarded, exceptionally, as a stabilizing factor; elsewhere (e.g. *Discourses* I.55) they are denounced as wreckers of any true republic because of their idleness and their landed interests which keep them, both physically and psychologically, outside the city proper.
6. Francesco Valori took the lead in the expulsion of the Medici from Florence in 1494 and was leader of the popular party which supported Savonarola. But he was murdered on the overthrow of Savonarola – earlier in the same year when Machiavelli entered the service of the new republican government.
7. At various times between 1250 and 1477 Florence had a 'Captain of the People' and other *Podestà* who were supposed to be

impartial 'foreigners', i.e. Italians other than Florentines, who would judge disputes between citizens. They had a bad reputation, both for ignorance and corruption.

8. 'The strong indictment of tyranny in this discourse makes it clear how intensely Machiavelli hated tyranny, and hence the last thing he had in mind in composing *The Prince* was to help would-be princes to set up a tyranny. He believes that autocracy is called for in certain circumstances, and that these circumstances were realized in the Italy of his day, but never tyranny.' (Walker, Vol II, pp. 26–7.) Machiavelli's positive values come out very clearly in the first paragraph of this discourse. And notice, technically, that here he distinguishes both republics and kingdoms from tyrannies.

9. Lucius Sergius Cataline attempted to seize the Consulship by conspiracy and then force when Cicero was Consul in 64 B.C., rallying a small army of adventurers and malcontents. He was defeated and killed. But Caesar is more disliked by Machiavelli simply because he *succeeded* in destroying the republic and its liberties; he was, in a word, a tyrant, therefore detestable and traditionally the proper object of assassination.

10. Dante, *Il Purgatorio*, Canto VII, 121–3.

11. Here is not an outright denunciation of Christianity, rather an argument that if the original spirit of Christianity had been kept up by Christian rulers as well as the spirit of Paganism had been by the ancient Romans, Christian states and republics would be far more united. Pastor in his monumental *History of the Popes*, Vol. V, p. 169 ff., typically calls Machiavelli's view of the corruption of the Church a 'caricature', but then goes on to describe the 'Court of Rome' of the early sixteenth century, rather than 'the Church' (perhaps too fine a distinction for Machiavelli), in essentially similar terms.

12. *Discourses* I.17. The distinction is vital, even if the criteria by which to make it are left vague, between inhabitants who have utterly lost their original *virtù* (assuming they ever had it) and those with enough left to be regenerated, given strong leadership.

13. Lucius Junius Brutus, who took part in the expulsion of the Tarquins and the establishment of the first republic in Rome

(c. 510 B.C.), was faced, when Consul, with a conspiracy of his own sons and others – disappointed at their lack of power in the new regime. According to Livy, not merely did Brutus consent to their death but he was present at their execution. Thus Machiavelli advises both princes and republics to spare no one, however honourable, who conspires against a new regime; and ideally to liquidate quickly those who plainly have an interest to do so, even if they have not yet done anything. In the eighteenth century the phrase 'sons of Brutus' was often used mistakenly of Marcus Brutus, Julius Caesar's assassin, as if to say that 'those who live by the sword shall perish by the sword' or that tyrannicides, however noble, are not comfortable people to have around after the revolution. But these are not Machiavelli's reasons. His practical point is 'get in first' and his sociological point is, as it were, 'watch especially the children of the ruling class, even in a republic'.

14. It seems that Machiavelli often, but not consistently, distinguishes between a 'king' and a 'prince', a king being a ruler of a well-ordered state, himself succeeding to the throne or being appointed to law, who is willing to be limited by the traditional laws – except where the laws themselves make his power absolute (usually, in the feudal theory of kingship, absolute to defend the realm and to enforce the laws, but not to make or even, alone, to declare law); and a prince is then one who does, or has to, set the laws aside (See *Discourses* I.10 and Footnote 8 above.) But there are instances of princes who turn themselves into kings, and of kings who have to act as princes, indeed degenerate into tyrants. Thus formally Machiavelli wobbles between a two-, a three- and a four-way distinction of types of government: principalities and republics; kingdoms, principalities and republics; and kingdoms, principalities, tyrannies and republics (the tyranny being the prince – or even a king – who uses power for its own sake, not for the preservation of the state; or who acts arbitrarily, but not just in the sense of breaking the law, but of going against the 'necessity' of a situation or further than it rationally demands). The essential distinction is, however, always clearly that between power exercised by one person and by many.

Which is best depends on the circumstances of a particular case – which will best ensure the immediate safety and the preservation of the state and its preservation through time. (See Walker, Vol. II, pp. 41–2 and Charles MacIlwain, *Constitutionalism, Ancient and Modern*, generally for medieval and early modern ideas on kingship and law.)

15. In this paragraph, says Walker, are compressed three basic principles: that class-conflicts are an advantage to a state when properly controlled; that a form of government can only be imposed if there is the right human material; and that in time of emergency one man must be in control. (Vol. II, p. 44.)

16. In *Discourses* I.18, i.e. the very next one – one sign, among many, that Machiavelli never finally decided on the best order in which to present his material.

17. *Discourses* I.16, 17 and 18 all show how Machiavelli would handle the transition from servitude to freedom and republican institutions according to the basic principle, set out most clearly in *Discourses* III.9, of conformity with 'the times' or circumstances. The difficulties are great, as he says in *Discourses* I.17 and 18 and in I.49, so great that 'quasi-regal' power may be needed to contain dissident elements during the transition (see also *Discourses* I.55). But this is fully consistent both with what he says about the need for dictatorship in times of emergency and his general view that a '*potestà regia*' is one of the '*qualità*' in the mixture of elements that go to make up even (or particularly) a flourishing republic.

18. 'So Jeroboam and all Israel came and spoke to Rehoboam, saying, "Thy father made our yoke grievous: now therefore ease thou somewhat the grievous servitude of thy father ... and we will serve thee" ... And Rehoboam took counsel with the old men that had stood before Solomon his father while yet he lived, saying, "What counsel give ye me to return answer to this people?" And they spake unto him, saying, "If thou be kind to this people, and please them, and speak good words to them, they will be thy servants for ever." ... [But] King Rehoboam forsook the counsel of the old men, and answered them after the advice of the young men, saying, "My father made your yoke heavy,

but I will add thereto: my father chastised you with whips, but I will chastise you with scorpions." ... And Israel rebelled against the House of David unto this day.' (2 *Chronicles*, 10.)

Foolish and headstrong Rehoboam to ignore the political or truly Machiavellian advice of the old men and thus to lose nine tenths of his kingdom!

19. He must be referring to Henry VIII's short-lived invasion of France in 1513, the Battle of the Spurs and all that, the magnificence and grandiosity of which would have appealed to him. But the theoretical example is sounder than the actual history. England had been at war twenty, not thirty years before, to defend the independence of Brittany; and hardly lacked military experience and preparation so close to the Wars of the Roses – internal fear, not simply general prudence, would have been the more accurate account.

20. Again 'tyranny' is sharply distinguished from 'principate'. The prince, if he is wise, will rule according to the interest of the state; but the tyrant rules simply according to his own interest. Hence Walker translates '*potestà assoluta*' in this context as 'despotism' to make the point clear; but, of course, '*potestà assoluta*' or absolute power can be properly used by a prince, or indeed by a dictator in a republic (see Footnote 25 below).

21. Walker points out that this is a misquotation from the Magnificat and is not said of David but of the Lord. 'Machiavelli would often have heard the Magnificat sung, but appears to have but a hazy notion of what it is all about.' (Walker, Vol. II, p. 53.)

22. See *Discourses* I.6 and II. 3, 4, 19, 23 and 30.

23. See *Discourses* I.30 and 58.

24. Philip V of Macedon against whom the Romans fought from from 200–196 B.C., not, of course, the father of Alexander the Great.

25. A sweeping generalization indeed; but Machiavelli is right to insist that the Roman dictatorship was a constitutional office and that some such institution is needed in all republics – whether called by that name or 'emergency powers'. See Clinton Rossiter's interesting *Constitutional Dictatorship* (Princeton, 1948) and Walker II, pp. 63–5.

26. See also *Discourses* II.19, III.16 and 25. Walker (Vol. II, p. 67) quotes Cato's speech in Sallust's *Cataline*: ' ... we now have luxury and avarice, a needy public, but in private opulence.' Shades, or rather ancestors, of Galbraith. Machiavelli plainly believes in the virtues of frugality and simplicity among the ruling political classes – a classical tradition that affected deeply both Jacobin and early American republican thought. But if he lacks any modern sense of either management of the economy or of the conditioning of thought by economic factors, yet his political realism about the power of the poor and the reasons he gives for detesting the gentry go farther than most classical authors – even if his solutions are vague or purely prescriptive.

27. Notice always the images of the *power* of the people, never the rights (he lived before Rousseau, as Gramsci sometimes forgot): better to have them on your side than the nobles, because of their greater power – if well led or if they are rendered desperate. But the maxim is relevant to principalities and republics alike. The example he gives in the previous paragraph is, after all, of a tyrant who would have done better for himself to have wooed the people rather than the nobles. Thus the people can easily be misled and popular government is not necessarily either republican or free government. Aristotle also advised the tyrant to cultivate the people (*Politics* V.9, 1310a). Machiavelli's thoughts on '*il popolo*' could be summed up in three ways: how strong are the people! (e.g. *Discourses* I.5, 6, 57 and 58); 'how easily men may be corrupted' (the heading of *Discourses* I.42); and a 'crowd is useless without a head' (the heading of *Discourses* I.44).

28. Appius Claudius introduced yet more sex into the class war by trying to use his high office of censor to seize Virginia, the daughter of an honest soldier and the betrothed of a former tribune of the people; to save her from his clutches, her father killed her; and the plebs marched out of the city in protest and were joined by the army (according to Livy, III.44–8). If only rulers would stick to their job! Both Machiavelli and Aristotle ostentatiously warn tyrants about the disproportionate amount of trouble that mucking about with the women of their subjects can cause (*Discourses* I.2, III.6 and 26; *Politics* V).

29. He makes the same general point in *Discourses* III.28 and 49, but he mentions no specific institution. He almost certainly had the Roman censors in mind. Livy (IV.8) thought that the censorship was founded in 443 B.C., the year after the tribunes of the people had been given consular power: that is that they were part of the original republican institutions. The institution began, he said, in a small way, but from undertaking a census it grew to control the correct position of people in it and the behaviour appropriate to their order or class: 'to such an extent that Roman customs and discipline came under its control. The honour of belonging to the Senate and to the centuries of the knights and the disgrace of being degraded, fell under its jurisdiction ...' Machiavelli noted (*Discourses* I.49) that the censors 'constituted a very powerful instrument which the Romans used in order to postpone the advent of corruption', but apart from this one passage there is only a single glancing reference to the institution (III.46). This is curious, since he places so much weight upon and refers so often to the institution of dictatorship. Dictatorship is to preserve the state in time of crisis; but the real power of the state depends on the *virtù* of its citizens. And if *virtù* is not simply military in character, but rather man militant in civic life as well as in the field, then Machiavelli neglects the institutional entailments of his own argument: the censorship should have been every bit as important as the dictatorship.

30. See Footnote 29 above.

31. *Discourses* I.16–18.

32. Walker mildly remarks that 'The eulogy of German towns ... has given rise to much controversy ... that Machiavelli has made some mistakes here cannot be denied.' (Walker, II, p. 85.) But, once again, it is the relevance, not the historical truth, of the examples which throw light on Machiavelli's theories of government: he could just as well have cited Rehoboam and Jeroboam again or the kingdom of Farëie.

33. The relevance of the fanciful Germanic examples is now, and in the next passage, made grimly clear: with an almost Lenin-like terseness and (perhaps) pseudo-practicality, Machiavelli says 'purge the gentry'. The social prejudice shows through of the

city-dweller and the maker of things as against the countryman and the inheritor of things, as well as the political-sociological argument. People who do not work and improve their property should lose their lives, says Machiavelli; should lose their property, says gentler Locke: but the bourgeois thought is essentially the same.

34. I would say that this is the most important discourse in the whole book. Walker shows the close correspondence of Machiavelli's concepts to those of Aristotle on 'equality' and on 'mixed government' (Walker, II, pp. 86–7). But in going back we witness the birth, in the fusion of ideas, of a genuinely political sociology, not that rigid and implacable modern bastard, the sociology of politics. The terrible difficulties, says Machiavelli, of changing a regime against its circumstances or social context; the greatness of doing it to make a republic, the foulness of doing it to make a tyranny; man must be 'scientific' about the contextual probabilities, but they never finally decide what is best or what otherwise *might* work – only a fool ignores them, but only a coward lets them decide for him: therein lies, for good or evil, our human freedom.

35. His optimistic view of '*il popolo*' (see Footnote 27 above) is not contradicted even in *The Prince*, although there their fickleness and unpredictability – from the point of view of a prince – is naturally stressed. (See *Prince* 6, 9 and 17.)

36. Machiavelli does not in fact explain why the masses should ruthlessly defend the common good while a prince is more likely to fight back for his own good. But, of course, there never is any philosophical discussion of the meaning of 'common good'; it never seems to occur to Machiavelli that the phrase could have any meaning apart from, in some sense, the aggregation of the interests of the actual inhabitants. His philosophical simplicity saved him from a lot of irrelevant nonsense.

In this discourse, however, both his thesis about the most appropriate circumstance for which type of government gets stated at its most general, and we see him introducing the dimension of *time* as the solvent of apparent contradictions: 'If princes are superior to populaces in drawing up laws, codes of civic life, statutes and new institutions, the populace is ... superior in sustaining what has been instituted.' Amid all the 'political development' literature of today, I still suspect that there are general grounds for thinking this proposition (albeit at a high level of abstraction) is true.

37. *Discourses* I.26 describes, in the last two paragraphs, Philip's terrible resolution – to be condemned by Christian and non-Christian alike; but he commonly succeeded, unlike those who pursued a middle course. See Introduction, p. 64 above.

38. *Prince* 3 and 5.

39. Now usually called '*Hiero*'. And note how carefully in this discourse Machiavelli raises, without committing himself in any way, perhaps the most difficult question of political philosophy, and one close to its cultural roots: tyrannicide.

40. See Footnote 11 above. Again not a rejection of Christianity as such, simply a criticism of it for not having sustained and developed the *virtù* of the ancients. Whether it would then be 'truly' Christian or not hardly worries Machiavelli; he was concerned with religion as a state institution.

41. Compare to *Prince* 4 where three methods are suggested of dealing with a conquered people who have been used to their own laws.

42. Machiavelli really did believe that there had been something called 'Paganism' as much one religion and as institutionally unified as (just) Christianity in his day. Perhaps this explains his strange under-emphasis of the importance of the Roman institution of censorship (see Footnote 29 above). He may have assumed that the maintenance of *virtù* was quite simply part of *the* religion and needed little else.

43. For Machiavelli as a strategic thinker, see Neal Wood's Introduction to Machiavelli's *The Art of War* (New York, 1965). In *The Art of War* he expresses the same opinion about money more moderately: 'Men, steel, money and provisions are the sinews of war, but of these four the two first are the most necessary, for men and steel will always find money and provisions.' Generally if Machiavelli failed to see the significance of the cannon and the birth of the big technology of war, his perception of the import-

ance of citizen armies as against professional armies was relevant
even into the nineteenth century, with Napoleon and the vast
armies of the American Civil War, hardly irrelevant to the two
World Wars of the twentieth century and still grimly relevant
to the evident superiority of the North Vietnamese over the
Americans.

44. Compare to the famous metaphors of *Prince* 18 of Chiron the
centaur and the lion and the fox. The prince needs to know how
to be half-man and half-beast, as Chiron, tutor of Achilles,
symbolized; and must have the strength of the lion but also the
cunning of the fox – otherwise the strongest lion falls into
traps.

45. Walker argues at some length (II, pp. 114–16) that the examples
used by Machiavelli from Livy do not, in fact, bear out his
point: they only show that Rome was accused of fraud. Certainly
Machiavelli is oddly careless, certainly unusually brief, on what
might seem such an important 'Machiavellian' point. One
suspects a deliberate melodrama as if he constantly remembers his
reputation for being 'tough-minded'. Otherwise the argument
is purely *post hoc propter hoc*, i.e. fraud is good if you can get away
with it. For once his friend Guicciardini seems wiser: 'But, as to
fraud, it is open to question whether it is always a good means
to arrive at greatness; because, though by deceit many neat
strokes are often brought about, getting a name for acting
fraudulently often deprives one of the chance of attaining one's
ends' (quoted by Walker, *loc. cit.*). And see *Discourses* III.20 for a
completely contradictory example, and see Footnotes 66 and 71
below.

46. *Discourses* 16–18 are closely related to the far more extended
argument of his *Art of War*. But they are emphatically not to be
skipped: the technical basis of his argument in favour of militia
furnishes, to him, one of the strongest grounds for the presumed
greater power of well-ordered republics compared to principalities.

47. In his *Art of War* (ed. Neal Wood), pp. 92–100, he repeats his
scepticism about the changes that some claimed artillery would
bring. Good infantry – loyal, trained, citizen infantry – he

repeats, and repeats, is the key. Although he strives for a balanced
view, as in the last sentence of *Discourses* II.17, some contempt for
gadgets as against men shows through. He associates artillery
with mercenaries and stateless technicians.

48. And some social contempt shows through here too: generally
infantry are a more solid sort of people than the *gentiluomini* on
horses. Admiration, however, in *Discourses* II.18, for Carmignuola who was adaptable enough (one of the great Machiavellian
virtues) to come down off his high horse and get under the Swiss
pikes on foot.

49. *Discourses* I.6.

50. *Prince* 12 and 13.

51. Walker comments (Vol. II, p. 129) of this dictum: 'Contrary to
the famous dictum of Aristotle that "virtue lies in the mean",
Machiavelli holds that in many cases it lies in the extremes.' (See
especially *Discourses* I.6, 26 and 55; III.21 and 22.) But Walker
here seems to confuse policy with form of government. Certainly
Machiavelli counsels extreme action, to princes and republicans
alike; but he is thoroughly golden-meanish in his account of the
mixture of elements in a republic which give it such an adaptability. That it is an amalgam of different principles and extreme
type of governments is exactly the Aristotelian idea of 'mean' –
emphatically not a 'mere compromise', or that famous 'middle
point between extreme views' which now the television inter-
viewer regards as objective truth and often himself inhabits,
alone. (See Introduction, pp. 25–26, and 29–31).

52. The Roman concept of the '*ius gentium*', those positive laws
which it appeared, in Roman eyes, all known states observed in
their political and commercial relations which each other. The
sanctity of ambassadors was held to be a particularly clear
example of, as it were, international common law.

53. This advice, to arm the people and to avoid mercenaries like the
plague, is not, of course, limited to republican governments. In
The Prince 20 he writes: 'A new prince has never [*sic, should* never
have] been known to disarm his subjects, on the contrary, when
he has found them disarmed he has always armed them, for by
arming them these arms become your own, those that you

suspected become faithful and those that were faithful remain so, and from being merely subjects become your partisans.'

54. Thus he can hardly have been rationally disappointed at not getting a job in Rome in the days of his exile. But the practice of deliberately employing foreigners in the courts and palaces of autocracies was too widespread to be brushed aside this easily. As Wittfogel points out in his *Oriental Despotism*, there were sound reasons for this practice: the foreigner had no local political support, so was entirely dependent on the ruler – only the eunuch was more dependable. Machiavelli's example only points to a narrower truth: don't trust a foreigner as an authority on his own former country (a truth that the C.I.A. have been slow to appreciate). With all his admiration of Rome, it is curious that Machiavelli never thought that it was part of the strength of the early republic that it was so remarkably *un*-ethnocentric, that Rome extended citizenship to able foreigners who wished to be Romans. (Indeed, in the very last paragraph of the whole work, he criticizes 'the generous way in which the Romans used to grant citizenship to foreigners'.) Part of her strength was a genuine civic ideology that transcended the habitual tribal or ethnic divisions of classical antiquity. (See Sir Charles Adcock, *Roman Political Ideas*, Cambridge University Press, 1959.) Here his main source let him down: Livy was a bit of a snob, unusual among Roman historians in that he made no play with the famous myth of the foundation of Rome by Romulus and Remus as a refuge for outlaws.

55. For 'the sons of Brutus' see Footnote 13 above and *Discourses* I.16, III.1, 5 and 6, to which Walker refers, but I think it more likely that Machiavelli is referring to chapters 5–8 of *The Prince*, which deal with the different types of problem facing a new princely regime.

56. If indeed it is true that more princes fall by conspiracies than by war, then the importance of the matter alone explains the abnormal length of this discourse, three times the length of the next longest chapter and eight times the average (calculates Walker). But is there any significance in the fact that all this vital piece of mechanics gets tacked on so near the end, virtually an

afterthought? Again, I surmise, the reputation of *The Prince* must have lain heavily on Machiavelli. After writing so much about *why* institutions change and *how* they can be preserved, particularly republican ones, he may suddenly have realized that he had said very little about *how* they can be changed, particularly against the odds. This chapter alone in the *Discourses* would justify Cassirer's image of Machiavelli the political technician, the author of that do-it-yourself political sex-manual hidden in the secret drawers of respectable Tudor statesmen, etc. I read Machiavelli as having an intense interest in such matters, but on a much more frivolous, both gay and morbid, level than that of the basic structure of his argument, serious and profound. I do not mean to imply that he thought conspiracies unimportant, but simply that their importance is as part of the *Fortuna* in affairs rather than the *Necessità*: therefore one can endlessly illustrate their occurrence, but not generalize about them. No generaliz-ations can be drawn from his examples except that principalities are more prone to fall by conspiracy than republics, less able to adapt themselves to changing *Fortuna*. A conspiracy in favour-able circumstances is only the rather melodramatic consequence of more basic factors for change, not the cause; and a conspiracy in the teeth of circumstances is, Machiavelli – if not the Machia-vellians – must believe, exceptional (see especially *Discourses* III, 7–9, which all treat of the need for adaptation to environment). I suspect, in other words, that Machiavelli would have read with great delight books like Curzio Malaparte's classic, *Technique of the Coup d'État*, or Mr Edward Luttwak's recent *Coup d'État: a Practical Handbook*, but would have regarded them as obsessionally specialized literature, a little suspect even of being political pornography.

57. An odd sort of example if no one is to emulate it. But no one can be rationally expected to emulate it since it went so greatly against circumstances; yet nothing more marvellous than to succeed in such an 'impossible' enterprise. Morally the Pagan ethic of 'fame' and the humanist ethic of 'prudence' pull Machiavelli in two ways, or he shows the dilemma between them: Pelopidas was both great and foolish.

58. See *Discourses* I.34 and III.6. And notice how this chapter by implication severely qualifies the importance of conspiracies in republics, as treated in *Discourses* III.6 'On Conspiracies'.

59. See *Discourses* I.7 and 52, but especially III.3, where his good nature is praised, but his failure to act drastically against conspirators is condemned. Piero Soderini was appointed Gonfalonier, or President, of the Florentine Republic in 1502 for life, but he was deposed in 1512 by the Medici backed by the Spaniards. Machiavelli served under him, became an intimate friend, and was imprisoned and tortured on his fall.

60. See *Discourses* I.18 and 49, and III.1.

61. On the role of the tribunes of the people see *Discourses* I.3, 37 and 39.

62. See especially *Discourses* I.32, 38 and 51; and *Prince* 15, 18 and 25. The 'moral philosophers' are probably, says Walker, Aquinas in *de Regime Principum* I.1 and possibly Aristotle in *Politics* I.2.

63. And so, continues Livy (IV.31), the people of Rome insisted on the appointment of a dictator. War is always, of course, the supreme example of a state of emergency that calls for such power, even in republics.

64. And see *Discourses* III.47, 'That a Good Citizen out of Love for his Country ought to ignore Personal Affronts'. cf. Lincoln: 'A man has not the time to spend half his life in quarrels. If any man ceases to attack me, I never remember the past against him.'

65. See *Prince* 17, 'Of Cruelty and Clemency, and Whether it is Better to be Loved or Feared'.

66. Both this discourse and the previous one (II.19) either contradict or severely qualify II.1.3, 'Men rise from a Low to a Great Position by Means rather of Fraud than of Force' (see Footnote 45 above); and they certainly reduce some of the overstatement of *Prince* 17 to proportion. There Machiavelli does say that 'it is much safer to be feared than loved', after having said that it is better to be loved and feared, but very difficult; but he goes on to draw a distinction between being feared and being hated. And the latter must be avoided even by a prince, cf. *Prince* 19, 'That We Must Avoid Being Despised and Hated'. Or perhaps the fault is not in Machiavelli but in commentators who so often quote 'better to

be loved than feared', a misquotation anyway, out of context. But if one strikes off such epigrams one can hardly help them being quoted, etc.

67. 'Note,' observes Walker (II, p. 189), 'the inconveniences each alternative entails; if quick conquests, then prolonged commissions and ultimately servitude; if no prolonged commission, then slow conquests.' Here is a genuine dilemma, for once, with no real hint as to its resolution; and the germ of that opinion which was to dominate the teaching of English classics in the late nineteenth century that 'the lesson of Rome' was that imperialism ultimately threatened free institutions in the homeland (see Alfred North Whitehead, *Essays in Science and Philosophy*, New York, 1947, p. 39).

68. Walker says (II, p. 193) that he could equally accurately have rendered '*dai principi*' as 'due to their *rulers*', since '*principi*' can equally well be the rulers of a republic; but in fact the examples given are of princes proper. 'Note, too, the implication that men are prone not merely to evil, but also to good, and that which is brought out will depend largely upon the way in which they are treated.'

69. No discourse, either before or after this, in fact deals with the problem of how to do something new by many hands (i.e. on his main argument such things are best done by one hand). Perhaps he is referring to *Prince* 9, 'Concerning the Civic Principality', but that had already been written and, in any case, deals mainly with the relationship between the prince and the people, as against his relying on the nobility, not with rule by citizens. This is probably another indication that the whole work may have been unfinished, almost certainly unrevised.

70. See Introduction, p. 52.

71. See Footnotes 45 and 66 above. But this treatment of the legitimate and even 'glorious' use of 'fraud' (something admitted to be 'dishonourable') both narrows the grounds to war and to states of emergency, and, compared to *Prince* 18, specifically excludes failure to keep one's pledged word and the breaking of promises as legitimate types of fraud. Perhaps 'fraud' (*la fraude*) is too specific a word; Machiavelli frequently substitutes '*astuzia*'

for it, so 'trickery' or 'sharp practice' may carry his meaning better.

72. This passage is often seized on to argue that Machiavelli taught a rigid 'Scientism'. I think, in fact, if all the qualifications are carefully read, it is more like a platitude. And, anyway, even if 'character' and 'passion' are relatively fixed throughout the ages, the form that they take in action, his whole theory presupposes, is shaped by circumstances. What is decisive to Machiavelli, as to Shakespeare, is the *interplay* between the two presumed forces of character and circumstance, not the fixity of either. If he had meant to say that human nature is everywhere the same, in a strong rather than a weak sense, then he would, presumably have laid out schematically what types of human nature there are, or what basic humours. Plato had done so, and the Medieval allegorists. There was ample precedent to do so, if that was what he meant. I think that he meant something either as profound or as banal, according to the context, as Hannah Arendt's remark in her *The Human Condition*, that nothing in nature is more alike than one man to another, and yet nothing more totally distinct from each other. Anyway, he constantly argues that failure to adapt one's nature to changing circumstances spells political ruin.

73. The theme of this last discourse, the restoration of old virtues, occurs strongly in both *Discourses* I.1 and *Discourses* III.1, thus suggesting, despite other signs of incompleteness or lack of revision (see Footnote 69), that this was the point at which and on which he aimed, indeed, to return and conclude.